Computational Intelligence in the Internet of Things

Hindriyanto Dwi Purnomo
Satya Wacana Christian University, Indonesia

A volume in the Advances in
Computational Intelligence and
Robotics (ACIR) Book Series

Published in the United States of America by
    IGI Global
    Engineering Science Reference (an imprint of IGI Global)
    701 E. Chocolate Avenue
    Hershey PA, USA 17033
    Tel: 717-533-8845
    Fax: 717-533-8661
    E-mail: cust@igi-global.com
    Web site: http://www.igi-global.com

Library of Congress Cataloging-in-Publication Data

Names: Purnomo, Hindriyanto Dwi, 1980- editor.
Title: Computational intelligence in the Internet of things / edited by
   Hindriyanto Dwi Purnomo.
Description: Hershey PA : Engineering Science Reference, [2019] | Includes
   bibliographical references.
Identifiers: LCCN 2018041833| ISBN 9781522579557 (hardcover) | ISBN
   9781522579564 (ebook)
Subjects: LCSH: Computational intelligence. | Internet of things.
Classification: LCC Q342 .C658 2019 | DDC 006.3--dc23 LC record available at https://lccn.loc.
gov/2018041833

This book is published in the IGI Global book series Advances in Computational Intelligence and Robotics (ACIR) (ISSN: 2327-0411; eISSN: 2327-042X)

British Cataloguing in Publication Data
A Cataloguing in Publication record for this book is available from the British Library.

For electronic access to this publication, please contact: eresources@igi-global.com.

Advances in Computational Intelligence and Robotics (ACIR) Book Series

ISSN:2327-0411
EISSN:2327-042X

Editor-in-Chief: Ivan Giannoccaro, University of Salento, Italy

MISSION

While intelligence is traditionally a term applied to humans and human cognition, technology has progressed in such a way to allow for the development of intelligent systems able to simulate many human traits. With this new era of simulated and artificial intelligence, much research is needed in order to continue to advance the field and also to evaluate the ethical and societal concerns of the existence of artificial life and machine learning.

The **Advances in Computational Intelligence and Robotics (ACIR) Book Series** encourages scholarly discourse on all topics pertaining to evolutionary computing, artificial life, computational intelligence, machine learning, and robotics. ACIR presents the latest research being conducted on diverse topics in intelligence technologies with the goal of advancing knowledge and applications in this rapidly evolving field.

COVERAGE

- Artificial Life
- Computational Logic
- Heuristics
- Natural Language Processing
- Computational Intelligence
- Machine Learning
- Robotics
- Fuzzy Systems
- Adaptive and Complex Systems
- Intelligent control

IGI Global is currently accepting manuscripts for publication within this series. To submit a proposal for a volume in this series, please contact our Acquisition Editors at Acquisitions@igi-global.com or visit: http://www.igi-global.com/publish/.

The Advances in Computational Intelligence and Robotics (ACIR) Book Series (ISSN 2327-0411) is published by IGI Global, 701 E. Chocolate Avenue, Hershey, PA 17033-1240, USA, www.igi-global.com. This series is composed of titles available for purchase individually; each title is edited to be contextually exclusive from any other title within the series. For pricing and ordering information please visit http://www.igi-global.com/book-series/advances-computational-intelligence-robotics/73674. Postmaster: Send all address changes to above address. ©© 2019 IGI Global. All rights, including translation in other languages reserved by the publisher. No part of this series may be reproduced or used in any form or by any means – graphics, electronic, or mechanical, including photocopying, recording, taping, or information and retrieval systems – without written permission from the publisher, except for non commercial, educational use, including classroom teaching purposes. The views expressed in this series are those of the authors, but not necessarily of IGI Global.

Titles in this Series

For a list of additional titles in this series, please visit:
https://www.igi-global.com/book-series/advances-computational-intelligence-robotics/73674

Artificial Intelligence and Security Challenges in Emerging Networks
Ryma Abassi (University of Carthage, Tunisia)
Engineering Science Reference • ©2019 • 293pp • H/C (ISBN: 9781522573531) • US $195.00

Emerging Trends and Applications in Cognitive Computing
Pradeep Kumar Mallick (Vignana Bharathi Institute of Technology, India) and Samarjeet
Borah (Sikkim Manipal University, India)
Engineering Science Reference • ©2019 • 300pp • H/C (ISBN: 9781522557937) • US $215.00

Predictive Intelligence Using Big Data and the Internet of Things
P.K. Gupta (Jaypee University of Information Technology, India) Tuncer Ören (University
of Ottawa, Canada) and Mayank Singh (University of KwaZulu-Natal, South Africa)
Engineering Science Reference • ©2019 • 300pp • H/C (ISBN: 9781522562108) • US $245.00

Advanced Metaheuristic Methods in Big Data Retrieval and Analytics
Hadj Ahmed Bouarara (Dr. Moulay Tahar University of Saïda, Algeria) Reda Mohamed
Hamou (Dr. Moulay Tahar University of Saïda, Algeria) and Amine Rahmani (Dr. Moulay
Tahar University of Saïda, Algeria)
Engineering Science Reference • ©2019 • 320pp • H/C (ISBN: 9781522573388) • US $205.00

Nature-Inspired Algorithms for Big Data Frameworks
Hema Banati (Dyal Singh College, India) Shikha Mehta (Jaypee Institute of Information
Technology, India) and Parmeet Kaur (Jaypee Institute of Information Technology, India)
Engineering Science Reference • ©2019 • 412pp • H/C (ISBN: 9781522558521) • US $225.00

Novel Design and Applications of Robotics Technologies
Dan Zhang (York University, Canada) and Bin Wei (York University, Canada)
Engineering Science Reference • ©2019 • 341pp • H/C (ISBN: 9781522552765) • US $205.00

For an entire list of titles in this series, please visit:
https://www.igi-global.com/book-series/advances-computational-intelligence-robotics/73674

701 East Chocolate Avenue, Hershey, PA 17033, USA
Tel: 717-533-8845 x100 • Fax: 717-533-8661
E-Mail: cust@igi-global.com • www.igi-global.com

Table of Contents

Detailed Table of Contents

Chapter 1

Sergei Savin, Innopolis University, Russia

In this chapter, the problem of motion planning for an in-pipe walking robot is
studied. One of the key parts of motion planning for a walking robot is a step
sequence generation. In the case of in-pipe walking robots it requires choosing a
series of feasible contact locations for each of the robot's legs, avoiding regions on
the inner surface of the pipe where the robot cannot step to, such as pipe branches.
The chapter provides an approach to localization of pipe branches, based on deep
convolutional neural networks. This allows including the information about the
branches into the so-called height map of the pipeline and plan the step sequences
accordingly. The chapter shows that it is possible to achieve prediction accuracy
better than 0.5 mm for a network trained on a simulation-based dataset.

Chapter 2

Soumen Mukherjee, RCC Institute of Information Technology, India
Arup Kumar Bhattacharjee, RCC Institute of Information Technology,
India
Debabrata Bhattacharya, RCC Institute of Information Technology,
India
Moumita Ghosal, Serampore Girls' College, India

In this chapter, data mining approaches are applied on standard IoT dataset to identify relationship among attributes of the dataset. IoT is not an exception; data mining can be used in this domain also. Various rule-based classifiers and unsupervised classifiers are implemented here. Using these approaches relation between various IoT features are determined based on different properties of classification like support, confidence, etc. For classification, a real-time IoT dataset is used, which consists of household figures collected from various sources over a long duration. A brief comparison is also shown for different classification approaches on the IoT dataset. Kappa coefficient is also calculated for these classification techniques to measure the robustness of these approaches. In this chapter, standard and popular power utilization in household dataset is used to show the association between the different intra-data dependency. Classification accuracy of more than 86% is found with the Almanac of Minutely Power Dataset (AMPds) in the present work.

Chapter 3

The aim of this chapter is to describe and analyze the application of machine learning for anomaly detection. The study regarding the anomaly detection is a very important thing. The various phenomena often occur related to the anomaly study, such as the occurrence of an extreme climate change, the intrusion detection for the network security, the fraud detection for e-banking, the diagnosis for engines fault, the spacecraft anomaly detection, the vessel track, and the airline safety. This chapter is an attempt to provide a structured and a broad overview of extensive research on anomaly detection techniques spanning multiple research areas and application domains. Quantitative analysis meta-approach is used to see the development of the research concerned with those matters. The learning is done on the method side, the techniques utilized, the application development, the technology utilized, and the research trend, which is developed.

Chapter 4

In recent years, internet of things (IoT) has expanded due to very good internet infrastructure everywhere. IoT has the ability to create a network of physical things that use embedded technologies in order to sense, converse, cooperate, and team up with other things. IoT-based applications require scalability and fault tolerance, which is very difficult to implement in centralized systems and computing environments. Distributed computing is an ideal solution to implement IoT-based applications.

The chapter starts with the basics of distributed computing where difference with centralized computing, challenges, and types of distributed computing applications are discussed. The chapter deals with the role of distributed computing for IoT based on advantages, issues, and related IoT-based applications. The chapter discusses the recent topic of distributed computing—FOG computing—in connection with IoT-based applications. At last, the chapter addresses research and interest trends about distributed computing and IoT.

Chapter 5

    Panagiota Papadopoulou, National and Kapodistrian University of Athens, Greece
    Kostas Kolomvatsos, National and Kapodistrian University of Athens, Greece
    Stathes Hadjiefthymiades, National and Kapodistrian University of Athens, Greece

Internet of things (IoT) brings unprecedented changes to all contexts of our lives, as they can be informed by smart devices and real-time data. Among the various IoT application settings, e-government seems to be one that can be greatly benefited by the use of IoT, transforming and augmenting public services. This chapter aims to contribute to a better understanding of how IoT can be leveraged to enhance e-government. IoT adoption in e-government encompasses several challenges of technical as well as organizational, political, and legal nature, which should be addressed for developing efficient applications. With the application of IoT in e-government being at an early stage, it is imperative to investigate these challenges and the ways they could be tackled. The chapter provides an overview of IoT in e-government across several application domains and explores the aspects that should be considered and managed before it can reach its full potential.

Chapter 6

    Ramgopal Kashyap, Amity University Chhattisgarh, India

The vast majority of the examination on profound neural systems so far has been centered on acquiring higher exactness levels by building progressively vast and profound structures. Preparing and assessing these models is just practical when a lot of assets; for example, handling power and memory are easy run of the mill applications that could profit by these models. The system starts handling the compelled gadget and depends on the remote part when the neighborhood part does not give a sufficiently precise outcome. The falling system takes into account a new ceasing component amid the review period of the system. This chapter empowers an entire assortment of independent frameworks where sensors, actuators, and registering hubs can cooperate and demonstrate that the falling design takes into account a free change in assessment speed on obliged gadgets while the misfortune in precision is kept to a base.

Jay Rodge, Illinois Institute of Technology, USA
Swati Jaiswal, VIT University, India

Deep learning and Artificial intelligence (AI) have been trending these days due to the capability and state-of-the-art results that they provide. They have replaced some highly skilled professionals with neural network-powered AI, also known as deep learning algorithms. Deep learning majorly works on neural networks. This chapter discusses about the working of a neuron, which is a unit component of neural network. There are numerous techniques that can be incorporated while designing a neural network, such as activation functions, training, etc. to improve its features, which will be explained in detail. It has some challenges such as overfitting, which are difficult to neglect but can be overcome using proper techniques and steps that have been discussed. The chapter will help the academician, researchers, and practitioners to further investigate the associated area of deep learning and its applications in the autonomous vehicle industry.

Keshav Sinha, Birla Institute of Technology, India
Partha Paul, Birla Institute of Technology, India
Amritanjali, Birla Institute of Technology, India

Distributed computing is one of the thrust areas in the field of computer science, but when we are concerned about security a question arises, "Can it be secure?" From this note, the authors start this chapter. In the distributed environment, when the system is connected to a network, and the operating system firewall is active, it will take care of all the authentication and access control requests. There are several traditional cryptographic approaches which implement authentication and access control. The encryption algorithms such as Rijndael, RSA, A3, and A5 is used for providing data secrecy. Some of the key distribution techniques have been discussed such as Diffie Hellman key exchange for symmetric key, and random key generation (LCG) technique is used in red-black tree traversal which provides the security of the digital contents. The chapter deals with the advanced versions of the network security techniques and cryptographic algorithms for the security of multimedia contents over the internet.

Chapter 9

Namrata Dhanda, Amity University, India
Stuti Shukla Datta, Amity University, India
Mudrika Dhanda, Royal Holloway University, UK

Human intelligence is deeply involved in creating efficient and faster systems that can work independently. Creation of such smart systems requires efficient training algorithms. Thus, the aim of this chapter is to introduce the readers with the concept of machine learning and the commonly employed learning algorithm for developing efficient and intelligent systems. The chapter gives a clear distinction between supervised and unsupervised learning methods. Each algorithm is explained with the help of suitable example to give an insight to the learning process.

Chapter 10

Kristoko Dwi Hartomo, Satya Wacana Christian University, Indonesia
Sri Yulianto Joko Prasetyo, Satya Wacana Christian University,
Indonesia
Muchamad Taufiq Anwar, Satya Wacana Christian University,
Indonesia
Hindriyanto Dwi Purnomo, Satya Wacana Christian University,
Indonesia

The traditional crop farmers rely heavily on rain pattern to decide the time for planting crops. The emerging climate change has caused a shift in the rain pattern and consequently affected the crop yield. Therefore, providing a good rainfall prediction models would enable us to recommend best planting pattern (when to plant) in order to give maximum yield. The recent and widely used rainfall prediction model for determining the cropping patterns using exponential smoothing method recommended by the Food and Agriculture Organization (FAO) suffered from short-term forecasting inconsistencies and inaccuracies for long-term forecasting. In this study, the authors developed a new rainfall prediction model which applied exponential smoothing onto seasonal planting index as the basis for determining planting pattern. The results show that the model gives better accuracy than the original exponential smoothing model.

Chapter 11

A. Surendar, Vignan's Foundation for Science, Technology & Research
(Deemed to be University), India

Digital data transformation is most challenging in developing countries. In recent days, all the applications are functioning with the support of internet of things (IoT). Wearable devices involve the most insightful information, which includes individual healthcare data. Health records of patients must be protected. IoT devices could be hacked, and criminals use this information. Smart cities with IoT use information technology to collect, analyze, and integrate information. Smart reduces the network traffic using the ground sensors, micro-radars, and drones monitor traffic to the traffic controller based on that signals are designed. The data collected includes the images and convey information to smart vehicles, which in turn, if data are hacked, may affect many people. Smart city includes important features such as smart buildings, smart technology, smart governance, smart citizen, and smart security. Cyber threat is a challenging problem, and usage of apps may increase malware that affects various customers.

Chapter 12

Machine learning (ML), neural network (NN), evolutionary algorithm (EA), fuzzy systems (FSs), as well as computer science have been very famous and very significant for many years. They have been applied to many different areas. They have contributed much to developments of many large-scale corporations, massive organizations, etc. Lots of information and massive data sets (MDSs) have been generated from these big corporations, organizations, etc. These big data sets (BDSs) have been the challenges of many commercial applications, researches, etc. Therefore, there have been many algorithms of the ML, the NN, the EA, the FSs, as well as computer science which have been developed to handle these massive data sets successfully. To support for this process, the authors have displayed all the possible algorithms of the NN for the large-scale data sets (LSDSs) successfully in this chapter. Finally, they have presented a novel model of the NN for the BDS in a sequential environment (SE) and a distributed network environment (DNE).

Preface

Intelligence computing is an emerging research area that covers various fields such as machine learning, neural network, evolutionary algorithm, fuzzy system as well as computer science. Intelligence computing has been used to investigate, simulate, analyze and solve real-world problems. It ability to deal with uncertainty and imprecision problem has attract researchers and practitioner to develop this field.

In recent year, computational intelligence has been used to deal various daily problems. The need for smart device has increase continuously in the range from personal business assistant to entertainment. Digital camera, wireless communication, sensors and multimedia become a common technology that equips the devices. The sensor help the device to collect data and the wireless communication enable the device to communicate with other device in their network to exchange information as well as receiving instruction. This has encouraged the development of Internet of Things that bring enormous applications to support our daily live.

Internet of Things refers to the interconnection of devices where the devices able to exchange and consume data with minimal human intervention. It integrates new technologies especially computing and communication technology. Internet of Things supports the collaboration environment between industries, researchers as well as policy makers. It has created new market that significantly change the economic and society globally.

This book discussed various issues related to the development of researches and application of Computational Intelligence and Internet of Things. There are 12 outstanding chapters in this book out of 25 chapter proposal submission. Each chapter addressed specific issues such as robotic, industrial application, government enhancement, security and weather. The brief overview for each chapter is given below.

Chapter 1 discusses the motion planning for in-pipe walking robots. The robots allow performing inspections of the inner surface of the pipe, which comes in direct contact with the transported material. The robot very useful for periodic inspection and repairs of pipelines that is labor-intensive and not always possible without the use of robots. Motion planning for walking robots requires step sequence generation. The sequence can be generated using lite algorithm that exploits the specific geometric representation of the pipeline. The algorithm can generate step sequence for pipes with obstacle. However, this approach has limitation, as it requires the knowledge of the obstacles locations as well as pipe branches. In order to solve this limitation, a new algorithm that facilitates motion planning for in-pipe walking robot that able to detect and localizing branches is proposed. The algorithm relies on the use of deep learning convolution neural network. The input data to the network is an array of points detected by a LIDAR-like sensor. The output of the network is the prediction of the origin of the pipe branch. The network includes 5 convolutional layers and 3 fully connected layers and uses ReLU activations for all layers. The results show the possibility of using convolution neural networks as a part of motion planning for in-pipe robots. For future research, there is a need to improve the control workflow on in-pipe walking robots. Machine learning has the potential to achieve robust control for the robots. A lot of progress has been made related to the use of numerical optimization algorithm. There is a need to use new methods such as reinforcement learning as well as convolution neural network.

Chapter 2 describes data mining approach to identify relationship among attributes of data, including data generated by Internet of Things. The authors provide various explanations of rule-based classifier and unsupervised classifiers. There are two main category of application of Internet of Things mentioned in the chapter; household application such as traffic monitoring systems and industrial application such as skin testing of airplane and mobile wallet. Internet of Things is applied in many high tech industries to increase sales. The application IoT may bring a major change in industry but it may also suffer from different problems such that performance of IoT is fully dependent of Internet. An example of relation between numerous features for electricity consumption in varying time is given in the chapter. The result can be used as thumb rule to find the influenced of electricity equipment on equipment. This is a new dimension that still needs to be explored. There are several issues that still need to be addressed such as fluctuation of Internet connection, range of distance of various devices and high investment cost.

Chapter 3 provides a structured and a broad overview of extensive research on anomaly detection techniques spanning multiple research areas and application domains. The study regarding on the anomaly detection is a very important thing in the life of human being. Some examples of study on anomaly detection are: network intrusion detection, tracking and safety field, climate prediction, cellular technology, medical, spatial detection and diagnosis for the engine. The Anomaly Detection System is generally designed using four methods: statistical, data mining, machine learning and graphical modeling. Currently, the most popular methods are data mining (45%), followed by machine learning (29% utilization). In order to improve the accuracy for anomaly detection, this study suggest to using a hybrid approach in data mining to combine the modified version of already existing algorithms. Hybrid approaches provide better results, higher accuracy and detection rate as well as reduction in the mean-time of false alarm rate.

Chapter 4 talks about distributed computing for internet of things. The internet has changed the computing paradigm from centralized to decentralized or distributed. In the distributed computing, a problem is divided into many tasks and each one is solved by one or more computational entities. Distributed computing is one of the most challenging research fields in computer science. Besides traditional topics such as synchronization, currently it is enriched with numerous topics from modern technologies such as wait-free consensus, oblivious routing, adverse cooperative computing, scheduling issues, task allocation, etc. The Internet of Things (IoT) builds on the idea of the original Internet. It encompasses, of networking, computing nodes that all linked together via global networks. It is widely adopted by every domain of applications due to familiarity of Internet. At the core of IoT are millions of devices that pass on data and carry out actions based on Internet connectivity. Internet is distributed in nature so applications based on IoT follow distributed architecture. The chapter has described advantages, issues and applications of IoT in terms of distributed computing. Fog computing is a new platform for distributed computing that is used in all most all IoT based applications. Some challenges for future research are: the need for identity of devices globally, research on architecture with distributed characteristics and encompasses of heterogeneity, issues on scalability and interoperability of communication, efficient chip based communication architecture, etc.

Chapter 5 proposed a new approach on the application of internet of things to enhance e-governance. In this chapter, the authors mentioned how Internet of Things (IoT) brings unprecedented changes in our lives, as they can be informed by smart devices and real-time data. The authors said that e-government seems to be one that can be greatly benefited by the use of IoT. The use of IoT in e-government can be extremely valuable as it offers the possibility for a wide range of applications and services that can be available to the public. IoT-based systems can enable the provision of new, innovative e-government services or ameliorate and complement the existing ones. Such systems and services can be even more important when used within critical security and safety contexts, allowing for the protection of the public and the prevention of disasters. Beside the opportunities, there are also challenges that need to be addressed technically and non-technically. Examples of technical challenges are the heterogeneity of the devices; incorporation of Artificial Intelligence (AI) in e-government applications; data interoperability that facilitates the exchange of information between public and private bodies and security. Examples of non-technical challenges are: organizational, political, financial and legal issues. Such issues can affect the decisions that need to be made and the actions that will follow them at strategic, tactical and operational level regarding the utilization of IoT technology for e-government purposes. Example case is given to offer useful insights that can be of interest for both researchers and practitioners and can serve as a starting point for further study and work in this field.

Chapter 6 outlines the deep learning application on internet of things. The chapter describes various issues regarding the application of deep learning on internet of things, such as deep learning model and architecture, IoT data characteristics, requirement analytics, quick and spilling information on IoT, profound learning as well as security. The chapter also mentions challenges of IoT such as security, gadget constraint in term of computational ability and idleness as well as communication. Overall, the chapter mentioned that profound learning can effectively manage IoT security. The authors proposed a new profound learning based steering assault recognition. The learning procedure yields the IoT assault location show and tried the model against various test situations for more exact estimation of exactness and review.

Chapter 7 provides a comprehensive overview of Neural Networks and Its application in Autonomous Vehicles. Neural Networks has been the one of the buzzwords in the last few years and are used in Deep Learning to solve complex problems which cannot be solve by traditional Machine Learning models and algorithms. Its popularity rises mainly because of the computing power and the data availability. One of the very famous applications of neural networks is in the fields of autonomous vehicle. Objet detection is used to view the outside the worlds as humans do. Using the object detection algorithms, the system can detect various objects including vehicles, human and traffic signs. Beside object detection, the autonomous vehicle also needs path planning to find the shortest as well as optimal path between two points ensuring less turning, less braking, and avoiding traffic. Both object detection and path planning requires powerful computing resources to process big data. Therefore, the autonomous vehicles are one of the best practical applications of the deep learning algorithms as it requires quick decisions to be made. The research in the autonomous vehicles industry has been tremendous in the last few years and continuously getting better. As a developing field, there are several issues that need to be addressed such as safety of the passengers, response times during accidents and emergency situations.

Chapter 8 describes the network security approach in distributed environment. Security is one of the main issues in the distributed environment. There are various data exchanged in the distributed environment. Multimedia data is one of the data that are widely used in many fields such as education, business, military as well as entertainment. Therefore, it is essential to secure the sensitive data before transmission or distribution. In this chapter, the authors the uses of RSA and RC6 encryption algorithm for secure multimedia transfer. The Red-Black substitution tree technique is used for key distribution. Three case studies are conducted to give insight on the performance of these algorithms. The first study aims to demonstrate the basic working principle of the RSA algorithm. The second study represents the key distribution technique using a Red-Black tree. The third study represents the security of data in GSM network. The case studies show how data can be secured in different ways. Various researches show that the demand for robust security mechanisms is growing rapidly and the use of intelligence algorithm is expected can enhance the security of data.

Chapter 9 enlightens the concept of machine learning and the commonly employed learning algorithm for developing efficient and intelligent systems. Common machine learning algorithms are explained in the chapter, such as linear regression, linear support vector machine, clustering algorithm as well as association algorithm. The authors also explained two type of learning process; supervised learning and unsupervised learning. Several problem examples help the readers to understand the learning algorithms mentioned in the chapter.

Chapter 10 proposed a new model of rainfall prediction for determining planting pattern. An accurate rainfall prediction model is needed to overcome the problem of shifting rainfall patterns. The proposed model of rainfall prediction use Exponential Smoothing Seasonal Planting Index (ESSPI). The proposed model is assessed using rainfall data in Boyolali, Indonesia from 2003 to 2014. The data is grouped for each district in Boyolali. The experiment result shows that the proposed methods provide better accuracy than the original exponential smoothing model. In the future, the model needs to be assessed in more various data and conditions.

Chapter 11 addressed the issue of computer forensic investigation in cloud of things. Recently, many applications are functioning with support of Internet of Things (IoT). The issue arises as IoT devices easier to hack and could trigger criminal misuse these information. Two important applications that are vulnerable from the hack are discussed in the chapter. The applications are health records from the wearable device and smart cities devices to collect information, analyze and integrate the information. Smart city include important features such as smart network traffic management, smart building, smart technology, smart governance, smart citizen and smart security. The authors mentioned that there is limitation in the current available forensic tools. The limitation refers to the unfit of existing of digital forensic tool with the heterogeneous infrastructure of IoT environment. This limitation will bring new challenges in the aspect of collecting evidence from distributed IoT infrastructures. Moreover, the extracting evidence from the IoT devices may not be acceptable in law court as the hacker can monopolize the evidence.

Chapter 12 explains the application of neural network for big data. Lots of information and massive data sets have been generated from big corporations or organization. These big data sets have been the challenges of many commercial applications, researches and organization. The enormous development of intelligence computing has attracted many practitioners and researches apply intelligence method on big data sets. In this chapter, a new model of Neural Network for big data sets in a sequential environment and distributed network is proposed. Based on the experiment results, the authors mentioned that the new model successfully applied on big data sets. In the near future, the model will be applied in billions of English documents in both the sequential environment and the parallel network environments.

The editor of this book would like to thanks to all contributors for their outstanding chapters that making this book a global reference. This book is suitable for scientist, engineer and practitioner in the field computational intelligence and Internet of Things.

Hindriyanto Dwi Purnomo
Satya Wacana Christian University, Indonesia

Acknowledgment

In this great opportunity, we would like to thank to all colleagues and friends for their unwavering supports, encouragement and helps of this book chapter. Their idea, feedback and suggestion have significantly improved the quality of the book. All chapters in this book have been rigorously reviewed. We gratefully acknowledge the constructive comments from all reviewers for the improvement of the overall outstanding chapters of the book.

We also sincerely thanks to the IGI Global at Hershey PA, USA for their unlimited help and support on this book chapter's project. In particular, special thanks to Ms. Jan Travers and Ms. Jordan Tepper for their guide and cooperation.

Hindriyanto Dwi Purnomo
Satya Wacana Christian University, Indonesia
January 2019

Chapter 1

Motion Planning Method for In-Pipe Walking Robots Using Height Maps and CNN-Based Pipe Branches Detector

Sergei Savin

(iD) https://orcid.org/0000-0001-7954-3144
Innopolis University, Russia

ABSTRACT

In this chapter, the problem of motion planning for an in-pipe walking robot is studied. One of the key parts of motion planning for a walking robot is a step sequence generation. In the case of in-pipe walking robots it requires choosing a series of feasible contact locations for each of the robot's legs, avoiding regions on the inner surface of the pipe where the robot cannot step to, such as pipe branches. The chapter provides an approach to localization of pipe branches, based on deep convolutional neural networks. This allows including the information about the branches into the so-called height map of the pipeline and plan the step sequences accordingly. The chapter shows that it is possible to achieve prediction accuracy better than 0.5 mm for a network trained on a simulation-based dataset.

INTRODUCTION

Pipelines are an important part of modern engineering and transportation infrastructure. Replacing aging pipelines is costly, which motivates performing periodic inspections and repairs in order to prolong the use of the existing ones (Ilg

DOI: 10.4018/978-1-5225-7955-7.ch001

et al., 1997). However, this activity is labor-intensive and is not always possible without the use of in-pipe robots (Tătar et al., 2007; Chatzigeorgiou et al., 2011).

In-pipe robots allow performing inspections of the inner surface of the pipe, which comes in direct contact with the transported material. In-pipe robots can be viewed as transportation systems carrying a suit of sensors or a specialized equipment designed for the inspection or repair tasks. The task of the in-pipe robots is then to move from point to point or along a given trajectory inside the pipe. This includes moving through pipes with changing diameter, pipes with horizontal and vertical sections, pipes with branches, T-junctions and L-turns (Roslin et al., 2012). The complex geometry of the inner surface of pipelines makes the problem of motion planning more difficult for in-pipe robots, compared with robots and vehicles moving on the ground.

One of the standard approaches to designing in-pipe robots is to use structures that make the problem of contact interaction with the inner surface of the pipe simpler. Examples of such designs include robots with passive or active parallel structures that press the robot's wheels or tracks against the inner surface of the pipe (Roh & Choi, 2005, Ryew et al., 2000; Jun et al., 2004). There are also examples of robots using loaded springs to directly push the robot's wheels against the inner surface of the pipe (Chatzigeorgiou et al., 2015; Horodinca et al., 2002). Some of the robots of this type have demonstrated the ability to move through pipelines with bends, and with horizontal and vertical sections (Tătar et al., 2007). The robot shown in (Nishimura et al., 2012) demonstrated the capability to move through T-junctions. These types of designs might also require the use of an additional steering mechanism (Choi & Roh, 2007). Advantages of these designs include reliable contact with the inner surface of the pipe, relatively simple control and relatively few motors required. The disadvantages of these designs include relatively small range of pipe diameters that a particular robot can navigate, limited possibilities in traversing sharp bends and turns, difficulties in moving through pipes with non-circular diameters, or equivalently, pipes contaminated with material deposits on their inner surface (Singh et al., 2017). There are also examples of in-pipe robots with wheels and tracks that do not use additional mechanical structures to improve the contact with the inner surface of the pipe (Ong, 2003). These types of robots are not capable of moving in vertical sections of pipelines.

One of the ways to improve the capabilities of in-pipe robots is to use designs that facilitate agile locomotion. One of such designs is in-pipe walking robots (Gálvez et al., 2001; Pfeiffer, 2007; Silva & Tenreiro, 2007). Examples of such robots can be found in (Zagler & Pfeiffer, 2003; Roßmann & Pfeiffer, 1996, 1998), where an eight-legged prototype was shown, in (Savin et al., 2017a) where a six-legged robot moving in spatially curved pipes was discussed, and in (Savin & Vorochaeva, 2017b, 2017c) where a four-legged robot designed for planar pipelines was considered.

Other alternative designs include in-pipe robots with flexible elements (Fukuda et al., 1989; Jatsun et al., 2012), robots with magnetic wheels (Tâche et al., 2007) and others. The discussion of their properties is beyond the scope of this chapter.

The advantages of in-pipe walking robots include their ability to navigate pipes with changing diameters, the possibility to directly control the reaction forces, their ability to move through horizontal and vertical sections of pipelines and their independence of the geometry of the pipe's cross-section. However, the control problem for this type of robots is challenging. It requires producing a trajectory which would be feasible in terms of the robot's dynamics and in terms of contact interactions. This leads to the problem of planning a step sequence on the inner surface of the pipe and then using this step sequence to generate trajectories for the robot's feet and the robot's body. These problems can be solved with computationally intensive specialized algorithms. They are discussed in more detail in the next section.

In paper (Savin & Vorochaeva, 2017a) it was shown that a step sequence for an in-pipe walking robot can be generated using a relatively simple and computationally lite algorithm, which exploits a specific geometric representation of the pipeline, allowing the pipeline to be "unwrapped" and transformed into a so-called height map. This algorithm can be used to generate step sequences for pipes with obstacles. Here an "obstacle" refers to a region on the inner surface of the pipe, where the robot should avoid stepping to. Examples of such regions are contaminant deposits on the inner surface of the pipe or the part of the pipe where it is connected to a branch. One of the limitations of this approach is that it requires the knowledge of the obstacle locations, including pipe branches, in order to generate the step sequence.

In this chapter, this limitation is addressed. The aim of the chapter is to provide an algorithm that can facilitate the motion planning for in-pipe walking robots by detecting and localizing the branches in the pipeline using the data from the robot's on-board sensors. The use of this algorithm is not limited to walking robots or footstep sequence generation. It can also be used to map the pipeline, localizing the branches, and it can be used as a part of navigation procedure for moving from the main pipe to a branch.

BACKGROUND

Motion Planning for Walking Robots

Motion planning for walking robots is often decomposed into a step sequence generation and trajectory planning. In this case, the step sequence generation procedure needs to provide a step sequence, feasible with respect to the environment as well as the robot's kinematics and dynamics. Examples of step sequence generation algorithms for legged robots can be found in (Short & Bandyopadhyay, 2018; Jatsun et al., 2017b). Trajectory planning procedure is required to provide trajectories for individual points (the edges of the robot's feet, the robot's center of mass or others) and motions of individual links which would implement a given step sequence. One of the well known types of trajectory generation algorithms are zero-moment point (ZMP) algorithms, which provide a criteria for maintaining vertical balance for the robots walking over flat terrain (Kajita et al., 2003; Vukobratović & Borovac, 2004).

The step sequence generation problem is often solved by projecting the supporting surface onto a two-dimensional map and planning the sequence of footholds on that map. The map can also be represented as a set of two-dimensional regions (Deits & Tedrake, 2014). In the case when the original surface is not horizontal, the feet might need to be oriented according to its local geometric properties after the step sequence is planned (Jatsun et al., 2017a). This approach allows simplification of the planning procedure, since local geometric properties of the supporting surface are excluded from the step sequence generation problem formulation. This approach allows the use of a number of planning methods, such as rapidly exploring random trees (RRT), probabilistic road maps, optimization-based methods and combinations of map discretization and graph search methods, such as A*.

The use of optimization-based methods is particularly interesting, as it allows introducing the notion of optimality into the planning problem formulation without having to discretize the map or rely on random search techniques. Optimization-based methods for step sequence generation are computationally expensive but they have been shown to be feasible for bipedal humanoid robots (Kuindersma et al., 2016). It should also be noted that the maps which include obstacles are usually not used directly in the optimization-based planning procedures, as it would lead to non-convex optimization problems which could produce local minima and could present numerical difficulties. Instead, such maps are decomposed into convex obstacle-free regions, which are then used as constraints in the optimization. The resulting optimization problem can be formulated as a mixed-integer quadratic program (MIQP), which can be solved by branch and bound algorithms implemented in available numerical solvers (specialized software packages) such as Gurobi or MOSEK (Aceituno-Cabezas, 2018). The decomposition of the map into convex obstacle-free regions can be done using a number of the existing methods, as discussed in (Deits & Tedrake, 2015; Savin, 2017, 2018a).

It should be noted that some of the planning methods, such as RRT, could be used directly on the original supporting surface, as it was done in (Savin, 2018b).

The main issue with applying the discussed above methods to the control of in-pipe walking robots is the fact that the geometry of the inner surface of the pipe is significantly different from the geometries of the supporting surfaces encountered by walking robots moving over the ground. Papers (Savin & Vorochaeva, 2017a, 2017b) discuss algorithms that exploit specific geometric descriptions of the pipes in order to generate a map, which can be used by the step sequence planners developed for on-ground walking robots. The algorithm presented in (Savin & Vorochaeva, 2017a) provides a so-called height map of the pipe by "unwrapping" it. The branches and material deposits on the inner surface of the map can then be treated as obstacles. It was shown in the paper that the resulting step sequences follow the geometry of the pipe and allow for feasible gaits.

In practice however, detailed maps of the inner surface of the pipe might not be available. In order to generate step sequences that take into account the pipeline branches, those need to be mapped. This motivates the use of localization and mapping algorithms for in-pipe robots. In (Thielemann et al., 2008; Tsubouchi et al., 2000) pipe recognition algorithms based on the use of camera images are discussed. These algorithms aim to address the localization problem for the robot and to recognize particular types of branches. The effectiveness of the recognition algorithms for the pipe branches might be improved by the use of neural networks, which is discussed in the following section.

Neural Networks-Based Computer Vision Methods Applied to In-Pipe Robots

The use of neural networks in computer vison has a long history. The relative advantage of the use of neural networks over traditional computer vision algorithms has been shown in image categorization tasks (Krizhevsky et al., 2012). One of the advantages of neural networks is associated with their ability to improve the prediction quality when more labeled training data is available. This allows to change the focus in the algorithm development from manually designing input data processing in order to account for all known cases and exceptions to gathering and labelling training data. In some cases, this might make the original task simpler, especially if gathering and labeling the training data is not labor-intensive. Additionally, experiments with transfer learning (methods for using a pre-trained neural network to improve the training process of a different neural network) had shown that it is possible to use a neural network trained on a big dataset to improve the performance of a different neural network, for which there might not be as much training data available (Huh et al., 2016). This is often explained by the fact that neural networks learn to recognize features that are similar to different tasks, and therefore transferring the knowledge of these features might speed up the learning process of a new neural net.

One of the most successful types of neural networks used for computer vision tasks are convolutional neural networks (CNN). CNN include convolutional layers, which can be viewed as sets of filters. The these filters are specified by the tunable parameters that the neural net learns during training. The advantages of this type of neural networks include small number of tunable parameters compared with dense neural networks, as well as their focus on extracting information from the spatially connected data (Goodfellow et al., 2016).

The success of neural networks is associated with the wide availability of tools for their design and training. Such tools include software packages such as Tensorflow, Caffe, PyTorch and their versions (Abadi et al., 2016; Jia et al., 2014; Collobert et al., 2002). The training of deep neural networks became feasible with the use of specialized GPU-enabled (where GPU stands for a graphic processor unit) mathematical libraries, supporting massive parallelization of the computations associated with the network training.

In this chapter, a convolutional neural network-based predictor is designed for the pipe branches detection. The gathering and labeling of the training dataset, the proposed structure of the network and the approaches to its training are discussed in the following sections.

Feedback Control for In-Pipe Walking Robots

In order to implement the step sequences and the trajectories generated for an in-pipe robot, feedback controllers are used. However, it requires controller design that can work with constrained mechanical systems. Such controllers are discussed in a number of works where feedback control of bipedal walking robots is studied (Mason et al., 2014; Kuindersma et al., 2016). Their application to in-pipe walking robots is studied in (Savin & Vorochaeva, 2017c; Savin et al., 2017b).

Other issues associated with feedback control, such as state estimation, model parameter estimation and others are also similar for the in-pipe walking robots and the on-ground walking robots (Savin et al., 2018a). Detailed discussion of the practical aspects of these issues for on-ground walking robots can be found in the reports on the DARPA Robotics Challenge and other sources.

IN-PIPE WALKING ROBOT DESIGN

In this chapter, we consider a walking in-pipe robot consisting of a body and a number of identical legs. The algorithms presented in the chapter pose a few requirements on the particular properties on the robot, which are discussed below.

Figure 1 shows a general diagram for an in-pipe walking robot.

In the figure 1, points K_i represent contact points of the legs. The robot shown in the figure has six legs, although different design choices are possible. The legs

Figure 1. In-pipe walking robot

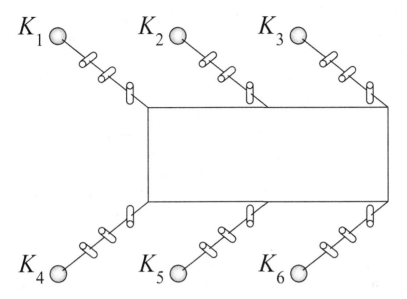

of the robot shown in the figure consist of three sequentially connected links. Each pair of connected links is joined by a rotational joint.

The leg structure shown in the figure 1 is one of many possible ones. Some alternative leg structures are shown in the figure 2 and in figure 3.

rotational joints, K are contact elements. The leg shown in figure 2 (a) is limited in its mobility, as it only can move its contact point K relative to its base point B along a plane. Therefore, it can only be used when such planar motion is sufficient. Such cases are studied in (Savin et al., 2017b; Savin & Vorochaeva, 2017b, 2017c).

The leg designs shown in figure 2 (b) and (c) are capable of moving their contact points relative to the base point in a given volume, determined by the lengths of the links and the joint limits. The difference between these two designs lies in the fact

Figure 2. Leg structures with point contact for in-pipe walking robots; (a) is the case when the leg has 2 degrees of freedom, (b) and (c) are cases when the leg has 3 degrees of freedom

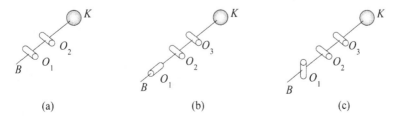

both have different additional kinematic singularities with respect to the task of moving the point K. These singularities occur when the point K lies on the axis of the joint O_1. In that position, the motion in joint O_1 does not affect the position or velocity of the point K.

In figure 3, the same notation is used as in figure 2, except in this case K_i represent the edges of the robot's foot. One of the differences between the leg structures shown in figure 2 and figure 3 lies in the contact interaction regimes they support. The designs shown in figure 2 support point contacts, where as the designs shown in figure 3 support distributed contact. From the walking robotics, it is well known that both point feet and feet supporting distributed contact can be used in practical applications. Traditionally, point feet have been widely used with quadrupeds, while distributed contact feet had been a part of the majority of humanoid robot designs. The advantage of distributed contact feet is associated with richer contact interactions. In particular, a single foot with distributed contact can produce a six-dimensional reaction wrench (including three-dimensional reaction force and torque), subject to the friction cone constraints. An ideal point foot on the other hand would only be able to produce a three-dimensional reaction force, also subject to the friction cone constraints. The disadvantage of using distributed contact feet is associated with the additional task of generating feasible orientation for them as a part of the step sequence generation procedure.

In bipedal robotics, legs similar to ones shown in figure 3 (a) are used often. They have 5 degrees of freedom, and are capable of placing and orienting the foot. However, since a free body position and orientation in the space is described by 6 independent parameters, a leg with only 5 degrees of freedom cannot implement all desired motions, and is constrained to a subset of possible positions and orientations. In practice, this constraint is often placed on the rotation of the foot along the axis normal to the plane of the foot. The structure shown in figure 3 (b) on the other

Figure 3. Leg structures with feet for in-pipe walking robots; (a) is a 5 degrees of freedom case, (b) is a 7 degrees of freedom case

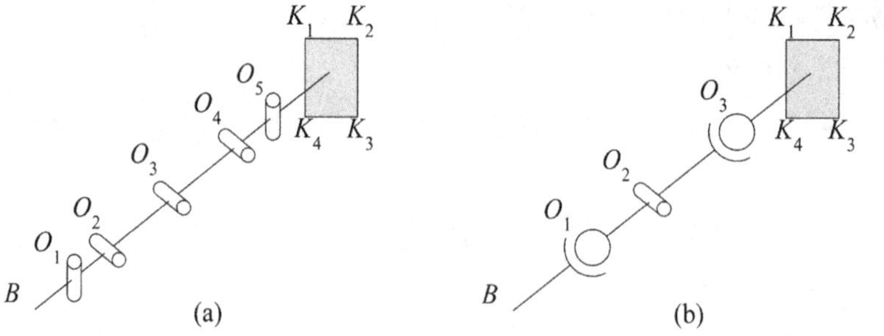

hand can provide arbitrary placement and orientation of the foot, within a given volume in the space of positions and orientations. It has one redundant degree of freedom, which can be seen as allowing the robot to orient the joint O_2 (the robot's knee).

In terms of planning step sequences, the designs shown in figure 2 (b) and (c) are the simplest, as they do not require additional constraints associated with the limited mobility of the leg (as in the case of the foot shown in figure 2 (a)), and they do not require additional considerations associated with the orientation of the robot's feet. The following sections are focused on this case. However, the step sequence generation algorithms discussed here can easily be extended to handle the case of distributed contact feet, same as it is done for bipedal walking robots (Kuindersma et al., 2016).

HEIGHT MAP-BASED STEP SEQUENCE GENERATION

In order to simplify the task of step sequence generation for an in-pipe robot, the height map-based approach proposed in (Savin & Vorochaeva, 2017a) is used. That approach requires a specific geometric description of the pipe and relies on the concept of a centerline.

The centerline of a pipe is a curve that passes through the centers of all circular cross-sections of the pipe. Let us define the centerline as the following parametric curve:

$$\xi(s) = \begin{bmatrix} \xi_x(s) & \xi_y(s) & \xi_z(s) \end{bmatrix}^{\mathrm{T}}, \tag{1}$$

where s is a parameter of the curve. The diameter of the pipe can also be defined as a function of s: $d = d(s)$. We require that $\xi(s)$ and $d(s)$ are differentiable. If it is desirable for s to be interpretable as a distance traveled along the centerline, we can additionally require that $\left\| d\xi/ds \right\| = 1$.

This allows us to define a height map of the pipe:

$$h(s, \varphi) = -d(s), \tag{2}$$

where φ is the angular coordinates defining the position of a point on the cross section of a pipe. The resulting surface is illustrated on the figure 4.

Figure 4. A pipeline and its height map

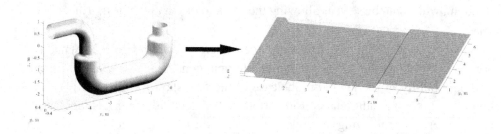

The height map can be used to plan a sequence of steps and then transform them back onto the inner surface of the original pipe. In order to perform this transformation, in (Savin & Vorochaeva, 2017a) it was proposed to use local coordinate systems placed along the center line. Let $e_1(s)$ be a unit vector tangent to the centerline $\xi(s)$ and let $e_2(s)$ and $e_3(s)$ be unit vectors orthogonal to $e_1(s)$ and to each other. We require $e_1(s)$, $e_2(s)$ and $e_3(s)$ to be smooth functions of the parameter s. Then they provide local orthonormal coordinate systems along the centerline. They can be used to perform the transformation from the centerline to the original pipe as follows:

$$p(s,\varphi,h) = \xi(s) - hT(e_1,\varphi)e_2,\tag{3}$$

where $T(e_1,\varphi)$ is a matrix that performs rotation around axis e_1 by an angle φ.

The height map can be used to plan sequences of steps in coordinates (s,φ), for example by incrementing the s coordinate by the value Δs for every next step. The resulting step sequence will follow the geometry of the pipe, spacing out the steps such that the legs do not drift apart from each other during the motion (Savin & Vorochaeva, 2017a).

IN-PIPE ROBOT'S SENSOR MODEL AND TRAINING DATASET GENERATION

Pipeline and Sensor Models

In this work, the training dataset is generated using a model of the pipeline and the sensor. This approach allows to explore the properties of the detection procedure and allows for faster experimentation, as the collection and labeling of the training dataset can be done automatically. However, it also limits the applicability of the achieved results, since the actual pipes might include features that might hinder the work of the predictor trained on a simulated data. The pipe model used here had been discussed in (Savin et al., 2018b), where it was used to test a pipeline classification algorithm.

To describe a pipe with a single branch we use the following set of parameters: unit vectors n_m and n_b which define the direction of the main pipe and its branch, points p_m and p_b which define the origin of the main pipe and of its branch and radii R_m and R_b of the main pipe and the branch respectively.

We consider the case when the robot is equipped with a sensor, which allows calculating distance to the nearest object along a given ray. An example of such sensor is a LIDAR system. The position of the sensor is given by p_s and the direction of the sensor's ray is given by a unit vector n_s.

In order to find the point of intersection of the ray with the inner surface of the main pipe, the following system of equations is solved:

$$\begin{cases} \alpha n_s = \beta n_m + p + (p_m - p_s) \\ p^{\mathrm{T}} n_m = 0 \\ p^{\mathrm{T}} p = R_m^2 \\ \alpha \geq 0 \end{cases}, \tag{4}$$

where α and β are scalar parameters and p is a slack variable. The parameter α can be seen as a distance between the sensor and the intersection point along the direction n_s. We assume that the sensor is only capable of measuring distances in one direction, therefore α is always positive. The scalar β represents the distance along the direction n_m that needs to be traversed in order to reach the intersection point.

Equations (4) are quadratic with respect to p and have two solutions, representing two intersection points of a line and a cylinder. In the general case, one of these solutions does not satisfy the condition $\alpha \geq 0$, so only a single solution is available.

The coordinates of the intersection point are then given as follows:

$$p_I = p_s + \alpha n_s. \tag{5}$$

We denote this solution as p_1. The ray might also intersect the branch. In order to find the intersection points with the branch, the following system of equations is solved:

$$\begin{cases} \alpha n_s = \beta n_b + p + (p_b - p_s) \\ p^T n_b = 0 \\ p^T p = R_b^2 \\ \alpha \geq 0 \\ \beta \geq 0 \end{cases} \qquad (6)$$

In the system (6) both α and β are required to be positive scalars. This is due to the fact that the branch only goes into a single direction. In case the branch goes through the pipe and continues in both directions, the restriction on β can be lifted. System (6) in general has two solutions, and any number of them can satisfy the conditions $\alpha \geq 0$, $\beta \geq 0$. Using the formula (5), up to two additional intersection points p_2 and p_3 can be found.

The geometry of the problem discussed above is illustrated in the figure 5.

Figure 5 illustrates that although there are up to three different points of intersection between the ray and the inner surface of the pipeline, only one of them is valid, since the ray cannot leave the inner volume of the pipeline. In figure 5, the parts of the ray that leave the inner volume are shown in red. Additionally, the point of intersection of the ray with the main pipe can lie within the branch. This means that this point is fictitious, as the part of the inner surface of the main pipe where it is connected to the branch is removed hence the ray cannot intersect it. The same is true for the intersection points with the inner surface of the branch that lie within the volume of the main pipe.

In order to remove infeasible solutions from the obtained set, the following procedure can be used (Savin et al., 2018b):

Figure 5. A pipe with a branch intersected by a ray from a sensor

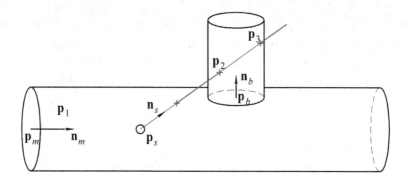

$$minimize \quad \|p_t\|$$

$$subject\ to: \quad \begin{cases} p_t \in \{p_1, p_2, p_3\} \\ \left\| (p_t - p_m) - (n_m^{\mathrm{T}}(p_t - p_m))n_m \right\| \geq R_m + \varepsilon \\ \left\| (p_t - p_b) - (n_b^{\mathrm{T}}(p_t - p_b))n_b \right\| \geq R_b + \varepsilon \end{cases} \qquad (7)$$

where ε is a small scalar constant that determines the margin of error in the procedure. It is needed to account for numeric round-off errors, which may lead to the drift of the intersection points towards the inner volume of the pipeline and then being rejected as infeasible.

Training Dataset Structure

The training dataset consists of arrays of point coordinates found by implementing the procedure discussed in the previous section. The array is generated by changing the direction of the sensor's ray, so that the rays are distributed uniformly on a grid. Here, 50 by 50 arrays of points are used. In order to provide the robot with a sense of depth, three separate arrays produced from different origin points p_s for the sensor are generated.

The resulting dataset sample is a matrix of dimensions $50 \times 50 \times 9$, since each point has three coordinates and there are three arrays stacked on each other. The label for each sample is the true position of the origin of the branch p_b. For each sample, the parameters describing the pipe are randomized. In total, 1000 samples are generated. Points that lie further than the distance $L_{\max}$ from the sensor are moved to be lying at that distance exactly. The data points in the set are normalized.

Figure 6 shows one array of points gathered by the sensor. The points in the figure are not normalized.

We can observe that the pipe appears to be capped. This is the result of the convention of moving intersection points that lie further than the distance $L_{\max}$ from the sensor. This is done in order to simplify the normalization of the data. To illustrate why this needs to be done, we can consider an intersection point obtained by a pointing the sensor into the direction arbitrary close to n_m. This would result in an intersection point arbitrary far away from p_s. If that point remains in the dataset and is not discarded as an outlier, it would require large scaling coefficients in order to normalize the data. This in turn might make all other data points bunch up close together, which is not desirable from the training perspective.

Figure 6. A set of intersection points gathered by the sensor

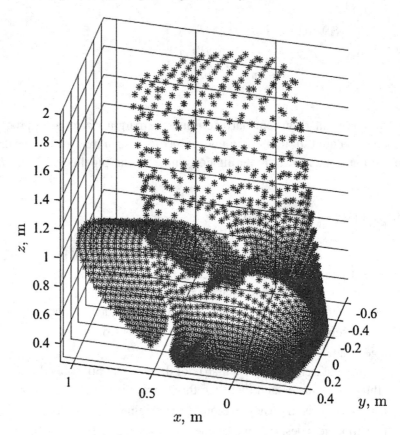

NEURAL NETWORK DESIGN AND TRAINING

In this section, the design of the proposed neural network is discussed. The task of the neural network is to predict the position of the origin of the pipe branches. The proposed design is a convolutional neural networks segmented into five identical modules, similar to the designs shown in (Savin et al., 2018b, Savin, 2018a). Each module includes a convolutional layer with 64 3x3 filters and a rectified linear unit (ReLU) activation function. The convolutional layer is followed by a max pooling layer with strides 2. Ioffe-Szegedy batch normalization is used (Ioffe & Szegedy, 2015). The output of the last module is flattened and fed into a dense (fully connected) layer with 32 elements and ReLU activation. Two of such layers are used, followed by a dense layer with 3 elements, used as an output.

The structure of the proposed network is shown in figure 7.

Figure 7. Structure of the proposed neural network

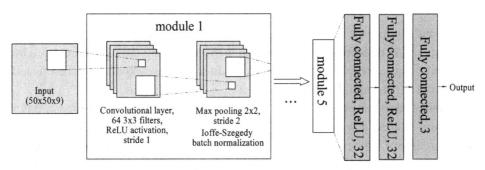

The proposed network is implemented using machine learning library Tensorflow and a high level deep learning library Keras. The model was trained with Adam optimization algorithm using decreasing learning rates, starting with $5 \cdot 10^{-3}$ and gradually decreasing it to $2 \cdot 10^{-5}$. The model was trained on 900 samples and 100 samples were used in verification, using mini batches of size 64.

The loss function dynamics during training is shown in the figure 8.

As figure 8 shows, it was possible to bring the loss down to less than 0.5 mm. It should be noted that the loss could be brought down further by longer training sessions with further decreasing learning rates, or by increasing the number of samples in the training set. However, it is not clear if it will lead to a significant performance improvement in terms of gate generation when the task is to avoid stepping into the pipe branch. With this type of task, robustness of the algorithm might be a more important criterion, as long as a certain precision threshold is reached.

Figure 8. Loss function dynamics during the network training

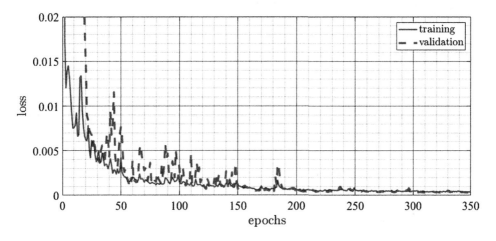

FUTURE RESEARCH DIRECTIONS

As of now, the in-pipe walking robots are in the beginning of their development and many of the questions associated with their design and control still need to be answered. Furthermore, additional research directions are expected to be opened when more experimental studies of such robots have been conducted.

Among of the most interesting research directions associated with in-pipe walking robots are: designing sensing and control algorithms for robust foot placements on the inner surface of the pipe, designing walking gaits capable of moving from the main pipe into a branch, designing walking gaits for the robots moving in pipes with arbitrary cross sections and others.

In general, there is still a need for improvement in the control workflow of in-pipe walking robots. The use of machine learning algorithms might be one of the directions towards achieving practical and robust control for these robots. The use of reinforcement learning in gait generation and feedback control for in-pipe walking robots have not been studied yet and the use on convolutional neural networks as a part of the computer vision system for such robots had only seen a few studies.

It should also be noted, that a lot of progress made in the walking robotics is related to the use of numerical optimization algorithms as part of the control loops. This might indicate one of the possible directions for further research in the in-pipe walking robotics. Same as the use of neural networks, optimization-based control algorithms require significant computational capabilities and place high demands on the on-board computer of the robot. These demands need to be addressed in implementations of their control system. The topic control system implementations for the in-pipe walking robots is especially interesting from the perspective of optimization of the physical parameters of the robot, including its weight and size. Thus, the optimal composition of the control system implementation for the walking in-pipe robots is another interesting research direction.

CONCLUSION

In this chapter, a motion planning workflow for in-pipe walking robots is discussed. In order to solve the step sequence generation problem, a height map-based algorithm was used, which allows to unwrap the pipe the pipe and generate the step sequence on a two dimensional map. The generated step sequence can then be mapped back onto the original pipe. Associated transformations can be done with the use of simple linear algebra computations.

In order to generate pipe branches-aware step sequences and avoid unintentionally stepping into the branches, a detection procedure was proposed. The procedure relies on the use of deep convolutional neural networks. The input data to the network is an array of points detected by a LIDAR-like sensor. The output of the network is the prediction of the origin of the pipe branch. The network includes 5 convolutional layers and 3 fully connected layers and uses ReLU activations for all layers.

The training data was generated using a model of the pipe and the sensor. The formulations used to generate the data are presented in the chapter. The network was trained across multiple sessions with diminishing learning rates. The training results showed that the network was capable of achieving accuracy within millimeters, which is enough for the discussed task.

The results shown in this chapter demonstrate the possibility of using convolutional neural networks as a part of motion planning for in-pipe robots. The network-based predictors could compliment the hand-written motion planning algorithms, taking care of the motion planning asks which are inherently data-driven

ACKNOWLEDGMENT

This work is supported by the Presidential Grant MK-2577.2017.8.

REFERENCES

Abadi, M., Barham, P., Chen, J., Chen, Z., Davis, A., Dean, J., . . . Kudlur, M. (2016, November). Tensorflow: a system for large-scale machine learning. In OSDI (Vol. 16, pp. 265-283). Academic Press.

Aceituno-Cabezas, B., Mastalli, C., Dai, H., Focchi, M., Radulescu, A., Caldwell, D. G., ... Semini, C. (2018). Simultaneous Contact, Gait, and Motion Planning for Robust Multilegged Locomotion via Mixed-Integer Convex Optimization. *IEEE Robotics and Automation Letters*, *3*(3), 2531–2538.

Chatzigeorgiou, D., Youcef-Toumi, K., & Ben-Mansour, R. (2015). Design of a novel in-pipe reliable leak detector. *IEEE/ASME Transactions on Mechatronics*, *20*(2), 824–833. doi:10.1109/TMECH.2014.2308145

Chatzigeorgiou, D. M., Youcef-Toumi, K., Khalifa, A. E., & Ben-Mansour, R. (2011, January). Analysis and design of an in-pipe system for water leak detection. In *ASME 2011 International Design Engineering Technical Conferences and Computers and Information in Engineering Conference* (pp. 1007-1016). American Society of Mechanical Engineers. 10.1115/DETC2011-48395

Choi, H. R., & Roh, S. G. (2007). In-pipe robot with active steering capability for moving inside of pipelines. In *Bioinspiration and Robotics Walking and Climbing Robots*. InTech.

Collobert, R., Bengio, S., & Mariéthoz, J. (2002). *Torch: a modular machine learning software library (No. EPFL-REPORT-82802)*. Idiap.

Deits, R., & Tedrake, R. (2014, November). Footstep planning on uneven terrain with mixed-integer convex optimization. In *Humanoid Robots (Humanoids), 2014 14th IEEE-RAS International Conference on* (pp. 279-286). IEEE. 10.21236/ADA609276

Deits, R., & Tedrake, R. (2015). Computing large convex regions of obstacle-free space through semidefinite programming. In *Algorithmic foundations of robotics XI* (pp. 109–124). Cham: Springer. doi:10.1007/978-3-319-16595-0_7

Fukuda, T., Hosokai, H., & Uemura, M. (1989, May). Rubber gas actuator driven by hydrogen storage alloy for in-pipe inspection mobile robot with flexible structure. In *1989 IEEE International Conference on Robotics and Automation* (pp. 1847-1852). IEEE. 10.1109/ROBOT.1989.100242

Gálvez, J. A., De Santos, P. G., & Pfeiffer, F. (2001). Intrinsic tactile sensing for the optimization of force distribution in a pipe crawling robot. *IEEE/ASME Transactions on Mechatronics*, 6(1), 26–35. doi:10.1109/3516.914388

Goodfellow, I., Bengio, Y., Courville, A., & Bengio, Y. (2016). *Deep learning* (Vol. 1). Cambridge, MA: MIT Press.

Horodinca, M., Doroftei, I., Mignon, E., & Preumont, A. (2002, June). A simple architecture for in-pipe inspection robots. In Proc. Int. Colloq. Mobile, Autonomous Systems (pp. 61-64). Academic Press.

Huh, M., Agrawal, P., & Efros, A. A. (2016). *What makes ImageNet good for transfer learning?* arXiv preprint arXiv:1608.08614

Ilg, W., Berns, K., Cordes, S., Eberl, M., & Dillmann, R. (1997, September). A wheeled multijoint robot for autonomous sewer inspection. In *Intelligent Robots and Systems, 1997. IROS'97., Proceedings of the 1997 IEEE/RSJ International Conference on* (Vol. 3, pp. 1687-1693). IEEE. 10.1109/IROS.1997.656584

Ioffe, S., & Szegedy, C. (2015). *Batch normalization: Accelerating deep network training by reducing internal covariate shift.* arXiv preprint arXiv:1502.03167

Jatsun, S., Savin, S., & Yatsun, A. (2017, August). Walking pattern generation method for an exoskeleton moving on uneven terrain. *Proceedings of the 20th International Conference on Climbing and Walking Robots and Support Technologies for Mobile Machines (CLAWAR 2017).* 10.1142/9789813231047_0005

Jatsun, S., Savin, S., & Yatsun, A. (2017, September). Footstep Planner Algorithm for a Lower Limb Exoskeleton Climbing Stairs. In *International Conference on Interactive Collaborative Robotics* (pp. 75-82). Springer. 10.1007/978-3-319-66471-2_9

Jatsun, S., Yatsun, A., & Savin, S. (2012). Pipe inspection parallel-link robot with flexible structure. In Adaptive Mobile Robotics (pp. 713-719). Academic Press. doi:10.1142/9789814415958_0091

Jia, Y., Shelhamer, E., Donahue, J., Karayev, S., Long, J., Girshick, R., ... Darrell, T. (2014, November). Caffe: Convolutional architecture for fast feature embedding. In *Proceedings of the 22nd ACM international conference on Multimedia* (pp. 675-678). ACM. 10.1145/2647868.2654889

Jun, C., Deng, Z., & Jiang, S. (2004, August). Study of locomotion control characteristics for six wheels driven in-pipe robot. In *Robotics and Biomimetics, 2004. ROBIO 2004. IEEE International Conference on* (pp. 119-124). IEEE.

Kajita, S., Kanehiro, F., Kaneko, K., Fujiwara, K., Harada, K., Yokoi, K., & Hirukawa, H. (2003, September). *Biped walking pattern generation by using preview control of zero-moment point* (Vol. 3). ICRA. doi:10.1109/ROBOT.2003.1241826

Krizhevsky, A., Sutskever, I., & Hinton, G. E. (2012). Imagenet classification with deep convolutional neural networks. In Advances in neural information processing systems (pp. 1097-1105). Academic Press.

Kuindersma, S., Deits, R., Fallon, M., Valenzuela, A., Dai, H., Permenter, F., ... Tedrake, R. (2016). Optimization-based locomotion planning, estimation, and control design for the atlas humanoid robot. *Autonomous Robots, 40*(3), 429–455. doi:10.100710514-015-9479-3

Mason, S., Righetti, L., & Schaal, S. (2014, November). Full dynamics LQR control of a humanoid robot: An experimental study on balancing and squatting. In *Humanoid Robots (Humanoids), 2014 14th IEEE-RAS International Conference on* (pp. 374-379). IEEE.

Nishimura, T., Kakogawa, A., & Ma, S. (2012, August). Pathway selection mechanism of a screw drive in-pipe robot in T-branches. In *Automation Science and Engineering (CASE), 2012 IEEE International Conference on* (pp. 612-617). IEEE. 10.1109/CoASE.2012.6386388

Ong, J. K., Kerr, D., & Bouazza-Marouf, K. (2003). Design of a semi-autonomous modular robotic vehicle for gas pipeline inspection. *Proceedings of the Institution of Mechanical Engineers. Part I, Journal of Systems and Control Engineering, 217*(2), 109–122. doi:10.1177/095965180321700205

Pfeiffer, F. (1850). The TUM walking machines. *Philosophical Transactions of the Royal Society of London A: Mathematical Physical and Engineering Sciences, 365*(1850), 109–131. doi:10.1098/rsta.2006.1922

Roh, S. G., & Choi, H. R. (2005). Differential-drive in-pipe robot for moving inside urban gas pipelines. *IEEE Transactions on Robotics, 21*(1), 1–17. doi:10.1109/TRO.2004.838000

Roslin, N. S., Anuar, A., Jalal, M. F. A., & Sahari, K. S. M. (2012). A review: Hybrid locomotion of in-pipe inspection robot. *Procedia Engineering, 41*, 1456–1462. doi:10.1016/j.proeng.2012.07.335

Roßmann, T., & Pfeiffer, F. (1996). Control and design of a pipe crawling robot. *IFAC Proceedings Volumes, 29*(1), 8162-8167.

Roßmann, T., & Pfeiffer, F. (1998). Control of an eight legged pipe crawling robot. In *Experimental Robotics V* (pp. 335–346). Berlin: Springer. doi:10.1007/BFb0112974

Ryew, S., Baik, S. H., Ryu, S. W., Jung, K. M., Roh, S. G., & Choi, H. R. (2000). In-pipe inspection robot system with active steering mechanism. In *Intelligent Robots and Systems, 2000.(IROS 2000). Proceedings. 2000 IEEE/RSJ International Conference on* (Vol. 3, pp. 1652-1657). IEEE. 10.1109/IROS.2000.895209

Savin, S. (2017, June). An algorithm for generating convex obstacle-free regions based on stereographic projection. In *Control and Communications (SIBCON), 2017 International Siberian Conference on* (pp. 1-6). IEEE. 10.1109/SIBCON.2017.7998590

Savin, S. (2018). Enhanced Footsteps Generation Method for Walking Robots Based on Convolutional Neural Networks. In Handbook of Research on Deep Learning. Academic Press. (forthcoming)

Savin, S. (2018). RRT-based Motion Planning for In-pipe Walking Robots. In Dynamics of Systems, Mechanisms and Machines (Dynamics), 2018 (pp. 1-6). IEEE. doi:10.1109/Dynamics.2018.8601473

Savin, S., Ivakhnenko, A., & Medvedev, D. (2018). Pipeline branches detection using deep convolutional neural networks. Extreme Robotics 2018.

Savin, S., Jatsun, S., & Vorochaeva, L. (2017). Trajectory generation for a walking in-pipe robot moving through spatially curved pipes. In *MATEC Web of Conferences* (Vol. 113, p. 02016). EDP Sciences. 10.1051/matecconf/201711302016

Savin, S., Jatsun, S., & Vorochaeva, L. (2017, November). Modification of Constrained LQR for Control of Walking in-pipe Robots. In Dynamics of Systems, Mechanisms and Machines (Dynamics), 2017 (pp. 1-6). IEEE. doi:10.1109/Dynamics.2017.8239502

Savin, S., Jatsun, S., & Vorochaeva, L. (2018). State observer design for a walking in-pipe robot. In *MATEC Web of Conferences* (Vol. 161, p. 03012). EDP Sciences. 10.1051/matecconf/201816103012

Savin, S., & Vorochaeva, L. (2017, June). Footstep planning for a six-legged in-pipe robot moving in spatially curved pipes. In *Control and Communications (SIBCON), 2017 International Siberian Conference on* (pp. 1-6). IEEE. 10.1109/SIBCON.2017.7998581

Savin, S., & Vorochaeva, L. (2017, May). Pace pattern generation for a pipeline robot. In *Industrial Engineering, Applications and Manufacturing (ICIEAM), 2017 International Conference on* (pp. 1-6). IEEE. 10.1109/ICIEAM.2017.8076143

Savin, S., & Vorochaeva, L. (2017, May). Nested quadratic programming-based controller for pipeline robots. In *Industrial Engineering, Applications and Manufacturing (ICIEAM), 2017 International Conference on* (pp. 1-6). IEEE. 10.1109/ICIEAM.2017.8076142

Short, A., & Bandyopadhyay, T. (2018). Legged Motion Planning in Complex Three-Dimensional Environments. *IEEE Robotics and Automation Letters*, *3*(1), 29–36. doi:10.1109/LRA.2017.2728200

Silva, M. F., & Tenreiro Machado, J. A. (2007). A historical perspective of legged robots. *Journal of Vibration and Control*, *13*(9-10), 1447–1486. doi:10.1177/1077546307078276

Singh, A., Sachdeva, E., Sarkar, A., & Krishna, K. M. (2017). *Design and optimal springs stiffness estimation of a Modular OmniCrawler in-pipe climbing Robot.* arXiv preprint arXiv:1706.06418

Tâche, F., Fischer, W., Moser, R., Mondada, F., & Siegwart, R. (2007). Adapted magnetic wheel unit for compact robots inspecting complex shaped pipe structures. In Advanced intelligent mechatronics, 2007 IEEE/ASME international conference on (No. LSRO-CONF-2007-013, pp. 1-6). IEEE Press. doi:10.1109/AIM.2007.4412506

Tătar, O., Mandru, D., & Ardelean, I. (2007). Development of mobile minirobots for in pipe inspection tasks. *Mechanika, 68*(6).

Thielemann, J. T., Breivik, G. M., & Berge, A. (2008, June). Pipeline landmark detection for autonomous robot navigation using time-of-flight imagery. In *Computer Vision and Pattern Recognition Workshops, 2008. CVPRW'08. IEEE Computer Society Conference on* (pp. 1-7). IEEE. 10.1109/CVPRW.2008.4563167

Tsubouchi, T., Takaki, S., Kawaguchi, Y., & Yuta, S. I. (2000). A straight pipe observation from the inside by laser spot array and a TV camera. In *Intelligent Robots and Systems, 2000. (IROS 2000). Proceedings. 2000 IEEE/RSJ International Conference on* (Vol. 1, pp. 82-87). IEEE. 10.1109/IROS.2000.894586

Vukobratović, M., & Borovac, B. (2004). Zero-moment point—thirty five years of its life. *International Journal of Humanoid Robotics, 1*(1), 157-173.

Zagler, A., & Pfeiffer, F. (2003, September). "MORITZ" a pipe crawler for tube junctions. In *Robotics and Automation, 2003. Proceedings. ICRA'03. IEEE International Conference on* (Vol. 3, pp. 2954-2959). IEEE.

ADDITIONAL READING

Dertien, E., Stramigioli, S., & Pulles, K. (2011, May). Development of an inspection robot for small diameter gas distribution mains. In *Robotics and Automation (ICRA), 2011 IEEE International Conference on* (pp. 5044-5049). IEEE. 10.1109/ICRA.2011.5980077

Li, P., Ma, S., Li, B., Wang, Y., & Ye, C. (2007, October). An in-pipe inspection robot based on adaptive mobile mechanism: mechanical design and basic experiments. In *Intelligent Robots and Systems, 2007. IROS 2007. IEEE/RSJ International Conference on* (pp. 2576-2581). IEEE.

Mateos, L. A., & Vincze, M. (2011, December). DeWaLoP-monolithic multi-module in-pipe robot system. In *International Conference on Intelligent Robotics and Applications* (pp. 406-415). Springer, Berlin, Heidelberg. 10.1007/978-3-642-25486-4_41

Nakazato, Y., Sonobe, Y., & Toyama, S. (2010). Development of an in-pipe micro mobile robot using peristalsis motion. *Journal of Mechanical Science and Technology*, *24*(1), 51–54. doi:10.100712206-009-1174-x

Roh, S. G., Ryew, S., Yang, J. H., & Choi, H. R. (2001). Actively steerable in-pipe inspection robots for underground urban gas pipelines. In *Robotics and Automation, 2001. Proceedings 2001 ICRA. IEEE International Conference on*(Vol. 1, pp. 761-766). IEEE. 10.1109/ROBOT.2001.932642

Schempf, H., Mutschler, E., Gavaert, A., Skoptsov, G., & Crowley, W. (2010). Visual and nondestructive evaluation inspection of live gas mains using the Explorer™ family of pipe robots. *Journal of Field Robotics*, *27*(3), 217–249.

Suzumori, K., Wakimoto, S., & Takata, M. (2003, September). A miniature inspection robot negotiating pipes of widely varying diameter. In *Robotics and Automation, 2003. Proceedings. ICRA'03. IEEE International Conference on* (Vol. 2, pp. 2735-2740). IEEE. 10.1109/ROBOT.2003.1242006

Tâche, F., Fischer, W., Siegwart, R., Moser, R., & Mondada, F. (2007, October). Compact magnetic wheeled robot with high mobility for inspecting complex shaped pipe structures. In *Intelligent Robots and Systems, 2007. IROS 2007. IEEE/RSJ International Conference on* (pp. 261-266). IEEE. 10.1109/IROS.2007.4399116

KEY TERMS AND DEFINITIONS

Centerline: A curve passing through the centers of circular cross sections of the pipe.

In-Pipe Robot: An autonomous or a semi-autonomous vehicle designed to move in the inner volume of a pipeline.

L-Turn: A section of a pipeline when the pipe bends, changing its direction by 90 degrees, producing a shape similar to letter L.

Step Sequence: A sequence of positions on the supporting surface where the robot needs to come into contact with it.

T-Junction: A pipeline junction where two perpendicular pipes are joined together, producing a shape similar to letter T.

Training Dataset: A set of labeled samples used by on optimizer algorithm to update the weights of a neural network, so as to enable it to better predict correct labels, given the samples.

Validation: A procedure of computing a performance metric for a neural network, using samples that were not used in the network training.

Chapter 2
Analysis of Industrial and Household IoT Data Using Computationally Intelligent Algorithm

Soumen Mukherjee
RCC Institute of Information Technology, India

Arup Kumar Bhattacharjee
RCC Institute of Information Technology, India

Debabrata Bhattacharya
RCC Institute of Information Technology, India

Moumita Ghosal
Serampore Girls' College, India

ABSTRACT

In this chapter, data mining approaches are applied on standard IoT dataset to identify relationship among attributes of the dataset. IoT is not an exception; data mining can be used in this domain also. Various rule-based classifiers and unsupervised classifiers are implemented here. Using these approaches relation between various IoT features are determined based on different properties of classification like support, confidence, etc. For classification, a real-time IoT dataset is used, which consists of household figures collected from various sources over a long duration. A brief comparison is also shown for different classification approaches on the IoT dataset. Kappa coefficient is also calculated for these classification techniques to measure the robustness of these approaches. In this chapter, standard and popular power utilization in household dataset is used to show the association between the different intra-data dependency. Classification accuracy of more than 86% is found with the Almanac of Minutely Power Dataset (AMPds) in the present work.

DOI: 10.4018/978-1-5225-7955-7.ch002

INTRODUCTION

In recent time the use of computational intelligence in every aspect of life is increasing day by day. New research findings from different types of computational intelligence domain like machine learning, neural network, meta heuristic algorithm, fuzzy systems are emerging at a very fast rate. In recent times smart devices are also being connected in Internet of Things (IoT) in a fast rate (Atzori, et al., 2010). Data collected from those smart devices can show important relationship and data analytic (Mohammadi & Al-Fuqaha 2018).

IoT is a network of objects e.g. vehicles, appliances, mobile phones, cameras, instruments, buildings etc (Parker 2014). These devices are all connected, doing communication and sharing information based on some protocols to achieve secure control of all the devices. There are certain characteristic of IoT like Interconnectivity, Heterogeneity, Scalability, Safety and Connectivity. Some of the application areas of IoT are Smart Appliances Control, Smart Intrusion Detection, Smart Energy Use, Smart Transportation and Parking, Smart Waste Management, Smart Pollution Control, Smart Fire Detection, Smart Wildlife Protection, Smart Protection from Hazardous and Explosive Gases, Smart Patients Monitoring, Smart Power Controllers, Smart Animal Farming, Smart Child Care etc.

Kevin Ashton at MIT's AutoID Lab around early 2000 A.D. pioneered the key concept to IoT (Internet of Things) (Barnaghi, et al., 2012). He thought of a system where information would be collected from the RFID tags attached to a host of connected devices and then this information would be linked to the Internet. Since then the concept has grown to such a stage that it encompasses the most modern ubiquitous paradigm and aim i.e. any device, anywhere, anytime can be connected to any other devices/equipments/people/systems through any means of communication mode to share and exchange information (Patel & Patel, 2016).

So the IoT is a hardware-software enabled behemoth network of physical objects in real life domain that connects a host of devices may be, computers and non-computers, living or inanimate, all sorts and forms to one another through a set of agreed, diverse standard data communication protocols sharing and updating data via wired and wireless connectivity (Sleman & Moeller 2008). This interconnected network of physical objects naturally has devices of all sizes, features and types, like mobile phones, data tablets, vehicles, home appliances, cameras, imaging systems, medical instruments, domestic and industrial components and systems, people, tree, water, roads, buildings, bridges, animals etc.

Till date about 5 billion devices have been deployed and connected in this interconnected scenario, but according to Cisco's IOTG (Internet Of Things Group), there will be over 50 billion connected devices in the world by 2020 (CISCO Report).

That poses enormous challenges on the design, development and deployment of all such devices using all the communication, control and automation and security standard technologies and protocols. Each object can be attached with a sensor to collect data. This data will then be shared and communicated amongst themselves over wired and wireless connectivity protocols enabling data security norms.

Conceptually IoT could be broken into three levels viz. i) people to things/ machines ii) people to people and iii) things/machines to other things/machines. They all connect among themselves through the Internet. Through the use of this system, smart positioning, tracking, safety, control and management including real-time online monitoring can be achieved. Thus this concept embraces "pervasive computing" to create a future safe, secure, intelligent co-operative environment to foster a harmonious global human living where energy, transport, mining, patient care, food and agriculture, cargo movement and fleet management, alarm systems and a lot of other sectors will all be integrated (Patel & Patel, 2016). There are lots of works done in Internet of Things (IoT) in machine learning domain. In their work Din et al. (Din et al., 2017) select different features using a bio inspired metaheuristic algorithm Ant Colony Optimization from massive IoT data. They remove noise from the data using Kalman filter and used MapReduce to enhance efficiency of the data. Pedestrian identification done by Lwowski et al. (Lwowski et al., 2017) using convolution neural networks (CNN) with a classification accuracy of 95.7% using IoT data. Anthi et al. has done (Anthi et al., 2018) a work on Intrusion Detection System for IoT, using Machine Learning (ML). Osuwa et al. (Osuwa et al., 2017) has developed an artificial intelligence application using IoT. Polyakov, et al. (Polyakov, et al., 2018) discussed the importance of voice assistants and pros and cons with a review in their paper. The motivation of the present work is to show how machine learning and computational intelligence can be used to the smart management of the Internet of Things data. The present work suggests how the association rule can be used to find out the relation between the IoT data which is very essential in machine learning domain.

This article shows how to apply different classification unsupervised techniques and rule based classifiers on the IoT dataset. Using these classifiers the articles wants to find relation between various features of the devices which are having IoT Enabling Technologies. Apriori and FP Growth Algorithm are used here on these data to find the relationship between various features. Also different classifiers are applied on these data, namely, Decision Table Classifier, Random Tree Classifier and Multi-Layer Perceptron and their degree of correct classification, various errors and statistical measures are shown. The chapter is arranged in the following manner. In the next section IoT Architecture is discussed then in the consecutive section IoT Enabling Technologies, IoT Characteristics, Scope of IoT are discussed. In the literature survey section to domains are discussed IoT in household and IoT in industry. In the next section basic concepts of the used technologies are discussed. Finally in the proposed work section details of the work is given. Finally conclusive remarks are given on the results found.

BACKGROUND

This background section is divided with IoT Architecture, IoT Enabling Technologies, IoT Characteristics and Scope of IoT.

IoT Architecture

IoT is envisaged to have a layered architecture. The many layers are cited below:

1. **Smart Devices/Sensors Layer:** This is at the base (ground) level. The IoT enabled products employ embedded technology due to the continued technological progress. Processors from 16-1500 MHz acting as intelligent nodes in a energy-harvested Wireless Sensor Network (WSN) to super processors in a multi-core environment could all fit into the scenario. The design and power management issues of these devices are very important here.
2. **Gateways and Networks Layer:** This involves different protocols in networks and gateways. Data passing, verification and conversion must all be seamlessly integrated.
3. **Management Service Layer:** These can be achieved via proper analysis, security measures, process modeling and device control. The M2M management is one great big area where it is impacting a big change.
4. **Application Layer:** This layer involves applications in smart environments/ spaces.

Authors have shown a conceptual IOT architecture by dividing the whole matter into different phases. In the very first Phase, sensor network attached with the IoT system gather data from the local environment. The phase 2 is for converting the analog data to digital. Next phase is concern with the preprocessing of collected data and at the final phase the data is stored finally in the database. Pictorial representation of this architecture is shown in Figure 1.

Figure 1. IoT Architecture

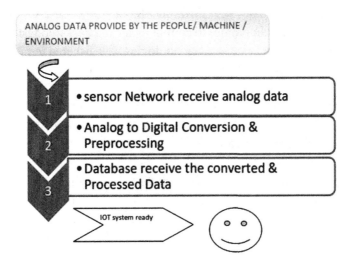

IoT Enabling Technologies

All existing technologies e.g 2G/3G/4G, starting from RFID, Bluetooth, NFC, Wi-Fi, Zigbee to GSM,GPRS,GPS,LTE, wireless sensor networks (WSN), microcontrollers, microprocessors and many new upcoming ones will enable IoT implementation (Lopez Research Report, 2013).These technologies must enable the real-life "things" i) to capture contextual information ii) to process those information locally iii) to improve security, privacy of data and iv) to update and share the data always in real-time mode. So the entities always stay current, up-to-date, "live" in the environment. They gather, pass and sense information to/from the environment and enable humans to sense, control and program them as required. As an example illustration, the RFID technology which had been in use since 1990s enables steps as below: i) a scanner(RFID Reader) captures information from the RFID tag attached to the object through radio waves ii) In the Reader a microprocessor controls a transceiver to process the information iii) The Transponder (tag, contactless card) communicates to the Reader through sharing of data(both-ways), energy and clock(from RFID-reader to Transponder) iv) the RFID-Reader finally stores the data to the application/ database server. By processing the information, the database system will be able to store and get all information related to the Identification Code. Barcode technology had been in use for a long time allowing Item Topology Identification wherein a 96-bit EPC (Electronic Product Code) designed and devised in MIT in 1999 had been used. Here the EPC Manager (28 bits) and Object Class (24 bits) play major roles in identification. In Bluetooth, short-distance RF communication (within may be 400-500 m) using piconets takes place between IT-enabled objects to gather, pass, share information. Likewise, GSM, GPRS, and GPS use 2-G, 3-G and 4-G mobile communication technologies to communicate the data amongst the different nodes. Beyond that 5-G and even 6-G technologies have ushered to take advantage of the broad spectrum of band usage and allowing enough bandwidth to individual devises/users.

So the approach should be: i) define what data we want from the sensors and design them likewise ii) build a security-enabled IoT network iii) collect as much data as possible from the sensors iv) arrange to pass these data to the various processors and then to the Internet (could be on servers or even on the Cloud Storage) and v) review the size and scale of IoT providers (the M2M-device management platform, the solution delivery platform and the apps sitting and acting on the "radio" or "sensor" data all should act hand-in-hand with one another (Lopez Research Report).

IoT Characteristics

Since IoT includes numerous applications in various domains and connections among them, we can segregate the whole scenario between vertical and horizontal application domains on the Internet. There should be a balance between these two. New web-based services like ITTT.com and zAPI.com have been formed to connect vertical integrations (Chase, 2013).

At the lowest layer, the technology must address the following issues

- **Connectivity:** Different wired and wireless standards.
- **Power Management:** Battery-powered or local energy-stored WSNs.
- **Security:** Built in hardware security and connectivity security protocols.
- **Heterogeneity and Complexity:** diverse structural and complex elements possible (no single technology is the champion here).
- **Ubiquity:** the sub-systems and devices always to be connected, available to all any time (24x7)
- **Transparency:** from the users'(devices) perspective, data passed and presented should be seamless and transparent hiding all the underlying complexities/transformations/translations/conversions and source/origin/ intermediaries
- **Dynamic Nature:** the enabled systems-devices may be dynamic, meaning no. of devices may change (on person, place and time), state of devices may vary (connected/disconnected, sleeping/wake-up etc.), context of devices (on location, temperature, speed)

- **Massive Scaling:** With a multitude of devices being connected to each other, the size requirements will be much higher order of magnitude than the Internet. So managing such larger size will be a real big design challenge.

Tomorrow's IoT will be the ideal mix of vertical and horizontal domains. In the vertical domain, various application portfolios may exist while in the horizontal level, IoT may have the largest system architecture. Here (in the horizontal level) mostly the sub-systems will be connected and information passed among them seamlessly, ubiquitously, invisibly in all applications. A global common data language (at least to many standards and interfaces) mostly may emerge (Chase, 2013). But designing and appropriating such a common data language is a real big daunting task.

The vertical domain applications may be linked to each other in data sharing, passing, verification and validation through Application Programming Interfaces (APIs). Examples of vertical domain applications could be portals on insurance, healthcare, home safety and security, finance, production, supply-chain management, efficient power control and management, home automation, BlockChain etc.

As another example, we may have a 5-layered pyramid structure of design architecture of a cyber-physical systems-enabled manufacturing system. Here from the bottom to the top layers would be 1) Smart Connection level 2) Data-to-Information Conversion level 3) Cyber level 4) Cognition level 5) Configuration level. One salient feature in each level may be plug-and-play, smart analytics for component machine health, twin models for components and machines, Integrated simulation and synthesis, self-configure for resilience and self-adjust for variations respectively.

Scope of IoT

IoT targets to permeate every sphere of human life in a productive, creative, synergistic way. The three C's of IoT are Communication, Control and Automation and Cost Savings. IoT can be applied to so many spheres of real-life (Lopez Research Report, 2013), e.g.

1. Smart Home (lighting, temperature, HVAC, etc. control, safety and intrusion prevention, auto on-off of domestic appliances effecting consumer power savings).
2. Transportation and Logistics (cargo, asset tracking for better position control, fleet management and aiming zero loss).
3. Smart City (within this it may include infrastructure improvement for charging electric vehicles, smart metering, remote patient monitoring (diabetes), smart retail, smart-bank branches, lane and highway management for car movements

etc.). It also may involve monitoring and controlling applications like bridges, railway tracks, on-and-offshore wind-farms etc.

4.   Smart Factory (automated production, inventory and sales management).
5.   Retail (brand and vendor management, sales tracking, giving customer's value-for-money).
6.   Environment (safe disposal of waste, possible recycling, eco-habitat, a clean and green surrounding).
7.   e-Health (all critical patient-care systems, smart patient monitoring (diabetes, cancer, AIDS to name a few), remote monitoring and administration of all critical hospital sub-systems including patients, doctors, nursing staff, medicines and hospital equipment) etc.

All businesses will profit from the successful deployment of IoT (Internet of Things). Their bottom line surely will improve. Apparently the barrier line between analog and digital world is fast eroding.

An ordinary production, inventory and sales management system may capture production data (Batch no. individual device id, date, other statistics etc.) from some tag attached to the device and pass it on a computer to store and process data from a database/application server. Then such information could be shared amongst various nodes for effective decision making and data analytics. Let us take the case of smart Production Management Systems. Such smart systems may use digital control systems to automate process controls, operation tools and service information systems to optimize plant safety and security. Smart industrial management systems may also be connected to the "smart grid" to optimize real-time energy. Measurements, automated controls, plant optimization, health and safety management are to be provided by a large number of networked sensors (Ersue et al. 2014). Industrial IoT (IIoT) is a subset of IoT and industries are expected to generate $12 trillion of global GDP by 2030 by employing IIoT (Daugherty et al. 2016).

CISCO has expanded IoT to IoE (Internet of Everything) which includes places, objects, things and people. Basically anything to which we can attach a sensor and establish connectivity can be a part of this new ecosystem. IoT has a glorious, challenging future for the benefit of humankind.

LITERATURE SURVEY AND FUTURE RESEARCH DIRECTIONS

Internet of thing is one of the emerging research domains in Computer Science (Feng & Liang, 2010). The application areas of this field can be vast from human body to street (Gubbia et al. 2013). The applications of IoT can be classified into two categories.

Applications of IoT in Household

According to (Anand & Susan, 2015) implementation of IoT can be done by Radio Frequency Identification (RFID) - it is nothing but a wireless device which is workable at electromagnetic fields. Objects are connected with this device must have a tag. Another technique is Near Field Communication. By this method smarts phones which are communicating are under the IoT. The third method is M2M i.e. Machine to machine information exchange method, by connecting lots of wireless sensor network and finally there is another method which is basic tool for IoT is IPV6 addressing scheme. To apply IoT in industry (Gupta, 2015) designed a framework of the flexible Network using intelligent data. Now, what is intelligent data? Objects in the real worlds are represented in the network are referred to as intelligent data. According to them their framework first addresses the problem, provides the reference and finally provides a uniform solution using IoT. This framework architecture flexible in the sense that the data used in the framework is authentic and secured. It also supports large scale devices when it uses large scale platforms. The framework as described by the (Gupta, 2015) the system is able to manage the unstable condition of a large network. IoT can be viewed as two types of architecture. Authors (Maranda & Kaczmarek, 2015) described that 3-layer architecture of IoT consists of perception layer, followed by transport layer then followed by application layer. In perception layer data collection from the real world is done. The action taken by transport layer is process of data from sensor and transfers them to the third layer. The last layer is responsible for delivery of applications which is the most important part of the architecture. The second type of architecture i.e. 5 layer architecture consists of perception layer, gateway layer, network layer, middleware layer and application layer. The first layer is just similar to the first layer of previous architecture. And perform the same work that is collect data from real world. The next two layers are used to transfer data between the intelligent objects. The next layer, middleware layer adds some flexibility to the interface between hardware and software. And finally we get application from the application layer.

Al-Sakran (Al-Sakran, 2015) proposed an agent based IoT framework. A Software agent is a executable entity. A multi-agent communication system is also introduced. This agent based system is applied on monitoring and controlling traffic using IoT. Traffic controlling system with image processing suffers many limitations where IoT based system offers some advantages. To introduce a traffic monitoring system, different categories of agents are used. Namely, Traffic Mobile Agent helps to send all data to the traffic management system. Second agent is user agent. By its name it directly communicates with the user. Next, monitor agent detects emergency situation (Lynggaard, 2013). RFID as stated above adds tags. Sensor Agent related with sensor. It receives data and processes it. Traffic Light Agent and Camera Agent are used to controlling traffic light and capturing image.

The whole traffic control System is mainly designed with RFID tag. The vehicle having RFID tag while passes through a road all the information related to a vehicle is saved in the system. At the same time GPS system obtains its position parameter.

Applications of IoT in Industry

Internet of Things can be broadly applied in industry (Evans & Annunziata, 2012). It offers lower production cost but it increases the efficiency of the product (Khan & Bhat, 2014). According the report (European Commission, 2017) IOOT can be introduced in aerospace industry. In this report the author thought IoT as a key element of smart factory in Industry 4.0.Designing and manufacturing an airplane or different parts of air bus is too much lengthy and difficult process. It is now fully, dependent of human being. In smart factory, the main aim is that IoT can support the human worker. This application can be done in the field of skin testing of airplane, measurement of rotation force as well as keep the regulation of construction. Thus overall performance of aircraft can be increased by this way. As its obvious result it can have a new impact on the business model and economic system. The researchers (Deshpande et al., 2016) observed that the use of CCTV is not enough to increase the quality in industry. Because it cannot generate any signal or alert (Zu, 2014). If different sensors such as Temperature sensor, Pressure sensor etc. will be used in the industry or hospital or in home, it will generate far better result. Sensors will produce analog signal and that signal will be sent to the android device. When an uneven situation arises, it will inform admin. By this method, hospital service can be improved significantly. If a sensor will be attached to a patient body, continuous monitoring by Doctor becomes very easy. This approach can also be applied widely in other industry. In this paper authors introduced a mathematical model to apply IoT easily. They consider some dataset and some functions to implement the data sets. According to cognizant report (Lucio, 2013) IoT depicted as combinations of four systems – The IP addressable things, Intermediate phase between things and cloud i.e. gateway, Networking components i.e. routers, aggregators, gateways, repeaters and so many devices which are used as a connecting device. And the last system is cloud storage. Applying IoT many more new models in hi-tech business can be achieved and that will increase sale of a company. Examples of hi-tech improvement are performance of mobile wallet can be more efficient by the use of sensor, shopping will be more interesting by the use of sensor in smart phone. Researchers (Beier, 2018) made a case study on China about creating digitalized Industry using IoT (Chen et al., 2017). In China many factories are closed due to negative environment pollution. In this country if IoT will be introduced in factory a transparent report can be generated to manage pollution and precautions can be taken. More over overproduction leads to unnecessary hazards. If availability and demand of customers are maintained digitally, the overproduction can be prohibited easily and environment will be managed efficiently. IoT also offers the advantage of saving energy, combine it with the digital approach and make a renewable energy system. In an article (Mohammeda & Ahmedb, 2017) the authors are concerned to manage weather, climate and agriculture by Internet of Things. Sensors, connected in IoT can measure the pollutant particle and give suggestion people what to do. IoT system is also able to monitor water pollution and pollution due to wastage. Weather forecast in more efficient manner only possible by using IoT. Radiation management which is the main reason for global warming can be done by IoT sensor smartly. IoT can provide its service in announcing natural disaster include floods, volcanic eruptions, earthquakes, hurricanes in advance and can save lives by its network with police station or hospitals. Smart agriculture is also an application field of IoT. Monitoring fields, weather, managing production everything is possible by the sensor of IoT.

From the above report, we can conclude that the application IoT may bring a major change in industry but it may also suffer from different problems such that performance of IoT is fully dependent of internet. So fluctuation in internet connection may affect it. Range of distance is another issue of IoT. Third point is the companies must have an early investment to introduce and maintain Internet of Things in their service.

In this work, authors have tried to find the relationship between various attributes of the IoT devices. Previously various works has been done to measure the harmful effect of the IoT devices on environment as well as to measure and control mechanism of IoT devices is also a huge area of research. Electronic gadgets, their working principles used in IoT technology is also important point of discussion. Here we have applied different association rule mining techniques as well as different classifiers to measure the influence of different features of these IoT devices on each other.

BASIC CONCEPTS

In this section authors have introduced some fundamental terms of rule based and unsupervised classifiers used in this work.

Association Rule Mining

Association rule can be represented as A->B, where A & B are disjoint item sets. The association rule can be generated based on the value of support and confidence. Frequency of a rule in a given dataset is known as Support and Confidence determines the frequency of item B in a transaction that contain A.

Association Rule Discovery

In a set of transaction, the rules which have support value greater than equal to the minimum threshold support and the confidence value greater than equal to the minimum threshold confidence can be discovered.

There are two steps of mining association rules frequent itemset generation and rule generation. In frequent itemset generation, itemsets with support value equal or greater then minimum support are considered. In rule generation high confidence rules from frequently appearing itemset is selected.

There are quite a few algorithms present for the generation of association rules:

Apriori Algorithm

It is developed by Agrawal in the year 1994 (Agrawal and Srikant, 1994) to find large scale association rules which multiple items. The disadvantage of this rule is it requires several iterations, it requires uniform minimum support and it is very difficult to find infrequent occurring events. In this algorithm some itemsets with minimum support are selected. Subsets with frequent set of items must be a frequent set of items. Iteratively frequent set of items are found with cardinality 1 to m. These sets of item are used in association rules (Liu et al.1998).

Consider two item X and Y, then various properties used to generate Association Rules are

Support = Frequency (X, Y)/ N

Confidence = Frequency (X, Y)/ Frequency (X)

Lift = Support (X, Y)/ (Support (X) * Support (Y))

The use of association rule mining is to find relation between various attributes and as well as to find the relation between various attributes and the class.

FP Growth

The FP Growth algorithm permits frequent sets of item detection without candidate set of items generation (Han et al. 2000). This is a two-step algorithm where in the 1st step a compact FP-tree data structure is build and in the 2nd step FP-tree is traversed to find frequent set of items. It is faster than Apriori but the space complexity is present in this algorithm.

Decision Table

It is a method of learning for discrete cost value target which can be modeled by a decision table. Any if-then rule (Hahsler, 2005) can be represented as decision table. This represents disjunction of conjunctions of constraints of the attributes (Kohavi, 1995).

Random Forest

Multiple decision tree predictors are present in Random forest. The classification accuracy increases in ensembles of trees which are identical but independent. Random vectors are used to control the growth of each tree in the forest (Breiman, 2001).

Multi-Layer Perceptron

Multi-Layer Perceptron (MLP) (Collobert and Bengio, 2004) is a type of neural network classifier which has a single input layer, single output layer and multiple hidden layers.

PROPOSED WORK

Through this work, authors have tried to apply different classification techniques unsupervised and rule based classifiers on the IoT dataset. Here author have considered dataset containing data about electricity metering of different appliances during certain time duration. Classification is a data mining technique that maps items with some class. The objective of classification is to predict the target class for some unknown data. In this work emphasis will be given to rule based classifier. Rule uses IF-THEN constraint for classification where condition known as antecedent are the various meter values and conclusion known as consequence is the target class or other relevant attributes. The dataset considered here in described below.

Association rule mining has been applied on the features of the IoT devices and to find relationship among them. Novelty of the work is to apply rule mining and classification techniques on IoT devices. Also validation of the data sets has been made using various error checking techniques used in the classification techniques.

Dataset Used

The Dataset used in this work is collected from UCI data repository (Makonin et al., 2013). This dataset is commonly known as "Almanac of Minutely Power Dataset (AMPds)" which includes utilization of water and natural gases. This dataset consist of household data gathered for multiple years in the area of Vancouver, Canada. This house is renovated in the year 2006 and got a rating more than 80% by Govt. of Canada. This data includes electric, water and gas consumption at 60 second interval. Electric voltage and current measurement is done by DENT Power Scout metering, gas measurements are done by an Elster AC250 and Elster BK-G4 metering; water measurements are taken by Elster or Kent V100 metering; and RS-485 network is used for data collection. The data are collected as Internet of Things (IoT) data. The dataset is taken in different timestamp in America time-zone. Details about the different data collected from the IoT devices used in the work are given in Table 1.

Rule based classifiers are applied to this dataset to find the relationship between various features. Rules generated may be used to predict the relation between the features and to interpret which feature may influence other features. Also few other unsupervised classifiers are applied, namely, Decision Table, Random Tree and Multi-Layer Perceptron. These classifiers are used to test the accuracy of predicting features from the given data set.

Table 1. Details about the different data collected from the IoT device used in the work.

Sl No.	Data/Feature Description	Voltage (Volt)	Current (Ampere)/ Breaker Type
1.	Full House Meter	240	200/Double Pole
2.	Garage Meter	240	60/Double Pole
3.	Security and Network Equipment	120	15/Single Pole
4.	Forced Air Furnace devices Fan and Thermostat	120	15/Single Pole
5.	Heat Pump Generator	240	40/Double Pole
6.	Dining Room Plug	120	15/Single Pole
7.	Kitchen Fridge	120	15/Single Pole
8.	Hot Water Generating Unit	120	15/Single Pole
9.	Entertainment devices like Television, PVR and AMP	120	15/Single Pole

Result and Discussion

In this work, authors have applied various association rule mining techniques, namely, Apriori and FP-Growth Algorithm for generating various rules based on confidence value. These rules represent the relation between various features. The list of features is specified in Table 1. Different parameter values considered for applying Apriori algorithms are shown in Table 2. For all the experiments Weka version 3.8 is used. Weka is a very popular tool for data mining. The entire experiment is done using association rule mining tab and classification tab of Weka.

For each rule, confi represents confidence of the rule, lift (in rules abbreviated as li) is measured by result of the confidence divided by the proportion of all features that are included in the consequence. Leverage (in rules abbreviated as le) Conviction (in rules abbreviated as con) is another measure of departure from independence. Conviction is given by P (antecedent) P (! consequence) / P (antecedent,! consequence). Rule

$$1 = 0 \; 4 = 0 \; 6259 ==> 5 = 0 \; 6259 \; <confi \; (1)> \; li \; (1.36) \; le \; (0.17) \; [1656 \; con$$
$$(1656.3)$$

represents Feature 1(Full House Meter) and Feature 4 (Forced Air Furnace) in 6259 transactions can predict the feature 5 (Heat Pump) with 100% confidence.

$$1 = 0 \; 4 = 0 \; 8 = 0 \; 5733 ==> 5 = 0 \; 5733 \; <confi \; (1)> \; li \; (1.36) \; le \; (0.15) \; [1517 \; con$$
$$(1517.1)$$

Table 2. Parameters values considered for Apriori Algorithm

Sl. No.	Features	Value
1	Type of metric considered for rule generation	Confidence
2	Minimum Support	0.1
3	Value by which support is decremented Iteratively	0.05
4	Number of rules generated	2000
5	Number of missing data	0
6	Upper bound value for minimum support	1.0
7	Number of instances	9999
8	Number of attributes	9
9	Number of cycles executed	18
10	Minimum confidence	0.9

represents Feature 1(Full House Meter) and Feature 8 (Hot Water Generating Unit) in 5733 transactions can predict the feature 5 (Heat Pump) with 100% confidence.

Hence from these rules it can be determined that which equipment (considered as antecedent in the rule) is influencing the working of other equipment (consequence in the rule).

Similarly other rules are generated showing the relation between different attributes. Here only top 20 rules are shown.

Top 20 rules generated by Apriori Algorithm on the said data based on the parameter values provided in Table 1 with confidence = 1 are as follows–

1. 1 = 0 4 = 0 6259 ==> 5 = 0 6259 <confi (1)> li (1.36) le (0.17) [1656 con (1656.3)

2. 1 = 0 4 = 0 8 = 0 5733 ==> 5 = 0 5733 <confi (1)> li (1.36) le (0.15) [1517 con (1517.1)

3. 1 = 0 4 = 0 9 = 0 5517 ==> 5 = 0 5517 <confi (1)> li (1.36) le (0.15) [1459 con (1459.94)

4. 1 = 0 3 = 1 4 = 0 5436 ==> 5 = 0 5436 <confi (1)> li (1.36) le (0.14) [1438 con (1438.51)

5. 1 = 0 4 = 0 6 = 0 5242 ==> 5 = 0 5242 <confi (1)> li (1.36) le (0.14) [1387 con (1387.17)

6. 1 = 0 4 = 0 8 = 0 9 = 0 5033 ==> 5 = 0 5033 <confi (1)> li (1.36) le (0.13) [1331 con (1331.86)

7. 1 = 0 3 = 1 4 = 0 8 = 0 5020 ==> 5 = 0 5020 <confi (1)> li (1.36) le (0.13) [1328 con (1328.42)

8. 1 = 0 4 = 0 6 = 0 8 = 0 4811 ==> 5 = 0 4811 <confi (1)> li (1.36) le (0.13) [1273 con (1273.12)

9. 1 = 0 3 = 1 4 = 0 9 = 0 4782 ==> 5 = 0 4782 <confi (1)> li (1.36) le (0.13) [1265 con (1265.44)

10. 1 = 0 4 = 0 6 = 0 9 = 0 4684 ==> 5 = 0 4684 <confi (1)> li (1.36) le (0.12) [1239 con (1239.51)

11. 1 = 0 3 = 1 4 = 0 6 = 0 4534 ==> 5 = 0 4534 <confi (1)> li (1.36) le (0.12) [1199 con (1199.82)

12. 1 = 0 3 = 1 4 = 0 8 = 0 9 = 0 4398 ==> 5 = 0 4398 <confi (1)> li (1.36) le (0.12) [1163 con (1163.83)

13. 1 = 0 4 = 0 7 = 0 4288 ==> 5 = 0 4288 <confi (1)> li (1.36) le (0.11) [1134 con (1134.72)

14. 1 = 0 4 = 0 6 = 0 8 = 0 9 = 0 4276 ==> 5 = 0 4276 <confi (1)> li (1.36) le (0.11) [1131 con (1131.54)

15. 1 = 0 3 = 1 4 = 0 6 = 0 8 = 0 4193 ==> 5 = 0 4193 <confi (1)> li (1.36) le (0.11) [1109 con (1109.58)

16. $1 = 0 \ 3 = 1 \ 4 = 0 \ 6 = 0 \ 9 = 0 \ 4022 ==> 5 = 0 \ 4022$ <confi (1)> li (1.36) le (0.11) [1064 con (1064.33)

17. $1= 0 \ 4 = 0 \ 7 = 0 \ 8 = 0 \ 3951 ==> 5 = 0 \ 3951$ <confi (1)> li (1.36) le (0.1) [1045 con (1045.54)

18. $1 = 0 \ 4 = 0 \ 7 = 0 \ 9 = 0 \ 3733 ==> 5 = 0 \ 3733$ <confi (1)> li (1.36) le (0.1) [987 con (987.85)

19. $1 = 0 \ 2 = 1 \ 3713 ==> 5 = 0 \ 3713$ <confi (1)> li (1.36) le (0.1) [982 con (982.56)

20. $1 = 0 \ 2 = 1 \ 4 = 0 \ 3704 ==> 5 = 0 \ 3704$ <confi (1)> li (1.36) le (0.1) [980 con (980.18)

It is also found that applying Apriori Algorithm with multiple filters or all filters available in Weka generates same set of rules as mentioned above for same set of parameters as mentioned in the above Table 2.

Another association rule generated is applied called FP-Growth. Different parameter values considered for these algorithms are shown in Table 3.

Top 20 rules generated by FP-Growth Algorithm on the said data based on the parameter values given in Table 2 with confidence = 1 are found as follows–

1. $2 = 1 \ 5 = 1 \ 1329 ==> 1 = 1 \ 1329$ <confi (1)> li (2.68) le (0.08) con (833.5)
2. $1 = 1 \ 4 = 1 \ 2644 ==> 5 = 1 \ 2644$ <confi (1)> li (3.78) le (0.19) con (1944.33)
3. $3 = 1 \ 2 = 1 \ 5 = 1 \ 1125 ==> 1 = 1 \ 1125$ <confi (1)> li (2.68) le (0.07) con (705.56)
4. $3 = 1 \ 1 = 1 \ 4 = 1 \ 2271 ==> 5 = 1 \ 2271$ <confi (1)> li (3.78) le (0.17) con (1670.03)
5. $2 = 1 \ 1 = 1 \ 4 = 1 \ 1328 ==> 5 = 1 \ 1328$ <confi (1)> li (3.78) le (0.1) con (976.58)

Table 3. Parameters values considered for FP-Growth Algorithm

Sl No.	Feature	Value
1	Type of metric considered for rule generation	Confidence
2	Minimum Support	0.1
3	Value by which support is decremented Iteratively	0.05
4	Number of rules generated	36
5	Number of missing data	0
6	Upper bound value for minimum support	1.0
7	Number of instances	9999
8	Number of attributes	9

6. 2 = 1 4 = 1 5 = 1 1328 ==> 1 = 1 1328 <confi (1)> li (2.68) le (0.08) con (832.87)
7. 3 = 1 2 = 1 1 = 1 4 = 1 1124 ==> 5 = 1 1124 <confi (1)> li (3.78) le (0.08) con (826.56)
8. 3 = 1 2 = 1 4 = 1 5 = 1 1124 ==> 1 = 1 1124 <confi (1)> li (2.68) le (0.07) con (704.93)
9. 5 = 1 2646 ==> 1 = 1 2645 <confi (1)> li (2.68) le (0.17) con (829.74)
10. 5 = 1 2646 ==> 4 = 1 2645 <confi (1)> li (3.76) le (0.19) con (971.58)
11. 1 = 1 5 = 1 2645 ==> 4 = 1 2644 <confi (1)> li (3.76) le (0.19) con (971.21)
12. 4 = 1 5 = 1 2645 ==> 1 = 1 2644 <confi (1)> li (2.68) le (0.17) con (829.42)
13. 3 = 1 5 = 1 2273 ==> 1 = 1 2272 <confi (1)> li (2.68) le (0.14) con (712.77)
14. 3 = 1 5 = 1 2273 ==> 4 = 1 2272 <confi (1)> li (3.76) le (0.17) con (834.62)
15. 3 = 1 1 = 1 5 = 1 2272 ==> 4 = 1 2271 <confi (1)> li (3.76) le (0.17) con (834.25)
16. 3 = 1 4 = 1 5 = 1 2272 ==> 1 = 1 2271 <confi (1)> li (2.68) le (0.14) con (712.46)
17. 2 = 1 5 = 1 1329 ==> 4 = 1 1328 <confi (1)> li (3.76) le (0.1) con (487.99)
18. 2 = 1 5 = 1 1329 ==> 1 = 1 4 = 1 1328 <confi (1)> li (3.78) le (0.1) con (488.79)
19. 2 = 1 1 = 1 5 = 1 1329 ==> 4 = 1 1328 <confi (1)> li (3.76) le (0.1) con (487.99)
20. 5 = 1 2646 ==> 1 = 1 4 = 1 2644 <confi\ (1)> li (3.78) le (0.19) con (648.78)

From the results of Apriori and FP-Growth Algorithm, it can be found that which feature in AMPds influences other features in the dataset also the number of transactions which supports the rules. As well as lift, leverage and conviction is displayed for each rule.

On the same dataset different classifiers are applied and there percentage of correct classification is also measured. In addition Kappa statistic, Mean absolute error, Root mean squared error, Relative absolute error, Root relative squared error are also determined for these classifiers (Table 7). Different classifiers used here are Decision Table, Random Tree and Multi-Layer Perceptron and their different features considered are shown in Table 4, Table 5 and Table 6 respectively.

From Table 6, it is found that Random Tree has classified more accurately than other two approaches. As the data are different IoT devices so relation between them is not so consistent, hence kappa coefficient values are not in perfect agreement, which measures the disagreement between features. Mean absolute error shows the measure of difference between two continuous features which forecast the error and for all the classifiers, value for mean absolute error is approximately same. Similarly root mean squared error, relative absolute error and root relative squared error also

Table 4. Parameters and their values considered for Decision Table Classifier

Sl. No.	Feature	Value
1	Size of each Batch	100
2	Number of folds for cross validation	10
3	Measure used to evaluate the performance of attribute combinations	RMSE
4	Search Method	Best First
5	Number of instances	9999
6	Number of attributes	9
7	Search Direction	Forward

Table 5. Parameters and their values considered for Random Tree Classifier

Sl. No.	Feature	Value
1	Size of each Batch	100
2	Training set size	100
3	Maximum depth of the tree	Unlimited
4	Number of Random Number of seed	1
5	Number of instances	9999
6	Number of attributes	9
7	Number of folds for cross validation	10
8	Number of Iteration	100

Table 6. Parameters and their values considered for Multi-Layer Perceptron

Sl. No.	Feature	Value
1	Size of each Batch	100
2	Number of Hidden Layers	(Number of Attributes + Number of Classes)/ 2
3	Learning Rate	0.3
4	Validation Threshold	20
5	Number of instances	9999
6	Number of attributes	9
7	Number of folds for cross validation	10
8	Number of Iteration	100

Table 7. Results for different classifiers

Result	Decision Table	Random Tree	Multi-Layer Perceptron
Correctly Classified Instances	8661 (86.6187%)	8671 (86.7187%)	8666 (86.6687%)
Incorrectly Classified Instances	1338 (13.3813%)	1328 (13.2813%)	1333 (13.3313%)
Kappa statistic	0	0.0629	0.0807
Mean absolute error	0.2319	0.2164	0.2202
Root mean squared error	0.3405	0.3307	0.332
Relative absolute error	100.0012%	93.3179%	94.9731%
Root relative squared error	100%	97.147 %	97.5136%

give similar result for all three classifier. Thus based on accuracy, random forest has given accuracy for the considered dataset. Hence these classification techniques can be used to determine the relation between features.

CONCLUSION

Association Rule mining and classification can be used to determine the relation between various features and class of datasets. In this work various classifiers are applied on different features of IoT dataset and to find the relation between them. This approach may be used to find the various devices used in IoT environment. Also some classifiers are applied on the same dataset to find accuracy in classification as well as various error parameters are measured for the classifiers. This work finds relationship between various features for electricity consumption of appliances with varying time. Rules generated may be used as thumb rule to find the influence of electrical equipment on equipment. This is a new dimension which may explore the use of data mining in the domain of IoT. Advantage of this approach is that here association rule mining has been applied on the features of the IoT devices and to find relationship among them. Also different classifies have been applied on these devices to measure their degree of correct classification.

REFERENCES

Agrawal, R., & Srikant, R. (1994). Fast algorithms for mining association rules. *Proceedings of the 20th International Conference on Very Large Data Bases*, 487-499.

Al-Sakran, H.O. (2015). Intelligent Traffic Information System Based on Integration of Internet of Things and Agent Technology. *International Journal of Advanced Computer Science and Applications, 6*(2).

Anand, M., & Susan, C. (2015). Artificial Intelligence Meets Internet of Things. *IJCSET, 5*(6), 149-151.

Anthi, E., Williams, L., & Burnap, P. (2018). Pulse: An adaptive intrusion detection for the Internet of Things. Living in the Internet of Things: Cybersecurity of the IoT - 2018, 1-4.

Atzori, L., Iera, A., & Morabito, G. (2010). *The Internet of Things: A survey*. Elsevier.

Barnaghi, P., Wang, W., Henson, C., & Taylor, K. (2012). Semantics for the Internet of Things. Early progress and back to the future. *International Journal on Semantic Web and Information Systems, 8*(1), 1–21. doi:10.4018/jswis.2012010101

Beier, G., Niehoff, S., & Xue, B. (2018). More Sustainability in Industry through Industrial Internet of Things? *Appl. Sci., 8*(2), 219. doi:10.3390/app8020219

Breiman, L. (2001). Random Forests. *Machine Learning, 45*(1), 5–32. doi:10.1023/A:1010933404324

Chase, J. (2013). *The Evolution of the Internet of Things*. Strategic Marketing, Texas Instruments.

Chen, Y., Meng, F. W., & Guo, H. C. (2017). Design of detection system for mine oxygen concentration based on Internet of Things. *Electronic Design Engineering, 69*(12), 50–56.

Collobert, R., & Bengio, S. (2004). Links between Perceptrons, MLPs and SVMs. *Proc. Int'l Conf. on Machine Learning (ICML)*.

Daugherty, P., Negm, W., Banerjee, P., & Alter, A. (2016). *Driving Unconventional Growth through the Industrial Internet of Things*. Accenture.

Deshpande, A., Pitale, P., & Sanap, S. (2016). Industrial Automation using Internet of Things (IOT). *International Journal of Advanced Research in Computer Engineering & Technology, 5*(2).

Din, S., Paul, A., Guizani, N., Ahmed, S. H., Khan, M., & Rathore, M. M. (2017). Features Selection Model for Internet of E-Health Things Using Big Data. *GLOBECOM 2017 IEEE Global Communications Conference*, 1-7.

Dwyer, B., & Hutchings, K. (1977, September). Flowchart Optimisation in Cope, a Multi-Choice Decision Table. *Australian Computer Journal*, *9*(3), 92.

Ersue, M., Romascanu, D., Schoenwaelder, J., & Sehgal, A. (2014). *Management of Networks with Constrained Devices: Use Cases*. IETF Internet Draft.

European Commission. (2017). *Digital Information Monitor: Industry 4.0 in Aeronautics: IoT applications*. Author.

Evans, P. C., & Annunziata, M. (2012). *Industrial Internet: Pushing the Boundaries of Minds and Machines*. General Electric.

Feng, D. L. Y., & Liang, Y. D. (2010). A Survey of the Internet of Things. *The 2010 International Conference on E-Business Intelligence*.

Grandinetti, L. (2013). *Pervasive Cloud Computing Technologies: Future Outlooks and Interdisciplinary Perspectives*. IGI Global.

Gubbia, J., Buyya, R., Marusic, S., & Palaniswami, M. (2013). Internet of Things (IoT): A vision, architectural elements, and future directions. *Future Generation Computer Systems*, *29*(7), 1645–1660. doi:10.1016/j.future.2013.01.010

Gupta, R. M. (2015). *Intelligent Data In The Context Of The Internet Of Things*. Academic Press.

Hahsler, M., Grün, B., & Hornik, K. (2005). Introduction to a rules – A computational environment for mining association rules and frequent item sets. *Journal of Statistical Software*, *14*(15). doi:10.18637/jss.v014.i15

Han, J., Pei, J., & Yin, Y. (2000). Mining frequent patterns without candidate generation. *Proceedings of the 2000 ACM-SIGMID International Conference on Management of Data*, 1-12.

Ho, T. K. (1995). Random Decision Forests. *Proceedings of the 3rd International Conference on Document Analysis and Recognition*, 278–282.

Khan, S. R., & Bhat, M. S. (2014). *GUI Based Industrial Monitoring and Control System*. IEEE.

Kohavi, R. (1995). The Power of Decision Tables. *8th European Conference on Machine Learning*, 174-189.

Kundra, A., & Maheshwari, A. (2016). Design of Intelligent Traffic Management Systems using Computer Vision and Internet of Things. *International Journal of Information & Computation Technology, 6*(1), 11-18.

Liu, B., Hsu, W., & Ma, Y. (1998). Integrating Classification and Association Rule Mining. *Fourth International Conference on Knowledge Discovery and Data Mining*, 80-86.

Lopez Research. (2013). *An Introduction to the Internet of Things (IOT)*. Author.

Lwowski, J., Kolar, P., Benavidez, P., Rad, P., Prevost, J. J., & Jamshidi, M. (2017). Pedestrian detection system for smart communities using deep Convolutional Neural Networks. *12th System of Systems Engineering Conference (SoSE)*, 1-6.

Lynggaard, P. (2013). *Artificial intelligence and Internet of Things in a "smart home" context: A Distributed System Architecture* (PhD dissertation). Aalborg University, Copenhagen, Denmark.

Makonin, S., Popowich, F., Bartram, L., Gill, B., & Bajic, I. V. (2013). AMPds: A Public Dataset for Load Disaggregation and Eco-Feedback Research. In *Electrical Power and Energy Conference (EPEC)*. IEEE. 10.1109/EPEC.2013.6802949

Maranda, A. P., & Kaczmarek, D. (2015). Selected methods of artificial intelligence for Internet of Things conception. *Proceedings of the Federated Conference on Computer Science and Information Systems, ACSIS, 5*, 1343–1348.

Mohammadi, M., & Al-Fuqaha, A. (2018). Enabling Cognitive Smart Cities Using Big Data and Machine Learning: Approaches and Challenges. *IEEE Communications Magazine, 56*(2), 94–101. doi:10.1109/MCOM.2018.1700298

Mohammadi, M., Al-Fuqaha, A., Sorour, S., & Guizani, M. (2018). Deep Learning for IoT Big Data and Streaming Analytics: A Survey. *IEEE Communications Surveys and Tutorials, 20*(4), 2923–2960. doi:10.1109/COMST.2018.2844341

Mohammeda, Z. K. A., & Ahmedb, E. S. A. (2017). Internet of Things Applications, Challenges and Related Future Technologies. *World Scientific News, 67*(2), 126–148.

Osuwa, A. A., Ekhoragbon, E. B., & Fat, L. T. (2017). Application of artificial intelligence in Internet of Things. *9th International Conference on Computational Intelligence and Communication Networks (CICN), Girne*, 169-173.

Parker, R. (2014). *Internet of Things in Manufacturing: Driving Revenue and Improving Operations*. Academic Press.

Patel, K. K., & Patel, S. M. (2016). IOT: Definition, Characteristics, Architecture, Enabling Technologies. Application & Future Challenges. IJESC, 6(5).

Polyakov, E. V., Mazhanov, M. S., Rolich, A. Y., Voskov, L. S., Kachalova, M. V., & Polyakov, S. V. (2018). Investigation and development of the intelligent voice assistant for the Internet of Things using machine learning. *2018 Moscow Workshop on Electronic and Networking Technologies (MWENT)*, 1-5. 10.1109/MWENT.2018.8337236

Sleman, A., & Moeller, R. (2008). Integration of Wireless Sensor Network Services into other Home and Industrial networks. *IEEE conference paper in 3rd International Conference on Information and Communication Technologies: From Theory to Applications.*

Zu, L. D. (2014, November). Internet of Things in Industries: A Survey. *IEEE Transactions on Industrial Informatics*, 10(4).

KEY TERMS AND DEFINITIONS

Apriori Algorithm: Apriori algorithm is developed by Agrawal in the year 1994 to find large-scale association rules with multiple items.

Association Rule Mining: Association rule can be represented as A->B, where A & B are disjoint item sets. The association rule can be generated based on the value of support and confidence.

Decision Table: It is a method of learning for discrete cost value target which can be modeled by a decision table.

FP Growth: The FP growth algorithm permits frequent sets of item detection without candidate set of items generation.

IoT: IoT is a network of objects (e.g., vehicles, appliances, mobile phones, cameras, instruments, buildings, etc.).

Multi-Layer Perceptron: Multi-layer perceptron (MLP) is a type of neural network classifier which has a single input layer, single output layer, and multiple hidden layers.

Random Forest: Multiple decision tree predictors are present in random forest. The classification accuracy increases in ensembles of trees which are identical but independent.

Chapter 3
Machine Learning Applications for Anomaly Detection

Teguh Wahyono
Satya Wacana Christian University, Indonesia

Yaya Heryadi
Bina Nusantara University, Indonesia

ABSTRACT

The aim of this chapter is to describe and analyze the application of machine learning for anomaly detection. The study regarding the anomaly detection is a very important thing. The various phenomena often occur related to the anomaly study, such as the occurrence of an extreme climate change, the intrusion detection for the network security, the fraud detection for e-banking, the diagnosis for engines fault, the spacecraft anomaly detection, the vessel track, and the airline safety. This chapter is an attempt to provide a structured and a broad overview of extensive research on anomaly detection techniques spanning multiple research areas and application domains. Quantitative analysis meta-approach is used to see the development of the research concerned with those matters. The learning is done on the method side, the techniques utilized, the application development, the technology utilized, and the research trend, which is developed.

INTRODUCTION

The aim of this chapter is to describe several applications of machine learning for anomaly detection. Although has received considerable attention from many researchers since 90's, the anomaly detection problem remained an interesting

DOI: 10.4018/978-1-5225-7955-7.ch003

problem in computer vision field. Its wide potential applications ranging from climate change, computer network intrusion detection, financial transaction fraud detection, engines fault detection, spacecraft anomaly detection to vessel track and the airline safety detection. The emerging applications of machine learning methods in the past ten years has received great interests from many researchers to adopt machine lerning to address anomaly detection.

This paper started with literature review using quantitative analysis meta approach to analyze the main research progress, opportunities and trends, and research applications in the anomaly detection field. This systematic literature review will identify the most significant journals in the anomaly detection field, the opportunities and trends for anomaly detection method, identify research applications and trends in anomaly detection system and give the proposed method improvements for anomaly detection in the future.

This chapter is an attempt to provide a structured and a broad overview of extensive research on anomaly detection techniques spanning multiple research areas and application domains. quantitative analysis meta approach to see the development of the research concerned with those matters. The learning is done both on the method side, the techniques utilized, the application development, the technology utilized and the research trend which is developed.

BACKGROUND

Anomaly, also known as outliers, is a term refers to irregularity or deviation from the normal pattern (Chandola, et al., 2007). Yang (2007) refered the term anomaly to observation data that strongly inconsistent with the previous compiled data. Recently, Bloomquist (2015) defined anomaly as *"patterns or data points that do not conform to a well defined notion of normal behaviour."*

Anomaly detection problem refers to the task of finding patterns in data that do not conform to expected behavior (Chandola, 2007). The problem is an interesting computer vision problem with many potential applications ranging from climate change detection, anomaly detection of fault tolerant robotic system (Jakimovski, 2011) to fraud transaction detection. In the past decade, anomaly detection problem has raised wide attention from various research domains due to its potential applications for recognizing indication that the underlying process that induces the data does not happen as expected. Depending on the context of the data, the detected anomalous data can be interpreted as either extreme climate change (Kawale, 2011), network security intrusion (Tsai, et al., 2010), medical diagnosis (Park, et al., 2015), engines fault (Djurdjanovic, et al., 2007), spacecraft anomaly detection (Fujimaki, et al.,

2007), Mobility-Based Anomaly Detection in Cellular Mobile (Sun, et al., 2006) or vessel track and the airline safety diagnosis (Budalakoti et al., 2009).

Despite many studies have been reported, anomaly detection remained a challenging problem. A prominent study reported by (Chandola, et al., 2007) summarized several challenges in detecting anomaly as follows.

1.   Defining a normal region which encompasses every possible normal behavior is very difficult. In addition, the boundary between normal and anomalous behavior is often not precise. Thus an anomalous observation which lies close to the boundary can actually be normal, and vice-versa.
2.   When anomalies are the result of malicious actions, the malicious adversaries often adapt themselves to make the anomalous observations appear like normal, thereby making the task of defining normal behavior more difficult.
3.   In many domains normal behavior keeps evolving and a current notion of normal behavior might not be sufficiently representative in the future. In medical research domain, concluded that the general pattern to be used as the expected behavior or reference is often unavailable.
4.   The exact notion of an anomaly is different for different application domains. For example, in the medical domain a small deviation from normal (e.g., fluctuations in body temperature) might be an anomaly, while similar deviation in the stock market domain (e.g., fluctuations in the value of a stock) might be considered as normal. Thus applying a technique developed in one domain to another is not straightforward.
5.   Availability of labeled data for training/validation of models used by anomaly detection techniques is usually a major issue.
6.   Often the data contains noise which tends to be similar to the actual anomalies and hence is difficult to distinguish and remove.

There are two prominent applications of anomaly detection. *First*, detecting climate change. Climate anomaly refers to the irregularity of climate patterns that occurred in a region over a particular period (Kawale, 2011). The oddity or deviation of the climate from the previous patterns strongly affected variation and inconsistency of some other weather variables. Due to its important effect to various aspect of human life, climate anomaly has raised research attention from various research communities. In Indonesia, for example, one of the anomalies phenomenons is the occurrence of an extreme climate change called El Nino and La Nina. This phenomenon strung out the season irregularity. For example: rainfall declines between 40-80% of the normal circumstances, the air temperature increases sharply accompanied by various extreme phenomenons, such as whirlwind, dryness and declining in the food production (Prasetyo, et al., 2011).

Second, detecting computer network security violation. Many reports showed some evidences that the advent of computer network has to be followed by the technical development of the data securing (Yang, et al., 2015). The security of a network is often interrupted by the presence of a threat from inside or from outside of the network. That offensive can be hacker attacks which purposely to damage the network, or an intruder who is going to steal the important information which is available on the network. The anomaly detection method is very instrumental to analyze the beginning conditions of the emergence of an attack; capturing the suspicious packets of data in order that the system can anticipate the occurrence of an intrusion.

This chapter starts with a detailed analysis of various methods for anomaly detection using quantitative analysis meta-approach to analyze the development of the research on anomaly detection. The analysis will emphasize on several aspects mainly: theoretical, applications, and the research trend. Next, some machine learning methods for addressing one-class classification will be discussed.

LITERATURE REVIEW

Anomaly

Chandola, Banerjee & Kumar (2011) classified anomalies into four wide categories as follows.

Point Anomalies

A point anomaly is a single point that is classified to have a different value from the common data group. The example of the point anomaly can be seen in Figure 1, in which the single point A and the single point B have deviant values from the rest.

Contextual Anomalies

A contextual anomaly happens if the data is called as anomaly based on a context, whereas on another context, it is considered normal. A simple illustration on the contextual anomaly is the number of access on a server when the university students register their lessons in the beginning of the semester. The number of access will increase significantly in the registration period. In the context of the registration periode, this occurrence cannot be said as an anomaly, but when it is an anomaly when it happens outside the registration periode (Figure 2).

Figure 1. Point anomalies represented by A and B

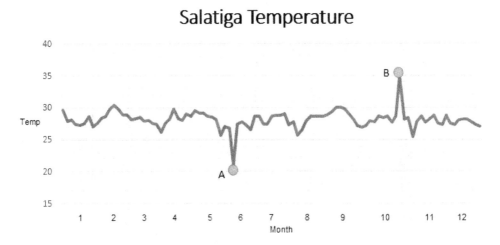

Figure 2. Contextual anomalies

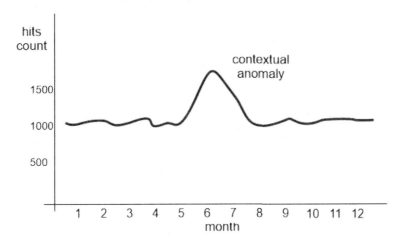

Collective Anomalies

A collective anomaly happens when it seen individually, the data is considered as normal, but it becomes anomaly when it happens simultaneously for a long period of time, longer from the same range of the other data surrounds it. The example of the point anomaly can be seen in Figure 3.

On the other hand, Xie et.al. said that anomaly can be classified into four types (Xie, et al., 2015):

Figure 3. Collective anomalies from stackexchange.com
(Stack Exchange, 2017)

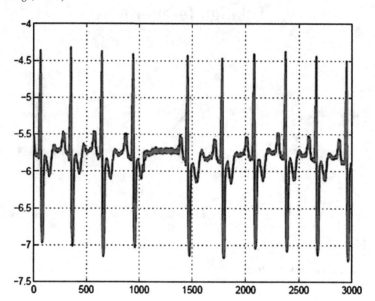

1. **Constant**: The anomaly happens when sequential observations show constant values.
2. **Burst**: The anomaly happens when the observation data shows significant bursts in some points.
3. **Small Noise**: The anomaly happens when the observation data shows small noise that can influence the variance.
4. **Large Noise**: The anomaly happens when a large noise appears and increase the variance value.

Further, detection is seen as a process to check something by using a specific way or technique. This detection can be done for various problems, such as a disease detection system, where the system identifies the problems connected to a disease, which is common to be called as symptoms. In this context, detection is used to find the anomaly in a group of data.

Methods, Applications, and Technological Issues

We have done a survey paper to know the method used, application and technological issues in anomaly detection. Following Kitchenham (2007) and Adisasmito (2007), literature mapping is implemented using systematic literature review (SLR) method. Several finding from literature review are as follows.

Figure 4. Four types of anomaly
(Xie, et al., 2015)

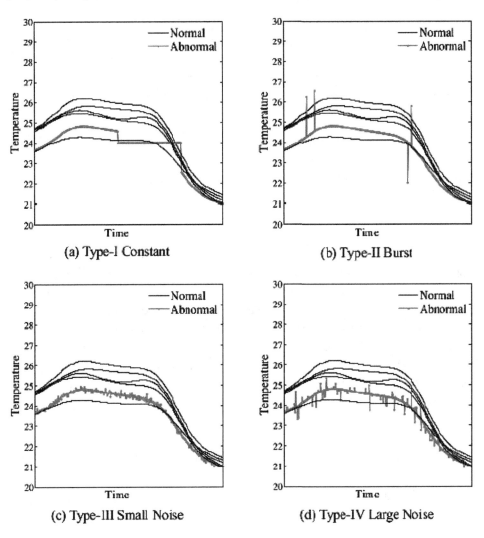

(a) Type-I Constant

(b) Type-II Burst

(c) Type-III Small Noise

(d) Type-IV Large Noise

Research Question

Research Question is a beginning part and a running basic of SLR. Research Question is used to guide the seeking process and the literature extraction. The analysis and the synthesis of data, as a result of SLR, is the answer from Research Question which we decide on the front. The Research Question formulation should be based on the five elements which come to be called PICOC criteria consisted

Table 1. PICOC criteria

Population	software, anomaly detection system
Intervention	anomaly detection technique, prediction methods, application area, technological issues
Comparison	n/a
Outcomes	Performance
Context	studies in academia, small and large datasets

of: Population, Intervention, Comparison, Outcomes, and Context. Table 1 shows PICOC criteria in this research.

There are five research question in this study as shown in Table 2.

Search Strategy

The searching strategy is started from the source determination of the literature headed for. In this research, it is determined six sources as follow: (1) IEEE Explore Digital Library (ieeexplore.ieee.org), (2) ACM Digital Library (dl.acm.org), (3) Semantic Scholar (www.semanticscholar.org), (4) Science Direct (sciencedirect. com), (5) Springer Link (springerlink.com), and (6) EBSCO (www.ebscohost.com).

The next stage is the determination stage of keyword (search string) from the literature searched accordance with the PICOC which had been designed before. The selection of the right keyword will determine the level of the literature accuracy discovered.

The following search string in this research was eventually used:

(anomaly OR outlier* OR intrusion OR security) AND (detect* OR predict* OR prone* OR probability OR assess* OR estimat* OR classificat*) AND (system OR software OR application OR methods)

Table 2. Research questions

ID	Research Question	Motivation
RQ1	Which journal is the most significant with anomaly detection field?	Identify the most significant journals in the anomaly detection field.
RQ2	What kind of methods are used for anomaly detection system?	Identify opportunities and trends for anomaly detection method
RQ3	What kind of research applications are selected by researchers in anomaly detection field?	Identify research applications and trends in anomaly detection system
RQ4	Which method performs best when used for anomaly detection?	Identify the best method for anomaly detection
RQ5	What kind of method improvements are proposed for anomaly detection?	Identify the proposed method improvements for anomaly detection

Significant Journal Publications

This research discovers 28 articles related to the Research Question that has been defined previously. Those articles come from a variety of digital library website which has been predetermined with the compositions such as in Figure 5 below.

Figure 6 shows the paper's distribution by the year of publication. From those data can be seen that every year, there are always be the research related to the anomaly detection of data. That matter shows that this research was conducted continuously and growing from year to year.

Figure 5. The composition of the article based on a data source

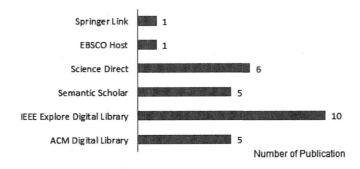

Figure 6. Distribution of selected paper over the year

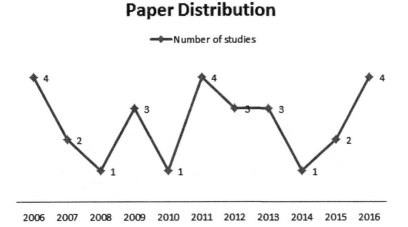

Methods Used in Anomaly Detection System

Anomaly Detection Systems are generally designed using four methods to execute the predictions, those are; statistical, data mining, machine learning, and graphical modeling as shown in Figure 7. The most popular method and used a lots are data mining (45% utilization), followed by machine learning (29% utilization).

The statistical method is the most basic method for used in the forecasting study. This study discovers two statistical methods used, those are; regression modeling and exponentially weighted moving average. A multinomial logistic regression modeling approach is used for detecting the attacks on the computer networks (Wang, 2005). Whereas the exponentially weighted moving average approach is used for enhancing security using mobility-based anomaly detection system (Sun, et al., 2006).

The data mining method is most widely used in the study of this anomaly detection. The various methods used are seen in Figure 8. There are seven data mining methods used in these studies, namely Clustering and outlier detection, DBScan, Fuzzy Logic, Genetic Algorithm (GA), Hidden Markov Models (HMM), Selection Criteria and Support Vector Machines (SVM). Fuzzy Logic and SVM are the most widely used methods, that is each at 25% of the researches by the method of data mining.

Data mining is a method that concerned with uncovering patterns, associations, changes, anomalies, and statistically significant structures and events in data (Grossman, 1997). Data mining can help improve the process of intrusion detection by adding a level of focus to anomaly detection (Patcha, 2007). Table 3 shows list of the papers that using data mining in their research, with the highlighting features and specific methodology.

Figure 7. Methods used in anomaly detection system

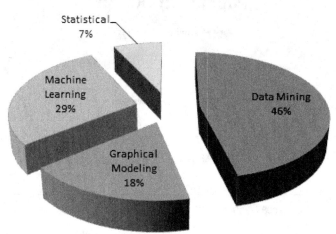

Figure 8. The various methods of data mining are used

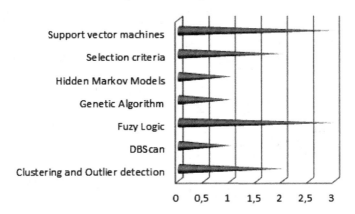

The machine learning methods used in this research can be seen in Figure 9. There are five methods which are used, namely semi-supervised learning, Discrete Wavelet Transform (DWT), decision tree, Principal Component Analysis (PCA) and Bayesian approach. Bayesian approach is the most widely used methods, that is 40% of the existing research.

Basically, machine learning is a computer process to learn from the data. It is a type of Artificial Intelligence (AI). With machine learning, systems have the ability to change their execution strategy on the basis of newly acquired information (2007). Machine learning system can automatically build the model based on the training dataset, which contains data instances that can be described using a set of attributes and associated labels (2013). Table 4 shows list of the papers that using machine learning in their research, with the highlighting features and specific methodology.

The researches which are using a graphical modeling and spatio-temporal approach are the latest researches in the imaging field, satellite imagery and several papers with a spatio-temporal thematic. Rembold (2013) using low-resolution satellite imagery for yield prediction and yield of anomaly detection. Another papers are imaging of neuronal activity (Park, 2015), visual anomaly detection in spatio-temporal (Alcaide, et al., 2016), and spatio-temporal graphical modeling approach to anomaly detection in distributed cyber-physical systems (Liu, 2016).

Research Application in Anomaly Detection System

Anomaly detection system so far has been applied in a variety of applications. Figure 6 showing that there are seven applications which are implementing this model. This research is applied in various fields such as Network Intrusion Detection, Spatial

Table 3. A summary of data mining based anomaly detection

Reference	Highlighting Features	Specific Methodology
Abadeh, et.al (2007)	This research is design and analysis of genetic fuzzy systems, implemented for intrusion detection in computer networks	Genetic Fuzzy
Ensafi et.al (2008)	It is optimizing Fuzzy K-means for network anomaly detection using PSO	Fuzzy Swarm Intelligent
Kawale et.al (2011)	Anomaly Construction in Climate Data	Selection Criteria
Das and Parthasarathy (2009)	It detects anomaly Detection and Spatio-Temporal Analysis of Global Climate System	Spatial-Temporal
Kao et.al (2009)	It is motivating Complex Dependence Structures in Data Mining: A Case Study with Anomaly Detection in Climate	dependence structure and the use of copulas
Budalakoti (2009)	Anomaly Detection and Diagnosis Algorithms for Discrete Symbol Sequences with Applications to Airline Safety	Sequence Miner vs Hidden Markov Models
Tsai et.al (2010)	A triangle area based nearest neighbors approach to intrusion detection	Triangle area based nearest neighbors (TANN)
Horng et.al (2011)	A novel intrusion detection system based on hierarchical clustering and support vector machines	Support Vector Machines
Yi et.al (2011)	Incremental SVM based on reserved set for network intrusion detection	Support Vector Machines
Celik et.al (2011)	Anomaly Detection in Temperature Data Using DBSCAN Algorithm	DBScan
Kavitha et.al (2012)	An ensemble design of intrusion detection system for handling uncertainty using Neutrosophic Logic Classifier	Fuzzy (Neutrosophic Logic Based Classifier)
Fu et.al (2012)	A Hybrid Anomaly Detection Framework in Cloud Computing Using One-Class and Two-Class Support Vector Machines	One Class and two Class SVM
Karami et.al (2016)	A fuzzy anomaly detection system based on hybrid PSO-Kmeans algorithm in content-centric networks	Fuzzy- Kmeans algorithm

Detection, Medical, Diagnosis for Engine, Tracking and Safety, Climate Data and Cellular Mobile.

The Most field which is using anomaly detection system is a field of the Network Intrusion Detection that is as many as 12 papers or 43% of all the exciting papers. Next came after by the research topics in the field of Tracking and Safety along with Climate Data that each at 15% of the existing research.

Figure 9. The various methods of machine learning are used

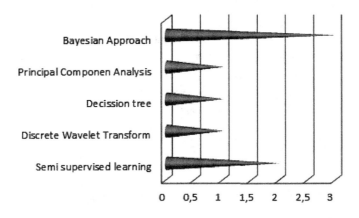

Performance Methods Used in Anomaly Detection

At this section will be selected the papers which are discussing up to the performance of each of the methods applied for the anomaly detection. After a further selection, there were elected 10 papers that have a discussion up to the performance testing, shown with the value of the Detection Rate. The exciting data shows in Table 5 that the anomaly detection by using Data Mining-Genetic Fuzzy approach has the highest level of the detection rate that is at 99,53.

Table 4. Summary of machine learning based anomaly detection

Reference	Highlighting Features	Specific Methodology
Fujimaki et.al (2006)	An Approach to Spacecraft Anomaly Detection Problem Using Kernel Feature Space	Principal Component Analysis
Yairi et.al (2006)	Telemetry-mining: A Machine Learning Approach to Anomaly Detection and Fault Diagnosis for Space Systems	Dynamics Bayesian Networks
Djurdjanovic et.al (2007)	Immune Systems Inspired Approach to Anomaly Detection and Fault Diagnosis for Engines	Exponentially Weighted Moving Average (EWMA)
Farid et.al (2010)	Combining Naive Bayes and Decision Tree for Adaptive Intrusion Detection	Naïve Bayes and Decision tree
Chitrakar et.al (2012)	Anomaly-based Intrusion Detection using Hybrid Learning Approach of combining k-Medoids Clustering and Naïve Bayes Classification	k-Medoids Clustering and Naive Bayes Classification
Gornitz et.al (2013)	Toward Supervised Anomaly Detection	semi-supervised anomaly detection
Mascaro et.al (2014)	Anomaly detection in vessel tracks using Bayesian networks	Bayesian Networks
Casas et.al (2016)	Machine-Learning Based Approaches for Anomaly Detection and Classification in Cellular Networks	Discrete Wavelet Transform

Figure 10. Research application in anomaly detection system

Strategy to Improve Accuracy for Anomaly Detection

According to the selected papers in this study, anomaly detection systems are generally designed using four methods to execute the predictions, those are; statistical, data mining, machine learning, and graphical modeling. To improve the accuracy for anomaly detection, the researchers proposed some strategy.

The first, if anomaly detection system using a machine learning method, note that there are two techniques in the application of machine learning. Both of these techniques are supervised and unsupervised learning. The results of several studies indicate that the supervised learning methods significantly outperform the unsupervised ones if the test data contains no unknown attacks (Omar, 2013). Among the supervised methods, the best performance is achieved by the non-linear methods, such as Support Vector Machines methods (Horng, et al., 2011; Yi, et al., 2011).

Table 5. Performance methods by detection rate

Author	Method	Detection Rate
Gornitz et.al (2013)	Machine learning-semi supervised anomaly detection	70,00
Casas et.al (2016)	Machine learning-Discrete Wavelet Transform	80,00
Kavitha et.al 2012)	Data Mining-Fuzzy Neutrosophic Logic Based	99,02
Abadeh, et.al (2007)	Data Mining-Genetic Fuzzy	99,53
Tsai et.al (2010)	Data Mining-Triangle area based nearest neighbors	99,27
Ensafi et.al (2008)	Data Mining-Fuzzy Swarm Intelligent	95,88
Horng et.al (2011)	Data Mining-support vector machines	95,70
Yi et.al (2011)	Data Mining-support vector machines	81,38
Chitrakar (2012)	Machine learning - k-Medoids Clustering and Naive Bayes	99,43
Farid et.al (2010)	Machine learning-Naïve Bayes and Decision tree	99,00

Secondly, data mining has been used in anomaly detection system by many researchers in recent years (Agrawal, 2015). In this area, hybrid approaches provide better results and overcome the drawback of one approach over the other (Fu, et al., 2012; Agrawal, 2015; Karami, et al., 2016). In hybrid approaches, researchers can combine the modified version of already existing algorithms. For example, there are one-class and two-class Support Vector Machines for a hybrid anomaly detection framework (Fu, et al., 2012) and a novel fuzzy anomaly detection based on Hybrid PSO-Kmeans (Karami, 2016). Chitrakar (2012) using a hybrid approach to combine Support Vector Machine classification and K-Medoids clustering for the network intrusion detection system. The experimental results demonstrate that hybrid approach performs high performance, higher accuracy, increase in detection rate and reduction in mean time of false alarm rate.

MACHINE LEARNING CONCEPT

Definition of Machine Learning

Machine learning is an emerging research field which has raised wide attention in the past ten years due to many successfull reports to address many problems, such as classification, using big data. As a branch of Artificial Intelligence [42. 43], machine learning focuses on the development of algorithm that automatically improves its performance with experiences. Specifically, Mitchell (1997) defined machine learning as algorithms that "*learn from experience E with respect to some class of tasks T and performance measure P, if its performance at tasks in T, as measured by P, improves with experience E.*" In the machine learning context, the process in which an algorithm improving its performance with experiences commonly refers to learning process.

Following Mitchell (1997), the learning process of a machine learning algorithm can be characterized by the following factors.

1. Training experience which depends on the following factors. *First*, the type of training experience from which a machine learning algorithm will learn. *Second*, the degree to which the learning algorithm controls the sequence of training examples. *Third*, how well the training dataset represents the distribution of examples over which the final system performance P must be measured.
2. Target function.
3. Representation of the learned function.
4. Learning algorithm.

Issues in Machine Learning

According to Mitchell (1997) the main issues in using machine learning approach can be summarized into Table 6.

Types of Learning

Learning types in machine learning can be categorized as shown in Figure 11.

Supervised Learning

Supervised learning uses the training data in performing prediction or classification. The data in the supervised learning is labeled data. The final purpose of this method is to identify the new input label by using the existing feature in the new data.

Some algorithms include in the supervised learning are:

- Multiple Regressions
- Decision Tree.
- Random Forest
- Naive Bayes Classifier

Table 6. Main issues in machine learning

Categories	Issues
Learning algorithm	• What algorithms exist for learning general target functions from specific training examples? • In what settings will particular algorithms converge to the desired function, given sufficient training data? • Which algorithms perform best for which types of problems and representations?
The size of training dataset	• How much training data is sufficient? • What general bounds can be found to relate the confidence in learned hypotheses to the amount of training experience and the character of the learner's hypothesis space?
Prior knowledge	• When and how can prior knowledge held by the learner guide the process of generalizing from examples? • Can prior knowledge be helpful even when it is only approximately correct?
Model testing	• What is the best strategy for choosing a useful next training experience, and how does the choice of this strategy alter the complexity of the learning problem?
Target function representation	• What is the best way to reduce the learning task to one or more function approximation problems? • What specific functions should the system attempt to learn? • Can this process itself be automated?
Optimization algorithm	• How can the learner automatically alter its representation to improve its ability to represent and learn the target function?

Figure 11. Types of machine learning

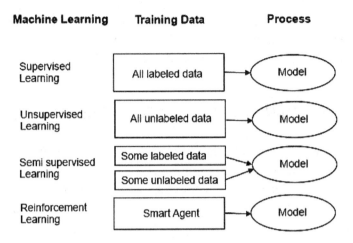

- Nearest Neighbor Classifier
- Support Vector Machine
- Artificial Neural Network

Unsupervised Learning

Unsupervised learning does not use training data in prediction or clarification. In the unsupervised learning, the system learns unlabeled data based on the features of the data. This algorithm does not have target variable and aims to classify almost similar objects in a specific area. For an example, if we want to classify the customers of a company based on similar traits like age, education, and hobby, we do not need any training data.

Some algorithms include in the unsupervised learning are:

- Hierarchical Clustering
- K-Means
- DBSCAN
- Fuzzy C-Means
- Self-Organizing Map

Semi-Supervised Learning

Semi-supervised Learning combines supervised and unsupervised learning. In this process, the system learns the labeled data and unlabeled data simultaneously to be made as training data.

Reinforcement Learning

Reinforcement learning is a method that teaches us how to act to face a problem, in which the action has impacts. This method is applied in a smart agent so that it can adapt with the condition in its environment.

MACHINE LEARNING APPROACH TO ANOMALY DETECTION

A plethora of machine learning methods to address anomaly detection tasks can be categorized broadly into supervised and unsupervised method categories (Park, 2015; Rembold, 2016). The supervised methods view anomaly detection as classification problem in which converting the problem into one or binary classification problem. The unsupervised methods, on the other hand, convert the problem into clustering task followed by apply thresholds to decide whether or not the data conform the "normal" data.

The term one-class classification was coined by Moya et.al (1996) refers to a task of "*learning to characterize the target class by examining only target data without requiring training samples of non-target data.*" This task can be viewed as a special type of classification problem. However, in contrast to binary or multi-class classification, one-class classification typically uses only samples from the assigned class called target class. In anomaly detection problem, as an example of one-class classification problem, the target class is typically called "normal" classes. Any sample which does not conform the "normal" class is categorized as "anomaly" data.

Wide potential application of one-class classification have gained research interest resulted in a plethora of proposed methods. Among the prominent methods based on support vector machine were proposed by Schölkopf *et al.* (2000) and Tax *et al.* (2004).

K-Nearest Neighbor

k-Nearest Neighbor (kNN) is a prominent machine learning method categorized as a supervised learning algorithm. Given n-samples

$$S = \left\{ \left(x_1, y_1 \right), \left(x_2, y_2 \right), \ldots, \left(x_n, y_n \right) \right\} \subseteq \mathcal{R}^m \times Y$$

as input data such that each $x_i \in \mathcal{R}^m$ represented by m-atributes (feature) a_j as follows:

$$x_i = a_1\left(x_i\right), a_2\left(x_i\right), \ldots, a_m\left(x_i\right)$$

where: $y_i \in Y = \left\{v_1, v_2, \ldots, v_p\right\}$ are x_i labels. The objective of k-NN method is to approximate a target function $f : \mathcal{R}^m \to Y$ with an approximation function $h : \mathcal{R}^m \to Y$ such that for a new data x, $h\left(x\right) = \hat{f}\left(x\right)$.

Many studies have adopted k-NN as a classifier to categorize samples into either normal or anomaly class. Following Yang & Liu (1999) the decision rule in k-NN can be written as:

$$y\left(x, c_j\right) = \sum_{d_i \in kNN} sim\left(x, d_i\right) y\left(d_i, c_j\right) - b_j$$

where: $y\left(x, c_j\right) \in \left\{0, 1\right\}$ the classification for sample d_i with respect to category c_j; $sim\left(x, d_i\right)$ be similarity between the test sample x and the training data d_i which can be measured using various distance functions such as: Euclidean distance between x and d_i points, cosine value between x and d_i vectors; and b_j is the optimal threshold for binary decisions which can be learned from training dataset. From learning process, the value of b_j is selected from all possible values that give the best performance of k-NN. From eq (1), the thresholding parameter (b_j) is very instrumental to categorize data as normal data or anomaly data in anomaly detection (Liao, et al., 2002).

The advantages of k-NN for anomaly detection are mainly: (1) no prior probabilities required, and (2) the algorithm is computationally efficient compared to other methods such as Bayesian classifier. The main computation is finding the k-nearest neighbors for the test data that involves sorting training data.

One-Class SVM

One-class Support Vector Machine (OCSVM) model proposed by Schölkopf (2000) is a kernel-based techniques for supervised learning. In general, the objective of this model is to estimate functions that describes the underlying distributions of the input data which have been mapped into a feature space using a kernel. Next, the knowledge about the data distribution can be used to address problem on the basis of the raw data. In the context of anomaly detection, the estimated function describe distribution of the target (normal) dataset. So that, any data does not conform the estimated distribution of the dataset is categorized as anomaly data.

In general, the OCSVM algorithm works by firstly mapping the target data into the feature space $\mathcal{F}$ corresponding to the kernel k followed by separating the data in feature space $\mathcal{F}$ using a hyperplane from the origin with maximum margin. Finally, the algorith returns a function f that takes the value +1 in a region capturing most of the data points, and -1 elsewhere. For a new point x, the value $f(x)$ is determined by evaluating which side of the hyperplane it falls on in the feature space $\mathcal{F}$.

The OCSVM model can be viewed as an adaptation of SVM (Vapnik, 1998) for one-class classification problem. In contrast to binary/multi-class SVM model, which is trained using dataset with two (or more) classes, the OCSVM model is trained using only one class dataset called "normal" or target samples to learn pattern of the given samples. Having been trained using the normal cases, the model is then used to predict new samples.

The term "planar OCSVM" often used in literature to differentiate the model (Schölkopf, 2000) from similar model proposed (Tax, 2004). The former model estimates a hyperplane to separate data in feature space that maximized the margin between the target data and the origin point; whilst, the later model estimates the smallest hypersphere that encloses the target data points. The later model will be described in 3.

The theoretical foundation of OCSVM can be described as follows. Consider some samples $x_1, x_2, \ldots, x_l \in \mathcal{X} \subseteq \mathcal{R}^{\mathbb{N}}$ where l is the number of samples are samples drawn from an unknown underlying probability distribution P. Mathematically, the aims of OCSVM algorithm is to estimate a set S so that a new, previously unseen, pattern x_{l+1} lies in S with an apriori-specified probability. The OCSVM model training comprises of several steps. *First*, mapping the data into the feature space $\mathcal{F}$ using kernel k. Consider ϕ be a feature map, $\phi : \mathcal{X} \to \mathcal{F}$ such that the image of ϕ (the dot product in $\mathcal{F}$) can be computed using kernel:

$$k(x,y) = \left(\phi(x) \cdot \phi(y) \right) \tag{1}$$

For example: Gaussian kernel which can be formulated as:

$$k(x,y) = e^{\frac{-x-y^2}{c}} \tag{2}$$

where c is a kernel parameter.

Second, minimizing the objective function which can be represented as follows.

$$\min_{w \in \mathcal{F}, \xi \in \mathcal{R}^n, \rho \in \mathcal{R}} \frac{1}{2} w^2 + \frac{1}{\upsilon l} \sum_i \xi_i - \rho \tag{3}$$

subject to:

$$\left(w \cdot \phi\left(x_i\right) \right) \ge \rho - \xi_i \text{ for all } i = 1, 2, 3, .., l \tag{4}$$

$$\xi_i \ge 0 \text{ for all } i = 1, 2, 3, .., l \tag{5}$$

where: w be the weight vector parameters, $\upsilon \in \{0, 1\}$ is a parameter, ρ be the offset parameterizing a hyperplane in the feature space $\mathcal{F}$ associated with the kernel k, and ξ_i or slack variable are penalized in the objective function. The minimization problem can be solved by setting out Lagrangian multipiers $\alpha_i, \beta_i \ge 0$.

$$\mathcal{L}\left(w, \xi, \rho, \alpha, \beta\right) = \frac{1}{2} w^2 + \frac{1}{\upsilon l} \sum_i \left(\xi_i - \rho\right) - \sum_i \alpha_i \left(\left(w \cdot \phi\left(x_i\right)\right) - \rho + \xi_i\right) - \sum_i \beta_i \xi_i \tag{6}$$

where: ξ_i or slack variable are penalized in the objective function. The coefficient α_i can be computed as the solution of the dual problem:

$$\sum_i \alpha_i = 1 \tag{7}$$

$$\min_{\alpha} \frac{1}{2} \sum_{i,j} \alpha_i \alpha_j \phi\left(x_i, x_j\right) \text{ subject to } 0 \le \alpha_i \le \frac{1}{\upsilon l} \tag{8}$$

If w and ρ solve this problem then the decision function is:

$$f\left(x\right) = \text{sgn}\left(\sum w.\phi\left(x\right) - \rho\right) \tag{9}$$

By using substitution,

$$f(x) = \text{sgn}\left(\sum_i \alpha_i \phi(x_i, x) - \rho\right) \tag{10}$$

where:

$$\rho = \sum_j \alpha_j \phi(x_j, x_i) \tag{11}$$

The function f will be positive (+1) for most examples x_i contained in the training dataset and negative (-1) elsewhere.

The immediate advantages of OCSVM models are: (1) the model required less number of samples in compared to binary/multi-class SVM; and (2) highly applicable for detecting anomaly data when there was only a small proportion of labeled data from the whole dataset (Chen, et al., 2001); and (3) the model can handle imbalanced data.

Support Vector Data Description

Support Vector Data Description (SVDD) is a model proposed Tax and Duin (2004) to address one-class classification problem. The proposed model estimates a hypersphere, characterized by center a and radius $R > 0$, that gives a closed boundary around the normal data points in feature space $\mathcal{F}$ with minimum diameter.

Consider l-samples $x_1, x_2, \ldots, x_l \in \mathcal{X} \subseteq \mathcal{R}^{\mathbb{N}}$ as target data for which we want to obtain a description. Consider the error function:

$$F(R, a) = R^2 + C\sum_i \xi_i \text{ for } 1 = 1, 2, .., l \tag{12}$$

subject to:

$$x_i - a^2 \leq R^2 + \xi_i \text{ for } 1 = 1, 2, .., l. \tag{13}$$

where: $\xi_i \geq 0$ be slack parameter, and C be penalty parameter to control the trade-off between the volume and the errors. This problem can be transformed into minimization problem using Lagrangian multiplier $\alpha_i \geq 0$ and $\gamma_i \geq 0$ as follows.

$$\mathcal{L}\left(R, a, \alpha_i, \gamma_i, \xi_i\right) = R^2 + C\sum_i \xi_i - \sum_i \alpha_i \left\{R^2 + \xi_i - \left(x_i^2 - 2a \cdot x_i + a^2\right)\right\} - \sum_i \gamma_i \xi_i$$

(14)

By minimizing $\mathcal{L}$ with respect to R, a and ξ_i; and maximizing $\mathcal{L}$ with respect to α_i and γ_i followed by setting partial derivatives to zero gives the constraints:

$$\sum_i \alpha_i = 1$$

(15)

$$a = \sum_i \alpha_i x_i$$

(16)

$$C - \alpha_i - \gamma_i = 0 \text{ or } \alpha_i = C - \gamma_i$$

(17)

Since $\alpha_i \geq 0$ and $\gamma_i \geq 0$, by substitution, $0 \leq \alpha_i \leq \gamma_i$.
Further substitution resulted:

$$\mathcal{L}\left(R, a, \alpha_i, \gamma_i, \xi_i\right) = \sum_i \alpha_i \left(x_i \cdot x_i\right) - \sum_{i,j} \alpha_i \alpha_j \left(x_i \cdot x_j\right)$$

(18)

Equation (16) shows that the center of the sphere is a linear combination of the data points. However, for data description, only data points x_i with $\alpha_i > 0$ are needed. These data points are called the support vectors of the description (SV's). By definition, R^2 is the distance from the center of the sphere a to (any of the support vectors on) the boundary.

Testing a new data point z is implemented in two steps as follows. *First*, the distance of the data point to the center of the sphere $\left(a\right)$, $d\left(z, a\right)$, has to be calculated using the following formula.

$$d\left(z, a\right) = \left(z.z\right) - 2\sum_i \alpha_i \left(z.x_i\right) + \sum_{i,j} \alpha_i \alpha_j \left(x_i.x_j\right)$$

(19)

Finally, a test data point z is accepted when this distance is smaller or equal than the radius. Hence, $d(z,a) \leq R^2$

$$R^2 = \left(x_k . x_k\right) - 2\sum_i \alpha_i \left(x_i . x_k\right) + 2\sum_{i,j} \alpha_i \alpha_j \left(x_i . x_j\right) \tag{20}$$

where: x_k is any support vector whose $\alpha_k < C$.

Zero-Boundary Long Short-Term Memory Model

Anomaly detection task from discrete sequence (time-series) of data has gained considerable attention from many researchers due to its wide applications in various fields such as cybersecurity and weather analysis. The study from Chandola (2012), for example, reviewed some prominent anomaly detections from time-series data. The main objective of anomaly detection from discrete sequence is locating a segment of data sequences that does not follow the pattern in a normal dataset.

Zero-boundary Long Short-term Memory Model was proposed by Roberts & Nair (2018). Architecture of the proposed model comprises of two parts. The first part (encoder) is based on Long Short-term Memory model and the second part (decoder) is based on one-class SVM model. Having this architecture, the model can be viewed as a mixed of LSTM model proposed by Hochreiter & Schmidhuber (1997) and one-class SVM model (2000).

The proposed model comprises of a modified LSTM autoencoder and an array of One-Class SVMs. The LSTM takes in elements from a sequence and creates context vectors that are used to predict the probability distribution of the following element. These context vectors are then used to train an array of One-Class SVMs. These SVMs are used to determine an outlier boundary in context space.

The mathematical foundation for this model can be described as follows. Let $D = \left\{x_1, x_2, \ldots, x_n\right\}$ is n-samples where $x_i = x_{i1}, x_{i2}, \ldots, x_{2m} \in \mathcal{R}^m$ for $i = 1, 2, .., n$ be a discrete sequence with length m. Let's define a language as a finite subset $L \subseteq \mathcal{R}^m$. A discrete sequence x_i is categorizd as normal if $x_i \in L$; otherwise it is categorized as anomaly. If x_i as an anomaly data then there exists $x_{ij}, 1 \leq j \leq m$ such that $P\left(x_{ij} \mid x_{i1}, \ldots, x_{i,j-1}; L\right) = 0$. Following this definition, machine learning algorithm aims to appriximate the target function $f(x, L)$ where:

$$f(x,L) = \begin{cases} 1, & \textit{if there is } x_{ij} \textit{ such that } P\left(x_{ij} \mid x_{i1}, \ldots, x_{i,j-1}; L\right) = 0 \\ 0, & \textit{otherwise} \end{cases} \tag{21}$$

Figure 12. Architecture of Zero-Boundary LSTM
(Roberts & Nair, 2018)

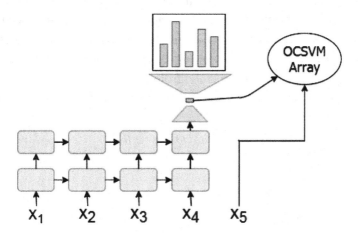

Since $P\left(x_{ij} \mid x_{i1},\dots,x_{i,j-1};L\right)=0$ then $P\left(x_{i1},\dots,x_{i,j-1} \mid x_{ij};L\right)=0$. Consequently:

$$f\left(x,L\right)=\begin{cases}1, & \text{if there is } x_{ij} \text{ such that } P_{x_{ij}}\left(x_{i1},\dots,x_{i,j-1};L\right)=0 \\ 0, & \text{otherwise}\end{cases} \qquad (22)$$

where: $P_{x_{ij}}$ be the probability under a specified x_{ij}.

The objective function of the model can be represented as follows.

$$\mathcal{L}=\sum_{i=1}^{n-1}-\log\left(P\left(x_{i+1} \mid D\left(E\left(x;\theta_E\right)_i;\theta_D\right)\right)\right) \qquad (23)$$

where:

$$E\left(x;\theta_E\right):\Sigma^n \rightarrow \mathcal{R}^{n\times e} \text{ is LSTM encoder} \qquad (24)$$

$$D\left(y;\theta_D\right): \mathcal{R}^e \rightarrow \mathcal{R}^{|\Sigma|} \text{ is MLP decoder} \qquad (25)$$

$$O_\sigma\left(cv\right): \mathcal{R}^e \rightarrow \mathcal{R} \text{ is OCSVM for element } \sigma \in \Sigma \qquad (26)$$

The LSTM autoencoders are trained by reconstructing their own input. Output of the encoder is the expected probability distribution for the $i+1$ element given the first i elements. The model is trained using stochastic gradient descent learning algorithm to learn θ_E and θ_D with the cross entropy as the objective function.

We can then train each OCSVM O$\sigma \in$ O with the context vector set from the corresponding Y$\sigma \in$ Y using the method from Schölkopf (2000). We now describe how to approximate the function f(x). Given, θ0 E and O, we define $g \approx f$ as

$$g\left(x\right) = \begin{cases} 1, & if\ there\ is\ x_i \in x\ such\ that\ O_{x_i}\left(E\left(x;\theta'_E\right)_{i-1}\right) < t_\alpha \\ 0, & otherwise \end{cases} \tag{27}$$

where: t_α be a threshold hyperparamater.

CONCLUSION

The study regarding on the anomaly detection is a very important thing in the life of human being. The various phenomenon often occurs related to the anomaly study. The network intrusion detection is the most widely fields using the technique of the anomaly detection. Followed by the tracking and safety field, climate prediction, cellular technology, medical, spatial detection and diagnosis for the engine.

The Anomaly Detection System are generally designed using four methods to execute the predictions, namely statistical, data mining, machine learning and graphical modeling. The most popular method and widely used are data mining (45%), followed by machine learning (29% utilization). Whereas the approach of graphical modeling used in the latest researches at the field of imaging, satellite imagery and several researches with a spatiotemporal thematic.

Machine learning is basically the process by which a computer learns from the data. Anomaly detection is an interesting problem in machine learning with any applications. Two most effective machine learning techniques used to detect anomaly are supervised and unsupervised learning. For supervised learning anomaly detection case, the detection is done by training the data points so that the can be classified into two groups of anomaly and non-anomaly, while in the unsupervised learning, we can apply a threshold to decide whether or not the data is anomaly.

Furthermore, to improve the accuracy for anomaly detection, this study suggest to using a hybrid approach in data mining to combine the modified version of already existing algorithms. Hybrid approaches provide better results, higher accuracy, increase in detection rate and reduction in mean time of false alarm rate.

REFERENCES

Abadeh, M. S., Habibi, J., & Lucas, C. (2007). Intrusion detection using a fuzzy genetics-based learning algorithm. *Journal of Network and Computer Applications*, *30*(1), 414–428. doi:10.1016/j.jnca.2005.05.002

Adisasmito, W. (2007). Systematic Review Penelitian Akademik Bidang Kesehatan Masyarakat. Jurnal Makara Kesehatan, 11.

Agrawal, S., & Agrawal, J. (2015). Survey on Anomaly Detection using Data Mining Techniques. International Conference on Knowledge Based and Intelligent Information and Engineering Systems. *Procedia Computer Science*, *60*, 708–713. doi:10.1016/j.procs.2015.08.220

Alcaide. (2016). Visual Anomaly Detection in Spatio-Temporal Data using Element-Specific References. *2016 IEEE VIS*.

Blomquist, H., & Moller, J. (2015). *Anomaly detection with Machine learning.* Uppsala Universitet.

Budalakoti, S., Srivastava, A. N., & Otey, M. E. (2009). Anomaly Detection and Diagnosis Algorithms for Discrete Symbol Sequences with Applications to Airline Safety. *IEEE Transactions on Systems, Man, and Cybernetics Part C*, *39*(1), 101–113.

Casas, P. (2016). *Machine-Learning Based Approaches for Anomaly Detection and Classification in Cellular Networks. 2016 The Traffic Monitoring and Analysis workshop.* TMA.

Celik, M., Dadaser-Celik, W., & Dokuz, A. S. (2011). Anomaly detection in temperature data using DBSCAN algorithm. *11 International Symposium on Innovations in Intelligent Systems and Applications*. 10.1109/INISTA.2011.5946052

Chandola, V., Banerjee, A., & Kumar, V. (2007). *Anomaly detection – a survey.* Technical Report 07-017. Computer Science Department, University of Minnesota.

Chandola, V., Banerjee, A., & Kumar, V. (2012). Anomaly detection for discrete sequences: A survey. *IEEE Transactions on Knowledge and Data Engineering*, *24*(5), 823–839. doi:10.1109/TKDE.2010.235

Chen, Y., Zhou, X. S., & Huang, T. S. (2001). One-class SVM for learning in image retrieval. In *Image Processing, 2001. Proceedings 2001 International Conference on* (Vol. 1, pp. 34-37). IEEE.

Chitrakar, R., & Chuanhe, H. (2012). Anomaly detection using Support Vector Machine classification with k-Medoids clustering. *Proceedings of IEEE Third Asian Himalayas International Conference on Internet (AH-ICI).* 10.1109/AHICI.2012.6408446

Das, M., & Parthasarathy, S. (2009). Anomaly detection and spatio-temporal analysis of global climate system. In *Proceedings of the Third International Workshop on Knowledge Discovery from Sensor Data.* ACM. 10.1145/1601966.1601989

Djurdjanovic, D., Liu, J., Marko, K. A., & Ni, J. (2007). Immune Systems Inspired Approach to Anomaly Detection and Fault Diagnosis for Engines. *2007 International Joint Conference on Neural Networks.* 10.1109/IJCNN.2007.4371159

Ensafi, R., Dehghanzadeh, S., Mohammad, R., & Akbarzadeh, T. (2008). Optimizing Fuzzy K-means for network anomaly detection using PSO. *Computer Systems and Applications, IEEE/ACS International Conference.*

Farid, D. M., Harbi, N., & Rahman, M. Z. (2010). Combining naive bayes and decision tree for adaptive intrusion detection. *International Journal of Network Security & Its Applications, 2*(2).

Fu, S., Liu, J., & Pannu, H. (2012). A Hybrid Anomaly Detection Framework in Cloud Computing Using One-Class and Two-Class Support Vector Machines. In *Advanced Data Mining and Applications.* Springer Berlin Heidelberg. doi:10.1007/978-3-642-35527-1_60

Fujimaki, R., Yairi, T., & Machida, K. (2005). An approach to spacecraft anomaly detection problem using kernel feature space. In *Proceedings of the eleventh ACM SIGKDD international conference on Knowledge discovery in data mining (KDD '05).* ACM. 10.1145/1081870.1081917

Gornitz, N., Kloft, M., Rieck, K., & Brefeld, U. (2013). Toward supervised anomaly detection. Journal Artificial Intelligence. *Intestinal Research, 46,* 235–262.

Grossman, R. (1977). *Data Mining: Challenges and Opportunities for Data Mining During the Next Decade.* Academic Press.

Hochreiter, S., & Schmidhuber, J. (1997). Long short-term memory. *Neural Computation, 9*(8), 1735–1780. doi:10.1162/neco.1997.9.8.1735 PMID:9377276

Horng, S.-J., Su, M.-Y., Chen, Y.-H., Kao, T.-W., Chen, R.-J., Lai, J.-L., & Perkasa, C. D. (2011). A novel intrusion detection system based on hierarchical clustering and support vector machines. *Expert Systems with Applications, 38*(1), 306–313. doi:10.1016/j.eswa.2010.06.066

Jakimovski, B. (2011). Biologically Inspired Approaches for Anomaly Detection within a Robotic System. In Biologically Inspired Approaches for Locomotion. Anomaly Detection and Reconfiguration for Walking Robots (pp. 127-150). Springer. doi:10.1007/978-3-642-22505-5_7

Kao, A. R., Ganguly, S. C., & Steinhaeuser, K. (2009). Motivating Complex Dependence Structures in Data Mining: A Case Study with Anomaly Detection in Climate. *2009 IEEE International Conference on Data Mining Workshops*, 223-230. 10.1109/ICDMW.2009.37

Karami, A. (2016). *A Novel Fuzzy Anomaly Detection Algorithm Based on Hybrid PSO-Kmeans in Content-Centric Networking. In Handbook of Research on Advanced Hybrid Intelligent Techniques and Applications*. IGI Global.

Kavitha, B., Karthikeyan, D. S., & Maybell, P. S. (2012). An ensemble design of intrusion detection system for handling uncertainty using Neutrosophic Logic Classifier. *Knowledge-Based Systems*, *28*(0), 88–96. doi:10.1016/j.knosys.2011.12.004

Kawale, J. (2011). *Anomaly Construction in Climate Data: Issues and Challenges. Technical Report*. Department of Computer Science, University of Minnesota.

Kitchenham, B., & Charters, S. (2007). *Guidelines for performing Systematic Literature Reviews in Software Engineering*. EBSE Technical Report Version 2.3.

Liao, Y., & Vemuri, V. R. (2002). Use of k-nearest neighbor classifier for intrusion detection. *Computers & Security*, *21*(5), 439–448. doi:10.1016/S0167-4048(02)00514-X

Liu, C., Ghosal, S., Jiang, Z., & Sarkar, S. (2016). An unsupervised spatiotemporal graphical modeling approach to anomaly detection in distributed CPS. In *Proceedings of the 7th International Conference on Cyber-Physical Systems (ICCPS 2016)*. IEEE Press. 10.1109/ICCPS.2016.7479069

Mascaroa, S., Nicholson, A., & Korb, K. (2014). Anomaly detection in vessel tracks using Bayesian Networks. *International Journal of Approximate Reasoning*, 55.

Michell, T. (1997). *Machine Learning*. Mc Graw Hill.

Moya, M., & Hush, D. (1996). Network constraints and multi- objective optimization for one-class classification. *Neural Networks*, *9*(3), 463–474. doi:10.1016/0893-6080(95)00120-4

Omar, S. (2013). Machine Learning Techniques for Anomaly Detection: An Overview. *International Journal of Computer Applications, 79*(2).

Park, Y., Wang, H., Nobauer, T., Vaziri, A., & Priebe, C. E. (2015). Anomaly Detection on Whole-Brain Functional Imaging of Neuronal Activity using Graph Scan Statistics. *Computer Networks*, *51*, 3448–3470.

Prasetyo, S.Y.J.P., Subanar, W. E., & Daryono, B.S. (n.d.). ESSA: Exponential Smoothing and Spatial Autocorrelation, Methods for Prediction of Outbreaks Pest In Indonesia. *International Review Computer and Software*.

Rembold. (2013). Using Low Resolution Satellite Imagery for Yield Prediction and Yield Anomaly Detection. *Yaogan Xuebao*, *5*, 1704–1733.

Roberts, C., & Nair, M. (2018). *Arbitrary Discrete Sequence Anomaly Detection with Zero Boundary LSTM*. arXiv preprint arXiv:1803.02395

Schölkopf, B., Williamson, R. C., Smola, A. J., Shawe-Taylor, J., & Platt, J. C. (2000). Support vector method for novelty detection. *Advances in Neural Information Processing Systems*, 582–588.

Stack Exchange. (2017). *Difference between contextual anomaly and collective anomaly*. Retrieved from https://stats.stackexchange.com/questions/323553

Sun, B., Yu, F., Wu, K., Xiao, Y., & Leung, V. C. M. (2006). Enhancing Security Using Mobility-Based Anomaly Detection in Cellular Mobile Networks. *IEEE Transactions on Vehicular Technology*, *55*(4), 1385–1396. doi:10.1109/TVT.2006.874579

Tax, D. M., & Duin, R. P. (2004). Support vector data description. *Machine Learning*, *54*(1), 45–66. doi:10.1023/B:MACH.0000008084.60811.49

Tsai, C.-F., & Lin, C.-Y. (2010). A triangle area based nearest neighbors approach to intrusion detection. *Pattern Recognition*, *43*(1), 222–229. doi:10.1016/j.patcog.2009.05.017

Vapnik, V. (1998). *Statistical learning theory*. Chichester, UK: Wiley.

Wahyono, T. (2017). Anomaly detection to evaluate in-class learning process using distance and density approach of machine learning. *International Conference on Innovative and Creative Information Technology (ICITech)*. 10.1109/INNOCIT.2017.8319138

Wang, Y. (2005). A multinomial logistic regression modeling approach for anomaly intrusion detection. *Computers & Security*, *24*(8), 662–674. doi:10.1016/j.cose.2005.05.003

Xie, M., Hu, J., & Guo, S. (2015). Segment-based anomaly detection with approximated sample covariance matrix in wireless sensor networks. Parallel and Distributed Systems. *IEEE Transactions on*, *26*(2), 574–583.

Yairi, T., & Kawahara. (2006). Telemetry-mining: a machine learning approach to anomaly detection and fault diagnosis for space systems. *2nd IEEE International Conference on Space Mission Challenges for Information Technology (SMC-IT'06)*. 10.1109/SMC-IT.2006.79

Yang, Y., & Liu, X. (1999). A re-examination of text categorization methods. In *Proceedings of the 22nd annual international ACM SIGIR conference on Research and development in information retrieval* (pp. 42-49). ACM.

Yang, Z., Meratnia, N., & Havinga, P. (2007). *Outlier Detection Techniques For Wireless Sensor Networks: A Survey*. Department of Computer Science, University of Twente.

Yi, Y., Wu, J., & Xu, W. (2011). Incremental SVM based on reserved set for network intrusion detection. *Expert Systems with Applications*, *38*(6), 7698–7707. doi:10.1016/j.eswa.2010.12.141

APPENDIX

Case Study: Detecting Anomaly Data
Using Distance kNN Method

Wahyono et.al (2017) did a simple research to see the data anomaly of the students' grades, especially for Religion and Civics lessons of 140 students is a school in Salatiga. The research was implemented in an application by using an R Programming.

The program codes for the data initiation are shown in Box 1.

Those codes produced outputs sowed in the diagram below, which illustrate the plots of the students' grades' data (Figure 13).

The anomaly detection was done by using distance based approach, using *distance to k-Nearest Neighbor* (k-NN) as the outlier score. The algorithms from the anomaly detection by using distance based with k-NN as the outlier score were:

Box 1.

```
1    #Call Data Set Nilai.csv
2    set.seed(1000)
3    x1=rnorm(50)
4    y1=rnorm(50)
5    nilai <- "nilai.csv"
6    mydata1 <- read.csv(nilai)
7    plot(mydata1,pch=16)
```

Figure 13. Data plot

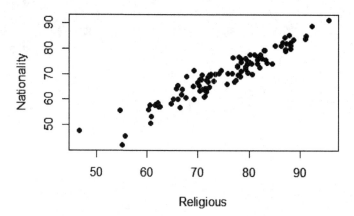

1. Determine the number of the closest neighbors ((k) parameter).
2. Determine the distance of every pair of data and sort them.
3. Determine the closest neighbor based on the minimum distance to –k.
4. Determine the category of the closest neighbors.
5. The conclusion was, a data can be called as anomaly if the point had the longest distance from the k of the clossest neighbors or if the point had largest distance average from the closest neighbors.

The program codes for determine distance matrix and distance to nearest neighbor are shown in Box 2.

Ordinary plot could be shown as in Figure 14.

The program codes for ploting with color determined by kdist are shown in Box 3.

Box 2.

```
 9  #Determine Distance Matrix and Distance to kth nearest neighbor (k=5)|
10  DMatrix=as.matrix(dist(mydata1))
11  kdist=1:140
12 ▾ for(i in 1:140){
13    kdist[i]=(sort(DMatrix[i,]))[6]
14  }
15
16  #Plotting data
17  library(ggplot2)
18  library(gridExtra)
19
20  #Ordinary plot
21  ggplot(data=mydata1,aes(x=Religious,y=Nationality,size=3))+geom_point()
```

Figure 14. Ordinary plot

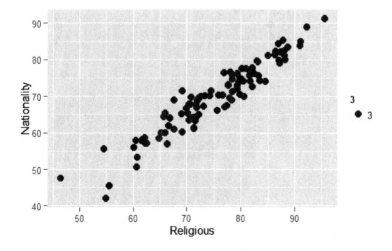

Gradient plot could be shown as in Figure 15.

By applying distance to k-Nearest Neighbor as the score, the Density Curve for the Outlier Score could be shown as in Figure 16.

Based on the above graphic, the lines perceives as outliers could further be found. Next, an analysis based on k-dist could provide Ggplot graphic shown in Figure 17.

Finding rows with outliers is shown in Box 4.

After finding rows with outliers were performed, it could also be concluded that the distance based model could identify 9 students whose grades could be seen as anomaly, which were students number 7, 30, 35, 98, 107, 110, 134, 138 dan 139.

Box 3.

```
26  #Plot with Color Determined by kdist
27  #and with Gradient Plot (Heatmap)
28  ggplot(data=mydata1,aes(x=Religious,y=Nationality,col=kdist,size=3))+geom_point()+
29    scale_colour_gradientn(colours=c("black", "red"))
30
```

Figure 15. Gradient plot

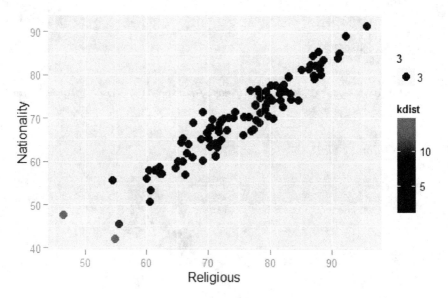

Figure 16. Density curved

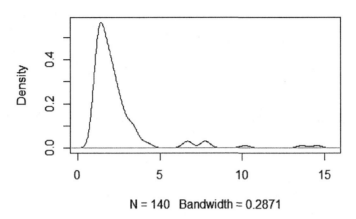

Figure 17. Ggplot analysis based on k-dist

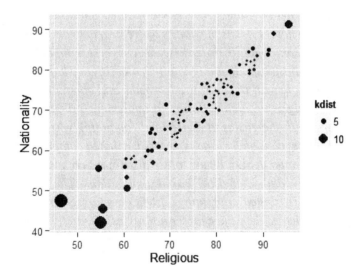

Box 4.

```
> #Finding Rows with Outliers
> (1:140)[kdist>=6]
[1]    7   30   35   98 107 110 134 138 139
```

Chapter 4
Distributed Computing for Internet of Things (IoT)

Dharmendra Trikamlal Patel
 https://orcid.org/0000-0002-4769-1289
Smt. Chandaben Mohanbhai Patel Institute of Computer Applications, India

ABSTRACT

In recent years, internet of things (IoT) has expanded due to very good internet infrastructure everywhere. IoT has the ability to create a network of physical things that use embedded technologies in order to sense, converse, cooperate, and team up with other things. IoT-based applications require scalability and fault tolerance, which is very difficult to implement in centralized systems and computing environments. Distributed computing is an ideal solution to implement IoT-based applications. The chapter starts with the basics of distributed computing where difference with centralized computing, challenges, and types of distributed computing applications are discussed. The chapter deals with the role of distributed computing for IoT based on advantages, issues, and related IoT-based applications. The chapter discusses the recent topic of distributed computing—FOG computing—in connection with IoT-based applications. At last, the chapter addresses research and interest trends about distributed computing and IoT.

INTRODUCTION TO DISTRIBUTED COMPUTING

Over the past several years, computing has undergone a series of changes from platform and environmental aspects. Due to the invention of the Internet, centralized computing became obsolete and new computing paradigm, in the form of distributed

DOI: 10.4018/978-1-5225-7955-7.ch004

was introduced. Distributed computing is a field of computer science and engineering that solves computational problems of distributed systems. Distributed computing divides problem in many tasks and each one is solved by one or more computational entities. Distributed computing involves several things: (a) Several autonomous computational entities with local memory (b) Communication among computational entities through message passing (c) Fault tolerance in each computing entity (d) Each computing element has limited view of the entire system. Distributed computing is essential in applications where data produced in one physical location and required by another location. Enigma@Home(Enima Website) project is the real application of distributed computing in cryptography. Enigma@Home is a wrapper between BOINC and Stefan Krah's M4 Project. The M4 Project is an effort to break 3 original Enigma messages with the help of distributed computing.

Distributed computing is the process of aggregating the power of several computing entities, which are logically distributed and may even be geologically distributed, to collaboratively run a single computational task in a transparent and coherent way, so that they appear as a single, centralized system. (Cao,2005)

Client -Server was the simplest model of distributed computing in the early days. The computing was distributed among the presentation layer and application layer. This kind of architecture has been widely used in the several applications such as ERP, billing and inventory applications. The main limitations of the Client-Server model are:

- Need of robust client systems as complex business processing done on client.
- It is very vulnerable to security breaches as logic depends on the client.
- Scalability Restrictions
- Difficulty in the maintenance and upgradation of client applications.

Object Management Group(OMG) has developed the next category of distributed computing architecture known as " Common Object Request Broker Architecture(CORBA"). It provides an object oriented solution. With the help of this architecture, the applications can run on any hardware platform anywhere on the network. Interface Definition Language (IDL) is designed to deal with methods of a remote object. It suffers from the following limitations:

- There is no CORBA standard is available to bind the Request Broker and its clients. We have to rely on vendor specific options.

- The interfaces of CORBA are very complex in comparison of traditional client-server architecture.
- Shipping of live objects are not feasible.
- Lacking in the implementation of CORBA services

JAVA RMI was another popular distributed architecture that was developed by the Sun Microsystems. It uses the lightweight object persistent techniques that makes the transaction among different components very efficiently. Like CORBA, it also uses the object oriented distributed computing. It supports the live shipping of the objects. However, it suffers from several drawbacks:

- It is specific to JAVA code
- Hard to implement callback methods over the Internet
- Security sometimes compromised, particularly when using dynamic class loading

Microsoft DCOM distributed architecture designed by the Microsoft specifically for the windows operating systems based software components. It is successful in providing distributed supports on windows platform. It has the following limitations:

- It is specifically for Microsoft languages
- Scalability issues
- Issues in session management

The modern era is of Internet of Things and distributed computing architectures discussed above are critical to the success of it. Data availability and usability are the major concern for the IoT . Distributed computing architectures play a vital role in the availability and usability of the data.

Centralized vs. Distributed Computing

In the early days of computer technology, the mainframe computer was used as centralized computing platform. Mainframe computer was physically large, held all of the computing power, memory and storage system. If it is managed wisely, it offers greater security. This kind of system relies totally on the central mainframe computer. The other thing is, centralized computing relies greatly on quality of management of resources provided to its users.

Table 1. Centralized vs. distributed computing

Sr.No	Parameter	Centralized Computing	Distributed Computing
1.	Data Computing	All computing is done on the central computing server.	The computing is distributed on multiple computing nodes.
2.	Single Point Failure	If a centralized server fails, the entire system crumples.	Each computing node survives on its own means there is no single point failure in this kind of model.
3.	Operational Cost	Lower, as it requires minimum hardware at each site.	Higher, as it requires computing hardware at each node.
4.	Reliability	Low, as it depends on a central node.	High, If one computing node fails, the other can do the specific task.
5.	Query Processing	Slow, as computing is done by single computing node.	Fast, as it allows parallel computing by several nodes.
6.	Autonomy	It has non-autonomous components.	It has autonomous components.
7.	Heterogeneity	Based on homogeneous technology.	Based on heterogeneous technology.
8.	Security	High, as all data resides on a central server.	May compromised as data travels among a number of computing nodes.
9.	Complexity	There is no complexity in calculation as all computation is done by central entity.	Huge complexity as computing done on different computing nodes.
10.	Replication	No method of replication.	Relies on master less peer-to-peer replication.
11.	User View	Use of central server is visible to the user.	Use of multiple computing elements is invisible to the user.

Contrary to centralized computing, distributed computing performs computing tasks on several computing entities. Distributed computing solves the problem of distributed system. A distributed system is an application in which single computational task runs on more than one computational node. The significant difficulty in distributed computing is to offer a user with a non distributed vision of a distributed system. Table 1 describes major differences between centralized computing and distributed computing.

Challenges of Distributed Computing

Distributed computing is one of the most challenging research fields in computer science. Besides traditional topics such as synchronization, currently it is enriched with numerous topics from modern technologies such as the Internet. Modern technology has given the birth of numerous challenges in this field. Following are several challenges due to the Internet:

Wait-Free Consensus

In distributed computing, to achieve reliability is a major apprehension in the existence of numerous flawed agents. The consensus problem requires agreement among a number of agents for a single data value. It is best suited for synchronization without mutual exclusion (Maurice,1991). If consensus is not achievable then execution of wait-free consensus is unworkable. A consensus protocol meets with consistency, termination and validity conditions(Benny,1987). Consistency condition is most vital as it guarantees the processor agrees. Termination condition determines that processor must finish in expected time, regardless of the action of the scheduler. Validation condition ensures the agreement among processors. Sometimes validity condition force processors to agree on some specific conditions that leads the problem in distributed computing. Shared coin is stronger primitive that provides a solution of validity condition. Shared coin mechanism satisfies the conditions of termination and probabilistic agreement. The probability agreement with 2δ probability indicates that the share coin protocol is agreed on by all processors. With probability $1 - 2\delta$, it is possible that all processors with not agree with each other at all. The more reliable and natural parameter instead of agreement is bias. In terms of bias, the probability that at least one processor decides on a given value is $\frac{1}{2} +$. It is considered as robust as it guarantees that all processor always agrees with the outcome of coin. The main limitation of share coin is, it gives too much power over the outcome of protocol to any processor at a given time. Consensus using random walk is an ideal solution to this situation. In any methodology, *the main challenge is the complexity of solving consensus.*

Oblivious Routing

The multi hop network is used in distributed system to communicate among any **n** numbers of computing elements. The computing elements communicate by exchanging messages in the form of packets. Routing selects an appropriate path of a packet that will follow in network. In a distributed system, oblivious routing is one type that is appropriate for dynamic packets. Oblivious routing makes decisions based on local knowledge. On traditional routing algorithms, the routing path chosen between source and destination depends on only those two entities. In (L.G Valiant et al., 1981) authors suggested efficient routing algorithms for hypercube and comparative ratio of these algorithms were O (log n). In (H. Racke,2002) oblivious routing algorithm with poly logarithm competitive ratio was shown. However, this result is not efficient as only exponential time algorithm was given. In (H.EI-

Sayed,2008) authors addressed the issue of previous work and showed the optimum oblivious routing scheme. The method given in (Y.Azae et al.,2003) did not give the likelihood to obtain general limits on the competitive ratio for defining types of graph. A polynomial time algorithm was given in (C.Harrelson et al.,2003) where they received competitive ratio of $O(\log^2 n \log \log n)$. In (Hiroshi et al.,2005) problem of oblivious routing for the directed graph was shown and they proved that we cannot obtain a competitive ratio better than $\Omega(\sqrt{n})$ and it is possible to achieve $\Omega(\sqrt{n} \log n)$. *The main challenge of this situation is to examine the circumstances in which congestion and stretch can be optimized simultaneously. Another thing is to identify classes of network where congestion and stretch can be minimized simultaneously.*

Adverse Cooperative Computing

In distributed computing, cooperative computing is required between number of computing elements. Sometimes due to processor failure, communication breakdown and unpredictable delay adverse affect done on cooperative computing. The basic problem of cooperation is divided among three aspects: shared memory, message passing and networks. *Developing efficient algorithms which solve adverse cooperative computing problem isa major challenge.*

Scheduling Issues

Broadcasting and multicasting are important processing in distributed systems. One of the significant purposes of parallel distributed systems is broadcasting. Broadcasting in a distributed system is used to deliver data over an entire system. There are various algorithms of broadcast scheduling, but shortest time scheduling is desirable in high performance distributed system. In (T.Casavant et.al,1988), (M. Arora et al,2002) and (Fatos et al.,2002) authors described different scheduling criteria, but they could be overlapped so it is very difficult to make them distinct. In distributed computing, minimum completion time and minimum execution time based scheduling algorithms are very important and desirable. In (R.F.Freund et al,1998, T.Casavant et al.,1988, T.W.Malone et al.,1998) author proposed a Minimum Completion Time algorithm in which it allocates tasks arbitrary for execution on a resource with minimum completion time. However, based on the above criteria of scheduling causes some tasks to be assigned for resources that haven't the minimum execution time in turn poorly consume some resources. *The main challenge of distributed scheduling is to achieve shorter time scheduling with optimum resource usage.*

Task Allocation

Efficient task allocation is very important in distributed computing in order to achieve performance and reliability (S.Kartic et al.,1995)(Veljko,et al.,1988). Task allocation can be done using a centralized agent (J.S. Rosenschein et al.,1988) or by collection of agents(R.G.Smith et al.,1983). The central crisis in the assignment of the tasks is that the agents have dissimilar abilities, and so each of the agents can execute only a subset of the tasks. The major goal of the agents is to take full advantage of the overall performance of the system, and to execute the tasks as soon as possible. The overall performance of the system is the sum of the performances of all the agents:

$$n = \Sigma ni = \frac{1}{time}\Sigma ni = \frac{N}{time} \tag{1}$$

The main challenge here is to optimize the behavior of the system and to minimize the time of performing all the tasks.

In addition, of the above mentioned challenges, distributed computing also has many traditional challenges such as:

- Scalability
- Security
- Concurrency
- Openness
- Design Challenges
- Extensibility
- Load balancing
- Observability

Types of Distributed Computing Applications

Distributed Computing based applications have certain characteristics. Not all applications are appropriate for distributed computing.

- Applications should have a potential to partition an application into autonomous tasks that can be computed independently.
- Applications with large databases that can be easily parsed for distributions.
- Applications with loosely coupled, non-sequential tasks and high compute-to-data ratio.

- Application with communication network to connect several computing elements.

    Distributed Computing applications may fall into different types depicted in Figure 1.

Internet Centric based distributed applications are in the scope of this chapter, the rest are out of the scope.

Internet Centric based distributed applications can be divided into three categories: network centric, server based computing and peer-to-peer computing.

In net centric computing, applications and data are downloaded from servers and exchanged with peers across a network when needed. The common net centric computing architecture supports access of information through multiple electronic channels. Net centric creates more flexible architecture that extends and evolves over time.

Raytheon Network Centric Systems provides systems integration for government and defense customers in the United States and the international marketplace. Used Klocwork's toolset on two defense programs: an aircraft multimode radar for military systems and a ground vehicle sensor. With Klocwork's tools, the developers were able to run "what if" scenarios to determine how the systems would react when several individual factors were integrated together. Raytheon was able to identify whether the radar's hardware requirements would change when the modes ran in parallel. Klocwork's tools are used to show a graphical view of all the sensors' elements, and ran feasibility tests to determine how those elements would interact with each other when integrated. This is a classical example of a net centric environment.

Figure 1.

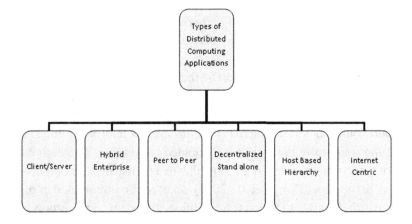

Internet of things (IoT) based applications are also considered as net centric applications as they extensively use RFID and sensor networks. The IoT conceptualized aim is to generate a whole network the facilitates objects to be connected anytime, anywhere, with anyone using any network. The ubiquitous composition of smart objects of IoT required wireless technology as a communication medium to exchange or collect data. The next topic will elaborate Internet of Things (IoT) in more detail.

ROLE OF DISTRIBUTED COMPUTING FOR IoT

The Internet of Things (IoT) builds on the idea of the original Internet. It encompasses, of networking, computing nodes that all linked together via global networks. IoT do not based on traditional communication paradigms. IoT is about data gathering from a good deal larger assortment of simple devices or sensors that communicate specific data to a centralized or semi-centralized collection point, and can obtain straightforward commands back from that central source. In comparison with traditional computing, networking nodes, sensor data are unstructured and less computing power and storage. The question arises that should we go for centralized or distributed architecture in the case of IoT? In the era of Internet, physical objects are no longer detached from virtual globe, but can be remotely controlled and can act as physical access points to Internet services so it resembles to distributed systems. Decentralized system of cooperating smart objects (SOs) is rising as an innovative archetype for IoT. Distributed computing is required in IoT to support rapid growth in data traffic and ability to control the data. IoT developer needs to distributed computing power to support the creation of apps and enormous amount of data crunching. IoT applications are closely related to cloud computing. Distributed computing is essential to apply computations from the cloud servers and to reduce the transmission bandwidth requirement. The Sensor is a vital part of IoT applications and distributed computing is essential for big data analysis problem in video sensor network. Highly distributed computing is required into sensors and aggregators of IoT based applications.

In the paper (Shao-Yi Chien et.al.,2015), the authors described that the centralized solutions on a cloud are not efficient to support the large scale data size and computation tasks. Internet of Things(IoT) based applications deal with the large scale data size and computation tasks so centralized solutions are not feasible at all. The authors described the solution in the form of distributed computing. The authors took an example of video sensing network to show the idea of distributed computing in IoT.

Authors in the paper (Singh et al., 2017), showed the importance of distributed intelligence in the Internet of Things and Multiagent systems. The authors described the major challenges in the context of decentralized intelligence from the perspective of Internet of Things based applications. The main focus of the paper was to explore the decentralized intelligence in distributed computing for the Internet of Things(IoT).

Wei Yu et al. (2017) did the literature survey on Edge Computing for the Internet of Things. The authors described that the a number of computation nodes distributed across the network in Internet of Things(IoT) based applications can offload the computational stress away from the centralized data center, and can significantly reduce the latency in the message exchange. They also narrated that the distributed structure can balance network traffic and avoid the traffic peaks in IoT networks, reducing the transmission latency between edge/cloudlet servers and end users, as well as reducing response times for real-time IoT applications in comparison with traditional cloud services.

The authors in the paper (Lin et al., 2017) had described that the distributed architecture provides an advantage of faster response and greater quality of service for IoT applications. The papers also described several applications based on the Internet of things in which distributed architecture leads to several advantages.

Nader Mohamed and his co-authors (2017) described a service oriented middleware for cloud and fog enabled smart city services. They described the distributed computing architecture that extends the traditional cloud computing centralized paradigm.

In 2018, Emanuele Di Pascale et al. (2018) published one paper in IEEE internet of things journal, in which a framework for distributed computing over IoT mesh network was presented. Authors concluded that by exploiting the principle of locality inherent to many IoT applications, a framework for distributed computing reduce the latency in the delivering processed information. Furthermore, it improves the distribution of energy consumption across the IoT network compared to a centralized processing scenario.

Advantages of Distributed Computing For IoT

- The Main intention of IoT based applications is atomization. Automation systems have multiple models and all requires integration in order to achieve correct and efficient output. Distributed computing provides controlling among all models in order to achieve correct results.
- Distributed computing acts as a bridge between IoT devices and remote data centers. IoT produce a huge data set that processed with distributed computing to achieve worth and consequence.
- IoT requires time critical tasks such as analysis and decision making and those can be efficiently handled by distributed computing.
- Distributed Computing can deal with high amount of traffic using smart filtering and careful transmission.

- Distributed Computing reduces the need for bandwidth by aggregating bits at certain access points and as a result lower cost and efficiencies of IoT based applications.
- IoT based applications require scalability and that can be achieved by distributed computing.
- IoT based applications need high security and for that breach and hacking must be avoided at any cost. Distributed computing nodes have the right mix of span of control, computing power and network connectivity that addresses many security problems.
- Many IoT based applications are expected to continue functioning in spite of the failure of the network link. The Distributed node provides backup and reliability as a result of an application may increase.

Issues of Distributed Computing in IoT

Internet is considered as an information hub based on the ideas of people, however, it is easily observed as physical world based on the advances of hardware and sensors. Internet of things (IoT) includes both Internet and physical objects with controllers, sensors and actuators. This additional layer of information brings new capabilities of capturing, processing and computing gigantic amount of semi structured and unstructured data. Computing is vital in terms of IoT as it controls data and serves as an integration medium among heterogeneous devices. There are several issues occur due to distributed computing.

- **Security:** Distributed computing does extremely large degree computations; there are several privacy and security issues that must be taken into consideration by developers of distributed computing systems. The Internet is a compulsory element of Internet of Things objects that allows a malicious penetrator at the most defectively confined location and attack all other computers in the network. One of the major concerns for nearly all distributed systems is hackers. Hackers can nastily molest the system by manipulating data and destroying results. In addition to hacker problem, data can be captured in transfer between the server and the client. In distributed system mechanism if the distributed software is downloaded from an unreliable location, clients are in the danger of opening up their machines to exterior individuals who desire to attack clients. In IoT more embedded systems are linked to the Internet, the probable damages from such vulnerabilities scale up considerably. Due to the birth of IoT, intelligence device based hacking is common. By using a cheap RFID scanner and low profile antennas, clone of half a dozen electronic passports in an hour is possible (J.Davis et al.,2009).

The majority accessible automotive, communication based on IoT systems are virtually unsecured against nasty violation (K.Lemke et al.,2006). Unfortunately, traditional security techniques are not capable of IoT based embedded systems (P.Koopman,2004).

U.S Veteran Affairs Department (VA) has launched a new project to guarantee linked medical devices are secluded. As IoT are more and more used in health applications, growingly connected devices are being worked in hospitals for patient monitoring and diagnosis. VA is concentrating more on boosting IoT security to secure IoT equipment on hospital networks from any malicious attacks. Recently, one attack was done on the MedStar Health network in Washington, D.C. that blocked patients' records. As additional devices turn into incorporated into health care services, security becomes vital. This concern was at the back of VA's new cybersecurity policy that focused on securing medical devices and general medical cybersecurity. VA's requirement for medical IoT security include: automation; scalability to millions of devices; consideration for device time lags; and the capacity to generate reports on protocols, threat indicators and device traffic volume.

- **Concurrency:** In IoT based applications, concurrency is the most vital element. Even if an application needs to forward data among sensors and actuators; several things needs to be done in parallel. IoT application gateways require intertwining collectively streams of actions that arrive at their interface. IoT are based on physical things and they are fundamentally concurrent. Physical things perform and react concurrently with any software that may be interacting with them. JavaScript is considered as an event based concurrency model and mostly applicable in IoT based applications. It follows asynchronous atomic callback (AAC) pattern of concurrency. AAC pattern is used extensively in Internet based programming for client/server model. It is also very helpful in embedded and in distributed computing (P.Levis et al.,2004)(T. Von et al.,1992). AAC patterns lessen the complexity of concurrent programming; however achieving coordinated action becomes challenging task. Coordination among physical objects is very necessary in IoT so AAC pattern is very difficult to implement. Integration of AAC with other concurrency model solves the above mentioned problem to some extent. Several works mentioned in (E.Kohler et al.,2000),(J.C.Corbett et al.,2013) (Y.zaho et al.,2007) tried to achieve concurrency in IoT ; based on a mixture of AAC with other mechanisms. Still researching is required on this issue to achieve cent percent concurrency with simplicity and less cost.

- **Fault Handling:** IoT based applications require to exchange messages among users, devices and service providers through web services. Due to instability of the Internet and nature of IoT based applications; reliability of message passing became a huge confront. Reliability becomes an essential requirement of IoT as it provides guarantees of message delivery among entities of IoT. There are two types of fault tolerance strategies used in any application: sequential and parallel (Z.Zheng et al.,2010). Parallel fault handling strategy is an ideal for IoT. When running a parallel query, some type of breakdown is expected to occur during query execution(J.Dean,2006). There are several solutions of parallel query based faults. First and simplest one is based on a parallel database management system in which it restarts queries if failures occur during their execution. The main limitation is only a single failure requires to restart the entire query. It is undesirable for long queries using a large number of servers. Map Reduce (J.Dean et al.,2004) technique materializes the output of each operator and restart individual operator when failures occur. This approach overcomes the limitation of a parallel database management system, but overhead is more to materialize all intermediate data. This approach avoids users to considering results incrementally. FTOpt is another fault tolerance method with works for heterogeneous computing elements. FTOpt chooses the fault-tolerance approach for every operator in a query plan to reduce the time to complete the query with failures. This technique is very complex to handle.

- **Quality of Service:** Quality of service is the most basic problem in both wired and wireless networks. IoT networking consists of heterogeneous environment and to maintain quality of service in such kind of environment is most challenging. Internet based Quality of Services(QoS) focuses on the performance requirement of end to end data transmission capacity. IoT can be seen as an Internet connecting things and besides Internet it consists of Mobile Communication Network, RFID, Sensors, Actuators, and Controllers, etc. Internet and Mobile Communication Network subsystems of IoT have mature QoS function (Braden et al.,1994) whiles other such as RFID,Sensors,Controllers, Actuators still have lack of QoS.Quality of System is based on an application of IoT. Basically IoT applications can be divided into three main tasks: inquiry, control and monitoring. The Inquiry task requires timeliness and reliability as Quality of Service. Timeliness and reliability should be reflected in monitoring and controlling task of an application. IoT applications also can be viewed as different perspectives such as the user layer, service layer and terminal layer. Quality of Service is a part of service layer and it should satisfy the customer. Service layer of IoT should have service attributes like service time, delay, accuracy and priority. Quality of Service is a most challenging task in IoT and it depends on the type of an application. For example in automatic parking management system quality depends on sensor coverage, reliability and system responsiveness. In multi access multi hop wireless networks there are several issues of QoS: Standard protocol for establishing QoS, Complexity of network dynamics and Reliable data delivery.

Issues of Distributed Computing in IoT are not limited up to the above mentioned topics, but they are most challenging in terms of IoT. In addition to them; deadlock, race condition, observability, controllability, design challenges, migration, load balancing are also issues in distributed computing, but they are rarely needed in IoT based applications.

IoT Applications Based on Distributed Computing

"The fourth industrial revolution" initiated by Germany in 2011 is really becoming a reality due to Internet of Things (IoT) based applications. At the core of IoT are millions of devices that transmit data and perform actions based on Internet connectivity. Every domain has a number of possibilities to implement such kind of IoT based applications. The Internet has distributed architecture in nature and it is one of the most important components of IoT based applications so distributed computing is an essential part of it. Herewith several domains of IoT are narrated in which distributed computing is required heavily.

- **Industrial Automation:** IoT is now widely used in the industrial automation industry. The objective of IoT is to get increased manufacturing performance and flexibility by applying efficient communications and interaction from manufacturing Input / Output devices, including sensors, actuators, analyzers, drives, and robotics. These devices are accessible using IP Communications and amalgamated using some software that runs on a large number of processors. Distributed computing is heavily used to process the data from such kind of devices. Industrial automation needs information in a timely manner and it is possible only through distributed computing. Distributed computing is also essential to integrate manufacturing unit with other organizational function. Industries need their distributed manufacturing and business processes and control systems to behave like a one single system. This objective of industry is fulfilled by the powerful computing in a distributed way.
- **Autonomous Driving:** Internet of Thing based autonomous driving requires complex algorithms of perception, localization, planning, and control.

These algorithms need data from many heterogeneous sensors, actuators, and computers. To manage the complexity of algorithms and heterogeneity of components, distributed system architecture is needed. Distributed architecture reduces the computational complexity of the system. Algorithms of autonomous driving are very large and complex, so single computing node is not enough to cover all complex computations. Efficiency and performance of the system can be improved by decentralizing the computational load into many computing nodes. Fault management is more convenient in distributed architecture rather than centralized architecture. Safety is the most important factor in autonomous driving and if system uses a single, centralized system, it is very dangerous if a single computing node fails due to hardware or software failure. Distributed architecture consists of several computing elements and each check the safety measures of other computing elements and keeps backups of failed element. The noise and cost of wiring can be reduced to a great extent by positioning distributed computing elements optimally. Reliability of the system can be improved a lot by using distributed architecture as computing elements are not dependent to others. Development efficiency is also improved as a developer can test the parallel system. The autonomous driving project is impossible without distributed computing.

- **Smart Healthcare:** IoT is a boon for the healthcare industry. It transforms healthcare industry by escalating competence, lowering cost and focuses on patient care. Smart healthcare requires real data and it is needed in a timely manner so parallel computing is required to obtain them. Patient data is very critical for hospitals so store them in single centralized computing element does not make any sense and it is prone to failure. Patient data must be stored in multiple computing elements, so if one fails data can be obtained from other. Smart health care needs integration of clinical functions with front end functions such as billing. Integration of functions needs to distribute architecture in order to get timely and efficient results. Analysis is very important part in health care and it is done by obtaining data from a multitude of devices. Processing data from multitude devices need distributed computing. Smart healthcare needs analytics of data and connect machine, data and people that can be deployed on machines or on premises or on a cloud so entirely it needs distributed architecture.

- **Smart City:** Smart city based IoT applications require integration of sensor networks with the cloud based platform. Smart City needs ability to virtualize sensors and IoT devices. A Cloud computing based on distributed platform is needed to implement the concept of similar physical and virtual interconnected things. Distributed computing is vital for real time interactions that exist in an application. Real time interactions involve the capability of an operating system and embedded devices involved in IoT paradigm. Smart city also requires multi model interactivity between end-users, which must achieve in a timely manner so distributed computing is vital in that sense. Scheduling and resource management is a crucial functionality of smart city. This functionality cannot be achieved using traditional way of computing. It takes into account shared access to IoT resources. The Integrated Cloud based platform is required in a smart city project that gathers the current states of available resources in the network and providing interface to computing heterogeneous data in timely manner by applying parallel computing kind of stuff. If one required resource is failed the system captures the data from backup resources as architecture is distributed. Without distributed computing, smart city project is like a dream of unrealistic thing.

- **Retail Industry:** Consumer acceptance of IoT devices is expected to rise quickly. The retail industry covers large spectrum of functionalities based on IoT applications. It includes product tracability, interactive consumer engagement, inventory management, smart payment, asset magement, etc. Huge efficiency is needed when data can be collected from numerous devices. Parallel computing is needed to get the processing efficiently and timely manner. Instead of encoded messaging, smart screens provide retail situation deeper information about what they're looking at, and controlling business decisions, including up-sells. To establish smart screen data must be processed from multiple heterogeneous locations and that is only achievable by distributed computing means. Retail industry needs some smart triggers such as which products are under performing, overstocked, out of the stock by taking data from multiple locations and in a timely manner. Distributed computing is the only means that generate such kind of smart triggers in a timely manner. Retailers also market and produce based on buying patterns of browsing behaviors of customers. Analytics of browsing behaviors is also heavily based on distributed computing. Every supplier is looking for ways to enlarge their trail with clients, and provide more services and that is not possible without distributed architecture of the system.

IoT are applicable for every domain and distributed computing is an inherent component of that. Not only above mentioned domains use distributed computing in case of IoT ; but all most all domains use that in any means. It is not possible to describe every domain in detail in terms of distributed computing. The Table 2 describes well known domains of IoT with distributed computing in brief.

Table 2. IoT based domains with distributed scenario

Sr. No	Emerging Domain	IoT Based Applications	Distributed Computing Scenario
1.	Smart Agriculture	• Controlling of climate conditions • Improvement in yield • Recommendations • Reduce water requirement • Forecasting	• Farm management using RFID tags needs distributed computing to get information timely manner • Agriculture E-Marketing needs to get and process data from multiple locations so require distributed computing. • Crop fault detection is done by using several sensors and that needs distributed environment. • Security of fields also needs data from multiple locations and required distributed computing.
2.	Wearable Devices	• Smart Glass • Smart Watch • Activity Tracker • Mail Notification	• Device to device interaction needs much more sharing and timely result, so require distributed computing.
3.	Education	• Interactive Environment • E-Learning • Report System • Collaboration	• Collaborative teaching-learning environment needs distributed processing. • To process and generates a huge amount of educational data, distributed processing is must.
4.	Military	• Real time Decision Making • Soldier Healthcare • Cost reduction through asset tracking • Military Logistics	• To process sensors data on timely manner parallel computing is needed. • To analyze enemy related information from huge data sets needs distributed computing.
5.	Environment	• Control air pollution • Determine patterns of land conditions • Fire detection of forest • Detection of Water Quality • Determine Soil Condition	• For environmental protection distributed computing is needed to process sensor data. • For emergency services for the betterment of an environment need faster executing type distributed computing.
6.	Manufacturing	• Automate Production Process • Reduction of maintenance cost • Controlling from remote • Analyzing data for processing	• Provide a broad picture of the entire manufacturing process distributed computing is needed to process the data of each unit. • Improve asset utilization and optimization, distributed computing is required.
7.	Smart Home	• Controlling Energy use • Remote control appliances • Intrusion Detection • Video Monitoring	• Distributed architecture is needed to control appliances of home remotely. • To investigate the circumstances of various home parameters distributed computing needed.

Layered Distributed Model of IoT

Internet of Things(IoT) based distributed model needs several layers. The Figure 2 describes the conceptual layered architecture of IoT.

The physical layer is the bottom layer. It comprises of devices, sensors, controllers, actuators, etc.. It consists of all main components of the Internet of Things. It provides the link to the next above layer.

Figure 2.

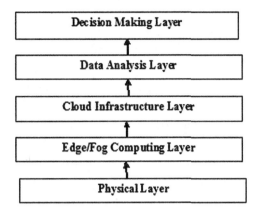

Edge computing layer is the real distributed paradigm of Internet of Things. It completely performs on distributed devices.Computational needs can be fulfilled at this layer where the user perform certain actions. It possesses, evaluates and acts on collected data so the performance of the system can be improved.Edge computing operates using local computing so require only local security boundaries.Edge computing decreases the response time to event by eliminating cloud infrastructure for immediate action.Edge computing is also known as fog computing, however there are subtle differences between them. In majority literature, these two terms are used interchangeably. Fog computing move forwards the intelligence to local area network while edge computing move forwards the intelligence directly into devices like controllers. In fog computing, data transfer form things to centralized architecture is very complex while the edge computing simplifies the communication chain and reduce the failure rate. Fog computing is described in the details in section-3.

Cloud infrastructure layer is responsible for data storage and further analysis. Applications on the cloud validates the data received from the physical devices.This layer is also responsible for the some sort of data analytics.

Data Analysis layer is very important for the Internet of Things as it is related to all aspects of data analytics. This layer has functions like data cleansing,transformation and data analytics and storage of data.

Decision Making layer uses the reporting tools to make an appropriate decision based on the data generated from below layer.

FOG COMPUTING

Fog computing is a model for analyzing and performing on Internet of Things (IoT) data. It consists of three main features in term of Internet of Things:

- Evaluate most time perceptive data close to where; it is generated.
- Acts on Internet of Things data very rapidly.
- Forward some data to cloud for long term storage and analysis.

Cloud architecture communicates only with IP and not with other protocols used in IoT devices. The ideal situation to process IoT data is nearer to device so computing that performs such situation is needed and that is termed as *Fog Computing*.

Fog Computing: A New Era of Distributed Computing

Traditional distributed architecture is not suitable for IoT based applications as they require processing the data nearer to devices. New computing paradigm is introduced to solve the issues of IoT that is termed as *Fog Computing*. Fog computing can be treated as a generally decentralized cloud, that function close to the level where data is generated and most often used. Fog Computing is an extension of cloud computing with one extra intermediate Fog layer. The Fog layer resides between device and cloud. This Fog layer is composed of geographically distributed Fog servers which can be deployed at the local premises of devices. Fog server consists of storage, computing and communication facility. Fog server can be adapted from existing network components and directly communicate with the device through WiFi, cellular or Bluetooth (I.Stojmenovic et al.,2015). Fog server can be connected to the cloud over Internet so rich computing advantage gained. Fog computing is a location awareness. Fog server is a much more dominant and flexible device managing three-dimensional resources and can deliver more smart and adaptive services to users. The Fog server acts as a proactive way and predict the user demand for information. Fog servers are an intelligent computing system. It performs local computations and data processing requests from users.

Benefits of Fog Computing

Fog computing has numerous advantages over traditional distributed computing. In the era of the Internet; Fog computing is required for many senses:

- It supports for mobility

- It provides low latency
- It improves quality of services
- It consists of location awareness
- It is well suited for real applications
- It generates fast processing due to proximity to end users
- Addresses security concerns
- Can operate reliably
- Move data to the best place for processing
- Lower Operating Expenses
- Easier to develop and deploy

How Does Fog Work?

Generally Fog computing works in concert with Cloud computing. Fog Computing promises to extend current cloud services. Emerging distributed services and applications at the edge of the network is an essence of Fog Computing. It provides hierarchical, virtualization, multi-tenancy and other distinctive features. Fog computing consists of several fog nodes. Fog nodes receive data from IoT devices using any protocol in real time. To achieve Fog Computing efficiently one extra layer in the form of intermediate layer is required. The intermediate layer is composed of several distributed servers. Fog server is a virtualized device with storage, communication and computing facility. The aim of fog server is to put storage, communication and computing nearer to the device so very fast computing can be achieved without sending data to cloud.

Role of Fog Computing In IoT

Internet of Things requires mobility support, location awareness, geo-distribution and low latency. Fog computing is a platform that provides above mentioned characteristics. Fog Computing consists of storage, compute and networking services between device and cloud computing data centers. Typically it is located at the edge of network. Fog Computing works in conjunction with cloud computing and optimizing the use of IoT resources. Fog computing permits computing and decision-making to happen by means of IoT devices and only drives relevant data to the cloud.

Chicago is equipped with one traffic light system based on IoT with several smart sensors. The open-source application developed to adjust light patterns and timing is running on each edge device. The application automatically makes adjustments to light patterns in real time, at the edge, working around traffic obstacle as they arise and lessen. Traffic delays are kept to a minimum so people spend less time in their cars and have more time to enjoy their big day. There is the smallest value in sending a steady stream of everyday traffic sensor data to the cloud for storage and analysis. It does predictive analysis to adjust and improve traffic application's response to future traffic anomalies.

RESEARCH AND INTEREST TRENDS ABOUT DISTRIBUTED COMPUTING AND INTERNET OF THINGS

Internet of Things is the future of the all domains of human life. It is going to make everything in our lives "smart". Several researches have been done already in this area, but there is a huge scope of research in almost all domains. There is a huge research scope in all domains in technology, architectural elements, communications, algorithms, hardware components, signal processing, security aspects and in standardization.

- Research is needed in new technologies of IoT that address the several issues like identity of devices globally, identity management, identity encoding, authentications of parties etc.
- Needed architecture with distributed characteristics and encompasses of heterogeneity, net neutrality, cloud computing, event driven architecture, synchronization and disconnected operations.
- Communication research is needed to fulfill the challenges of scalability, interoperability, energy efficient, and best performance.
- IoT require efficient chip based communication architecture and that is also a research challenge.
- Automatic computing and networking is also a research challenge in IoT.
- Algorithms for optimal assignment of resources in dynamic environment are a big challenge in IoT.
- Hardware component is required in which configuration is changed dynamically. This kind of hardware design is crucial for IoT related applications.
- Research is required in VLSI circuits with scalability issues.
- Designing of low cost, high performance IoT based devices is a major concern.
- Data and signal processing is required in IoT with semantic interoperability.
- Distributed repository for faster searching of a smart object is a main research problem.
- Incorporate minimum traffic and congestion is a big challenge in IoT applications.

- Modifications in traditional distributed database technology are required to address large number of things and this is a big challenge in a global information space.
- Research is also needed in area of dynamic security and privacy management.
- IoT use cloud computing so research is needed in security of cloud computing.
- Ontology based semantic standard is a big challenge in IoT.
- Standards for communication within and outside the cloud are one of the most research challenges of IoT.
- Creating knowledge and big data is an emerging research issue of IoT.

CONCLUSION

Internet of Things is widely adopted by every domain of applications due to familiarity of Internet. At the core of IoT are millions of devices that pass on data and carry out actions based on Internet connectivity. Internet is distributed in nature so applications based on IoT follow distributed architecture. The chapter has been started with basics of distributed computing where difference between centralized and distributed computing was discussed in length. Distributed architecture is beneficial in terms of IoT applications, but it consists of the number of challenges. The chapter also described a number of challenges of distributed computing. The chapter narrated several applications of distributed computing. Internet of Things based applications use distributed computing extensively. The chapter described advantages, issues and applications of IoT in terms of distributed computing. Fog computing is a new platform for distributed computing that is used in all most all IoT based applications. The chapter has describes in brief benefits, how it works and role of Fog Computing in Internet of Things(IoT). At the last chapter has been narrated with research direction of IoT with distributed computing paradigm.

REFERENCES

Arora, M., Das, S. K., & Biswas, R. (2002). A Decentralized Scheduling and Load Balancing algorithm for Heterogeneous Grid Environments. *Proc. Of International Conference on Parallel Processing Workshops (ICPPW'02)*, 499 - 505.

Azar, Y., Cohen, E., Fiat, A., Kaplan, H., & Racke, H. (2003). Optimal oblivious routing in polynomial time. *Proceedings of the 35th ACM Symposium on Theory of Computing*, 383–388.

Braden, R., Clark, D., & Shenker, S. (1994). *Integrated services in t he Internet architecture: An overview*. RFC1633.

Cao, Y. (2005). *Parallel and Distributed Computing techniques in Biomedical Engineering* (Ph.D thesis). National University of Singapore.

Casavant, T., & Kuhl, J. (1998). A Taxonomy of Scheduling in General Pupose Distributed Computing Systems. *IEEE Transactions on Software Engineering, 14*(2), 141–154. doi:10.1109/32.4634

Chien, S.-Y., Chan, W.-K., Lee, C.-H., & Srinivasa Somayazulu, V. (2015). Distributed computing in IoT: System-on-a-chip for smart cameras as an example. In *The 20th Asia and South Pacific Design Automation Conference*. IEEE.

Chor, B., Israeli, A., & Li, M. (1987). On Processor Coordination using asynchronous hardware. *Proceedings of Sixth ACM symposium on Principles of Distributed Computing, 86-97*. 10.1145/41840.41848

Corbett. (2013). Google's globally-distributed database. *ACM Transactions on Computer Systems, 31*(8).

Davis, J. (2009). *Attacks on Mobile and Embedded Systems: Current Trends*. Mocana whitepaper. Retrieved from www.mocana.com

Dean. (2006). *Experiences with MapReduce, an abstraction for large-scale computation*. Keynote I: PACT.

Dean, J., & Ghemawat, S. (2004). MapReduce: simplified data processing on large clusters. *Proc. of the 6th OSDI Symp.*

Di Pascale, Macaluso, Nag, Kelly, & Doyle. (2018). The Network As a Computer: A Framework for Distributed Computing Over IoT Mesh Networks. *IEEE Internet of Things Journal, 5*(3), 2107 – 2119.

El-Sayed, H., Mellouk, A., George, L., & Zeadally, S. (2008). Quality of service models for heterogeneous networks: Overview and challenges. *Annales des Télécommunications, 63*(11-12), 639–668. doi:10.100712243-008-0064-z

Freund, R. F., Gherrity, M., Ambrosius, S., Campbell, M., Halderman, M., Hensgen, D., ... Siegel, H. J. (1998). Scheduling resources in multi-user, heterogeneous, computing environments with SmartNet. *7th IEEE Heterogeneous Computing Workshop (HCW '98)*, 184-199. 10.1109/HCW.1998.666558

Harrelson, C., Hildrum, K., & Rao, S. (2003). A polynomial-time tree decomposition to minimize congestion. *Proceedings of the 15th Annual ACM Symposium on Parallel Algorithms and Architectures*, 34–43. 10.1145/777412.777419

Herlihy, M. (1991). Wait-Free Synchronization. *ACM Transactions on Programming Languages and Systems*, *11*(1), 124–149. doi:10.1145/114005.102808

Kartik, S., & Siva Ram Murthy, C. (1995). Improved Task- Allocation Algorithms to Maximize Reliability of Redundant Distributed Computing Systems, Wipro Infotech Limited, Bangalore Indian Institute of Technology, Madras. *IEEE Transactions on Reliability*, *44*(4). doi:10.1109/24.475976

Kohler, E., Morris, R., Chen, B., Jannotti, J., & Kaashoek, M. F. (2000). The click modular router. *ACM Transactions on Computer Systems*, *18*(3), 263–297. doi:10.1145/354871.354874

Koopman, P. (2004). Embedded system security. *IEEE Computer*, *37*(7), 95–97. doi:10.1109/MC.2004.52

Lemke, K., Paar, C., & Wolf, M. (Eds.). (2006). Embedded Security in CarsSecuring Current and Future Automotive IT Applications. Springer-Verilag.

Levis, P., Madden, S., Gay, D., Polastre, J., & Szewczyk, R. (2004). The emergence of networking abstractions and techniques in TinyOS. *First USENIX/ACM Symposium on Networked Systems Design and Implementation (NSDI 2004)*.

Lin, J., Yu, W., Zhang, N., Yang, X., Zhang, H., & Zhao, W. (2017). A survey on Internet of Things: Architecture enabling technologies security and privacy and applications. *IEEE Internet Things J.*, *4*(5), 1125–1142. doi:10.1109/JIOT.2017.2683200

Malone, T. W., Fikes, R. E., & Howard, M. T. (1988). A market-like task scheduler for distributed computing environments. In B.A. Huberman (Ed.), The Ecology of Computation. North-Holland.

Milutinovic. (1988). A Simulation Study of Two Distributed Task Allocation Procedures. *IEEE Transactions on Software Engineering, 14*.

Mohamed, N., Al-Jaroodi, J., Jawhar, I., Lazarova-Molnar, S., & Mahmoud, S. (2017). SmartCityWare: A service-oriented middleware for cloud and fog enabled smart city services. *IEEE Access: Practical Innovations, Open Solutions*, *5*, 17576–17588. doi:10.1109/ACCESS.2017.2731382

Racke, H. (2002). Minimizing congestion in general networks. In *Proceedings of the 43rd Symposium on Foundations of Computer Science*. IEEE Computer Society.

Rosenschein, J. S. (1988). Synchronization of multiagent plans. In A. H. Bond & L. Gasser (Eds.), *Readings in Distributed Arti_cial Intelligence* (pp. 187–191). San Mateo, CA: Morgan Kaufmann. doi:10.1016/B978-0-934613-63-7.50020-6

Singh & Chopra. (2017). The Internet of Things and Multiagent Systems: Decentralized Intelligence in Distributed Computing. *2017 IEEE 37th International Conference on Distributed Computing Systems (ICDCS).*

Smith & Davis. (1983). Negotiation as a metaphor for distributed problem solving. *Artificial Intell., 20,* 63-109.

Stojmenovic, I., Wen, S., Huang, X., & Luan, T. H. (2015). An Overview of Fog Computing and its Security Issues. *Concurrency and Computation.*

Tamura, Tasaki, Sengoku, & Niigata. (2005). *Scheduling Problems for a Class of Parallel Distributed Systems.* Institute of Technology, Faculty of Engineering, Niigata University.

Valiant, L. G., & Brebner, G. J. (1981). Universal schemes for parallel communication. *Proceedings of the 13th ACM symposium on Theory of Computing,* 263–277.

von Eicken, T., Culler, D. E., Goldstein, S. C., & Schauser, K. E. (1992). Active messages: A mechanism for integrated communication and computation. *SIGARCH Comput.Archit. News, 20*(2), 256–266. doi:10.1145/146628.140382

Xhafa, F., & Abraham, A. (2010). Computational models and heuristic methods for Grid scheduling problems. *Future Generation Computer Systems, 26*(4), 608–621. doi:10.1016/j.future.2009.11.005

Yu, Liang, He, Hatcher, Lu, Lin, & Yang. (2017). A Survey on the Edge Computing for the Internet of Things. *IEEE Access, 6,* 6900 – 6919.

Zhao, Y., Lee, E. A., & Liu, J. (2007). A programming model for time-synchronized distributed real-time systems. In *Real-Time and Embedded Technology and Applications Symposium (RTAS)* (pp. 259-268). IEEE. 10.1109/RTAS.2007.5

Zheng, Z., & Lyu, M. (2010). An adaptive QoS-aware fault tolerance strategy for web services. *Empirical Software Engineering, 15*(4), 323–345. doi:10.100710664-009-9126-8

KEY TERMS AND DEFINITIONS

Broadcast: It is a communication method where packet of information is sent from one sender to all receivers.

Fault Tolerance: It is an attribute of the system that enables it to carry on operating despite of the failures of some system components.

Internet of Things (IoT): It is a networking of physical devices embedded with intenet, electronics, sensors, software, actuators that enable devices to store and send the data.

Message Passing: It is the form of communication among entities of the network. Generally, it is used in interprocess communication and parallel computing.

Multi Hop Network: It is a network that consists of two or more hops to send packets from source to destination.

Multicast: It is a communication method where packet of information is sent from one or more senders to set of receivers.

Mutual Exclusion: It is the requirement of the system according to which only one process is able to access the shared resource at a time.

Observability: It is a measure that determines how inside conditions of system can be incidental by the facts of its external output.

Openness: The degree to which the system exhibits its own strategy.

RFID: It is a technology that automatically tracks tags attached to any object.

Scalability: It is the capacity of the system to handle increasing amount work without affecting existing system.

Shortest Time Scheduling: It is a scheduling algorithm in which the process with the smallest amount of time remaining for the completion is chosen for the next execution.

Synchronization: Process of coordinating two or more activities in time.

Chapter 5
Enhancing E–Government With Internet of Things

Panagiota Papadopoulou
National and Kapodistrian University of Athens, Greece

Kostas Kolomvatsos
National and Kapodistrian University of Athens, Greece

Stathes Hadjiefthymiades
National and Kapodistrian University of Athens, Greece

ABSTRACT

Internet of things (IoT) brings unprecedented changes to all contexts of our lives, as they can be informed by smart devices and real-time data. Among the various IoT application settings, e-government seems to be one that can be greatly benefited by the use of IoT, transforming and augmenting public services. This chapter aims to contribute to a better understanding of how IoT can be leveraged to enhance e-government. IoT adoption in e-government encompasses several challenges of technical as well as organizational, political, and legal nature, which should be addressed for developing efficient applications. With the application of IoT in e-government being at an early stage, it is imperative to investigate these challenges and the ways they could be tackled. The chapter provides an overview of IoT in e-government across several application domains and explores the aspects that should be considered and managed before it can reach its full potential.

DOI: 10.4018/978-1-5225-7955-7.ch005

INTRODUCTION

The Internet of Things (IoT) creates an emerging new era of the Internet, in which machines and objects get connected and equipped with sensors, surpassing their traditional role to constitute dynamic actors of networked environments with novel services. The ubiquitous nature of IoT brings dramatic changes to the way we work and live, with an increasing adoption in various domains of personal and organizational activity. According to industry reports, IoT is a very promising technology and is predicted to flourish within the next years, as 127 new devices connect to the Internet every second (McKinsey, 2018). It is expected that more than 24 billion IoT devices will exist by 2020, which will be four times the world population, while by 2018 IoT penetration will cover half of the world population. Investments on IoT are predicted to reach $5-6 trillion (Newman, 2017). More than half of major new business processes and systems will incorporate some elements of IoT (Gartner, 2017). As IoT advances it is applied in government and the public sector allowing for services that improve the lives of the citizens (IBM Industries, 2017). IoT can bring unprecedented benefits in government systems and services, making a shift from e-government to smart government, transforming G2C, G2B and G2G transactions and processes.

IoT-enabled government information systems and applications can extend the type and the quality of the services offered with innovative smart provisions in a wide spectrum of domains. IoT affects a number of sectors including health, transportation, environment, communications, security/safety, energy, defense and smart cities. In each of these sectors IoT can be used to provide e-government services that can be valuable and helpful to citizens, the society and the environment.

Security and safety are of critical importance to the society and can become even more significant if they are related to areas such as public health or the environment. IoT can allow for the effective treatment of security and safety needs of the public sector through the sensing, processing and communication capabilities of autonomous devices. Critical areas, in aerial, maritime and ground contexts, can be greatly benefited by being monitored with the use of IoT technology to facilitate appropriate and timely action. In particular, the use of mobile IoT devices can enable a wide range of activities related to security and safety, such as the surveillance and monitoring of areas, the detection of threats, the effective management of events, the fast response to emergency situations, the notification about security/safety alerts and the communication of current status to people. Such IoT empowered activities can be applied to a number of contexts such as border surveillance and control for trespassing, weather monitoring and forecasting for intense or dangerous phenomena, air pollution detection, fire detection in forests and rural areas, monitoring of water level in rivers, lakes and the sea for avoiding floods or quality control of water for drinking and agriculture. IoT enables advanced e-government services that can be sustainable and efficient and which could not be previously affordable or even possible.

In all these cases, IoT systems and applications enable the provision of advanced services to people and the society in general, that can enhance their security and safety against a number of threats and in diverse contexts. These electronic services are offered to the public by the government, allowing for a better quality of life by protecting citizens and the environment. In addition, thanks to the use of IoT, these electronic government-to-citizen and government-to-society services eliminate the risk of putting people that are responsible for dealing with such incidents in danger. We believe that these critical public services are where IoT can bring most value to e-government.

Despite the increasing progress and interest in both areas of IoT and e-government, research on their combined use is scarce; Although some studies such as AlEnezi et al.'s, (2018) and Brous and Janssen's (2015a, 2015b) can be helpful to our knowledge, how e-government can benefit and grow from IoT has not been adequately addressed yet. In order to gain a better understanding about how e-government can successfully leverage the IoT potential, a comprehensive approach of applying IoT in e-government is needed, covering both positive and negative aspects, technical and not-technical, associated with the combined use of e-government and IoT systems.

In this chapter an attempt is made towards setting a framework for designing and implementing smart government services with IoT-based systems. In this direction, after an overview of the research literature related to the topic, we describe several application scenarios for IoT in e-government, with a particular focus on critical services provision, in areas of public security/safety, utility network infrastructures such as water and electricity supply, weather monitoring and transportation management. Then, we identify the challenges, technical and non-technical, that can be encountered in the development of IoT e-government systems and we continue to propose solutions that can be used to tackle these challenges. The chapter proceeds to showcase the potential of IoT-based e-government as well as the challenges and how they should be addressed through an example scenario. Following the analysis of the example case, the chapter summarizes our findings and provides conclusions and guidelines. The chapter aims to contribute to a better understanding of how the IoT promise in government can be realized and to provide insights that can be of value for both researchers and practitioners active in the growing field of IoT and e-government.

BACKGROUND

IoT and e-government have been jointly studied as a topic that has recently received significant attention in a number of research works. AlEnezi et al. (2018) study smart government as the technological union of e-government and smart cities. Smart cities could incorporate an ICT infrastructure on top of the physical infrastructure that can involve sensors, actuators, network hardware, end users devices and so on. The authors, in their recent work, discuss three IoT-based smart government challenges, namely, mindscaping, investment and security and privacy, which are considered as of primary concern to the overall implementation success or failure of smart government.

Tang and Ho (2018) provide an empirical analysis of smart sensor adoption by US local governments. They examine two specific questions regarding sensor adoption: what factors affect the scope of sensor adoption by municipal governments and what factors affect the level of integration among sensors across different urban domains. Their results show that the change in smart sensor adoption in e-government is incremental. The study gives evidence that local governments' early adoption of smart sensors is likely to stem from their needs in specific policy domains. The authors also find that a local government's historical paths on urban sustainability and data-driven decision-making practices can predict its trajectory of sensor deployment, in terms of the scope and the integration of smart sensors across different urban domains. On the other hand, a local government's e-government progressiveness is not found to be a significant predictor of smart sensor adoption.

Brous and Janssen's (2015a) work was on the identification of the potential benefits of IoT in e-government applications. Drawing from a review of the research literature and using data from two case studies they found that e-government can be benefited from IoT at political, strategic, tactical and operational level. Their findings show that IoT enables effective knowledge management, sharing and collaboration between domains and divisions at all levels of the organisation, as well as between government and citizens. Specifically, according to the study, the IoT benefits for e-government include improved efficiency, effectiveness and flexibility of services, reduction of costs, improved citizen empowerment, improved government transparency, more efficient enforcement of regulations, improved planning and forecasting and improved health and safety measures.

The previous authors have also studied the impediments that block IoT adoption by governments in Brous and Janssen (2015b). Based on a literature review and two case studies they identify the main barriers of adopting IoT for government purposes, which are classified at the strategic, tactical and operational level. Specifically, impediments of IoT for e-government can be attributed to data privacy issues, data security issues, weak or uncoordinated data policies, weak or uncoordinated data governance, and conflicting market forces, costs, interoperability and integration issues, acceptance of IoT, and trust related issues, a lack of sufficient knowledge regarding IoT, IT infrastructural limitations, and data management issues.

Sideridis et al. (2015) provide an overview of Smart Cross Border e-Government Systems (SCBeG) making full use of ICT innovations in cloud computing, big data and IoT, based on the results of the EU project STORK 2.0. The authors propose the development of SCBeG systems in combination with e-identification platforms and their utilization in various application areas.

Sideridis and Protopappas (2015) have studied IoT in e-government focusing in life sciences. They discuss smart e-government systems as they are enabled by IoT and cloud computing technologies and they specifically examine the application of such systems in the domain of agriculture. In a similar vein, the work of Kumar (2017) investigates the use of IoT in e-governance, focusing on IoT services in the field of agriculture. The author presents the benefits of IoT for economy and sustainable development through a case study of agricultural production in India. The study suggests that IoT in agriculture can lead to better productivity and higher revenue which in turn can enhance the country's economy and lead to prosperity.

Schwertner et al. (2018) examine IoT as one of the technology components that are essential in Industry 4.0 and suggest an approach for its use in the context of natural disaster and crisis management, targeting data acquisition, management and analysis. The use of IoT-based systems for natural disaster detection and warning has also been the topic of several studies such as Alphonsa et Ravi, (2016), Amjath Ali et al., (2017) and Babu et al., (2018).

Haddadeh et al. (2018) propose an acceptance model for IoT smart devices in the context of public sector services. They present an empirically tested model on the perceived value and continuous use intention of public services enabled by IoT. Their findings show that citizens' perceived value of IoT can be influenced by empowerment, perceived use and privacy, resulting in affecting their continuous use intentions. Perceived value and continuous use intention of IoT in the context of public services were not found to be predicted by informational social support.

Thibaud et al. (2018) provide a comprehensive overview of publications on IoT-based applications in high-risk Environment, Health, and Safety (EHS) industries. They focus specifically on healthcare services, food supply chain (FSC), mining and energy industries (oil & gas and nuclear), intelligent transportation, and building and infrastructure management with emphasis on emergency response operations until 2016. They identify the main general characteristics of IoT applications by industry, specifically system architecture, sensor level, communication, back-end system and business/market aspects. They also provide a review of the challenges that IoT-based application need to deal with. These are grouped in technical and social and economic challenges. Technical challenges include energy efficiency, communication and data-related challenges (connectivity, latency, throughput, standardization), scalability (network size, interoperability), security and safety (reliability, privacy protection). Social and economic challenges that are identified comprise business model, standardization, compliance with regulatory and industry standards, community support and staff training, affordability vs. high cost of implementation, absence of global or national standards and regulation and time-to-market for IoT-based applications. For these challenges the authors present the main solutions proposed per industry in the reviewed literature, which are mostly focused on tackling the technical issues. The authors review also covers the future research trends and challenges in each EHS industry, which seem to concentrate mostly on technical challenges and trends, especially in communication and processing capabilities.

APPLICATION SCENARIOS

IoT adoption in e-government can be harnessed across a wide variety of sectors. Various e-government applications could be developed to make use of the data collected by the IoT devices. Each of them could aim to provide extended analytics services to support fast and informed decision making, which could of great value, especially for cases requiring emergency response.

In this section, indicative application scenarios IoT in e-government are described, focusing on areas that are related to public security and safety, and in particular in the domains of surveillance and control of critical security and safety areas, transportation and environmental monitoring. The latter is analyzed into environment pollution control and natural phenomena related to fire, earthquakes and the weather.

Surveillance and Control of Critical Security and Safety Areas

Security and safety are of major importance for citizens and the society. IoT can provide support for addressing various security and safety requirements. The autonomous nature of IoT nodes and the sensing and advanced onboard processing capabilities allow for tasks such as object detection and sensor information fusion.

IoT could be used to provide effective and efficient surveillance and control of critical security and safety areas. IoT nodes can be used to monitor country borders, land, maritime or aerial, or other sensitive areas in regards to public security and safety, such as airports, ports and train, metro or bus stations. IoT systems can also be employed for the control of other public places which are highly populated and receive large concentrations of people, especially in particular events or periods, such as popular squares and roads during Christmas holidays and various festivals, or venues and places like stadiums during concerts or games and other sports or art events. In addition, IoT capabilities can be valuable for the security and safety protection of critical infrastructure, such as energy plants for electrical power or water supply.

In each of these contexts, IoT nodes can work, both separately and in collaboration, to provide enhanced security and safety control and protection, and allow for detection and prevention of illegal trespassing, invasion or crimes. IoT nodes can collect data with the use of acoustic and motion sensors and cameras, which can be processed to provide information about the current status of the monitored area. Such information can be of great value to stakeholders to assess potential vulnerabilities and threats, handle dangerous incidents that may occur and facilitate their decision-making process regarding operations management and the course of action that should be taken. Public authorities, the police, command and control centers can be significantly benefited from the functional features and facilities of IoT systems and the amount and richness of the information they can provide.

Using IoT systems, the surveillance and control of critical areas can be done remotely and constantly, at any time, in ways that could be difficult if not impossible otherwise. Border control can be significantly improved and become more effective. Critical areas can easily be monitored and controlled, without putting humans in risk, as IoT nodes can be used anywhere, particularly mobile IoT devices and unmanned vehicles. Thus, IoT systems can allow for surpassing human limitations and enable immediate response to critical events to offer increased security and safety to countries and their citizens.

Traffic Control and Emergency Management in Transportation

IoT technology has already been adopted in transportation systems either in the available infrastructure (e.g., roads, buildings) or in the vehicles. Intelligent transportation systems such as in-car IoT systems, smart highways or route planning can assist users to deal with all the constraints associated with traffic, time, and cost. E-government services can be built on top of the collected data and provide functionalities related to traffic or emergency management. Traffic congestion is a growing problem in most urban areas across the world (Hounsell et al., 2009). Traffic management services can collect data from IoT sources, process and manage these data and use the delivered information to implement various measures to manage traffic. This will lead to a better flow of vehicles reducing the observed traffic jams and consequently eliminating the risk of accidents or facilitating the fast move of people or the police, ambulances and fire brigade in case of emergency.

IoT devices can report data related not only to vehicles but also to drivers. In any case, the in-vehicle devices can monitor drivers' status or the status of the vehicles in close distance and relay this data to the centralized infrastructure. The central system can have a view on the status of each vehicle being immediately informed about the presence of any emergency. In addition, the central system can have the overview of any area in the city and support services for long-term traffic management. Such emergency situations can be also identified by the in-vehicle devices forming a huge infrastructure of autonomous vehicles that can assist in emergency management.

Environmental Monitoring

Environmental monitoring is considered one of the top areas IoT can deliver the most value for in 2018 (Columbus, 2018). IoT, due to its autonomous nature, can provide support for environment monitoring and control where elaborate sensing, processing and possibly reacting are needed. IoT devices can be adopted for providing smart e-government services, by monitoring specific phenomena and, when needed, generating alerts or taking action. Such phenomena can be related to various facets of the environment covering a wide spectrum of incidents. The phenomena for which IoT could be used for e-government purposes can be grouped into two broad categories, environment pollution and natural phenomena. Natural phenomena include fire in forests and rural areas, earthquakes and weather phenomena.

Environment Pollution

IoT e-government systems can be used for the protection from environment pollution. They can involve applications such as monitoring of air quality, water quality, sea quality and soil quality. Environmental IoT systems can allow for activities such as air pollution detection, quality control of water for drinking and agriculture, soil quality control for agricultural purposes and sea quality control for swimming and fishing. E-government services for environment protection can also involve IoT devices for the monitoring of waste management and pollution coming from industrial or residential activity. Energy production plants and management can also be supported by IoT systems, allowing for the continuous risk-free provision of general public goods such as electricity or gas or water supply.

The critical issue in such e-government services is the efficient management of the collected data. Such management can assist in making long- or short-term decisions. For instance, short-term decisions could be related with taking immediate actions to avoid environmental pollution with negative consequences in people's lives. Long-term decisions can be related with the delivery of strategies to proactively avoid environmental pollution. The proactive decision making should be based on historical data but also on the estimation of the future trends in the observed information. In any case, the timely processing of the collected data should lead to a set of analytics designed by experts in order to support further decision making. Hence, the discussed e-government services should be designed having ICT experts cooperating with experts in other domains (e.g., environmental scientists) in order to conclude the best possible result.

Fire Detection in Forests and Rural Areas

IoT could be used for fire detection in forests and rural areas. For instance, a set of sensors could be adopted to monitor a forest for identifying fire events. Mobile IoT devices, particularly unmanned vehicles, could also be extremely valuable tools for fire protection. Such devices can be deployed for forest and rural areas monitoring, which can be used to contribute in fire prevention as well as in fire extinguishing. Hence, such services can assist in the proactive decision making together with the efficient situational awareness when an event is triggered. In particular, the autonomous functionality of IoT devices can be leveraged to allow for remote management of fire events. Beneficiaries of such a system could be the fire brigade, local authorities, municipalities, public authorities or citizens. In case of detecting a suspicious event the IoT-based system would be capable of generating fire alerts, informing the interested parties and also be connected with command and control systems of emergency management authorities. In particular, mobile IoT devices such as unmanned vehicles could serve as valuable actors for fire protection. For example, unmanned aerial vehicles (UAVs) can conduct regular flights above the area of interest to provide an aerial view allowing for complete and wide coverage of the area. UAVs can also serve as part of the operation for extinguishing a fire, providing valuable information that can be used for several purposes. Similarly, unmanned ground vehicles (UGVs) can assist in the better monitoring of land surfaces, especially those that are not easily accessible by humans and regular vehicles, contributing with the data that they can collect on the spot, to the prevention of fire incidents as well as to their management in case of occurrence.

Thus, IoT devices can greatly facilitate the difficult work of the fire brigade, at operational level, in locating areas that are in need and in planning their fighting against fire. IoT information can also be useful in informing citizens about fire events and also help the police, civil protection and local authorities in their decision-making about actions that need to be taken, for example the evacuation of an area.

Earthquake Alert

IoT capabilities can be particularly useful for the protection from earthquakes, a natural phenomenon to which it is still extremely difficult to react promptly and effectively and it is still debatable within the scientific community if it can be predicted and how reliable such predictions can be. Autonomous, distributed sensor systems can be used in order to monitor earth conditions for seismic activity. Examples of IoT systems for earthquake detection can be found in the works of Alphonsa et Ravi, (2016), Amjath Ali et al., (2017) and Babu et al., (2018). Such IoT systems can send warnings in the occurrence of an earthquake so as to inform people and government systems faster and allow for efficient response actions. These alerts can be generated and received by smart phones or other devices and systems early enough to prevent damages or human loss. In such cases, it is important is to enhance the situational awareness of possible damages or affected areas in order to assist public authorities in their first response. A challenge in this domain is to manage the heterogeneity of the external systems that should be informed when an event occurs. This kind of e-government services will act as the intermediary between the sensory infrastructure and systems of public authorities. Hopefully, IoT systems can also be used to contribute in the prediction of earthquakes and, consequently, help governments and the public in the timely reaction and protection from them.

Weather Monitoring and Forecasting for Intense or Dangerous Phenomena

IoT devices and systems can be used to monitor weather conditions for intense or dangerous phenomena, allowing for effective reaction against them. Such phenomena include storms, strong winds, floods, tsunamis and high rain or snowfall levels. Leveraging IoT capabilities can support the early detection of such phenomena, enabling disaster prevention or mitigation through provision of timely warnings and facilitation of immediate response (e.g. Amjath Ali et al., 2017). E-government services from meteorology offices can be greatly informed using the data that can be collected with IoT devices. The analysis of these meteorological data can enhance the accuracy and timeliness of weather forecasts and monitoring. In this way, IoT-based meteorological systems enable the provision of frequent and highly precise weather updates as well as the generation of alerts in case intense or dangerous weather phenomena are estimated to appear, providing rich information regarding their location, duration and intensity. IoT devices can be used for monitoring the water level in rivers, lakes or the sea, creating alerts when a rise is detected and notifying for evacuation plan of inhabited areas in case of flood possibility. IoT can also be valuable for e-government services in case of extreme weather phenomena such as hurricanes and tornados. Intense weather phenomena forecasting and the timely estimation of their consequences may positively affect various industries in addition to general populace safety. For instance, agriculture depends on precise up-to-date readings on soil, temperature and moisture while the identification of any dangerous situation seems to be imperative (Burkhalter, 2018).

CHALLENGES OF IOT IN E-GOVERNMENT

The adoption of IoT in e-government can be very promising as well as challenging at the same time. In this section, we focus on the challenges of the use of IoT in e-government which can be divided into technical and non-technical.

Technical Challenges

The central concept of the IoT era is that "things interact with each other'. Such interactions refer to peer to peer communication and data exchange as well as communication with back end systems usually found in the Cloud. The autonomous nature of IoT devices allows us to gain from the automation of various functionalities, the integration of data and services and the analysis of the behavior of autonomous entities and the collected data. It should be noted that IoT devices are characterized by two parameters, i.e., the type of the hardware they use and the type of the software they adopt. In the following paragraphs we provide our view on the technical challenges in the adoption of the IoT vision in E-government services.

Initially, the heterogeneity of the devices plays a crucial role in the provision of services that can be supported by the entire set of the available nodes. This way, we can have the opportunity to create universal services for 'injecting' E-government functionalities into the devices. The diversity of IoT devices poses difficulties in their connection and communication. Difficulties are further created by the lack of common standards for data exchange, which can refer to communication among devices and information systems, among information systems and end-users – citizens or organizational entities, and among different government entities and organizations. The key aspect in addressing these communication problems is the adoption of high quality protocols, metadata and algorithms to handle the discussed heterogeneity. The research community has already devoted attention on this challenge through the development of applications for heterogeneous devices. Middleware is significant to solved the aforementioned problem and facilitate the collection of data from homogeneous or heterogeneous IoT devices. The burden mainly lies in the collection of data from sensors and subsequently their transforming into a unified representation for further processing. On top of the unified data, efficient interfaces can be provided to facilitate the access to the collected data, thus, to generate knowledge over them. This way, end users can attach their devices to Cloud interfaces and 'upload' sensors measurements through lightweight APIs. It should be noted that in such cases, the management of large scale data is significant for further processing and delivering results that can be useful in E-gov applications.

Another challenge for adopting IoT in e-government lies in the incorporation of Artificial Intelligence (AI) in e-government applications. AI can provide the means for building intelligent applications over the collected data. With the adoption of AI, the provided e-government applications will be capable of supporting human-like activities. Machine learning may empower software components with the ability to detect patterns, take decisions autonomously or learn from the adopted models and adjust any decision based on the status of the environment. The benefit is that systems should not be fully 'programmed' in advance but they can learn the correct line of actions during their functioning. This ability to embed learning capabilities within the IoT device itself, and in addition, marry device-centric insights with aggregated intelligence in the Cloud, is expected to dramatically improve outcomes (Cooke, 2018).

Data interoperability facilitates the exchange of information between public and private bodies. This way, different bodies can share information and increase the efficiency through the mitigation of the inconsistencies. In addition, data interoperability can help in avoiding duplications of data, thus allowing for saving storage and resources. To support the 'connection' of heterogeneous data, different data models can be combined into a single model that covers the desired application domain. The delivered model should meet requirements like reliability, performance, scalability, heterogeneity coverage and interoperability. This way, we can deliver e-government services in the minimum time with high quality incorporating a low cost.

As described in Cenci et al., (2017), the European Interoperability Reference Architecture (EIRA) (Chou et al., 2015) uses a service-oriented architecture and the Open Group's Archimate ontology and tools as its reference model. EIRA interoperability is defined through a set of architecture building blocks, i.e,. technical, semantic, organizational and legal. Technical Interoperability involves the planning for technical issues involved in linking computer systems and services. Semantic Interoperability is related to giving precise meaning to the exchanged information while organizational interoperability refers to coordinated processes between different entities. Finally, legal interoperability refers to the aligned legislation so that exchanged data is accorded proper legal weight.

Security is another challenge for the adoption of the IoT in e-government. Numerous devices can have access to e-government services present in the Cloud, thus, it is imperative to secure the authorized access to data collected/generated/ inserted by a specific user. This aspect of the problem is more intense when we focus on sensitive personal data. Cloud architectures already provide security mechanisms for accessing their services, however, the autonomous nature of the IoT nodes imposes additional challenges. A lot of discussion can be done about the danger of the hacking of devices and systems to obtain information and data. Another danger is potential cyber-attacks against the devices themselves - attacks which take over control of the device and cause them to operate in dangerous and insecure ways. Due to the complexity of the architecture of the IoT e-government services, a solution for the security of the applications could be the adoption of multi-layered security services. Firewalls, security protocols, authentication, encryption and intrusion detection mechanisms can be employed to e-government IoT systems to provide the necessary level of security.

The use of IoT in e-government also poses a challenge related to the resources that are needed for data storage and processing. The plethora of data collected by sensors and IoT systems create the need for storage. IoT data storage in e-government implies requirements for storage infrastructure with high capacity to accommodate the volume of data as well as the speed with which they are generated. Access to IoT e-government data should be controlled and at the same time be fast and facilitate queries and response for efficient service provision.

Non-Technical Challenges

IoT in e-government goes beyond technical challenges and comprises non-technical ones which can include organizational, political, financial and legal issues. Such issues can affect the decisions that need to be made and the actions that will follow them at strategic, tactical and operational level regarding the utilization of IoT technology for e-government purposes. Decisions can concern the extension of current e-government systems and services or the development of new ones for utilizing IoT. Such decisions about plans and actions for pursuing e-government projects with IoT need not necessarily be driven by top government but they can rather start at local authority level. In any case IoT-based information systems and services should be designed so as to be aligned with government or local administration strategy and objectives.

Any IoT-based e-government application implies approval and acceptance by government administration, of local or greater level, depending on the aim and scope of the e-government system and the community or the society to which it is addressed. This requires changes in the mentality of the authorities and citizens that the IoT-oriented system serves and affects, in their mode of operation and work and even in individual lifestyle and behavior. As with any new technology introduced, resistance to change in organizations and citizens is hardly inevitable and should be taken into consideration in IoT e-government initiatives.

In addition, planning and implementation of IoT applications implies requirements and changes of organizational and economic nature, regarding processes, policies and investments, whilst setting the need for an appropriate legal and regulatory framework that enables the IoT e-government and the changes implied. All of these aspects, jointly and each of them separately, have are important contributors to the success of IoT-oriented e-government. This might request the co-operation of all involved parties from the public sector or the industry in a specific domain of interest for defining IoT vision and policies for e-government.

The introduction of IoT in e-government calls for organizational reform and process redesign, in order to allow for the adaptation of current government services or the introduction of new ones, based on IoT. This may entail the need for the creation of new government bodies and institutions or organizations as well as the formation of co-operations and coalitions that will facilitate the effective development and use of IoT-oriented e-government services.

The transition to IoT e-government requires the existence and availability of the appropriate infrastructure and resources, such as 5G telecommunication networks, which in turn require strategic investments for their implementation. Financial support for IoT e-government services, including funding as well as billing schemes, is essential for their feasibility and sustainability.

IoT-based information systems and services need to be formally acceptable and comply with regulations and fulfill legal requirements. The effective adoption of IoT in e-government requires strong institutional support. At the same time, institutions and legislation itself can drive IoT adoption by governments enforcing technological evolution. For example, Estonia as part of its program for 2020 plans to implement the "no legacy principle" which will be introduced by law, meaning that the public sector should not adopt any kind of Information Communication Technology solution that is older than 13 years (e-Estonia, 2018).

Security and privacy of data are aspects that cross horizontally almost every IoT e-government application. Apart from their technical characteristics, security and privacy are prominent issues of IoT e-government with aspects that also request a non-technical approach. Security is imperative for high risk services such as energy power production and management plants or environment protection. In addition to technical mechanisms, non-technical measures such as access control, management processes and security policies are also needed for risk mitigation. Similarly, the protection and control of personal data is also required in practically all sectors of IoT-based e-government, especially in healthcare applications. Regulations and procedures should be in place to ensure the availability, high quality and safe use of the provided IoT-oriented e-government services without jeopardizing security and data privacy. At the same time, imposing security and privacy rules and policies should not be in the expense of IoT-based systems usability.

The effectiveness of IoT adoption in e-government should be facilitated by being realized in cooperation with academic and research institutions and with synergies between the public and private sector. This will enable the development of IoT systems and services and the infrastructure needed for their effective support. Public-private sector partnerships are identified as an important factor for the successful use of IoT in e-government as shown in the World Bank Group (2017) report by lessons learnt during the actual implementation of IoT-oriented projects in several countries. Such partnerships can also help towards the development of IoT-based business models that allow for sustainability and affordability. This is highlighted in the previously mentioned report, which denotes a lack of IoT-specific government-to-business business models and policies. The same report also reveals that there is a lack of understanding of IoT and its data value and management. This implies a need for raising awareness and improving knowledge on IoT and the role it can have in government contexts. This can be addressed towards all potentially involved parties through education and partnerships among academic, government and business entities, constituting a vital component of governments strategic planning along with IoT-based project design and implementation.

APPLYING IOT-BASED E-GOVERNMENT: EXAMPLE CASE

Having discussed the challenges associated with the adoption of IoT in e-government, we return to the application scenarios of IoT-based e-government systems to examine them through a specific example. The following paragraphs describe the application of IoT in providing alerts for weather phenomena.

We assume a number of smart devices placed on a set of road vehicles. Such devices exhibit various functionalities, e.g., routing. End users may adopt these devices to calculate the shortest or the simplest path to perform their activities. In the central, cloud infrastructure, there is a service available, delivered by the Civil Protection department of the Ministry of Internal affairs, which is capable of processing meteorological data and derive decisions in relation to intense meteorological events. IoT devices are subscribed in the aforementioned service and are ready to receive data related to alerts for emergency or intense meteorological situations. As IoT devices are mobile, they should update their location in the central service. Actually, this is automatically performed through the exchange of light weight messages, thus, the central system is capable of knowing the location of the end users. Suppose the discussed service identifies intense meteorological events in a specific area. This area is continuously updated as the events are realized. The central system can perform a simple reasoning process and group the end users in a set of clusters according to the risk of being affected by the phenomenon. The groups are continuously updated to 'follow' the realization (e.g., change of location) of the phenomenon. Specific warning messages are delivered to users belonging to groups that are affected or will be affected by the phenomenon. IoT nodes after the reception of the aforementioned messages can easily update their operation, e.g., update the routing results and follow a different route.

Based on the above example, one can easily identify the two core dimensions of the mobile IoT - e-government synergy: the IoT nodes and the e-government services. Usually e-government services are placed at the Cloud to increase efficiency and be beneficial from the increased computational capabilities while IoT nodes are close to citizens and, usually, change their location. The most important issue in this setting is to model the interaction between the two parts and define schemes that allow for high quality services to end users.

E-government services can easily be combined with systems that monitor the activity of end users as they are moving around and utilize it not only to update their location but also to update the IoT node operation. The principles of offering location-based services can be easily incorporated in the IoT e-government systems. However, location-based models should be enhanced by techniques for handling the heterogeneity of the devices and the functions they perform. IoT nodes can also be grouped to be monitored by the e-government services for offering 'personalized' services and avoid network flooding. Spatio-temporal clustering can be adopted to continuously generate clusters of IoT nodes. In this way, e-government services can target specific groups of users and support multiple roles. The modular approach and a role-based infrastructure can increase the efficiency in the delivery of data creating the basis for personalized e-government services.

The data produced by e-government services can be pulled or pushed to the end devices according to the application domain. In the example, the 'push' model is adopted to send critical data to the IoT nodes. In this way, e-government services can trigger end users to perform some tasks. It should be noted that we can be based on the autonomous nature of the IoT devices, thus, end users will be only informed when the final results are delivered. In the 'pull' model, IoT nodes request data from the e-government services to complete their tasks. In any case, the exchanged data should be annotated in a way that facilitates the interaction between the two actors. In this point, there is an increased need for defining data description models designed for the interaction between the aforementioned actors. A common high-level data model will easily support the management of heterogeneity in the IoT nodes and their functionalities.

Addressing IoT Challenges

In this section we summarize the main challenges, technical and non-technical, associated with the described scenario and present the proposed solutions to address them. Technical challenges include the heterogeneity of the devices, data interoperability, security and the inclusion of additional functionalities. Non-technical challenges involve government administration support, legal coverage, privacy, IoT policy and organizational interoperability. Table 1 presents a potential solution for each challenge in the discussed scenario.

CONCLUSION

The use of IoT in e-government can be extremely valuable as it offers the possibility for a wide range of applications and services that can be available and beneficial to the public. IoT-based systems can enable the provision of new, innovative e-government

Table 1. IoT challenges and responses examples

Challenge	Response
Heterogeneity of the devices	The use of an end point where end users' devices can be 'hooked' and receive information. The end point will be controlled by the appropriate software while supported by a model for data exchange.
Data Interoperability	The use of a data model and software that will align the heterogeneous data in an automatic manner.
Security	The back end system should be secured against unauthorized access through the aforementioned techniques. In the discussed scenario this is very important due to the criticality of the application. In addition, the above discussed security mechanisms should also be applied on the end users devices to avoid the generation and spread of fake messages.
Inclusion of additional functionalities	AI can be included in the reasoning process for events identification as well as in the clustering of end users. Complex event processing, pattern identification, classification and prediction can assist in events detection that will fire the creation of messages for end users. In addition, clustering can be performed on top of multivariate data to depict not only the current position of users but personalized aspects like their ability to respond in emergency scenarios. For instance, the instructions to end users can differ based on their personal characteristics and their initial route.
Government administration support	A decision and support is needed by government administration for the use of IoT for the provision of e-government service for warning for weather phenomena
Legal coverage	A legal framework with the appropriate laws and regulations should be in place to allow the use of the service
Privacy	Enabling the collection and use of geo-positioning data and activity whilst protecting citizens privacy
IoT policy	Setting a policy for using IoT for e-government involving all interested parties and stakeholders in the domains of transportation, civil protection, meteorological services, telecommunications
Organizational interoperability	The provision of interorganizational services implies the need for interoperability not only of the data exchanged among involved entities but also of the organizations themselves, sharing processes and policies that enable their communication

services or ameliorate and complement the existing ones. Such systems and services can be even more important when used within critical security and safety contexts, allowing for the protection of the public and the prevention of disasters. This chapter seeks to contribute to a better understanding of the potential of IoT in e-government and how such potential could be reached. The aim is to examine IoT use from both a positive and a negative perspective, highlighting the benefits as well as the challenges that come with introducing it in e-government. The emphasis is placed in safety critical areas where the adoption of IoT-based systems can be most helpful, offering unprecedented functionalities that be life-saving. The analysis of IoT in e-government with regards to the application scenarios, the technical and non-technical challenges and the example case presented can offer useful insights that can be of interest for both researchers and practitioners and can serve as a starting point for further study and work in this promising field.

ACKNOWLEDGMENT

This work has received funding from the European Union's Horizon 2020 Research and Innovation Programme under Grant Agreement No. 645220 (Road-, Air- and Water-based Future Internet Experimentation, RAWFIE).

REFERENCES

AlEnezi, A., AlMeraj, Z., & Manuel, P. (2018). Challenges of IoT based Smart-government Development. *2018 IEEE Green Technologies Conference (GreenTech)*, 155-160. 10.1109/GreenTech.2018.00036

Alphonsa, A., & Ravi, G. (2016). Earthquake early warning system by IOT using Wireless sensor networks. *Proceedings of 2016 International Conference on Wireless Communications, Signal Processing and Networking (WiSPNET)*. 10.1109/WiSPNET.2016.7566327

Amjath Ali, J., Thangalakshmi, B., & Vincy Beaulah, A. (2017). IoT Based Disaster Detection and Early Warning Device. *International Journal of MC Square Scientific Research*, *9*(3), 20–25. doi:10.20894/IJMSR.117.009.003.003

Babu, A. S., Naidu, G. T., & Meenakshi, U. (2018). Earth Quake Detection And Alerting Using IoT. *International Journal of Engineering Science Invention*, *07*(05), 14–18.

Brous, P., & Janssen, M. (2015a). Advancing e-Government Using the Internet of Things: A Systematic Review of Benefits. In Lecture Notes in Computer Science: Vol. 9248. *Electronic Government. EGOV 2015*. Cham: Springer. doi:10.1007/978-3-319-22479-4_12

Brous, P., & Janssen, M. (2015b). A Systematic Review of Impediments Blocking Internet of Things Adoption by Governments. In Lecture Notes in Computer Science: Vol. 9373. *Open and Big Data Management and Innovation. I3E 2015*. Cham: Springer. doi:10.1007/978-3-319-25013-7_7

Burkhalter, M. (2018). How IoT infrastructure allows for more accurate weather forecasting. *Perle*. Available at https://www.perle.com/articles/how-iot-infrastructure-allows-for-more-accurate-weather-forecasting-40169629.shtml

Cenci, K., Fillottrani, P., & Ardenghi, J. (2017). Government Data Interoperability: A Case Study from Academia. *Proc. of the ICEGOV*. doi:10.1145/3047273.3047382

Chou, B. C. C. H., Chou, B. C. C. H., Archive, F. D., Archive, F. D., Goethals, A., & Goethals, A. (2015). *An introduction to the European Interoperability Reference Architecture v0.9.0*. EIRA.

Columbus, L. (2018). *Where IoT Can Deliver The Most Value In 2018*. Retrieved from https://www.forbes.com/sites/louiscolumbus/2018/03/18/where-iot-can-deliver-the-most-value-in-2018/

Cooke, A. (2018). Realising the future and full potential of connected IoT devices with AI. *Silicon Republic*. Available at https://www.siliconrepublic.com/enterprise/ai-iot-automation-ibm

e-Estonia (2018). *Internet of Things paves the way for smart B2G solutions*. Available at https://e-estonia.com/internet-of-things-way-for-b2g-solutions/

El-Haddadeh, R., Weerakkody, V., Osmani, M., Thakker, D., & Kapoor, K. K. (2018). Examining citizens' perceived value of internet of things technologies in facilitating public sector services engagement. *Government Information Quarterly*. doi:10.1016/j.giq.2018.09.009

Gartner. (2017). *Gartner Says By 2020, More Than Half of Major New Business Processes and Systems Will Incorporate Some Element of the Internet of Things*. Available at http://www.gartner.com/newsroom/id/3185623

Hounsell, N. B., Shrestha, B. P., Piao, J., & McDonald, M. (2009). Review of urban traffic management and the impacts of new vehicle technologies. *IET Intelligent Transport Systems*, *3*, 419–428.

Industries, I. B. M. (2017). *The incredible ways governments use the Internet of Things*. Available at https://medium.com/ibmindustrious/the-incredible-ways-governments-use-the-internet-of-things-1072d34b9821

Kumar, S. P. (2017). Internet of Things for sophisticated e-governance: A special focus on agricultural sector. *International Journal of Trend in Research and Development*.

McKinsey. (2018). *The Internet of Things: How to capture the value of IoT*. McKinsey & Company. Available at https://www.mckinsey.com/featured-insights/internet-of-things/our-insights

Newman, P. (2017). The Internet of Things 2017 Report: How the IoT is Improving Lives to Transform the World. *Business Insider*. Available at http://www.businessinsider.com/the-internet-of-things-2017-report-2017-1

Schwertner, K., Zlateva, P., & Velev, D. (2018). Digital technologies of industry 4.0 in management of natural disasters. *Proceedings of the 2nd International Conference on E-commerce, E-Business and E-Government*.

Sideridis, A., & Protopappas, L. (2015). Recent ICT Advances Applied to Smart e-Government Systems in Life Sciences. *Proceedings of the 7th International Conference on Information and Communication Technologies in Agriculture, Food and Environment (HAICTA 2015)*.

Sideridis, A. B., Protopappas, L., Tsiafoulis, S., & Pimenidis, E. (2015). Smart Cross-Border e-Gov Systems and Applications. In S. Katsikas & A. Sideridis (Eds.), *E-Democracy – Citizen Rights in the World of the New Computing Paradigms. e-Democracy 2015. Communications in Computer and Information Science* (Vol. 570). Cham: Springer.

Tang, T., & Ho, A. T.-K. (2018). A path-dependence perspective on the adoption of Internet of Things: Evidence from early adopters of smart and connected sensors in the United States. *Government Information Quarterly*. doi:10.1016/j.giq.2018.09.010

Thibaud, M., Chi, H., Zhou, W., & Piramuthu, S. (2018). Internet of Things (IoT) in high-risk Environment, Health and Safety (EHS) industries: A comprehensive review. *Decision Support Systems*, *108*, 79–95. doi:10.1016/j.dss.2018.02.005

World Bank Group. (2017). *Internet of Things: The New Government to Business Platform*. Available at: http://documents.worldbank.org/curated/en/610081509689089303/pdf/120876-REVISED-WP-PUBLIC-Internet-of-Things-Report.pdf

Chapter 6
Deep Learning:
An Application in Internet of Things

Ramgopal Kashyap

ⓘD https://orcid.org/0000-0002-5352-1286
Amity University Chhattisgarh, India

ABSTRACT

The vast majority of the examination on profound neural systems so far has been centered on acquiring higher exactness levels by building progressively vast and profound structures. Preparing and assessing these models is just practical when a lot of assets; for example, handling power and memory are easy run of the mill applications that could profit by these models. The system starts handling the compelled gadget and depends on the remote part when the neighborhood part does not give a sufficiently precise outcome. The falling system takes into account a new ceasing component amid the review period of the system. This chapter empowers an entire assortment of independent frameworks where sensors, actuators, and registering hubs can cooperate and demonstrate that the falling design takes into account a free change in assessment speed on obliged gadgets while the misfortune in precision is kept to a base.

INTRODUCTION

In previous years, profound fake neural systems have turned out to be particularly great for different machine learning assignments. Profound learning systems are as of now the best in class for different machine learning errands, for example, picture and discourse acknowledgment or normal dialect handling. While to a great degree skilled, they are additionally asset requesting, both to prepare and to assess. The

DOI: 10.4018/978-1-5225-7955-7.ch006

majority of the examination on profound learning centers on preparing these profound models. Progressively, profound and complex systems are built to be more exact on different benchmark datasets. Urgent for preparing these enormous models are graphical handling units. Top of the line GPUs were once saved for 3D displaying and gaming however their parallel engineering makes them likewise amazingly appropriate for profound learning. Most of the activities inside a profound neural system are framework duplications and increments, two writes of tasks for which a graphical processing unit (GPU) is requests of extent quicker than a focal handling unit. Preparing a profound neural system is computationally exceptionally costly however effective GPU executions currently make it plausible to prepare a model considered excessively troublesome to prepare in the past. The time expected to prepare a profound neural system is by and large not extremely basic (Hong & Lee, 2013). The assessment of a prepared model, be that as it may, can be amazingly time touchy. At the point when the system is utilized to manage a robot or to decipher voice orders from a client, it ought to have the capacity to work progressively. Any deferral will bring about poor client encounter or perhaps in unsafe circumstances when a robot or automaton is included. While preparing the system is regularly done on an elite framework, once prepared, the system must be utilized as a part of a certifiable condition the assets accessible to frameworks in these situations are much more restricted.

In this chapter, the main focus is in the center on picture order issues utilizing profound neural systems, the methods introduced here are, be that as it may, not restrict to this area but rather can be reached out to all profound learning grouping undertakings. Conceivable applications incorporate home computerization and security frameworks, savvy apparatuses, and family unit robots. The need to utilize profound neural systems on obliged gadgets that can't assess the whole system because of confinements in accessible memory, preparing force or battery limit. Current remote advancements are quick and sufficiently moderate to consider off-stacking every one of the calculations to a cloud back end as an answer. This presents an additional dormancy (10– 500 ms) and makes the gadgets subject to the system association; this reliance might be unsuitable now and again.

A robot, for instance, would end up inoperable when the server cannot become to, in this chapter this strikes a center ground. A neural system comprises of consecutive layers where each layer changes the yield from the past layer to a portrayal appropriate for the following layer. Each layer extricates more intricate highlights from its info the last layer utilizes the abnormal state highlights to arrange the info and misuse the characteristic consecutive plan of a neural system to empower an early-halting instrument to utilize the layers of a pretrained arrange as stages in a course. Each layer can catch extra multifaceted nature yet additionally requires extra assets, for example, processing time and memory to store the parameters. Each stage groups the info and returns certainty esteem and stops the assessment of more profound layers once a specific required certainty edge is come to. The decision of this limit esteem enables us to exchange off precision and speed.

The idea of a falling system and the developing enthusiasm for the Internet of Things (IoT) and its subsidiary huge information require partners to get it their definition, building squares, possibilities, and difficulties. IoT what's more, enormous information have a two-way relationship. On one hand, IoT is a primary maker of enormous information, and then again, it is a vital focus for huge information examination to enhance the procedures also, administrations of IoT (Sezer, Dogdu & Ozbayoglu, 2018). Additionally, IoT huge information examination has demonstrated to convey an incentive to the general public. For instance, it is revealed that, by recognizing harmed pipes and settling them, the Division of Park Management in Miami has spared about one million USD on their water bills. IoT information is unique in relation to enormous general information (Gomes & Mayes, 2014). To better comprehend the necessities for IoT information examination, to investigate the properties of IoT information and how they are extraordinary from those of general enormous information. IoT information displays the accompanying qualities:

- **Large-Scale Streaming Data:** A heap of information catching gadgets are dispersed and conveyed for IoT applications, what's more, produce floods of information consistently. This prompts a tremendous volume of persistent information.
- **Heterogeneity:** Various IoT information securing gadgets assemble diverse data bringing about information heterogeneity.
- **Time and Space Relationship:** In the vast majority of IoT applications, sensor gadgets are appended to a particular area, and hence have an area and time-stamp for every one of the information things.
- **High Clamor Information:** Due to minor bits of information in IoT applications, a significant number of such information might be liable to blunders, what's more, commotion amid securing and transmission. Despite the fact that getting concealed learning and data out of huge information is promising to improve the nature of our lives, it isn't a simple and direct assignment. For such a complex also, a difficult assignment that goes past the abilities of the conventional derivation and learning approaches, innovations, calculations, and foundations are required (Kashyap & Piersson, 2018). Fortunately, the ongoing advances in both quick processing and progressed machine learning strategies are opening the entryways for huge information investigation and learning extraction that is appropriate for IoT applications.

- Past the huge information investigation, IoT information requires another new class of examination, to be specific quick and spilling information investigation. To bolster applications with rapid information streams and requiring time-touchy i.e., ongoing or close constant activities without a doubt, applications, for example, self-ruling driving, fire forecast, driver/elderly stance and in this manner awareness as well as wellbeing condition acknowledgment requests for quick handling of approaching information and speedy activities to accomplish their objective. A few scientists have proposed methodologies and systems for quick gushing information examination that use the capacities of cloud foundations and administrations that as it may, for the previously mentioned IoT applications among others, require quick examination in little scale stages, i.e., at the framework edge or even on the IoT gadgets themselves (Chae & Quick, 2014). For instance, self-ruling autos need to settle on quick choices on driving activities, for example, path or speed change. In reality, this sort of choices ought to be bolstered by quick investigation of potentially multi-modular information spilling from a few sources, including the various vehicle sensors, e.g., cameras, radars, LIDARs, speedometer, left/right flags, and so on. Correspondences from different vehicles, and movement substances (e.g., activity light, activity signs) for this situation, exchanging information to a cloud server for investigation and returning the reaction is liable to inactivity that could cause petty criminal offenses or mishaps. A more basic situation would distinguish walkers by such vehicles. Exact acknowledgment ought to be performed in strict ongoing to forestall fatal accidents. These situations suggest that quick information investigation for IoT must be near or at the wellspring of information to evacuate pointless and restrictive correspondence delays.
- Better utilization of profound learning for distinguishing steering assaults that objective to IoT, before giving data about DL, ML ought to be disclosed to all the more likely get it DL since, ML can be viewed as the progenitor of DL.

MACHINE LEARNING

Machine Learning is one of the pathways in driving Artificial Intelligence (AI) inquire about. Fame of ML originates from two reasons or two undertaking must be finished by ML. First the undertaking that should be possible by machines, second the errand that can't be performed by people. Learning movement becomes a force to be reckoned with to be savvy what eludes a framework has capacity staying aware of changes of its condition. On the off chance that a framework can accord to the changes, this capacity can assist it with surviving. ML examines are put at the intersection territory of insights, computer science and engineering, it can likewise give answers for different controls. Since use of ML relies upon utilizing information that can be from back, geosciences or prehistoric studies. ML additionally delivers data from the information with the end goal that PCs utilize information while taking a shot at a procedure yet the information, typically, is useless from human point of view (Campbell & Ying, 2011) to take care of deterministic issues effortlessly for instance, a product to control lighting framework in a brilliant home can complete a decent work constantly, utilizing the action and sunshine. Yet, there are loads of non-deterministic issues that don't have enough data about or power and time to tackle to require measurements for taking care of these sorts of issues for example; demonstrating the dread of people against unforeseen circumstance is so difficult without measurements. Essentially, measurement manufactures numerical models and ML trains them. Starting here of view, ML has fundamentally the same as importance with traditional programming. This depiction have less demanding to see the effect between traditional programming and ML; a established program is sustained by information and manage as an info which change the appropriate response as an yield after the procedure, in the complexity, a ML calculation is nourished by information and reply, which is relied upon to comprehend the connection between them. This relationship can be utilized as a part of various types of information to assess their yields.

In ML, there isn't any express programming, it ought to be called 'preparing' as a result of the learning process. ML framework does not do anything with the exception of investigating the factual structure of given information. For instance, which is significant with the following assignment, the genuine information? For instance, somebody, who supposedly is our questioning Thomas, needs to know the reason for a specific movement that occurs in the evening around his home (Ksiezopolski, 2012). He puts reconnaissance cameras to specific purposes of his home and one of the vital highlights of the cameras is taking photographs and sparing them on the PC when they distinguish any movement with their sensors that as it may, the security arrangement of the house is extremely monotonous and exhausting, in light of the fact that the proprietor of the home needs to check all the photographs, of the previous evening, each day to be fulfilled about his home's security. On the off chance that wishes to set up a superior framework, it needs to caution Thomas when a genuine danger happens. The framework shouldn't give an alert when the night action happens on account of a feline or squirrel. Along these lines can give loads of cases of pictures to ML calculation, that are as of now labeled previously, called target variable, previously.

These objective factors incorporate the highlights, case pictures, called preparing set, incorporate objects of people, felines, leaf and so forth. At that point, the ML calculation learns measurable guidelines for corresponding clear picture to distinct labels and the yield is a ML show that points to recognize night action. At last, the framework breaks down throughout the night movement for every day over taken pictures and if there is a suspicious movement of intrigue, it gives a notice or an alarm, as our questioning Thomas needed from the earliest starting point. A few specialists think about on ML process in two sections; the adapting part and the inducing part. As specified previously, the adapting part is bolstering the ML calculation with the preparation set and the gathering part is making expectations about the reason for action by the framework (Ksiezopolski, 2012). Managed learning and unsupervised learning are fundamental kinds of ML, first of them are exist by utilizing completely named dataset while other one are exist completely unlabelled dataset. In managed taking in, the model gets datasets which incorporates a few highlights vectors and names that are the relating yields of highlight vectors. Consequently the model figures out how to deliver adjust yields because of given new information. Order and relapse are most famous result of regulated learning. In unsupervised taking in, the other path around, there is no chief who supplies the marks that incorporate right consequence of comparing contribution, to prepare the models. So the display has just information esteems, watches the consequences of its activity. In the other alluding, unsupervised learning is an undertaking to depict concealed examples from input information. Grouping and dimensionality diminishment are two basic unsupervised learning illustrations.

Deep Learning

Profound learning is a sort of Neural Networks (NN) preparing and has NN design contrast between 'old fashioned' NN and profound learning is that DL has many concealed layers. DL additionally takes in the highlights itself, which empowers the learning procedure to be more precise and furthermore it appears to be more productive and exact than shallow learning. DL has achieved accomplishment in the PC vision, design acknowledgment, picture and sound handling. It additionally empowered noteworthy change for arrangement and forecast issues. Complex profound neural calculations are prepared with the utilization of ground-breaking GPUs. For AI, DL speaks to the best in class, additionally to deal with big data particularly in regards to versatility and speculation. In directed learning, there are three kinds of datasets. In the first place, preparing set is one of the key terms of learning process. It is an empowering influence for learning calculation to be managed furthermore; it contains the normal outcomes under the name highlight (Vu et al., 2018). The weights of the interior layers of NN are resolved in light of the information and their normal outcomes. What's more, ideal weights are acquired. Another term is approval set that helps the learning procedure for tuning the parameters of capacities to get ideal weights. At long last, the test set is utilized for assessing the execution of preparing process. Before beginning the learning procedure, the dataset is isolated into the preparation set and the testing set, that approval dataset is part from the preparation set. While setting up the neural system calculation, ages are utilized as learning time. One age implies, the preparation set is gone through the system totally; NN preparing calculations plan to decide the 'best' conceivable arrangement of weight values for the issue under thought. Of course, deciding the ideal arrangement of weight is regularly an exchange off between limiting the system mistake, calculation time and keeping up the system's capacity to sum up.

Deep Learning Model

Two imperative upgrades over the customary machine learning approaches in the two periods of preparing are expectation to begin with, they diminish the need for hand created and designed capabilities to be utilized for the preparation. Subsequently, a few highlights that may not be evident to a human view can be removed effectively by DL models. Furthermore, DL models enhance the accuracy. In this chapter, audit an extensive variety of profound neural system models and investigate the IoT applications that have profited from DL calculations (Koakutsu, 2018). This chapter recognizes five principle central IoT administrations that can be utilized as a part of various vertical areas past the particular administrations in every space. It will likewise talk about the qualities of IoT applications and the manual for coordinating them with the most fitting DL demonstrate. The study does not cover conventional machine learning calculations for IoT information investigation as there are some different endeavors that have secured such methodologies. Besides, this overview too does not delve into the subtle elements of the IoT framework from an interchanges and systems administration point of view.

Deep Learning and IoT

There are few works exhibiting normal information mining and machine learning techniques that have been utilized as a part of IoT conditions. It tended to diverse arrangement, bunching, and visit design mining calculations for the IoT framework and administrations. Be that as it may, that work did not consider DL approaches, which is the core interest of our overview. Additionally, their attention is basically on disconnected information mining, while additionally think about learning and digging for both constant (i.e., quickly) and enormous information investigation. Machine learning approaches administered and unsupervised, rules, fluffy rationale, and so on in the thinking period of a context-aware registering framework, and have talked about the possibilities of applying those strategies in IoT frameworks. Regardless, they too did not think about the part of DL on the set thinking. The work gives a study of machine learning strategies for remote sensor systems (Li, Ota & Dong, 2018). In that work, the creators examined machine learning strategies in the useful parts of WSNs, for example, steering, limitation, furthermore, grouping, and also non-practical prerequisites, such as security and nature of administration. They investigated a few calculations in managed, unsupervised, and support learning approaches. This work centers around the framework of WSN which is one potential foundation for executing IoT applications, while our work isn't reliant on the wellsprings of information i.e., IoT foundations and spreads a wide scope of IoT applications and administrations. Besides, the core interest was on conventional machine learning techniques, while this article centers on cutting edge and DL strategies. At long last DL approaches in arrange movement control frameworks. While this work basically centers on the framework of system, it varies from our work that spotlights on the utilization of DL in IoT applications. In particular, they featured the association of diverse machine learning strategies with flag preparing advancements to process and dissect opportune huge information applications.

Commitments

IoT scientists and engineers who need to manufacture examination, AI frameworks, and learning arrangements over their IoT framework, utilizing the developing DL machine learning approaches. The commitments of this chapter can be outlined as takes after:

- Keeping in mind the end goal to embrace DL approaches in the IoT environments it recognizes the key attributes and issues of IoT information.
- Compared to some related work in writing that have tended to machine learning for IoT, audit the state of-the-craftsmanship DL strategies and their pertinence in the IoT area both for enormous information and spilling information investigation (Yao et al., 2018).
- Audit an extensive variety of IoT applications that have utilized DL in their unique circumstance likewise gives an examination furthermore, a rule for utilizing diverse kinds of DNN in the different IoT areas and applications.
- Audit the ongoing methodologies and innovations for conveying DL on all levels of IoT chain of importance from asset obliged gadgets to the mist and the cloud.

- Feature the difficulties and future research headings for the effective and productive converging of DL and IoT applications. It additionally incorporates a concise depiction of headways toward continuous and quick DL models and state-of the-craftsmanship calculations that are joint with DL. A brief audit of a few structures and devices with various capacities what's more, calculations that help DNNs is likewise exhibited. IoT applications in various areas e.g., medicinal services, agribusiness and so on.

IOT DATA CHARACTERISTICS AND REQUIREMENTS FOR ANALYTICS

IoT information can be spilled consistently or collected as a wellspring of enormous information. Spilling information alludes to the information created or caught inside small interims of time and need to be expeditiously broke down to remove quick bits of knowledge as well as settle on quick choices. Enormous information alludes to colossal datasets that the ordinarily utilized equipment and programming stages are not capable of storing, oversee, process, and break down. These two methodologies ought to be dealt with distinctively since their prerequisites for the explanatory reaction are not the same (Kim, Jeong & Kim, 2017). Understanding from enormous information investigation can be conveyed following a few long periods of the information age, be that as it may, understanding from spilling information investigation ought to be prepared in a scope of a couple of several milliseconds to few moments. Information combination and sharing assume a basic part in creating pervasive conditions in light of IoT information. This part is more basic for time-delicate IoT applications where an auspicious combination of information is expected to bring all bits of information together for investigation and thusly to give dependable and exact significant bits of knowledge.

IoT Quick and Spilling Information

Many research endeavors recommended gushing information examination that can be chiefly conveyed on superior figuring frameworks or cloud stages. The gushing information investigation on such systems depends on information parallelism and incremental preparing by information parallelism, a substantial dataset is apportioned into a few little datasets, on which parallel investigation are performed all the while. Incremental preparing alludes to getting a little clump of information to be prepared rapidly in a pipeline of calculation undertakings. In spite of the fact that these systems decrease time dormancy to restore a reaction from the spilling information diagnostic structure. They are not the most ideal arrangement for time-stringent IoT applications by bringing spilling information examination closer to the wellspring of information i.e., IoT gadgets or edge gadgets the requirement for information parallelism and incremental handling is less sensible as the extent of the information in the source enables it to be handled quickly (Mazzei, Baldi, Montelisciani & Fantoni, 2018). It may, bringing quick examination on IoT gadgets presents its own particular difficulties for example, confinement of figuring, stockpiling, and power assets at the wellspring of information.

IoT Big Information

IoT is not able to be one of the real wellsprings of huge information, as it depends on interfacing countless gadgets to the Internet to report their habitually caught status of their surroundings. Perceiving and extricating significant designs from gigantic crude information is the central utility of enormous information investigation as it brings about larger amounts of experiences for basic leadership and pattern expectation (Jang, 2015). Along these lines, separating these experiences and learning from the enormous information is of outrageous significance to numerous organizations, since it empowers them to increase upper hands. Sociologists thinks about the effect of enormous information examination to that of the development of the telescope and magnifying lens for cosmology and science, individually.

Profound Learning

DL comprises of managed or unsupervised learning systems in view of numerous layers of Artificial Neural Networks (ANNs) that can learn progressive portrayals in profound models. DL structures comprise of numerous handling layers. Each layer can deliver non-direct reactions in light of the information from its info layer. The usefulness of DL is imitated from the instruments of human cerebrum and neurons for preparing of signs. DL structures have increased more consideration as of late contrasted with the other customary machine learning approaches. Such methodologies are considered as being shallow-organized learning structures variants i.e., a constrained subset of DL (Rayner, 2011). In spite of the fact that ANNs have been presented in the previous decades, the developing pattern for DNNs began in 2006 when G. Hinton et al. exhibited the idea of profound conviction systems from that point. The state of-the-workmanship execution of this innovation has been watched in various fields of AI including picture acknowledgment, picture recovery, web crawlers and data recovery, and regular dialect preparing.

DL procedures have been produced over customary ANNs, Feed-forward Neural Networks (FNNs), Multilayer Perceptrons (MLPs) have been utilized as a part of the past decades to prepare frameworks, however when the quantity of layers is expanded, they end up hard to prepare. The little size of preparing information was another calculates that outcomes over fitted models. In addition, the restriction in computational abilities in those days denied the usage of productive more profound FNNs (Despotovic & Tanikic, 2017). These computational impediments have been settled of late because of equipment progresses as a rule and the advancement of Graphics Processing Units (GPUs) and equipment quickening agents particularly. Past the auxiliary perspectives and centrality of the profundity of DL models, and in addition equipment propels, DL strategies have profited from progressions in viable preparing calculations of profound systems including:

- Using Rectified Linear Units (ReLUs) as enactment work,
- Introducing dropout strategies,
- Random introduction for the weights of the system,
- Addressing the debasement of preparing precision by remaining learning systems,
- Solving vanishing angle issue and in addition detonating inclination issue by presenting and upgrading

One favorable position of DL designs, contrasted with the conventional ANNs, is that DL methods can learn concealed highlights from the crude information. Each layer prepares on an arrangement of highlights in view of the past layer's yields. The internal generally layers can perceive more mind-boggling highlights, since the total and recombine highlights from the past layers. This is called the pecking order of highlights for instance, if there should arise an occurrence of a face acknowledgment demonstrate, crude picture information of representations as a vector of pixels are encouraged to a model in its info layer (Carta, Cabrera, Matías & Castellano, 2015). Each concealed layer would then be able to take in more unique highlights from the past layer's yields, e.g., the primary shrouded layer distinguishes the lines and edges, the second layer recognizes con front parts, for example, nose, eyes, and so forth, and the third layer consolidates all the past highlights to produce a face. Nonetheless, the detailed upgrades of DL models are in view of experimental assessments, and there is still no solid expository establishment to answer why DL procedures beat their shallow partners. Additionally, there is no unmistakable limit amongst profound and shallow systems in light of the number of shrouded layers. For the most part, neural systems with two or on the other hand more shrouded layers that fuse the ongoing progressed preparing calculations are considered as profound models. Too, intermittent neural systems with one shrouded layer are considered as profound since they have a cycle on the units of the concealed layer, which can be unrolled to a proportionate profound system.

Deep Learning Models

In this area, introduce a concise review of a few normal DL models and additionally the most bleeding edge structures that have been presented as of late. Intrigued perusers can allude to other writing that overviewed the models and designs of DL in more subtle elements. A DNN comprises of an information layer, a few shrouded layers, also, a yield layer. Each layer incorporates a few units called neurons; a neuron gets a few sources of info, plays out a weighted Figure 1. Internet of things attacks like DDoS attack, routing attack, and social engineering attack is shown. Summation over its sources of info, at that point the subsequent whole experiences an actuation capacity to deliver a yield (Addo, Guegan & Hassani, 2018). Every neuron has a vector of weights related to its info measure and in addition, a predisposition that ought to be upgraded amid the preparation procedure.

In the preparation procedure, the information layer allows more often than not haphazardly weights to the information preparing information and passes it to the following layer. Each ensuing layer additionally relegates weights to their info and produces their yield, which fills in as the contribution for the accompanying layer. At the last layer, the last yield speaking to the model expectation is created a misfortune work decides the rightness of this forecast by registering the blunder rate between the anticipated and genuine qualities. An advancement calculation, for example, Stochastic Gradient Descent (SGD) is utilized to change the heaviness of neurons by figuring the slope of the misfortune work (Senov, 2015). The mistake rate is spread back over the system to the information layer known as back propagation calculation. The system at that point rehashes this preparation cycle, in the wake of adjusting

Figure 1. Internet of things attacks

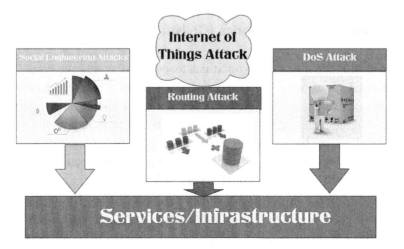

the weights on each neuron in each cycle, until the point that the blunder rate falls beneath a coveted edge. Now, the DNN is prepared and is prepared for surmising. In a general arrangement, DL models fall into three classifications, to be specific generative, discriminative, and half and half models. Despite the fact that not being a firm limit, discriminative models more often than not give administered learning approaches, while generative models are utilized for unsupervised learning. Half breed models consolidate the advantages of both discriminative and generative models.

In this investigation, Keras is used as a DL system since it guarantees numerous points of interest like its seclusion, and since it empowers us to construct and test complex neural systems rapidly. To start with, Keras is an open source DL library that incorporated into the Python biological community. Second, Keras additionally has a wide range network and a nitty-gritty client manual. From that point forward, Keras empowers to assemble a complex neural system effectively (B Arnold, 2017); Tensorflow is a system that is produced by Google for DL. It is reasonable for working with CPUs and GPUs. Tensorflow likewise contains a few usages to fabricate complex DL models. It is runnable on Mac, Windows and Linux, as a python bundle. It is likewise utilities with Keras. Initially the rearranged the dataset to enhance the profound model execution and abstain from over fitting and fabricated Neural Network as 7 layers the first layer is input layer that has 10 neurons, a number of information layer ought to be equivalent to the quantity of highlights sections in the dataset. The last layer is the yielding layer that has only 1 neuron. This is known as a Regression display. Our neural system has 5 concealed layers. First and fifth layers have 50 neurons and second and fourth layers have 100 neurons. Third layer has 300 neurons. The neural arrange layers are delineated in Figure 2. Prior to the preparation begins, the dataset is part again at the rate of 0.3 as approval dataset to tune the preparation execution of the model the neural system demonstrates appears in Figure 2.

Convolution Neural Networks (CNNs)

For vision-based errands, DNNs with a thick association between layers are difficult to prepare and don't scale well. One imperative reason is the interpretation invariance property of such models. They along these lines don't take in the highlights that may change in the picture e.g., the pivot of submitting posture recognition. CNNs have tackled this issue by supporting translation equivariance calculations. A CNN gets a 2-D input e.g., a picture or discourse flag and concentrates abnormal state highlights through a progression of shrouded layers (Fu, Li, Gao & Wang, 2018). Everyone is living in an information driven age, information has been finding or will find each purpose of our life. A great many people imagine that this impact is an outcome of industry 4.0 that makes our life speedier than before as all other

Figure 2. Deep learning model

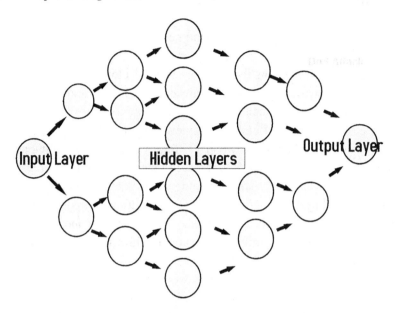

modern upsets. Industry 4.0 empowered the collaboration between PCs or digital area and physical frameworks.

This collaboration is called digital physical frameworks that point made the IoT by implanting sensors, controllers, and actuators. Another outcome of the upset the tremendous information that is produced and should be overseen, called big data. To build up effective correspondence of IoT is a troublesome point to accomplish and keep up, while the number of created information has been expanding, conditionally, the term information security has turned into a significant term particularly in regards to security of touchy information in arrangement with the three standards of data security classification, integrity, and availability. There are numerous assaults auto hacking, DDoS or physical assaults to IoT in view of, especially, an absence of strong steering conventions. The measurements guarantee that DDoS assaults expanded 91% of every 2017 because of the misuse of IoT gadgets (Vlajic & Zhou, 2018). IoT, which is in all branches of life, is powerless against a few sorts of assaults that as it may, there is likewise no successful answer for shielding our life from being influenced by these assaults. These days, machine learning (ML) is the most well-known examination theme for recognizing digital assaults for IoT security. Since ML-based arrangements can offer a vigorous framework to inconspicuous assaults. In actuality, the most concerning issue of research on IoT security is the absence of open datasets. Subsequently, there must be far-reaching thinks about to discover arrangements in these issues.

Deep Learning Model Architecture

It is required to assess a prepared profound neural system on a compelled gadget unfit to hold all the parameters in memory or unfit to play out the computations in the required time of off-stacking the whole system to a cloud back-end, we off-stack just a piece of the system. The main layers are assessed locally and the remote part is just required when these layers can't characterize an example with adequate certainty. This early-ceasing instrument amid the review period of the system ensures that just speak with the cloud back-end when it is totally required by staying away from superfluous information exchanges to the cloud can diminish the normal idleness and cost while assessing the system. It somewhat alters the standard design of a feed-forward neural system to empower the early-halting component. Rather than one yield layer a softmax classifier after the last shrouded layer and prepare different yield layers: one straightforwardly on the crude info information and one after each shrouded layer in the system (Jha & Kwon, 2017). This permits to quit spreading an example through the system once an adequately certain outcome is gotten to utilize a fascinating property of neural system classifiers expressing that they give yields which appraise Bayesian a posteriori probabilities, which means the yields can be translated as certainty measures i.e., how sure is the system that a specific example has a place with a specific class? (Shaoshi Yang, Tiejun Lv, Maunder & Hanzo, 2013). This approach is appeared in Figure 2 for a neural system with three shrouded layers. The procedure used to proliferate an example through the system the arrangement comprises of n concealed layers and n + 1 yield layers.

Training

A course arranges it is prepared as takes after that add extra yield layers all things considered or after a subset of the shrouded layers and utilize standard back propagation to prepare the layers. It is conceivable to prepare every one of the layers on the double. The blunder back propagated to a certain parameter is weighted of the mistake of each yield layer for that parameter. It is likewise conceivable to reuse a pretrained off-the-rack arrange. Research has demonstrated that the highlights learned by the primary layers of a profound neural system are frequently not particular to one issue yet can be summed up finished diverse datasets. A well-known way to deal with prepare a great system is to reuse the principal layers of a freely accessible pretrained organize and to supplant the layers toward the finish of the system. The system all in all is then calibrated on the issue of particular dataset. This procedure makes it conceivable to prepare a mind-boggling system on a moderately little measure of information since the primary layers of the system as of now are reasonable highlight extractors. Changing over a totally prepared conventional system to a course system should be possible fast at a little cost when keeping the weights settled and spread the preparation set information once through the system and store the inward portrayals after each concealed layer at that point prepare softmax yield layers to characterize the put away portrayals (Jha & Kwon, 2017). This second approach is utilized as a part of every one of our tests behind the remote cloud servers where space and vitality are inexhaustible. As a rule, neural systems are reenacted in programming on broadly useful equipment. While to a great degree adaptable, this worldview isn't the most proficient approach to assess a neural organize. Neuromorphic chips are equipment segments, uncommonly intended to suit a neural system. They require less capacity to run and can create a yield speedier. They are as yet costly and difficult to get right now and the measure of neurons they can contain is moderately little for any true system. The course design, in any case, would take into consideration a possibly ground-breaking crossbreed organize. The main layers are assessed on the quick neural system equipment. The more profound layers, reproduced in programming, are just required when the primary layers were not able to group the example certainly. Comparable engineering could fuse field-programmable entryway clusters to assess the first layers. The capability is to provide equipment quickening agent for profound neural systems has been very much reported however functional applications are still rather unprecedented. The falling worldview likewise takes into consideration a more strong blame tolerant framework. Web availability can be unsteady in numerous commonsense circumstances.

The course arranges whether to acknowledge or to dismiss a grouping in light of the edge esteem. This esteem isn't hard-coded into the system yet can be passed as a contention at runtime, autonomous for each example. This can be helpful in numerous useful circumstances since it permits an exchange off amongst exactness and speed. Correspondingly, the limit could rely upon different estimations, for example, arrange inactivity or the cost related with the arrange association WiFi versus portable associations. A conceivable engineering empowered by the course organizes the principal layers are assessed on the robot, either by an on-board neuromorphic chip or by the inserted CPU or GPU. Off-stacking the calculation is just required when these layers can't arrange the information. A nearby calculation hub (cloudlet) is utilized for the middle of the road layers. The cloudlet can become a nearby low inactivity organize the association. Sending information to the cloud presents a higher idleness and is just required when the more profound layers are required.

Security Problems of the Internet of Things

IoT is under hazard because of its heterogeneous structure which thus empowers collaboration of digital space and physical area. Vulnerabilities of IoT are recorded by OWASP. Inadequate validation, unreliable system administrations, absence of transport encryption furthermore, uprightness confirmation, security concerns, unreliable programming or firmware, poor physical security are in the rundown, moreover, lacking directing conventions can be added to the rundown and the situation of meeting up close and personal with the results of these specified vulnerabilities. In October of 2016, the biggest DDoS assault was completed by utilizing IoT botnets. PayPal, The Guardian, Netflix, Reddit and CNN, especially, turned into the objective. The botnets were made by a malware called Mirai. This malware misused the security weakness of IoT gadget's login information's. Abused gadgets were coordinated to the objectives. Utilizing default username, secret word, and non-special passwords also, absence of programming and firmware refreshes caused the Mirai assault.

The term of IoT is an arrangement of interconnected gadgets, machines and related programming administrations. It has been assuming an essential part in the cutting edge society since it empowered vitality effective robotization for upgrading personal satisfaction. Anyway IoT frameworks are an evident focus for digital assaults due to their impromptu and asset compelled nature. In this way, nonstop observing and examination is required for anchoring IoT frameworks (Weber, 2010). As a result of the huge measure of system and detecting information created by IoT gadgets and frameworks, big data and ML strategies are very viable in consistent checking and examination for the security of IoT frameworks. It is acquired a high level of preparing precision (up to 99.5%) and F1-scores (up to 99%). In this examination the main concentration is on particular IoT directing assaults, to be specific, diminished rank, rendition number change and hi surge. Frameworks security prerequisites depend to strength against steering assaults and profound learning-based for discovery for directing assaults to IoT. There are three principle interruption recognition approaches in writing; abuse location, inconsistency discovery, and particular based location. Moreover, cross breed based framework is additionally situated under the interruption discovery subject and it's, quickly, a blend of abuse identification and oddity recognition.

Abuse identification is exceptionally viable in identifying known assaults anyway it is deficient against obscure or novel assaults in light of the fact that their marks are not yet known. Furthermore, any alteration to the marks can cause an expansion in false caution rate and that will diminish viability and unwavering quality of the recognition framework. Particular based location plans to set specific conduct in light of the default deny standards. On the off chance that the determinations are abused, the framework will think there is an irregular circumstance. This approach is successful to covert the concealed assault that might be completed later on. Notwithstanding, setting specific details to the framework is a staggering errand in thinking about each extraordinary issue. Abnormality based recognition approach is, essentially, developed on typical action profile and it expects that any foe activity will strife with the typical movement. Peculiarity based identification is analyzed under four subheadings; progressed measurable models, control based systems, organic models and learning models. The learning models, in view of that regardless of whether abuse recognition can give quicker reaction. Learning models have a more hearty structure against obscure assaults than others. Customary ML strategies, for example, Bayesian Belief Networks (BBN), Support Vector Machines (SVM) have been connected for digital security, anyway the huge scale information age in IoT requires a profound learning-based strategy which performs better with huge information sizes and is versatile to distinctive assault situations (Datta & Das, 2015). IPv6 is a generally utilized convention in IoT and IPv6 based remote sensor systems (WSNs) are especially defenseless to steering assaults. IPv6 over Low-fueled Wireless Individual Area Networks (6LoWPAN) is an IPv6 based WSN convention. 6LoWPAN displays a few focal points as low power utilization, little, little impression, modest structure and simple support. In addition, WSNs incorporate numerous sensors which have constrained assets, for example, low memory, little transmission capacity and low vitality (Ahmed & AL-Shaboti, 2018). Areas of steering assaults in IoT additionally appear in Figure 3.

In our examination practicality of our system with reenactments up to 1000 hubs while the current investigations, for example the strategy with minimal number of hubs (up to 50), which is definitely not a reasonable approach for an IoT situation and to utilize the information created by genuine identical recreations in view of an absence of accessibility of open IoT assault datasets. The Cooja recreation produces crude bundle catch documents, which are first changed over into Comma Separated Values (CSV) records for content based handling. The CSV documents are then the contribution to the component pre-handling module of our framework. The highlights are ascertained in light of the activity stream data in the CSV documents. In the first place, include discussion process is connected to a few highlights, which is situated in crude datasets, at that point, recognized 12 includes as a starting hopeful list of capabilities. Subsequently, include standardization is connected to all datasets to lessen the negative impacts of minor qualities. In the pre-highlight choice advance, examined the significance of highlights by randomized decision trees, histograms and pearson rate estimation because of this examination, a portion of the highlights are dropped in the pre-include determination process after element preprocessing (Roh, Kim, Son & Kim, 2011), the datasets comparing to every situation is named

Figure 3. An overview of IoT attack

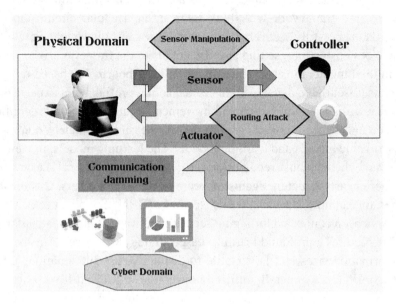

and blended to deliver a preprocessed dataset, comprising of a blend of assault and kindhearted information. These datasets are nourished into the profound learning calculation. Profound layers are prepared with regularization and dropout instruments, their weights are balanced and the IoT attack detection models are made.

Challenges of IoT

IoT gadgets have the capacity of information gathering, moving and handling in savvy applications. This information composes spread to numerous zones, for example, wellbeing, transportation, military and so on. Security of the touchy information, that is the greatest danger of IoT, comes into conspicuousness. This hazard establishes in two primary vulnerabilities. First; heterogeneous gadgets furthermore, between operable associations makes the administration of IoT frameworks more mind-boggling. Second; numerous gadgets have asset constraints, the absence of computational ability, low idleness. Second reason likewise makes the recognition of conceivable and obscure assaults to IoT gadgets troublesome (Lee & Lee, 2015). These reasons make the steering conventions powerless for instance, WSN comprise of hubs that incorporate at least one sensor which has minimal effort and constrained power. These sensors' goals are detecting nature and speaking with the base station, the base station has more vitality, correspondence and computational power than different hubs to guarantee the system between different hubs and end client. These capacities guarantee to check natural conditions by hubs. WSN has general attributes, for example, having modest number of hubs, control constrained hubs, dynamic system topology and huge size of sending. WSN has critical issues as delicate information insurance, protection and validation. Lamentably, the customary answers for these issues, as cryptography or key circulation conventions, couldn't be relevant due to the specified limitations of sensor devices. There are various steering conventions in WSN. Some of them based on asset mindfulness or vitality decrease; however none of them are hearty directing conventions against the IoT assaults, the system of IoT is shown in figure 4.

There are many sort of assaults to IoT that are physical assaults, observation assaults, DoS, get to assaults, assaults on security, digital wrongdoings, destructive assaults and SCADA. Steering assaults are performed at organize layer and they are more basic than other assaults, in other saying, they can be an initialize for rest of the assaults to IoT. RPL assaults can be analyzed under three classes relying upon the weakness which they expect to misuse. These classes are asset based, topology based and movement based. Asset based assaults intend to devour vitality, power and over-burden the memory. Topology-based assaults intend to upset the typical procedure of the system. This could cause that at least one hub are severed from the system. Moreover these assaults undermine the first topology of the system. Movement based assailant hubs point to join the system as a typical hub. At that point these assailants utilize the data of the organize activity to lead the assault directing

Figure 4. Systems of internet of things

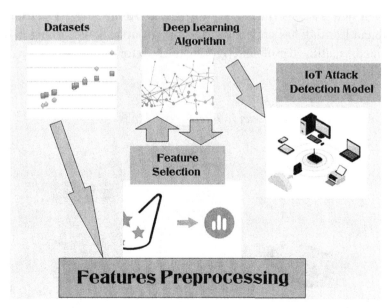

assaults happen at the system layer. IoT frameworks are for the most part powerless against directing assaults (Fattah, Sung, Ahn, Ryu & Yun, 2017). Among the most noteworthy directing assaults is diminished rank, hi surge and form number assaults.

Profound Learning-Based Detection of Steering Attacks

In this area, our profound learning-based steering assault recognition will be clarified and assess the significance of the highlights because of the dataset's record for choosing highlights to influence the figuring out how to process more exact. The highlights with too high and low significances are dropped with a specific end goal to avert over fitting. The datasets are standardized by a component standardization procedure to influence the preparation to process speedier (Subbulakshmi, 2017). The yield of the element preprocessing steps is preprocessed datasets which are taken into the profound learning calculation. The learning calculation is actualized by the assistance of Python libraries such as Keras, Scikit and Numpy. The learning procedure yields the IoT assault location show and tried the model against various test situations for more exact estimation of exactness and review.

Routing Attack Detection

Directing assaults can be distinguished by signature based arrangements and abnormality arrangements. Mark based arrangements are better against directing assaults that have little difference in its temperament. So abnormality based arrangements are superior to anything mark based arrangements about the recognition exactness of new assaults (Lachdhaf, Mazouzi & Abid, 2018). The examination that profound learning has preferable execution over shallow learning in the light of this brief data; utilized profound figuring out how to distinguish steering assaults as shown in figure 5.

Figure 5. Attacks detection model in Internet of Things

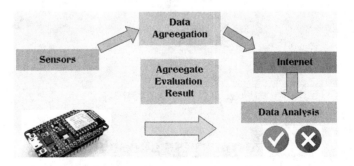

Neural Systems and Profound Learning

The fundamental engineering of neural systems goes back to the 1950s and the quintessence has not changed much since. A neural system contains interconnected layers of neurons. The knowledge of the network is stored in the weights of the connections between the nodes This hypothesis expresses that these basic neural systems can speak to each conceivable capacity at the point when given proper weights; it does, be that as it may, not state how to discover these parameters or what number of weights are required. Advances in innovation, for example, productive GPU usage and the accessibility of colossal marked datasets permitted to prepare progressively more profound and complex system designs. As of now to a great degree profound systems are the best in class procedure for picture furthermore, discourse acknowledgment for a more inside and out a review of the historical backdrop of neural systems what's more, profound realizing.

Resource Obliged Machine Learning

Both neural systems and other machine learning calculations and procedures require huge measures of assets, particularly memory and handling power. The preparation period of a neural system is the most computationally costly. The inclination drop calculation used to tune the weights of the system needs various disregards the preparation set and every cycle requires various framework increases and augmentations. A significant part of the examination on disseminated neural systems has in this way been centered around models for the circulated preparing of profound systems on immense measures of information. The most well-known case of this is the Google Map Belief framework, fit for preparing to great degree vast neural systems on 1000s of machines and 10,000s of CPU centers (Titanto & Dirgahayu, 2014). While the assets accessible when preparing a system are relatively boundless, the assessment of the prepared system is frequently done on a financial plan need to include the knowledge of a profound neural system to a compelled gadget. Here, inherent confinements on battery limit, handling force and memory, confine the size and many-sided quality of the system. Different works have proposed strategies to limit the cost while assessing a machine learning model.

Researchers show different topologies in which machine learning models can be joined to limit the cost while assessing the models. They portray how to develop a tree of classifiers where tests can take after an individual way. Every way takes a gander at particular highlights of the info information. A course can be viewed as a unique instance of tree topology. The method exhibit here varies from the past employment of a course topology in a machine learning model. Our course does not contain an arrangement of free element extractors but rather is prepared all in all, as one major model. By including an early-halting component in the shape of middle yield layers can reuse parts of the enormous model as a little model. As of late, different systems have been proposed to pack a prepared neural system, making it more reasonable for asset obliged gadgets, for example, cell phones, robots or rambles. The creators demonstrate that a shallow system can figure out how to mirror an extensive, profound system, adequately compacting the profound engineering in a little system with comparable properties. This enables the little system to get a superb execution at a much lower cost, both in memory required to store the weights and in preparing power expected to assess the system. It is additionally conceivable to pack a troupe of neural systems into one system to make a model more appropriate for dispersed assessment by presenting an early-halting system.

Image Segmentation and Ann

For the picture division errand, RCNN extricated two sorts of highlights for every locale: full district highlight and forefront highlight, and found that it could prompt better execution while linking them together as the area include. RCNN accomplished noteworthy execution enhancements because of utilizing the exceptionally discriminative CNN highlights. In any case, it likewise experiences three fundamental disadvantages for the division assignment, which roused huge research:

The element isn't good with the division undertaking. In spite of the fact that the CNN include has been over and again appeared to give higher execution when contrasted with ordinary hand-made highlights like SIFT and HOG, it isn't particularly intended for the picture division errand, RCNN used was in reality adjusted to characterize jumping boxes i.e., to separate full area highlights, making it imperfect to remove closer view highlights. To address this issue, they presented one extra system which was particularly tweaked on the area closer view and proposed to mutually prepare the two systems (Guo, Liu, Georgiou & Lew, 2017). For the proposition age, SDS supplanted particular hunt with MCG and announced better outcomes. Given pre-registered proposition, expected to consolidate the area characterization and semantic division together. It acquainted a differentiable locale with pixel layer which could delineate districts to picture pixels, making the entire system particularly calibrated for the picture division undertaking. On the off chance that can perform programmed picture explanation, at that point this can have both handy and hypothetical advantages. In exemplary protest acknowledgment outline a calculation which can investigate a sub-window inside the picture to distinguish a specific question. For instance, in the event that one has a great protest finder and a ten megapixel picture, at that point one would attempt to utilize the locator at all ten million areas in the picture which could without much of a stretch expect minutes to weeks contingent on the many-sided quality of the question identifier and the quantity of picture changes being viewed as, for example, turn and scale (Kashyap & Gautam, 2016).

On account of programmed picture division, rather than trying utilizing the protest finder at all pixel areas, now just need to attempt it for the quantity of fragments in the picture which is regularly somewhere in the range of 10 and 100 and surely requests of size not as much as the quantity of areas in a picture (Juneja & Kashyap, 2016). Moreover, one may likewise have a go at utilizing the question locator at various introductions which can likewise be mitigated by the picture division. The advantages are not constrained to only computational speed, but rather likewise to upgrading exactness. When one performs window-based question recognition, one regularly additionally needs to manage foundation clamor and distracters. At that point it will have naturally expelled the foundation commotion which will fundamentally expand the precision of the protest acknowledgment (Kashyap & Tiwari, 2018).

Moreover, programmed picture division can give us bits of knowledge into how the human visual framework can play out a similar assignment. It can give hypothetical defenses to the qualities and shortcomings of visual data frameworks; it can give us profound knowledge into the conditions when visual data frameworks won't have the capacity to effectively comprehend visual ideas or protests on the planet (Juneja & Kashyap, 2016). Robotized division can go past question acknowledgment and location in that it isn't required to know the protest or visual ideas heretofore. This can prompt real achievements as a rule PC vision since it enables new questions is found out by the framework. At the point when an obscure question is found and isn't ordered by the current database, at that point another passage can be made for the new obscure protest and this can prompt a genuinely broad PC vision framework (Kashyap & Tiwari, 2017). So the principle advantages of programmed picture division are as per the following: It can enhance computational effectiveness. It can enhance precision by taking out foundation commotion. It can give both hypothetical and profound bits of knowledge into both how visual frameworks function and what the constraints are. It can be broader than question location and acknowledgment.

CONCLUSION

This proposal is the evidence of the idea that profound learning can effectively manage IoT security. The steering assaults diminished rank assault; hi surge assault and form number assault are effortlessly distinguished by our proposed assault identification models. This proposition additionally fills an exceptionally vital hole of the steering assault location for IoT. The greatest issue of this sort of regions is the absence of datasets and furthermore the information isn't best when it has impossible substance. The significant preferred standpoint of this method is that it takes into consideration a runtime exchange off between precision and speed. An appropriate limit can be chosen in light of the required precision what's more, on the accessible assets as opposed to having one system with a settled precision and computational cost. The time expected to process one picture relies upon the multifaceted nature of the picture, though an ordinary usage of a neural system utilizes precisely the same for each picture paying little respect to the distinctive complexities. This idea of contingent calculation has been as of late proposed in different fills in too. The most important of these methodologies are the Big-Little neural systems where somewhat, quick to execute arrange is utilized to attempt to group an information test. The huge system is just utilized when the certainty of the little organize is not exactly a predefined limit. The falling engineering could be viewed as an extraordinary instance of a Big-Little system where a piece of the huge system is utilized as the little system, along these lines keeping away from the overhead of putting away two totally autonomous systems. Another favorable position of the course thought about the Big-Little design is that the calculations done by the principal organizer in the course are utilized by the last stages when required. The Big system in the Big-Little engineering, on the other hand, needs to begin again starting with no outside help when the little system can't characterize the info.

REFERENCES

Addo, P., Guegan, D., & Hassani, B. (2018). Credit Risk Analysis Using Machine and Deep Learning Models. *Risks*, 6(2), 38. doi:10.3390/risks6020038

Ahmed, A., & AL-Shaboti, M. (2018). Implementation of Internet of Things (IoT) Based on IPv6 over Wireless Sensor Networks. *International Journal of Sensors Wireless Communications And Control*, 7(2). doi:10.2174/221032790766617091 1145726

Arnold, T. (2017). kerasR: R Interface to the Keras Deep Learning Library. *The Journal Of Open Source Software*, 2(14), 296. doi:10.21105/joss.00296

Campbell, C., & Ying, Y. (2011). Learning with Support Vector Machines. *Synthesis Lectures On Artificial Intelligence And Machine Learning*, 5(1), 1–95. doi:10.2200/ S00324ED1V01Y201102AIM010

Carta, J., Cabrera, P., Matías, J., & Castellano, F. (2015). Comparison of feature selection methods using ANNs in MCP-wind speed methods. A case study. *Applied Energy*, 158, 490–507. doi:10.1016/j.apenergy.2015.08.102

Chae, J., & Quick, B. (2014). An Examination of the Relationship Between Health Information Use and Health Orientation in Korean Mothers: Focusing on the Type of Health Information. *Journal of Health Communication*, *20*(3), 275–284. doi:10.1080/10810730.2014.925016 PMID:25495418

Datta, S., & Das, S. (2015). Near-Bayesian Support Vector Machines for imbalanced data classification with equal or unequal misclassification costs. *Neural Networks*, *70*, 39–52. doi:10.1016/j.neunet.2015.06.005 PMID:26210983

Despotovic, V., & Tanikic, D. (2017). Sentiment Analysis of Microblogs Using Multilayer Feed-Forward Artificial Neural Networks. *Computer Information*, *36*(5), 1127–1142. doi:10.4149/cai_2017_5_1127

Fattah, S., Sung, N., Ahn, I., Ryu, M., & Yun, J. (2017). Building IoT Services for Aging in Place Using Standard-Based IoT Platforms and Heterogeneous IoT Products. *Sensors (Basel)*, *17*(10), 2311. doi:10.339017102311 PMID:29019964

Fu, R., Li, B., Gao, Y., & Wang, P. (2018). Visualizing and analyzing convolution neural networks with gradient information. *Neurocomputing*, *293*, 12–17. doi:10.1016/j.neucom.2018.02.080

Gomes, C., & Mayes, A. (2014). The kinds of information that support novel associative object priming and how these differ from those that support item priming. *Memory (Hove, England)*, *23*(6), 901–927. doi:10.1080/09658211.2014.937722 PMID:25051200

Guo, Y., Liu, Y., Georgiou, T., & Lew, M. (2017). A review of semantic segmentation using deep neural networks. *International Journal of Multimedia Information Retrieval*, *7*(2), 87–93. doi:10.100713735-017-0141-z

Hong, S., & Lee, Y. (2013). CPU Parallel Processing and GPU-accelerated Processing of UHD Video Sequence using HEVC. *Journal Of Broadcast Engineering*, *18*(6), 816–822. doi:10.5909/JBE.2013.18.6.816

Jang, Y. (2015). Big Data, Business Analytics, and IoT: The Opportunities and Challenges for Business. *Journal of Information Systems*, *24*(4), 139–152. doi:10.5859/KAIS.2015.24.4.139

Jha, D., & Kwon, G. (2017). Alzheimer's Disease Detection Using Sparse Autoencoder, Scale Conjugate Gradient and Softmax Output Layer with Fine Tuning. *International Journal Of Machine Learning And Computing*, *7*(1), 13–17. doi:10.18178/ijmlc.2017.7.1.612

Juneja, P., & Kashyap, R. (2016). Energy based methods for medical image segmentation. *International Journal of Computers and Applications*, *146*(6), 22–27. doi:10.5120/ijca2016910808

Juneja, P., & Kashyap, R. (2016). Optimal approach for CT image segmentation using improved energy based method. *International Journal of Control Theory and Applications*, *9*(41), 599–608.

Kashyap, R., & Gautam, P. (2016). Fast level set method for segmentation of medical images. In *Proceedings of the International Conference on Informatics and Analytics (ICIA-16)*. ACM. 10.1145/2980258.2980302

Kashyap, R., & Piersson, A. (2018). Big Data Challenges and Solutions in the Medical Industries. In Handbook of Research on Pattern Engineering System Development for Big Data Analytics. IGI Global. doi:10.4018/978-1-5225-3870-7.ch001

Kashyap, R., & Tiwari, V. (2017). Energy-based active contour method for image segmentation. *International Journal of Electronic Healthcare*, *9*(2–3), 210–225. doi:10.1504/IJEH.2017.083165

Kashyap, R., & Tiwari, V. (2018). Active contours using global models for medical image segmentation. *International Journal of Computational Systems Engineering*, *4*(2/3), 195. doi:10.1504/IJCSYSE.2018.091404

Kim, D., Jeong, Y., & Kim, S. (2017). Data-Filtering System to Avoid Total Data Distortion in IoT Networking. *Symmetry*, *9*(1), 16. doi:10.3390ym9010016

Koakutsu, S. (2018). Deep Learning - Current Situation and Expectation of Deep Learning and IoT. *The Journal Of The Institute Of Electrical Engineers Of Japan*, *138*(5), 270–271. doi:10.1541/ieejjournal.138.270

Ksiezopolski, B. (2012). QoP-ML: Quality of protection modelling language for cryptographic protocols. *Computers & Security*, *31*(4), 569–596. doi:10.1016/j.cose.2012.01.006

Lachdhaf, S., Mazouzi, M., & Abid, M. (2018). Secured AODV Routing Protocol for the Detection and Prevention of Black Hole Attack in VANET. *Advanced Computing: An International Journal*, *9*(1), 1-14. doi:10.5121/acij.2018.9101

Lee, I., & Lee, K. (2015). The Internet of Things (IoT): Applications, investments, and challenges for enterprises. *Business Horizons*, *58*(4), 431–440. doi:10.1016/j.bushor.2015.03.008

Li, H., Ota, K., & Dong, M. (2018). Learning IoT in Edge: Deep Learning for the Internet of Things with Edge Computing. *IEEE Network*, *32*(1), 96–101. doi:10.1109/MNET.2018.1700202

Mazzei, D., Baldi, G., Montelisciani, G., & Fantoni, G. (2018). A full stack for quick prototyping of IoT solutions. *Annales des Télécommunications*, *73*(7-8), 439–449. doi:10.100712243-018-0644-5

Rayner, M. (2011). The curriculum for children with severe and profound learning difficulties at Stephen Hawking School. *Support for Learning*, *26*(1), 25–32. doi:10.1111/j.1467-9604.2010.01471.x

Roh, Y., Kim, J., Son, J., & Kim, M. (2011). Efficient construction of histograms for multidimensional data using quad-trees. *Decision Support Systems*, *52*(1), 82–94. doi:10.1016/j.dss.2011.05.006

Senov, A. (2015). Improving Distributed Stochastic Gradient Descent Estimate via Loss Function Approximation. *IFAC-Papersonline*, *48*(25), 292–297. doi:10.1016/j.ifacol.2015.11.103

Sezer, O., Dogdu, E., & Ozbayoglu, A. (2018). Context-Aware Computing, Learning, and Big Data in Internet of Things: A Survey. *IEEE Internet Of Things Journal*, *5*(1), 1–27. doi:10.1109/JIOT.2017.2773600

Subbulakshmi, T. (2017). A learning-based hybrid framework for detection and defence of DDoS attacks. *International Journal of Internet Protocol Technology*, *10*(1), 51. doi:10.1504/IJIPT.2017.083036

Titanto, M., & Dirgahayu, T. (2014). Google Maps-Based Geospatial Application Framework with Custom Layers Management. *Applied Mechanics And Materials, 513-517*, 822-826. Retrieved from www.scientific.net/amm.513-517.822

Vlajic, N., & Zhou, D. (2018). IoT as a Land of Opportunity for DDoS Hackers. *Computer*, *51*(7), 26–34. doi:10.1109/MC.2018.3011046

Vu, H., Gomez, F., Cherelle, P., Lefeber, D., Nowé, A., & Vanderborght, B. (2018). ED-FNN: A New Deep Learning Algorithm to Detect Percentage of the Gait Cycle for Powered Prostheses. *Sensors (Basel)*, *18*(7), 2389. doi:10.339018072389 PMID:30041421

Weber, R. (2010). Internet of Things – New security and privacy challenges. *Computer Law & Security Review*, *26*(1), 23–30. doi:10.1016/j.clsr.2009.11.008

Yang, S., Tiejun, L., Maunder, R., & Hanzo, L. (2013). From Nominal to True A Posteriori Probabilities: An Exact Bayesian Theorem Based Probabilistic Data Association Approach for Iterative MIMO Detection and Decoding. *IEEE Transactions on Communications*, *61*(7), 2782–2793. doi:10.1109/TCOMM.2013.053013.120427

Yao, S., Zhao, Y., Zhang, A., Hu, S., Shao, H., Zhang, C., ... Abdelzaher, T. (2018). Deep Learning for the Internet of Things. *Computer*, *51*(5), 32–41. doi:10.1109/MC.2018.2381131

KEY TERMS AND DEFINITIONS

Artificial Intelligence: Computerized reasoning is insight shown by machines, rather than the characteristic knowledge showed by people and different creatures. In software engineering, AI =is characterized as the investigation of "keen specialists": any gadget that sees its condition and takes activities that amplify its risk of effectively accomplishing its goals. Colloquially, the expression "manmade brainpower" is connected when a machine impersonates "subjective" capacities that people connect with other human personalities, for example, "learning" and "critical thinking."

Artificial Neural Network: An artificial neural network (ANN) is a data handling worldview that is roused by the way organic sensory systems, for example, the cerebrum, process data. The key component of this worldview is the novel structure of the data handling framework. It is made out of an extensive number of exceptionally interconnected preparing components (neurones) working as one to take care of particular issues. ANNs, similar to individuals, learn by case. An ANN is designed for a particular application, for example, design acknowledgment or information grouping, through a learning procedure. Learning in natural frameworks includes changes in accordance with the synaptic associations that exist between the neurons.

IoT: The internet of things (IoT) is the system of physical gadgets, vehicles, home apparatuses, and different things installed with hardware, programming, sensors, actuators, and availability which empowers these things to associate and trade information, making open doors for more straightforward coordination of the physical world into pc based frameworks, bringing about proficiency upgrades, financial advantages, and lessened human intercession.

Chapter 7

Comprehensive Overview of Neural Networks and Its Applications in Autonomous Vehicles

Jay Rodge
Illinois Institute of Technology, USA

Swati Jaiswal
iD https://orcid.org/0000-0001-9671-534X
VIT University, India

ABSTRACT

Deep learning and Artificial intelligence (AI) have been trending these days due to the capability and state-of-the-art results that they provide. They have replaced some highly skilled professionals with neural network-powered AI, also known as deep learning algorithms. Deep learning majorly works on neural networks. This chapter discusses about the working of a neuron, which is a unit component of neural network. There are numerous techniques that can be incorporated while designing a neural network, such as activation functions, training, etc. to improve its features, which will be explained in detail. It has some challenges such as overfitting, which are difficult to neglect but can be overcome using proper techniques and steps that have been discussed. The chapter will help the academician, researchers, and practitioners to further investigate the associated area of deep learning and its applications in the autonomous vehicle industry.

DOI: 10.4018/978-1-5225-7955-7.ch007

INTRODUCTION

Neural Networks has been the one of the buzzwords from last 5 years. Neural Networks are used in Deep Learning (Yoshua Bengio 2015) which is a sub field of Machine Learning, and tries to solves complex problems which cannot be solve by traditional Machine Learning models and algorithms. It has rose to the popu;arity in last 5 years mainly because of the computing power and the data available. Neural Network require lots of Computing power to function since it has many mathematical operation which needs to be performed simultaneously. The image recognition problem was a big problem, it requires features to be detected such as curves, shapes etc., which was not possible by traditional machine learning algorithms. Neural Networks are good at recognizing the features by itself. In the given figure, it can be seen that, the neural network first tries to detect edges, then it tries to detect complex shapes using those edges, and then the objects get detected. For example, Convolutional Neural Networks or CNNs (Yann LeCun, 1994) is now used everywhere for object detection, video recognition, Natural Language Processing(NLP) (Wenpeng Yin 2017) and recommender systems.

Also, the results are very better when used Neural Networks as compared to Machine Learning model. And it takes lesser time to do the task once, the neural networks are trained (learning through examples). This characteristics of learning through examples has made the Autonomous Vehicles possible. There are many situations in which the severals controls has to be applied. Manually programming autonomous vehicles is not possible since it would take lot of time. Deep learning is the best possible solution since it learns the behavior through real world driving examples and has a ability get better over a period of time.

Figure 1. Detecting features
(Honglak Lee, 2011)

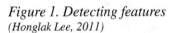

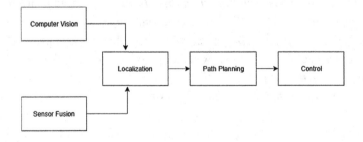

Neural Networks

Neural networks are also known as Artificial Neural Network(ANNs). Neural Networks generally tries to mimic the capability of neurons present in a human brain. A unit component of ANN is called a Neuron. Neurons are also called as a Unit or a Node. Multiple neurons connected in form of layers, construct a Neural Network. Mathematically, a neuron is a function which takes in a set of inputs and processes it through a set of functions. A typical structure of a neuron looks like:

A Neuron is represented mathematically as,

$$z = w1x_1 + w2x2_+ w_3x3 +_b y = f(z)$$

Here x1, x2, an$_d$ x3 are bei$_n$g multiplied by the weights w1, w2, an$_d$ w3 respect$_i$vely using matrix multiplication, and then added by a bias matrix 'b' (The weight matrices are initialized randomly and the bias matrices are initialized by a zero vector). Then, the resultant is passed through a Activation Function.

Activation Function

Neuron produces output based on a function called Activation Function. It takes a input and processes it using the mathematical function, then producing the output. Each neuron in the neural network uses Activation Function. It has There are various

Figure 2. Basic neuron

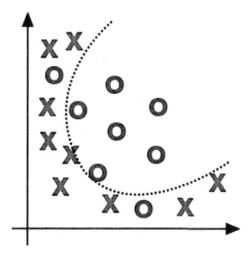

types of Automatic Functions which are used for different purposes. Most popular activation functions that are used in practice are as follows:

1. Sigmoid
2. Tanh
3. ReLU
4. Softmax

Sigmoid

The sigmoid activation is used when probability is required for a prediction. Also, it functions between the value of 0 and 1, which makes it idle choice for predicting probability as an output.

Sigmoid function is represented by:

$$f(z) = \frac{1}{1 + e^{-z}}$$

Tanh: Hyperbolic Tangent

Tanh is a modified form of Sigmoid, and performs better than Sigmoid. The range of Tanh is (-1, 1). Tanh is also sigmoidal or s-shaped like the sigmoid function.

It is presented by:

$$f(x) = \frac{e^{-2x}}{1 + e^{-2x}}$$

ReLU: Rectified Linear Unit

ReLU is the most used activation function by the practitioners as well as researchers and the simplest non linear activation function. Also, it is less computationally heavy as compared to Sigmoid and Hyperbolic tangent due to less mathematic operations since it is only has to choose a maximum value between two values.

ReLU is represented by:

$$(z) = \max(0, z)$$

Figure 3. Sigmoid Activation Function

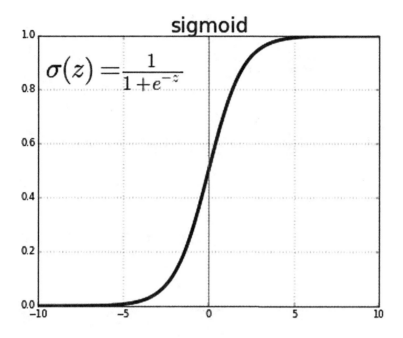

Figure 4. Hyperbolic tangent

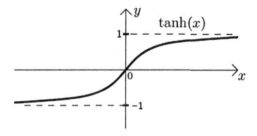

Softmax

Sigmoid function is used when we want to predict from two classes. But if there are more than two classes then Softmax Activation function is used. The output of this function is categorical probability distribution. Basically, it provides the probability of the classes and helps in predicting from a categorical data.

$$f(z)_j = \frac{e^{z_j}}{\sum_{k=1}^{K} e^{z_k}}$$

Figure 5. Rectified Linear Unit Function

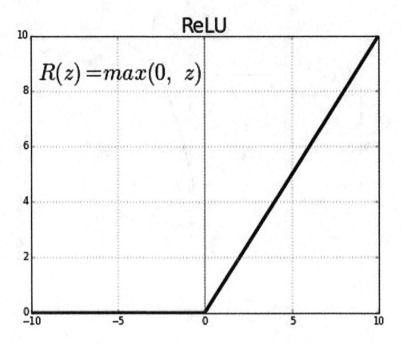

$$R(z) = max(0, \ z)$$

where z is a vector of the inputs to the output/final layer and j refers to the output nodes (j=1, ..,K). For example, In hand written digit classification from images, since there are 10 digits(0-9) there will be 10 output nodes in the output layer. Softmax Activation function will give a probability for each output layer node i.e. for each digit, and the sum of probabilities of all the nodes in output layer will add upto 1, therefore giving a probability of that particular category.

The Softmax Function can be used for any number of classes or categories. Therefore, it is mostly used Computer Vision, object detection algorithms where are many possible objects.

Like human brain, neurons are inter-connected in form of layers. The layers are categorized into three types:

- Input Layer
- Hidden Layer
- Output Layer

The input layers generally consist of the input data. The hidden layers perform the mathematical computations based on the input and activation function in each layer. The values computed by the hidden are then finally passed to the output layer which can one neuron or several neurons based on the application. The neural network having more than one hidden is called Deep Neural Network. Adding more hidden layers in neural network can improve the results significantly, but also requires huge computation power to train the neural networks.

The architecture of the neural network has to be designed considering the use case. We have to design the architecture which can include adding number of hidden layers, how many neurons should be there in each layers.

Training the Neural Network

This is the most difficult part of the Deep Learning. Because the training has to be performed on large and processed dataset. The dataset should be large enough so that the neural network can recognize a pattern and learn them. And it should also be cleaned i.e. it should not have any false positives or false negatives, which could affect the training and thereby affecting predictions and result.

The second most important part is the computation power. Deep Neural Network requires huge computation power depending on the number of hidden layers.

Challenges

- Data
- Overfitting
- Hyperparameter tuning
- High Performance systems

Figure 6. Structure of a neural network

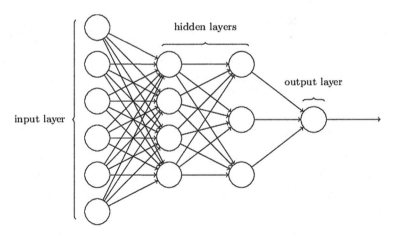

Data

Neural Networks generally require large amount of data to train. The data or dataset has to be large enough so that the model can find patterns and learn them. Less data can affect the performance of the model which yields less accuracy.

For example: Personal Assistants or speech recognition systems are trained large amount of data to build a system with higher accuracy since such systems have to work with more than one language.

The size of the data can be from terabytes to petabytes.

Also, the data should be evenly distributed, for example it should have almost same number of examples for true and false positives. Evenly distributed data helps the deep learning model generalize better with great accuracy.

Overfitting

Sometimes, there is a big difference in accuracy in training set and the testing test. This generally happens in complex algorithms and models, the reason being it memorizes the data instead of finding and then learning the pattern. Generally, a good deep learning model does not have a much difference in accuracy found in training set and testing set. If the difference is large then there's a problem with the deep learning model. For example, if the training accuracy is 90% and 60% on the unseen data, then this is causing due to overfitting.

Overfitting can be avoided using this popular Regularization techniques which are:

- **Dropout Layer:** Adding Dropout layer can significantly reduce the overfitting problem. Dropout layer mainly randomly removes or disables some nodes in the network at each training iteration. This generally helps in generalizing and optimizing the weights of the neurons and provides great results. It's mainly used in Convolutional Neural Networks.
- **Data Augmentation:** Sometimes, the reason for overfitting could be due to the less training examples for the algorithm to learn from. In this, the existing data could be modified slightly and added to the dataset. For Example: A image in the dataset could be cropped, rotated slightly etc. This will increase the number of the examples and thus preventing overfitting.

Hyperparameter Tuning

Hyperparameter tuning is another challenge in deep learning. The deep learning algorithms have lots of parameters which need to be tuned to get better accuracy. The slight difference in the parameter can yield huge change in terms of accuracy and performance.

Figure 7. Overfitting

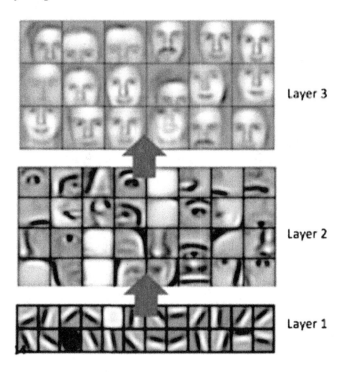

Figure 8. Dropout
(Hinton et al. 2014)

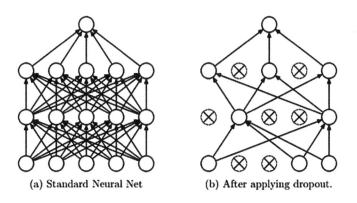

For Example: One of the Hyperparameter, known as learning rate (Hyperparameter to control how fast the neural network adjust the weights with respect to the loss) has huge impact when changed by decimals, as well as affects the time taken to the train the deep learning model.

Figure 9. Data augmentation

High Performance Systems

Deep Learning mainly consist of complex mathematical operations like matrix multiplication etc. This mathematical operation requires great processing power. Therefore, Graphics Processing Units (GPUs) are now used for training neural network as it has higher number of cores as compared to Central Processing Unit(CPU). The challenge here is GPUs are expensive and consumes lots of power, on the other hand, CPUs take lot of time to train as it has lesser number of cores.

APPLICATIONS

The research in autonomous vehicle has steadily increased due to the data available as well as the computing power available to process that data. Neural Networks algorithms are now being used in the Self Driving Cars mainly for Lane Detection, Object detection, and driving and making decisions based on the situation. An autonomous vehicle works as shown in the figure.

Figure 10. Working of an Autonomous Vehicle

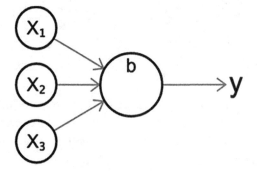

Basically it uses, Computer Vision to look around and detects objects in the environment mainly through camera. Sensor Fusion helps in getting the real time understanding of the environment using the sensors like lasers, LIDAR etc. Localization is used to get real location of the environment using the information from computer vision and sensor fusion. Path Planning uses the information, that is previously generated by Localization, and tries to decide or make a path based on the information and destination. Finally, control is used to apply the control on the hardware like steering wheel, brakes etc.

Mostly Neural Networks are used in Computer Vision and Path Planning part of the Autonomous Vehicle. Detecting objects in the environment is tricky, since there can be various kinds of objects which needs be detected and considered by the system while driving. Path Planning involves deciding and making a path for the autonomous vehicle considering the traffic rules, other vehicles, pedestrians etc.

Computer Vision for Autonomous Vehicle

Autonomous vehicle researchers and manufacturers are using object detection algorithms with the help of Computer Vision to view the outside the world as humans do. YOLO (Joseph et al. 2016) is the most used object detection algorithms. YOLO [You Only Look Once] can detect various objects including vehicles, human, traffic signs as shown in the Figure 11 which are necessary for the system to identify. YOLO works on Convolutional Neural Network which has 24 convolutional layers and 2 fully connected layers. Inspired by YOLO, the author Bichen Wu et al.(2017) made a SqueezeDet which works on low power and memory specially for Autonomous

Figure 11. Object Detection using YOLO

Driving. SINet(Xiaowei Hu et al. 2018) i.e. Scale Intensive Convolutional Neural Network for Fast Vehicle Detection also an object detection algorithm which solves some issue of large variance of scale of the objects and vehicles.

Path Planning for Autonomous Vehicle

Path planning is important part, as it finds the shortest as well as optimal path between two points ensuring less turning, less braking, and avoiding traffic. Path Planning is done based on the information collected by the camera, sensors and localization and accordingly takes control. There can be various situation in which the system needs to take decisions like lane changing, stopping when a pedestrian crosses the roads etc., this can be achieved by training the neural network with real human driving behavior. Neural Networks tracks the changes to generalize and learn what a human driver does on various obstacle like braking, overtaking etc. Due to this Neural Networks are trained on the large datasets of human driving behavior.

End to End Learning for Self-Driving Cars

The author Mariusz Bojarski et al. (2016) trained a Convolutional Neural Network which took pixels from the front facing camera in the car directly and corresponding steering commands as labels. The author trained the network with 100 hours of driving data. The results were interesting, as the car was able to operate in several conditions like on highways, local road as well as in sunny, and rainy weather. This was done without explicitly training about the road lanes, pedestrians, lane lines etc. They used NVIDIA DRIVE™ PX (computer system specially designed for the Self-Driving cars) which was connected to Cameras in the front, Storage as well as the Steering wheel to record the steering wheel angle corresponding to the camera footage.

Figure 12. Path planning

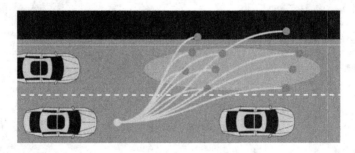

Figure 13. Data collection system
(Mariusz Bojarski et al. 2016)

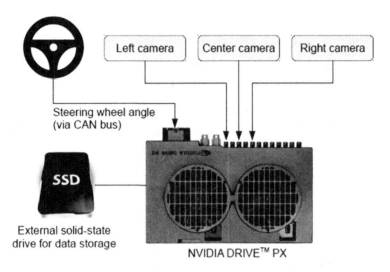

CONCLUSION

In the last few years, deep learning has been largely used in almost all possible areas due to the data available right now for research as well as the Computing power available to process the big data. It is trying now trying to automate the tasks which requires intelligence and with great accuracy. The Autonomous vehicles are the best practical application of the deep learning algorithms as it requires quick decisions to be made. The research by Mariusz Bojarski et al. (2016) in End-to-End Learning for Self Driving Cars shows the potential of Neural Network which can learn complex functions without being explicitly programmed which is much better than programming manually. The research in the autonomous vehicles industry has been tremendous in the last few years and keeps getting better, however there's still some issues which needs to be solved considering safety of the passengers and its environment such as response times during accidents and emergency situations. This is reason autonomous vehicles haven't been commercialized yet. But with continues research and training it can improve over time and then possibly will be seen on public roads.

REFERENCES

Abraham, A. (2005). 129: Artificial Neural Networks. Handbook of Measuring System Design.

Chen, Z., & Huang, X. (2017). End-to-end learning for lane keeping of self-driving cars. *IEEE Intelligent Vehicles Symposium (IV)*. 10.1109/IVS.2017.7995975

Cogswell, M., Ahmed, F., Girshick, R., Zitnick, L., & Batra, D. (2015). *Reducing Overfitting in Deep Networks by Decorrelating Representations*. arXiv:1511.06068

Heylen, J., Iven, S., De Brabandere, B., Jose, O. M., Van Gool, L., & Tuytelars, T. (2018). From Pixels to Actions: Learning to Drive a Car with Deep Neural Networks. *IEEE Winter Conference on Applications of Computer Vision*. 10.1109/WACV.2018.00072

Hu, Xu, Xiao, Chen, He, Qin, & Heng. (2018). SINet: A Scale-insensitive Convolutional Neural Network for Fast Vehicle Detection. *IEEE Transactions on Intelligent Transportation Systems*.

Kroumov & Yu. (2011). *Neural Networks Based Path Planning and Navigation of Mobile Robots*. DOI: doi:10.5772/26889

Le Cun, Y., & Bengio, Y. (1994). Word-level Training of a Handwritten Word Recognizer Based on Convolutional Neural Networks. *Proc. of the International Conference on Pattern Recognition*, 88-92.

LeCun, Bengio, & Hinton. (2015). Deep learning. *Nature, 521*(7553), 436.

LeCun, Y., & Bengio, Y. (1994). Word-level training of a handwritten word recognizer based on convolutional neural networks. In *Proc. of the International Conference on Pattern Recognition* (pp. 88-92). IEEE.

Lee, H., Grosse, R., Ranganath, R., & Ng, A. Y. (2011). Unsupervised Learning of Hierarchical Representations with Convolutional Deep Belief Networks. Communication of the ACM, 10(10).

Mochamad, V. G. A., Hindersah, H., & Prihatmanto, A. S. (2017). Implementation of Vehicle Detection Algorithm for Self-Driving Car on Toll Road Cipularang using Python Language. *4th International Conference on Electric Vehicular Technology (ICEVT)*.

Redmon, J., Divvala, S., Girshick, R., & Farhadi, A. (2016). You Only Look Once: Unified, Real-Time Object Detection. *IEEE Conference on Computer Vision and Pattern Recognition (CVPR)*. 10.1109/CVPR.2016.91

Redmon, J., Divvala, S., Girshick, R., & Farhadi, A. (2016). *You Only Look Once: Unified, Real-Time Object Detection.* arXiv:1506.02640

Srivastava, Hinton, & Krizhevsky, Sutskever, & Salakhutdinov. (2014). Dropout: A Simple Way to Prevent Neural Networks from Overfitting. *Journal of Machine Learning Research, 15*, 1929-1958.

Tariq, S., & Choi, H. (2016). Controlled Parking for Self-Driving Cars. *2016 IEEE International Conference on Systems, Man, and Cybernetics.*

Wu, B., Wan, A., Iandola, F., Jin, P. H., & Keutzer, K. (2016). *SqueezeDet: Unified, Small, Low power Fully Convolutional Neural Networks for Real-Time Object Detection for Autonomous Driving.* arXiv:1612.01051

Yin, W., Kann, K., Yu, M., & Schütze, H. (n.d.). *Comparative Study of CNN and RNN for Natural Language Processing.* arXiv:1702.01923

Chapter 8
Network Security Approaches in Distributed Environment

Keshav Sinha

ⓘ https://orcid.org/0000-0003-1053-3911
Birla Institute of Technology, India

Partha Paul
Birla Institute of Technology, India

Amritanjali
Birla Institute of Technology, India

ABSTRACT

Distributed computing is one of the thrust areas in the field of computer science, but when we are concerned about security a question arises, "Can it be secure?" From this note, the authors start this chapter. In the distributed environment, when the system is connected to a network, and the operating system firewall is active, it will take care of all the authentication and access control requests. There are several traditional cryptographic approaches which implement authentication and access control. The encryption algorithms such as Rijndael, RSA, A3, and A5 is used for providing data secrecy. Some of the key distribution techniques have been discussed such as Diffie Hellman key exchange for symmetric key, and random key generation (LCG) technique is used in red-black tree traversal which provides the security of the digital contents. The chapter deals with the advanced versions of the network security techniques and cryptographic algorithms for the security of multimedia contents over the internet.

DOI: 10.4018/978-1-5225-7955-7.ch008

INTRODUCTION

Cryptology is defined from Greek word kryptós and lógos which means hidden word. Cryptography and Cryptanalysis is an amalgamation of cryptology. The art of hiding the readable data (according to the perception of a human being) into a non-readable format is known as cryptography. Cryptanalysis is the opposite of cryptography, where it converts the non-readable data into readable form, without knowing the algorithm of encryption. The word cryptography is originated from the Greek word "kryptós", which means the art of writing or solving codes secretly. The first citation of the cryptography technique was in the form of hieroglyphics, dated back to 1900 B.C, that is during the time of Egyptian. In the year 1799, a French soldier found a black basalt slab, which was inscribed with the ancient script. The stone was in the form of irregular shape which contains three different types of scripts (i) Greek, (ii) Egyptian hieroglyphics, and (iii) Egyptian demotic. In the year 1790-1832, Jean-Francois Champollion was the first person who cracked the hieroglyphics code by using a Greek guide. Since the year 1802, the Rosetta stone has been kept in the British Museum, London. Modern day's cryptography is very different from ancient cryptography. Now the encryption algorithm is very complicated and require huge computational time. Cryptography algorithm uses the number of shift rounds and XOR operation for decipherment. Due to the advancement in computing power, the future cryptographic algorithm works on quantum computation speed allowing use of large key size. The DNA cryptography is one of the kind of cryptographic technique which uses the perplexing genetic data for hiding and improve the genetic secrecy in the sequencing process. The term cryptology is offend used in the field of data transmission and storage.

Principles of Security

There are several types of security attacks are performed by hackers in real life. To tackle those attacks, there are sets of security principles which will help us to understand and find the possible solutions to those problems which is caused by the attackers. There are six principles of cryptography and security.

1. **Confidentiality:** It specifies that only the sender and the authentic user should be able to access the data. No third party will access the data without authorization.
2. **Authentication:** It is the mechanism to establishing a secure (authentic) connection between sender and receiver. It is mainly used in electronic transactions, and network handshaking.

3. **Data Integrity:** When the sender sends a message to the recipient, and in between the communication channel the contents of a message is lost. Then it say that the integrity of the message is lost.
4. **Non-Repudiation:** This refers to the situation when a user sends the data and at a later stage it denies.
5. **Access Control:** It defines as what to access and who has given the right to access the data.
6. **Availability:** It specifies that all resources are available to the legitimate users at all time.

Cryptographic Techniques

Cryptography provides a secure data communication environment for the user. Where Encryption and decryption play a major role. Encryption algorithm uses a key to transform an original message into an encrypted cipher message. If the key is the same for encryption and decryption then the algorithm will always transform the plaintext into the ciphertext. The message is secure if an attacker cannot determine any properties of plaintext or key. There are different types of key selection techniques such as:

1. **Symmetric-Key Cryptography:** In this, both sender and receiver use a single key for encryption and decryption of the original message.
2. **Public-Key Cryptography:** It is also known as asymmetric key cryptography. Where it uses a pair of keys for encryption and decryption.
3. **Hash Functions:** In modern cryptography, the algorithms do not use keys for encryption. Instead of that, they generate a hash value for encryption.

Different researchers have developed several language sets for cryptography. In general, the english alphabet is used which consists of *26* letters for encryption and decryption.

Let us see, how the cryptography algorithm works. To encrypt the message (*M*) with an ASCII alphabet (*n*) the encryption work as:

Original Message (*M*): It consists of several sets of sub-messages { m_0, m_1, ..., m_{n-1} }, where

m = Finite set of letters

n = 2^r, fixed length sequences.

n = 2^7 for the ASCII alphabet and *n* = *26* for uppercase Latin letters (*A*, *B*, ..., *Z*).

This is the basic example, how cryptography is work.

Motivation and Purpose of the Work

The motivation of these work is to secure any format of multimedia data. Because the multimedia data is used in the various fields such as education, military, business, and entertainment. Therefore, it is essential to secure the sensitive data before transmission or distribution. An access right control method is used to authenticate the users and secure the data which undergoes various attacks during the transmission process. There are various requirements and challenges present in the field of multimedia security while sending any type of multimedia data through the communication channels. Users have to face different levels of security challenges such as:

• Lots of hackers are present on the web presently, who may use the digital content in illegal activities.
• Replication of digital content is very common problems for users and Digital Right Management (DRM) association.
• Digital Data piracy is another problem for any digital data distributer industries.
• Huge amount of data's are generated by satellites. And it required a secure channel to transmit that data to the authentic government.

These are the some of the challenges and problems of the multimedia security. There are series of problem present in cyber data security, and it will not be able to cover all the problems. And to provide security of multimedia there is no algorithm available in this world, which ensures that the security of all the type of multimedia data. Also, there are not any common algorithm present which provides security to all the types of multimedia data. So, there is a need to find the effective methods which can be used to solve the above problem. It should provide robustness and effectiveness to securely send the data through the communication channels.

BACKGROUND

When the term security of data is framed, then it first concerned about attacks. From a technical point of view, attacks are divided into two types (i) Active Attacks and (ii) Passive Attacks. In Active Attack, the attacker will modify the data and creates a wrong message, which is sent to the receiver side. This type of attack is very difficult to detect, and it causes serious harm in terms of financial and personal data losses in real life. There is a very familiar attack know as a DoS attack, where the attacker sends the multiple requests to the server which creates congestion for the legitimate request. Now, in Passive Attack the attacker just watches the network traffic and collect the important information from that. This type of attack doesn't harm the system, but it can track all the personal information form the system. From several years different techniques was developed by different researches to defend against active and passive attacks. In the year 1976, Whitefield Diffie and Martin Hellman proposed a first key exchange algorithm which works as a public-key system based on the Discrete Logarithm Problem (DLP). It is so powerful that, when two parties agree on the symmetric key exchange, and that time the attack will happen, then the attacker will not able to get the key or any information. In Table. 1 shows the Diffie Hellman key exchange steps.

1.   Find a large prime number p.
2.   Find the primitive element α of Z_p^* or subgroup of Z_p^*.

Therefore, the session key ($k_{Session}$) $= k_{S,R} = \alpha^{a_R \cdot a_S} = \alpha^{a_R \cdot a_S}$ mod p.

This system is work as public key cryptography, if the attacker tries to get the information then it should know (α, p, b_S, and b_R). The problem of this algorithm is the length of the key if the size of 'p' is less than 512 bits then the performance of the algorithm is reduced and there is a chance that the attacker will get the data. If the size of 'p' is greater than 2^{1024} bits, then it provides more security in the transmission. In the year 1977, one year after the Diffie Hellman algorithm, a new cryptosystem has been developed by three scientist name as Ron Rivest, Adi Shamir, and Leonard Adleman also know for RSA cryptosystem. RSA was first developed in the MIT lab in 1977, it is the most popular public-key cryptosystem. The main application of RSA methods is in encryption and in the digital signature. The working principle of RSA is on prime factorization. After that, several techniques were developed by different researchers which provide security in a distributed environment. J. Meyer and F. Gadegast (1995) implement the DES algorithm for MPEG-1 video, where it uses the stream header, DC/AC coefficient, frames, and blocks. The algorithm works on streaming videos and it provides complete encryption to the video. Spanos and Maples (1995) introduced a selective encryption technique which encrypts the

Table 1. Diffie Hellman key exchange

Sender		Receiver
Pick $k_{(private)\,S} = a_S \in \{2, 3, ..., \text{p-1}\}$ Compute $k_{(public)\,S} = b_S = \alpha^{a_S}$ mod p		Pick $k_{(private)\,R} = a_S \in \{2, 3, ..., \text{p-1}\}$ Compute $k_{(public)\,S} = b_R = \alpha^{a_R}$ mod p
Send b_S to the receiver	$b_S \rightarrow$	
	$b_R \leftarrow$	Send b_R to the sender.
$k_{SR} = b_R^{a_S} = (\alpha^{a_R})^{a_S}$		$k_{SR} = b_S^{a_R} = (\alpha^{a_S})^{a_R}$

intra-frame, video header and MPEG format code using the DES algorithm. Agi and Gong (1996) implement the Aegis Algorithm for MPEG video transmission. The algorithm works on video frames. The time complexity of Aegis algorithm is very less. Jakimoski and Kocarev (2001) introduce the chaotic block Cipher technique. It takes the byte operations for linear and differential probabilities of the original text. Soyjaudah et al. (2004) implements the Rijndael Algorithm for voice encryption. Using 128-bit block cipher for a speech on GSM network provides a high level of security and less time complexity for encryption. Yang et al. (2008) implements an S-modem based on Linear Predictive Coding (LPC) technique for encrypted speech transition on a GSM channel. It is used to transmit the encrypted data on GSM networks with sufficient accuracy. Zhang (2010) discuss in their research about security, trust and risk of multimedia. Zhu et al. (2011) introduce a novel multimedia cloud computing technique which provide storage and quality of service (QoS) for a distributed environment. To archive high, QoS for multimedia services author proposed a media-edge cloud (MEC) architecture. It uses the central processing unit (CPU), and graphics processing unit (GPU) for storage. And it also supports parallel processing and QoS for various devices. Gadea et al. (2011) introduced the cloud-based software architecture for multimedia which works on the web browser and it allows to collaborate over webcam chat for sharing of multimedia content in real-time. Diaz-Sanchez et al. (2011) introduce a media cloud. The working of media cloud is on UPnP or DLNA which distribute the media beyond the boundaries of the local network. Zhang (2011) present the survey on Digital Rights Management Ecosystem and how the multimedia data usage controls. The survey deals with risk free environment for multimedia content. Verma and Singh (2012) provide the review on Twofish, Rijndael, and RC6 algorithm. The study provides the comparison and performance evaluation of all three algorithms. Chumchu et al. (2012) implements an RC4 algorithm which provides simple and cheap end-to-end voice encryption over GSM-based Network. The algorithm works in real time and for full duplex communication. The voice quality decreases after applying the RC4 algorithm. Goswami et al. (2012) implements the Elliptic Curve and RSA Algorithm for GSM security. Using 3GPP encryption using public key cryptography will provide the better, faster and more secure way transmission but it is restricted to wireless communication. Zainuddin and Manullang (2013) implement the Rijndael algorithm for e-learning. The motive is to understand the standard encryption process by not only reading books but to do some practical work. Chouhan and Singh (2015) proposed the real-time encryption technique for voice signal on GSM network. The algorithm is used to remove the characteristics from the speech and send the distorted voice on GSM channel. Oishi et al. (2016) implements the RC6 and Blowfish for Wi-Fi security. The hybrid approach will provide a faster and secure way to communicate. As compared to the AES algorithm the hybrid approach is less secure in WAP and WAP2. Ming et al. (2018) proposed the chaotic system for the image encryption. It discretization the Ikeda map to the chaotic system. From the beginning of internet the e-content is distributed and exchange and for security and tracking of the data Digital Rights Management (DRM) technique is used. DRM is the organized approach for copyright protection of digital data. It also prevent from unauthorized redistribution of data. DRM was developed in response to control the online piracy of commercially data. In technical point of view, DRM is implemented by embedding code which prevents from copying, specifies a time period in which the content can be accessed or limits the number of devices the media can be installed on. It also provides a secure environment for the user to exchange data for the various distributed systems.

Weakness of Various Cryptographic Algorithm

Among the many existing cryptographic algorithms, DES, 3DES, BLOWFISH, IDEA, AES, RC6 and RSA are selected and compared on the basis of structure, security, flexibility to expand in future and limitations. Table 2, illustrates the comparative study on selected algorithms.

Random Number Generator

The cryptographic algorithm mostly works with random numbers. In mathematics, the series is said to be random iff it doesn't follow any sequence or any repetition. Such sequence are only be generated by some natural phenomena or some electrical devices. In many cases it observed that random numbers are not used for cryptographic

Table 2. Comparison of various cryptographic algorithm

Algorithm	Structure	Flexibility and Modification	Known Attacks
DES	Feistel	NO	Brute Force Attack
3DES	Feistel	YES, Extended from 56 to 168 bits.	Brute Force Attack, Chosen Plaintext, Known Plaintext
BLOWFISH	Feistel	YES, 64-448 key length in multiplies of 32.	Dictionary Attack
IDEA	Substitution-Permutation	NO	Differential Timing Attack, Key-Schedule Attack
AES	Substitution-Permutation	YES, 256 key length in multiples of 64	Side Channel Attack
RSA	Factorization	YES, Multi Prime RSA, Multi power RSA	Factoring the Public Key
RC6	Feistel	YES, 128-2048 key length in multiplies of 32	Brute Force Attack, Analytical Attack

purposes, so pseudorandom number generator is came into the frame. Pseudorandom number is generated by using algorithms that can generate long sequences of numbers with a great degree of randomness but ultimately, the sequence tends to repeat and hence the name is 'pseudorandom'. Now, there are several techniques to generate random number such as Monte Carlo, Linear Congruential Generator (LCG), Blum Blum Shub (BBS), chaotic maps etc.

Monte Carlo

Monte Carlo methods is used to generate the random sequences. The problem is described by a stochastic model such as random walk. Let 'X_n' be the position of a particle in the *x*-direction at time t_n. After some time the position is changed by ΔX_n at time t_{n+1}. Then particle is represent by Equation 1.

$$X_{n+1} = X_n + \Delta X_n \tag{1}$$

If the displacement ΔX_n is chosen randomly, then there is a random walk process.

Blum Blum Shub (BBS)

It is also a traditional pseudorandom number generator which uses the modulo function and seed value for sequence generation. Equation 2 is used for sequence of number generation.

$$X_{n+1} = \left(X_n \right)^2 \bmod m \tag{2}$$

Where, $m = p \times q$

'*p*' & '*q*' = two large prime numbers.
X_n is the nth number.

Chaos Theory

It is a branch of mathematics which observer the behavior of dynamical systems. In starting the behavior of chaotic systems are predictable but after some interval of time it appears to be random. For cryptography, user uses the chaotic map that exhibits chaotic behavior. Chaotic maps are may be of discrete-time or a continuous-time parameter. There are various mathematical models which use the chaotic map such as logistic map, tent map, etc.

1. Logistic Map: It is a polynomial mapping of degree 2. Mathematically, the logistic map is given by Equation 3.

$$x_{n+1} = rx_n (1 - x_n)$$

(3)

where, x_n = it represent between [0, 1].
    r = interval of [0, 4].

2. Tent Map: In mathematics, tent map is used the parameter μ from real-valued function $f_{1/4}$. Represent of the map is given by Equation 4.

$$f_\mu = \mu \min (x, 1 - x)$$

(4)

μ = parameter in-between [0, 2].
$f_{1/4}$ = Maps with unit interval [0, 1].

The Linear Congruential Generator

In the year 1949, D. H Lehmer introduced the linear congruential generator (LCG). The working of LCG is to generate a pseudo-random number. The LCG uses the two constraints upper and lower limit within the defined intervals. Generation of the random number is given by Equation 5.

$$X_i = ((a.X) + b) \bmod M$$

(5)

Whereas, 'M' and 'a' is a real number.

X_0 = seed value which is {$0 \leq X \leq M$-1}
a = Constant multiplier. {$1 \leq a \leq M$-1}.
b = Increment value. {$1 \leq b \leq M$-1}.

Eq.5, is used to find the least significant bit as the first random number. This process is repeated and until the required bit value is not achieved. The seed value is increment after each round is represented as Equation 6 and Eq.7.

$$X_{i+1} = ((a.X_i) + b) \bmod M \tag{6}$$

$$X_1 = ((a.X_{i+1}) + b) \bmod M \tag{7}$$

There is a certain limitation for LCG in seed value. The seed value is not much longer than the length of 'k' and pseudo bit string. The relationship between 'k' and 'L' is represented as Equation 8.

$$k = 1 + \log_2 L\,M. \quad \{k+1 \le L \le M\text{-}1\} \tag{8}$$

This type of generator is also known as k, L-linear congruential generator. It is not good for the cryptographic purposes because it is easy to predict. The result of LCG computes the integer value in the range of $[2^{l-1} < M < 2^l]$ along with a, b, X_0 (seed) values. Whereas, 'l' is the length of 1-bit string and 'n' is number of elements. The output is as follows:

```
Input positive integer l: 6
Input positive integer n: 17
x values: 9
3
27
13
69
9
3
27
13
69
9
3
27
13
69
9
3
27
```

These are overview regarding how the cryptography is work, what are the weakness against multimedia data. Now, case study is present on the basis of how the cryptography algorithm is work with combination of pseudo-random number and tree.

CASE STUDY 1: USING OF RSA AUTHENTICATION IN APACHE SERVER

In this case study, the flaws of the TCP protocol while sending the multimedia data on communication channel have been described and discusses the efficient use of the RSA algorithm for security of data. Before going into the topic, we have to learn about what are the threats present in the network. So firstly, we should know what the attacker will do with the network.

- It could intercept the packets, and also modify the packets.
- It can also inject the packets into the network.
- An attacker could hijack the computer.
- An attacker could participate in the protocol or in a distributed system.

There are several threats present in network security. Mostly the attacks are executed in the TCP protocol. So, to avoid this type of attacks, user have to know that, how the TCP sequence number works. Let's first understand how the TCP handshake is done. Actually, it will send three types of packets in order to create new TCP connection (i) Client Sequence Number (SN_c), (ii) Server Sequence Number (SN_S), and (iii) Acknowledgement (ACK ()). General steps for Handshake between Client (C) and Server (S) is given in Table 3.

Table 3. Handshake between Client (C) and Server (S)

C:	$C \rightarrow S$	SYN ($\boldsymbol{SN_c}$)
S:	$S \rightarrow C$	SYN (SN_S) ACK (SN_c)
C:	$C \rightarrow S$	SYN (SN_S)
C:	$C \rightarrow S$	Data (SN_c)

How it will work? First the client will send Client Sequence Number (SN_c) to the Server. The server will check the sequence number and then server will reply with the Server Sequence Number (SN_S) and Acknowledgement ACK (SN_c) to the client. Once the client will authenticate the server sequence number it will start sending the data with client SN_c to the server. This is the actual packet routine for TCP handshake, and it also provides initial security, up to some extent. Now the server assumes that it is pretty much connected with the legitimate user IP-address '*C*'. Now the question is arising that, how server knows that it is a right client? The answer is very simple because the client contains the server SN_S, which is send to the client during the time of handshake. The data are present in the *SYN* form which is automatically increment each time. So, that the server will trace the delay in the network and re-connect from the same position. The sequence number (*SN*) in TCP is consist of 32-bits. So, there is not that much of randomness and it is an easy environment for the attackers to generate and predict the sequence number. This is the whole scenario about, how the client and server will communicate with each other. If the attacker wants to connect the server as a legitimate user it has to predict the Server Sequence Number (SN_S). Let us see, how the attacker (*A*) will connect to the server is shown in Table. 4.

Now here the problem starts, the attacker has to wait for the SN_S, which is to be acknowledged by the client. Once the attacker will get the (ACK (SN_S)) of the client. The attacker will guess the next hop sequence number. TCP doesn't provide much more randomness and it will easily to generate the 64 bits or 128 bits of sequence number jump. Once the connection is established, the attacker will start sending packets to the server.

Table 4. Attacker (A) will connect to the server

A:	$C \rightarrow S$	SYN (SN_c)	The attacker generates normal Sequence Number.
S:	$S \rightarrow C$	SYN (SN_S) ACK (SN_c)	The server doesn't know that if it is an attack or not. So, it's connected normally.
A:	$C \rightarrow S$	ACK (SN_S)	
A:	$C \rightarrow S$	Data (SN_c)	

How RSA Algorithm Will Work for Server Authentication?

When the attack is executed on the network, the attacker will get only 1 to 2 μsec to capture the packets or alter the packets. In Figure. 1 shows that how information leaked by the server.

The RSA encryption is generally depending on three things:

1. Generate the key. $Keygen(p,q)$, $Primes \sim 512bits$, and $n = pq$.
2. Encryption, and
3. Decryption.

Now, the RSA encryption is done on the basis of prime factorization. And while using the large prime number it is possible that it will take more computation time during encryption. The encryption and decryption process of RSA algorithm is given by Equation 9 and Equation 10.

For Encryption,

$$Encry_{pt} = M \rightarrow M^e \bmod (n) = C \qquad (9)$$

And for decryption,

$$Decry_{pt} = C \rightarrow C^d \bmod (n) = M \qquad (10)$$

In encryption, user takes an original message (*M*), the encryption key (*e*), and multiplication product (*n*) to generate the ciphertext (*C*). Similarly, in decryption, the ciphertext (*C*), the decryption key (*d*) and multiplication product (*n*) are used to getting the original message. Now the question is arising, how the message is

Figure 1. A different form of information leaked by Server

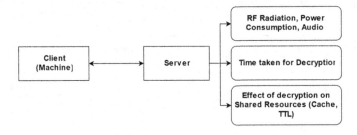

decrypted correctly? So, RSA have a very cool property of modulo function, if there is any message $\varphi(n)$ then it is represented as Equation 11 and Equation 12.

$$\left[X^{\varphi(n)} = 1\right] \bmod n \tag{11}$$

And, $\varphi = (p\text{-}1)(q\text{-}1)$
Then,

$$e \times d = \alpha\varphi(n) + 1 \tag{12}$$

Where,

$e =$ Encryption Key.
$d =$ Decryption Key.
$\alpha =$ Constant.
$\varphi(n) =$ Message.

So, basically the RSA encryption is given by Equation 13.

$$e \to d = \frac{1}{e} \bmod \varphi(n) \tag{13}$$

RSA Pitfalls

There are two different types of pitfalls for RSA encryption:

1. **Multiplicative**: Supposes there are two messages M_0 and M_1, and both message is encrypted by using RSA. Then what will happen, the Equation 14 and Equation 15 represent the original message and normal message creation.

Original Message: $M_0 \to M_0^{\ e} \bmod (n)$ (14)

Attacker Created Message: $M_1 \to M_1^{\ e} \bmod (n)$ (15)

Then from Equation (*14*) and (*15*)

$$\left(M_0 M_1\right)^e \bmod n \tag{16}$$

In Equation 16, you can see that M_0 is a message which send by the sender but M_1 is a message which is created by the attacker. Somehow, if an attacker can construct the message (M_1) that is similar to the message (M_0) then it is very simple to generate a whole original message. So, it is one of its kind of RSA encryption disadvantages. The second property of RSA are deterministic.

2. **Deterministic**: In RSA the encryption is very straight and it uses an encryption key (*e*), and multiplicative product (n) which is deterministic in nature.

$$\text{Original Message: } M \rightarrow M^e \bmod\left(n\right) \tag{17}$$

In Equation 17, shows that if the attacker will not construct the original message without having the private key. But, it can use hit and try the method, which allows encrypting a similar message by using same public key (*e*), and multiplicative product (*n*). Because public key and the multiplicative product are distributed to everyone. The attack can generate the similar message and compare with the encrypted message. If some of the parts is matched with ciphertext then the attacker can generate the whole message by using that reference. So, these are the two pitfalls of RSA which is to be consider for using the algorithm before encryption.

How to Avoid RSA Problem?

Before encrypting the message with RSA, the user will take a small function $\left(f\right)$ of the message and try to encrypt that function $\left(f\right)$ message by using Optimal Asymmetric Encryption padding (OAEP) method.

$$\text{Original Message: } M \rightarrow M^e \bmod\left(n\right)$$

By using OAEP method: $M \rightarrow f\left(M\right)^e \bmod\left(n\right)$

OAEP injects two properties to the message

1. **Randomness:** It allows to create a 1024-bit random number which is used for hiding the message.

Encrypted Message = [Randomness + Original Message $f(M)$ + Randomness]

$$(18)$$

Using the Equation 18, adding the randomness with the original message and then that message is encrypted with the public key. If the attacker wants to get that message, then it will create a similar message and encrypt that message with the same public key and multiplicative product and compare that message with the original message. But, the output of that message is not similar to the original message. Because of its randomness padding which will avoid the properties of deterministic and make the message secure.

2. **Fixed Padding:** It helps to avoid the multiplicative property of RSA. If a user adds the fixed padding with the original message and random values, then it can easily find out that what modification has been done on the original message by the attacker. Then the user will become aware that the message has been tempered by an attacker.

Encrypted Message = [Fixed Padding + Original Message $f(M)$ + Randomness]

$$(19)$$

Using the Equation 19, the fixed padding is placed with the message and the randomness. If there is attack on original message the user will check the message with the padding message, if the same message is not present as before encryption, then the user presumes that there is some tampering with the original message and if the message is same as original message then there is no attack on the message.

How to Use the RSA Encryption for Apache Server?

There are various ways to use RSA authentication for Apache server. The most optimized way is to use Chinese Remainder Theorem (CRT) in RSA authentication. The scenario for CRT is given in Equation 20 and Equation 21. If there is two number a_1 and a_2 that have some value 'X'.

$(X = a_1)$ mod p

$$(20)$$

$(X = a_2)$ mod q $\hspace{6cm}$ (21)

And if 'p' and 'q' are two prime number. Then it turns out that there is a unique solution X' of 'p' and 'q' then it is given in Equation 22.

$[X = X']$ mod p $\times$ q $\hspace{6cm}$ (22)

So, this unique X' is computed easily using CRT. Suppose, to compute the message M $= C^d$ mod $(p \times q)$. Then divide the message into two parts using the Equation 23 and Equation 24.

$$m1 = C^d \bmod (p) \hspace{5cm} (23)$$

$$m2 = C^d \bmod (q) \hspace{5cm} (24)$$

Then CRT is used to

- Compute M $= C^d$ mod (n) from m1, m2 which is unique and fast.
- Computing m1 and m2 are ~4x faster than computing the 'M' directly (~quadratic).
- Dividing the value of 'n' in the multiplicative product of (p and q).
- Computing M, from 'm1' and 'm2' using CRT is (~negligible) in comparison.
- So, roughly a 2x speedup is gain while using CRT optimization for RSA.

How CRT Helps in Securing Apache Web Server?

The unique feature of CRT is prime factorization and high-speed computation which will provide a robust system to the user. The man-in-a-middle attack is possible in the current scenario while using RSA. But, while using the CRT with RSA which provide 2x ~ times faster computation in comparison to normal RSA. It is a very weak system and the attacker is to gain the data in this scenario easily. In normal RSA the attacker will wait and get the chance to gain the data at the time of decryption. Computation of RSA will take much time in uniprocessors system. And it is to be concluded that decryption time very important for the server security. So, using CRT with RSA provides a high level of security to the server.

CASE STUDY 2: RED-BLACK TREE FOR KEY DISTRIBUTION

In this case study, it represent the different approach for key distribution for cryptographic algorithm which is used in securing the multimedia data. Now, the cryptography is divided into two parts (i) Key distribution strategy, and (ii) Cryptography Algorithm. According to Priya (2018), cryptographic algorithm is mostly depending on key distribution technique. Here a study demonstrated which deals with Red-Black Trees for key distribution. A Red-Black (R-B) tree is the self-balanced binary search tree. The feature of R-B tree is "colour" which is either red or black. The structure of (R-B) tree would be:

```
struct node
{
enum {red, black}
colour;
void *item;
struct node *left, *right, *parent;
   }
```

The leaves node is colored black and it is considered to be Null node and it is used for termination. There are some of the properties of the Red-Black tree is as follows:

- Every node must be either red or black.
- Every null node is black.
- Every red node is consisting of two black child nodes.

If the tree having the number of black nodes and height of the tree is from node 'x' to the leaf node and it is denoted by $bh(x)$. The height of a Red-Black tree with 'n' internal nodes is represented as $2\log(n+1)$. The time complexity of tree traversal is denoted in O ($\log(n)$). In RB traversal, the searching is done from left to right before moving to the next level which is shown in the Figure. 2.

Now the question is to raised, How the RB tree is used for encryption? So, for that author uses the three different level for encryption. The first level is used the Linear Congruential Generator (LCG) for random number generation, in second level RB tree data structure is applied, and the third level is used for encryption of the data based on the colour of the node. In level 1, the LCG is used to generate the sequence of random number and the seed value is used for initialization. The recursive relation is used to generate a random sequence which is given by Equation 25.

Figure 2. RB Traversal technique for next pointer

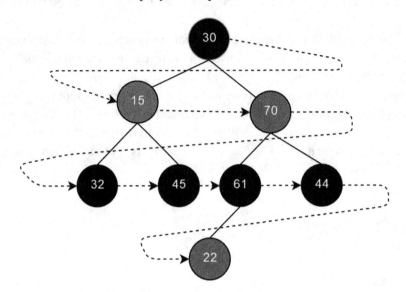

$$X_{i+1} = ((a.X_i) + b) \bmod M \qquad (25)$$

where, '*a*' is a multiplier, '*b*' is an increment, and '*M*' is modulus.

To generate the sequence uses the $a = 5$, $b = 3$, and $M = 16$. In Table 5, shows the randomly generated sequence number using LCG.

Now, the generated sequence number is used for mapping the text character. The mapping is bidirectional and it is shown as in Table 6.

After this level, the dictionary is created which is used to assign the text character with the RB tree. Now, rearrange the tree data and obtain the new order. The second level is to apply the coloring on the nodes. So, the top level is colored black after that it follows the RB colouring rule. There increment in node value after each assigning of character and it is used for the encryption. The encryption of character is initialized after applying the colour on the nodes. The block diagram represents the sender side encryption process.

In Figure. 3 represent the encryption process of the sender side. The process for encryption are as follows:

1. Generate Seed value for encryption and decryption.
2. Generate the table using LCG.
3. Use the table of encryption.
4. Construct the RB tree.

Table 5. LCG random sequence number

Input Number (X_{i+1})	Output Number (X_i)
0	3
3	2
2	13
13	4
4	7
7	6
6	1
1	8
8	11
11	10
10	5
5	12
12	15
15	14
14	9
9	0

5. Encrypt the Black node of the RB tree.
6. Rearrange the table.
7. Send the data to the receiver side.

Now, if you want to encrypt the characters "HI ITS ENCRYPTION" then it has to use the Table 6 for mapping character with the dictionary.

Step 1: Encrypt the message according to the LCG table.

Plain Message: "HI ITS ENCRYPTION"
Encrypted Message: "KLM AZUEL XLZHG MS"
Next step is to assign the node order with the encrypted character for traversal is shown in Table 7.

Step 2: Apply RB tree traversal

The RB traversal New-order is presented in the Figure. 4.

Table 6. Representation of Number with the text character

0	A	0	Q
1	B	1	R
2	C	2	S
3	D	3	T
4	E	4	U
5	F	5	V
6	G	6	W
7	H	7	X
8	I	8	Y
9	J	9	Z
10	K	10	
11	L	11	.
12	M	12	,
13	N	13	?
14	O	14	@
15	P	15	'

Figure 3. Encryption in the sender side

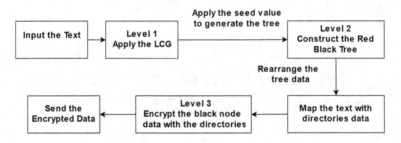

Table 7. Node order with the encrypted character

K	L	M			A	Z	U	E	L			X	L	Z	H	G			M	S
1	2	3	4	5	6	7	8	9	10	11	12	13	14	15	16	17	18	19	20	21

RB traversal: 4,2,8,1,3,6,10,5,7,9,11,15,20,13,17,19,21,12,14,16,18

Step 3: Encrypt the black node using a dictionary.

Rearrange the list: LU KMA LZ EZ MXG S LH
Encrypt the black Node only then

```
!ASPQA L!OF!ZMBT!D!LH!
```

After encryption, all the character in the message are altered and it is not in a readable format. The encrypted message is sent to the receiver side. Now, the decryption process is shown in Figure 5.

In Figure 5, represent the decryption process on the receiver side. The first step is to construct the RB tree whose length is equal to the length of the encrypted message. The decryption is just the opposite of encryption process so it has to follow the bottom-up approach to construct the tree. Steps for tree construction is as follows:

1. Construct the Red-Black tree.
2. Perform tree traversal.

Figure 4. Red black tree after encryption of character

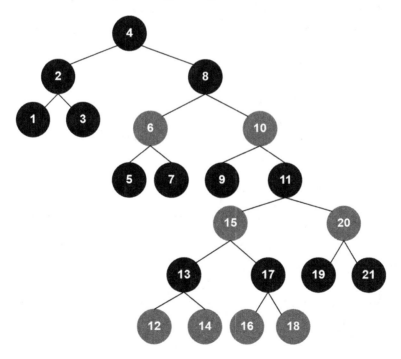

Figure 5. Decryption in the receiver side

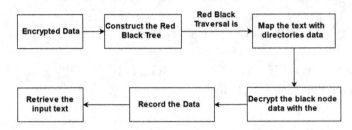

3.   Map the data with directory table.
4.   Decrypt the Black node.
5.   Rearrange the character table.
6.   Use the LCG table for final decryption.
7.   Generate the original text.

Once the tree is constructed to apply the decryption algorithm. Steps for decryption is as follows:

Cipher Message: !ASPQA L!OF!ZMBT!D!LH!

Step 1: Construct the Red Black Tree

The length of tree is (1 to 21). RB traversal nodes are 4,2,8,1,3,6,10,5,7,9,11,1 5,20,13,17,19,21,12,14,16,18

Step 2: Mapping of text shown in Table.8.

After decrypting the black nodes: LUKMALZEZMXGSLM

Step 3: Record the result and decrypt the data which is shown in Table 9.

Table 8. Mapping of text character with color Node

Encrypted Data	!	A	S	P	Q	A	L	!	O	F	!	Z	M	B	T	!	D	!	L	H	!
RB Traversal	4	2	8	1	3	6	10	5	7	9	11	15	20	13	17	19	21	12	14	16	18
Colour of Nodes	B	B	B	B	B	R	R	B	B	B	B	R	R	B	B	B	B	R	R	R	R
Decrypted Data		L	U	K	M	A	L		Z	E		Z	M	X	G		S		L	H	

Table 9. Decrypt the text character and record the result

Arrange in Ascending order	1	2	3	4	5	6	7	8	9	10	11	12	13	14	15	16	17	18	19	20	21
Associated Data	K	L	M			A	Z	U	E	L			X	L	Z	H	G			M	S

Step 4: Retrieve the input text

Cipher Text: "KLM AZUEL XLZHG MS"

Original (Decipher) Text: "HI ITS ENCRYPTION"

This is the overall scenario of encryption and decryption using the RB tree. In RB tree user uses the distribution and substitution technique to create the ciphertext which is one the different way of cryptography. It is not suitable for large datasets but it is good for 2^7 data length size. Moving forward, another case study is about security in GSM channel. The huge amount of user is using the GSM channel and sending their data in the form of a message (text) or in the call (speech). So, better sure that the communication channel is secure or not. From this note, let's start another case study which is based on the real-time problem for the user.

CASE STUDY 3: SECURITY IN GLOBAL SYSTEM FOR MOBILE COMMUNICATIONS (GSM) NETWORK

GSM security is one of the research area in telecommunication field. In the year 1975, Kieffer has first proposed the mobile spectrum of 900 MHz in Europe. Later on it was used for mobile communication. When you think in back 90s the user of the GSM network is very less than compared to the current scenario. In the present scenario, millions of users are connected with GSM network, which creates massive traffic in transmission of signal. Call drops and network congestion are some of the examples of GSM traffic. In this case study the primary focus is how to provide the security of data during transmission on GSM channels.

GSM Architecture

GSM consists of a different entity, which works together to form a GSM system. In Figure.6, represent the architecture of the GSM system. The GSM [22] system is made up of different layers. Technically GSM system is consisting of hardware and SIM (Subscriber Identity Module). The working of GSM is as follows: To launch the GSM services initially, the SIM starts to transmit the signal to the nearest MS

(Mobile Station). The work of Mobile Station is to check the IMEI (International Mobile Equipment Identity) registration and then send the acknowledgment to network service provider whether that device was stolen or not. The second part of GSM is the authentication process, which takes place in-between MS, BTS, MSC, and AuC. When the subscriber connects to the nearest mobile station it first sends the authentication requests and International Mobile Subscriber Identity (IMSI) to the MSC. The MSC collect the authentication triplets and IMSI request and forward to the HLR. When HLR receives the request then it first validates the IMSI with the database. Once this process is completed, it sends the IMSI and authentication triplets to the AuC. In AuC it checks the authentication key (k_i) which is related to the IMSI. The key (k_i) length is of 128 bits which are associated with IMSI. *A3* and *A8* are two cryptographic algorithms [23] present in AuC.

The decryption process is consisting of 32-bit Signed Response (SRES), 64 bits (k_c) cipher key, and it also generates 128-bits random number RAND. These are the three triplets used in *A5* encryption while transmitting the speech on the air-to-air interface.

In Figure. 7, represent the authentication process which consists of 64-bit of *A5* stream cipher encryption key. For many year KASUMI is used for GSM security. KASUMI is a block cipher technique which is used in Universal Mobile Telecommunications System (UMTS), GSM, and General Packet Radio Service (GPRS) mobile communications systems. In UMTS, KASUMI is used in confidentiality (*F8*) and integrity algorithms (*F9*) with names UEA1 and UIA1, respectively. In GSM, KASUMI is used in the *A5/3* key stream generator and in GPRS in the GEA3 key stream generator. But, for many years the *A5* encryption algorithm is made secret. But Briceno et al. (1999) has a reverse engineered *A5* algorithm and come up with updated *A5/1* and *A5/2* encryption algorithm for GSM security. Many cryptanalysts have try to reverse-engineer the *A5* algorithm. It is evidenced that *A5* algorithm is totally insecure for voice encryption. So, to remove those faults different researcher introduces a different encryption technique for GSM channel. After some time *A5/3* algorithm is introduced which highly secure against snooping and it is also suitable for GPRS (General Packet Radio Service), HSCSD (High-Speed Circuit-Switched Data) and EDGE (Enhanced Data Rates GSM Evolution). The advantage of the *A5/3* technique is to provide complete protection of mobile number, and speech which is usually transmitted on a radio signal. Later on, a different technique is developed to provide security on GSM network. *RC6* is another cryptographic technique which designed by Ron Rivest, Matt Robshaw, Ray Sidney and Yiqun Lisa Yin (1998) which is used for encryption. *RC6* uses the variable key length size of 128, 192, and 256 bits. Another cryptographic technique is Rijndael also known as Advanced Encryption Algorithm (AES). In the year 1988,

Figure 6. GSM architecture

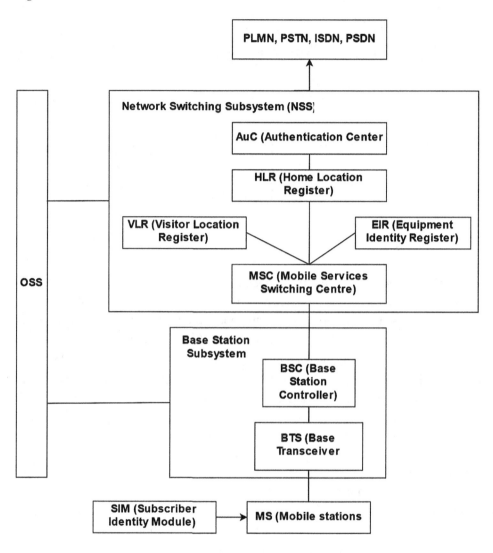

the two Belgian cryptographers Vincent Rijmen and Joan Daemen first proposed the Rijndael algorithm and their surnames are reflected in the cipher's name. It is a symmetric key block cipher technique which uses the 128, 192 and 256 bits key sizes. It also has a different number of rounds which totally depends on key/block sizes which are as follows:

- 9 rounds if the key/block size is 128 bits.
- 11 rounds if the key/block size is 192 bits.

Figure 7. GSM authentication model

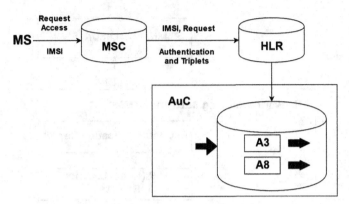

- 13 rounds if the key/block size is 256 bits.

Some of the key step used in Rijndael encryption are as follows:

It is a Feistel structure technique which uses the triple discrete invertible uniform transformations. The first round is a simple key addition which adds the security layer of N_{r-1} rounds to the final round. In the Rijindael algorithm, the block is divide into 32-bits length and each block is structure as 4×4 matrix. Similarly, the cipher key is also divided into 32-bits. The blocks are interpreted as multi-dimensional arrays of 4-byte vectors. In Figure. 8 shows the sub byte transformation of the block for Rijindael.

The sub-block transformation is nonlinear which operates each elements byte independently with invertible S-box (substitution table). In Figure. 9 represent the S-box table for the substitution process.

The figure 10, represents the shift row transformation of variable offsets. The offset values are reliant on block length.

The mix column transformation represents the polynomial characteristics over a Galois Field (GF) values (2^8), multiplied $x^4 + 1$ (modulo) with a fixed polynomial. Figure. 11 shows the mix column transformation.

Figure 8. Sub byte transformation

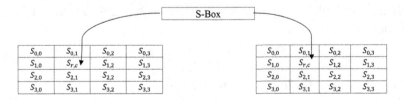

Figure 9. S-box table for the substitution

								Y								
		0	1	2	3	4	5	6	7	8	9	a	b	c	d	e	f
	0	63	7c	77	7b	8c	7c	7c	77	7b	77	63	7c	7b	7c	7c	77
	1	ca	82	c9	7d	8c	82	82	c9	7d	c9	ca	82	7d	82	82	c9
	2	b7	fd	93	26	8c	fd	fd	93	26	93	b7	fd	26	fd	fd	93
	3	04	c7	23	c3	8c	c7	c7	23	c3	23	04	c7	c3	c7	c7	23
	4	09	83	2c	1a	8c	83	83	2c	1a	2c	09	83	1a	83	83	2c
	5	53	d1	00	66	8c	d1	d1	00	66	00	53	d1	66	d1	d1	00
	6	d0	ef	aa	e5	8c	ef	ef	aa	e5	aa	d0	ef	e5	ef	ef	aa
X	7	51	a3	40	a5	8c	a3	a3	40	a5	40	51	a3	a5	a3	a3	40
	8	cd	0c	13	b9	8c	0c	0c	13	b9	13	cd	0c	b9	0c	0c	13
	9	e0	81	4f	26	8c	81	81	4f	26	4f	e0	81	26	81	81	4f
	a	e7	32	3a	b1	8c	32	32	3a	b1	3a	e7	32	b1	32	32	3a
	b	ba	c8	37	45	8c	c8	c8	37	45	37	ba	c8	45	c8	c8	37
	c	70	78	25	de	8c	78	78	25	de	25	70	78	de	78	78	25
	d	e1	3e	b5	29	8c	3e	3e	b5	29	b5	e1	3e	29	3e	3e	b5
	e	60	f8	98	97	8c	f8	f8	98	97	98	60	f8	97	f8	f8	98
	f	8c	a1	89	0d	8c	a1	a1	89	0d	89	8c	a1	0d	a1	a1	89

Figure 10. Shift row transformation

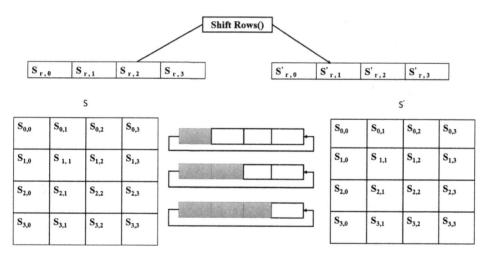

Finally, the transformed round key is XORed and the cipher key determines by the round key. In Figure. 12, illustrate the key transformation for the S-box.

Overall, the Rijndael algorithm demonstrates a high degree of modular design which is secure for any type of attack. These are some encryption technique which is used in the GSM system. Here in this case study, we restrict our boundary of

Figure 11. Mix column transformation

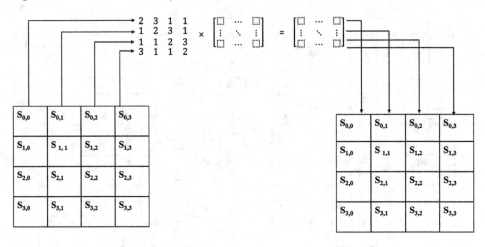

Figure 12. Add Round Key Transformation

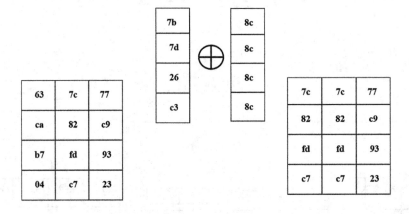

work. So, 128 bits size of the block and the key length is used for GSM encryption which provides an end-to-end voice/speech encryption. For our case study, *RC6* is considered for encryption and decryption purposes. The *RC6* algorithm is very similar to the *RC5* algorithm. In *RC5*, the data encryption is done by three simple steps (i) Independent rotation, (ii) Modular Addition, and (iii) XOR operation. In *RC6*, the process is similar to two parallel *RC5* algorithms. However, *RC6* use one extra multiplication process in order to create a rotation dependent. In *RC6* there are four w-bit (write) register *A, B, C, D* which contain 128 bits key expansion of input and output data. Due to the Feistel network structure, the input data is taken in the least significant bit and the key most significant bit. In GSM, AuC is consist of three triplets (*RAND*, K_i, and K_c) which is taken for encryption. Whereas,

RAND and K_i are engaged in *A8* algorithm and K_c (cipher key) is engaged in the *A5* algorithm. The cipher key is taken as an input in '*C*' and set standard 100 rounds for the simulation. The algorithm for *A5/3RC6* is as follow:

Initial Variants of RC6 –w r b is:

A + B = 2w modulo addition.

A - B= 2W modulo subtraction.

A $\oplus$ B= XOR of w-bit words.

A x B= 2w multiplication.

A <<< B = Rotate A to left.

A >>> B = Rotate A to right.

(A, B, C, D) = (B, C, D, A) Parallel phase

A5/3 is a 64-bit key expansion, so to convert the key to the 128-bits which uses in the *A5/3RC6* encryption.

Algorithm for Key Expansion

- **INPUT:** Kc cipher key in C, r = no of rounds, Word Array (*L*= 0, 1… c-1).
- **OUTPUT:** w-bit round key.

```
Start
{
S [0] =  Kw
For m = 1 to 2r+3, then
{
s [m] = s [m-1] + Lw
}
U = V = a = b = 0
Iter = 3 * max [C, (2r + 4)]
For n = 1 to Iter, then
{
U = S [a] = (S [a] + U + V) <<< 3
```

```
V = L [b] = (L[b] + U + V) <<< (U+V)
m = (a+1) mod (2r + 4)
n = (b+1) mod C
}
}
End;
```

RC6 Key-Expansion is similar to the *RC5* but the difference is that *RC6* will use (2r + 4) additive keys and in the *RC5* the key size will be 2(r + 1).

A5/3RC6 Encryption Algorithm

The Pseudo code for A5/3RC6 is

```
•           INPUT: A, B, C, D register, r-round, w-bit key
•           OUTPUT: Cipher Data
START
{
B + = S [0];
D + = S [1];
For m = 1 to r, then
{
K = (2B² + B) <<< lg W
L = (2D² +D) <<< lg W;
A = ((A ⊕ K) <<< L) + S [2i];
C = ((C ⊕ L) <<< K) + S [2i+ 1];
(A, B, C, D) = (B, C, D, A)
}
A + = 2S [r+1];
C + = S [2r+3];
}
End
```

Here, (A, B, C, D) and (B, C, D, A) stand for the parallel assignment. Where the original data is converted into the encrypted data. The algorithm uses 4 bits register for w-bit key expansion. The original data is taken as an input and divide it into four different variables A, B, C, D. Variable 'B' and 'D' is used for storing the key and after that start the simulation of the process. The variable 'K' and 'L' is used for bit round array and estimate the number of rounds. Variable 'A' and 'C' is used for XOR operation, the value range is from [2i to 2i+1] the encryption is run up to the last block.

A5/3RC6 Decryption Algorithm

Decryption is just a reverse process of encryption, where the encrypted data is taken as an input and converted into an original data. Using subtraction process conversion is done for a normal file. The pseudo code *A5/3RC6* is given below:

```
•           INPUT: Cipher in the register A, B, C, and D.
•           OUTPUT: Plain Data.
START
{
C - = S [2r + 3];
A - = 2S [r + 1];
For n = r to 1, then
{
(A, B, C, D) = (B, C, D, A)
K = (2D² + D) <<< lg W
L = (2B² + B)) <<< lg W
C = ((C - S [2i + 1]) >>> L) ⊕ K
A = ((A - S [2i]) >>> K) ⊕ L
}
D - = S [1]
B - = S [0]
}
}
End;
```

The RC6 algorithm mostly depends on sub-block generation and key rotation. Here, the original data is stored in the register and the shift operation is done by modulo operation. This case study showed how the encryption is done in a GSM system when the data is transmitted on the radio spectrum.

DISCUSSION AND CONCLUSION

There are several ways to secure the multimedia data on communication channels. In this chapter, author use to discuss a RSA and RC6 encryption algorithm for secure multimedia transfer and for key distribution author uses the Red-Black substitution tree technique. The case study 1, demonstrate the basic working principle of the RSA algorithm. Apache web server is an open source software which used for web services and application deployment. Most of the time prime factorization is the biggest problem for any uniprocessor system and its computation time is very high. Apache server runs on the standalone computers and sometime in the parallel environment also. So, to speed up the computational time of the server, the RSA is used with the Chinese Remainder Theorem (CRT). Working with CRT increases the computation up to 2x times. And while dividing the key value it cannot be hacked at the time of the attack. The case study 2, represents the key distribution technique using a Red-Black tree. By applying the tree structure, it provides three-tier security layers. If any intruder will access the first layer it will not be able to get the message of the next level. It also provides the information integrity at the time of hacking. One of the drawbacks of this algorithm is that it uses common special symbols. So, it may be chance that the hacker will guess the original message by analyzing the cipher message. Application of LCG creates a robust algorithm for encryption, because alone LCG is not a good random number creator, and it does not archive the requirement of encryption. But, applying the LCG with red-black tree will create the level of security abstraction which is not easily breakable. Future extension of this algorithm is to use all the special characters which will create a high degree of security. Cryptographer can also create the alternative method, which is on the basis of the Red-Black tree and LCG, which will increase the security of each level. The case study 3, represent the security of data in GSM network. The author tries to implement *RC6* algorithm to increase the security of GSM system. Already GSM consists of security algorithm for voice encryption. But those techniques are old and it doesn't provide a high level of security for different format of multimedia data. However, security in GSM, it means end-to-end voice encryption. Already, KASUMI is used with *A5/3* for providing voice security. The other algorithm such as Rijndael algorithm which demonstrates a high degree of modular design to secure any type of attack. But at restrict boundary work Rijndael will reduce the performance of security. Now, the encryption technique which is used in the GSM system will be light weight in nature and it will be reliable for all type multimedia data. While implementing the *RC6* with a traditional *A5/3* algorithm will improve the security level. *RC6* is a block cipher technique which provides the flexibility in key length and block size. It is important to know that *RC6* can be efficiently used in restricted memory environments such as in SIM and smart card. In the distributed environment, security of data is the major concern. The case studies show that how the data can be secured in different ways. Various researches shows that the demand for robust security mechanisms is growing rapidly in the era of Artificial Intelligence.

REFERENCES

Agi, I., & Gong, L. (1996). An Empirical Study of Secure MPEG Video Transmission. In *Proceeding of the Internet Society Symposium on Network and Distributed System Security (ISSoNDSS '96)*. IEEE. 10.1109/NDSS.1996.492420

Briceno, M., Goldberg, I., & Wagner, D. (1999). *Voice Privacy, A Pedagogical Implementation of the GSM A5/1 AND A5/2*. Retrieved from the Internet http://cryptome.org/gsm-aS12.htm

Chouhan, A., & Singh, S. (2015). Real Time Secure end to end Communication over GSM Network. In *Proceeding of the International Conference on Energy Systems and Applications (ICESA '15)*. Pune, India: IEEE. 10.1109/ICESA.2015.7503433

Chumchu, P., Phayak, A., & Dokpikul, P. (2012). A Simple and Cheap End-to-End Voice Encryption Framework over GSM-based Networks. In *Proceedings of the Computing, Communications and Applications Conference (ComComAp '12)*. Hong Kong, China: IEEE. 10.1109/ComComAp.2012.6154800

Diaz-Sanchez, D., Almenarez, F., Marin, A., Proserpio, D., & Cabarcos, A. P. (2011). Media cloud: An open cloud computing middleware for content management. *IEEE Transactions on Consumer Electronics*, *57*(2), 970–978. doi:10.1109/TCE.2011.5955247

Gadea, C., Solomon, B., Ionescu, B., & Ionescu, D. (2011). A collaborative cloud-based multimedia sharing platform for social networking environments. In *Proceeding of the International Conference on Computer Communications and Networks (ICoCCN '11)*, Maui, HI: IEEE. 10.1109/ICCCN.2011.6006079

Global System for Mobile Communications (GSM). (2017). *From GSM to LTE-Advanced Pro and 5G*, 1–70. DOI: doi:10.1002/9781119346913.ch1

Goswami, S., Chakraborty, S., Laha, S., & Dhar, A. (2012). Enhancement of GSM Security Using Elliptic Curve Cryptography Algorithm. In *Proceedings of the Third International Conference on Intelligent Systems Modelling and Simulation (ISMS '12)*. Kota Kinabalu, Malaysia: IEEE. 10.1109/ISMS.2012.137

Gupta, A., & Singh Chandel, P. (2014). Security Enhancement in GSM using A3 algorithm. *International Journal of Computers and Applications*, *108*(1), 18–20. doi:10.5120/18875-0138

Jakimoski, G., & Kocarev, L. (2001). Chaos and Cryptography: Block Encryption Ciphers Based on Chaotic Maps. *IEEE Transactions on Circuits and Systems Fundamental Theory and Applications*, *48*(2), 163–169. doi:10.1109/81.904880

Li, M., Fan, H., Xiang, Y., Li, Y., & Zhang, Y. (2018). Cryptanalysis and improvement of a chaotic image encryption by first-order time-delay system. *IEEE MultiMedia*, *24*(1), 1–1.

Meyer, J., & Gadegast, F. (1995). *Security Mechanisms for Multimedia Data with the Example MPEG_1 Video*. Berlin: Project Description of SECMPEG.

Oishi, J. N., & Mahamud, A. (2016). Short Paper: Enhancing Wi-Fi Security Using a Hybrid Algorithm of Blowfish and RC6. In *Proceeding of the International Conference on Networking Systems and Security (NSysS '16)*. Dhaka, Bangladesh: IEEE. 10.1109/NSysS.2016.7400706

Priya, A., Sinha, K., Darshani, M. P., & Sahana, S. K. (2018). A Novel Multimedia Encryption and Decryption Technique Using Binary Tree Traversal. *Proceeding of the Second International Conference on Microelectronics, Computing & Communication Systems (MCCS 2017)*, 163–178. DOI: 10.1007/978-981-10-8234-4_15

Rivest, L. R., Robshaw, B. J. M., Sidney, R., & Yin, L. Y. (1998). *The RC6 Block Cipher*. Version 1.1, Lab (M.I.T).

Soyjaudah, S. M. K., Hosany, A. M., & Jamaloodeen, A. (2004). Design and Implementation of Rijindeal Algorithm for GSM Encryption. In *Proceedings of the Joint IST Workshop on Mobile Future & Symposium on Trends in Communications (SympoTIC '04)*, Bratislava, Slovakia: IEEE. 10.1109/TIC.2004.1409510

Spanos, A. G., & Maples, B. T. (1996). Security for Real-Time MPEG Compressed Video in Distributed Multimedia Applications. In *Proceeding of the International Phoenix Conference on Computers and Communications (IPcCC '96)*. Scottsdale, AZ: IEEE. 10.1109/PCCC.1996.493615

Verma, K. H., & Singh, K. R. (2012). Performance Analysis of RC6, Twofish and Rijndael Block Cipher Algorithms. *International Journal of Computers and Applications*, *42*(16), 1–7. doi:10.5120/5773-6002

Yang, Y., Feng, S., Ye, W., & Ji, X. (2008). A Transmission Scheme for Encrypted Speech over GSM network. In *Proceeding of the International Symposium on Computer Science and Computational Technology (ISCSCT '08)*. Shanghai, China: IEEE. 10.1109/ISCSCT.2008.290

Zainuddin, Z., & Manullang, V. E. (2013). E-Learning Concept Design of Rijndael Encryption Process. In *Proceeding of the International Conference on Teaching, Assessment and Learning for Engineering (TALE '13)*. Bali, Indonesia: IEEE.

Zhang, Z. Y. (2010). Security, Trust, and Risk in the Digital Rights Management Ecosystem. In *Proceeding of the International Conference on High-Performance Computing and Simulation (HPCS '10)*. Caen, France: IEEE. 10.1109/HPCS.2010.5547093

Zhang, Z. Y. (2011). Digital Rights Management Ecosystem and its Usage Controls: A Survey. *International Journal of Digital Content Technology & Its Applications, 5*(3), 255–272. doi:10.4156/jdcta.vol5.issue3.26

Zhu, W., Luo, C., Wang, J., & Li, S. (2011). Multimedia cloud computing. *IEEE Signal Processing Magazine, 28*(3), 59–69. doi:10.1109/MSP.2011.940269

Chapter 9
Machine Learning Algorithms

Namrata Dhanda
Amity University, India

Stuti Shukla Datta
Amity University, India

Mudrika Dhanda
Royal Holloway University, UK

ABSTRACT

Human intelligence is deeply involved in creating efficient and faster systems that can work independently. Creation of such smart systems requires efficient training algorithms. Thus, the aim of this chapter is to introduce the readers with the concept of machine learning and the commonly employed learning algorithm for developing efficient and intelligent systems. The chapter gives a clear distinction between supervised and unsupervised learning methods. Each algorithm is explained with the help of suitable example to give an insight to the learning process.

INTRODUCTION

Can a person with both his legs amputated still drive a car, or a man with impaired vision can cross a busy road without assistance. The answer to these questions, which once seemed impossible, is in affirmative now. This has become possible due to machine learning. So what is machine learning then? It is a field of science which provides systems the ability to learn and adapt from the environment conditions. Here, the objective is to develop programmed models that can access data and further use them for improving their performance without much human intervention. So

DOI: 10.4018/978-1-5225-7955-7.ch009

straight away next question that comes into one's mind how these systems acquire intelligence? So the intelligence is acquired through learning. Learning is a very crucial component in developing an intelligent system. Learning may be supervised or unsupervised. Supervised learning refers to inferring a mapping function between input and output using a set of training data. Later the function can be employed for assessing testing data. Unsupervised learning refers to developing hidden structure in the input data. These learning models can be employed in developing a classifier or a predictor. As an example let us consider a person with impaired vision and he is wearing intelligent goggles while moving on the roads. The intelligent gadget in the form of goggles is continuously monitoring the scenario on the road. Now if the person has to cross the road these goggles would take the input in the form of image and classify whether the road in front of the person is busy or not and would help him in making the decision of whether to cross the road or not. It is often observed that if one has browsed for the flight cost from Delhi to Mumbai two three times on the home page of an air services, and the next time when he logs on to the site, he gets a display of prices offered by various air service provider along with their routes for round trip between Delhi and Mumbai. This is an example of adaptive learning or more specifically, learning from the query. Thus objective is to create intelligent systems that could assist human in the areas where human intelligence has limitation. Lot of researches and investigations are going across the globe to evolve new and better learning methods.

Machine learning is a field of Computer Science which often uses statistical techniques to give computers the ability to learn. It is closely related to artificial intelligence which is enabling computers to perform human-like activities. Machine learning is giving computers the ability to learn without being explicitly getting programmed. Thus, this chapter introduces the reader with commonly employed supervised and unsupervised learning algorithms.

The chapter is organized mainly in four sections: first section deals with the introduction to Machine Learning and how intelligent systems can work for the betterment of life. Second section deals with parametric and nonparametric algorithms. Third section discusses in details the commonly employed supervised learning algorithm with example to assist readers gain an insight towards learning techniques. Fourth section deals with unsupervised learning algorithms example clustering and a priori methods.

BACKGROUND

Tom M. Mitchell provided a widely quoted, more formal definition of the algorithms studied in the machine learning field: "A computer program is said to learn from experience E with respect to some class of tasks T and performance measure P if its performance at tasks in T, as measured by P, improves with experience E" (Mitchell, 1997). This definition of the tasks in which machine learning is concerned offers a fundamentally operational definition rather than defining the field in cognitive terms. This follows Alan Turing's proposal in his paper "Computing Machinery and Intelligence", in which the question "Can machines think?" is replaced with the question "Can machines do what we (as thinking entities) can do?" (Turing, 2009). In Turing's proposal the various characteristics that could be possessed by a thinking machine and the various implications in constructing one are exposed.

Machine learning is a technology that allows computers to learn directly from examples and experience in the form of data. Traditional approaches to programming rely on hardcoded rules, which set out how to solve a problem, step-by-step. In contrast, machine learning systems are set a task, and given a large amount of data to use as examples of how this task can be achieved or from which to detect patterns. The system then learns how best to achieve the desired output. It can be thought of as narrow AI: machine learning supports intelligent systems, which are able to learn a particular function, given a specific set of data to learn from. Machine learning has gained a significant importance in the recent years. A large number of applications have been developed using Machine Learning algorithms. Amongst several already existing applications, machine learning methods, in particular, help in coping up with large datasets (e.g., Clark & Niblett, 1989; Cohen, 1995; Dietterich, 1997; Mitchell, 1997; Michalski, Bratko, & Kubat, 1998).

PARAMETRIC AND NON PARAMETRIC ALGORITHMS

Before familiarizing readers with commonly employed learning algorithms, it is imperative to understand the terms parametric and non-parametric.

- **Parametric Algorithms**: Algorithms that simplify the function to a known form are called parametric machine learning algorithms. The algorithm involves two steps: first identification of the form of the function and second evaluating the coefficients of the function from the training data e.g is linear regression, logistic regression

- **Non Parametric Algorithms:** Algorithms that do not make any assumptions about the form of the mapping function are called nonparametric algorithms. Such algorithms have the flexibility to learn any functional form from the training data. However, such algorithms require large training dataset and take more time in learning e.g. support vector machine, kNN algorithm

SUPERVISED LEARNING ALGORITHMS

In supervised learning, idea is to learn a function that best maps input variable to the output variable. Here training data is in sets of input variables and their corresponding output. Thus the process of estimating a mapping function from the training dataset can be thought of as a teacher supervising the learning process. The algorithm iteratively makes predictions on the input training data (input data) and is corrected by the teacher (known output). Learning stops when the algorithm achieves an acceptable level of performance. Most commonly employed supervised algorithms are:

- Linear Regression
- Logistic Regression
- Linear Discriminant Analysis
- Linear Support Vector Machine
- K Nearest Neighbor Algorithm (KNN)

LINEAR REGRESSION

Linear regression is statistical approach to map input variable to their corresponding out. It is the a known and well understood algorithm in machine learning. Data can be modeled with simple linear equation as:

$$y = b_0 + b_1 x \tag{1}$$

This represent a line where y is the variable that we want to predict and x is the input attribute b_0 is the intercept and b_1 is called the slope. The coefficient b_0 and b1 are estimated using the labeled input and output variables. Once these coefficients values are estimated, the linear mapping function is ready to prediction for unknown input variables. If there were more input variable then this would become a multiple regression problem.

Example

For the given data develop a linear model of prediction
So, the aim to evaluate the linear coefficients b_0, b_1
We first evaluate the mean of x and y

Mean(x)= 3, Mean(y)=2.8

Error of each variable from the mean is then calculated as given in the table 2
Sum of the multiplication = (3.6-0.2+0.2+0+4.4)=10
Slope can be then evaluated as $b_1=8/10=0.8$
Intercept can be calculated as

b_0=mean(y)-b_1*mean(x)=0.4

So the linear model is given by:

y=0.8x+0.4

Table 1.

x	y
1	1
2	3
4	3
3	2
5	5

Table 2.

x	e_x	y	e_y	e_x, e_y
1	1-3=-2	1	1-2.8=-1.8	3.6
2	3-3=-1	2	3-2.8=.2	-0.2
4	3-3=1	4	3-2.8=.2	0.2
3	2-3=0	3	2-2.8=-.8	0
5	5-3-2	5	5-2.8= 2.2	4.4

LOGISTIC REGRESSION

Logistic regression can be employed for linearly as well as non-linearly separable problems. It is mostly employed for predicting the probability of an event. Application of logistic regression include: image segmentation, handwriting recognition etc.

So, Logistic regression is a statistical method for analyzing the given dataset in which more than one variable determine an outcome. The algorithm is mainly employed for classification purpose. The outcome is measured with a binary variable (either 0 or1). In Logistic regression a link is used to map the linear combination of independent variable onto Bernoulli distribution. This link is called 'logit' transformation. The equation is given as:

$$Logit(p) = b_0 + b_1 x_1 + b_2 x_2 \tag{2}$$

$$Logit(p) = ln(p/1-p) \tag{3}$$

$$ln(p/1-p) = b_0 + b_1 x_1 + b_2 x_2 \tag{4}$$

solving for p gives

$$p = e^{(b0+b1x1+b2x2)}/(1 + e^{(b0+b1x1+b2x2)}) \tag{5}$$

$$p = 1/(1 + e^{-(b0+b1x1+b2x2)}) \tag{6}$$

'p' refers to the probability of presence of the characteristics of interest.

So, modeling data in logistic regression refers to generating appropriate coefficients (b_0, b_1, b_2) of independent variables from the data set and estimate the probability of presence of new input data to a particular class.

Example

Develop a logistic regression model for the given data set (Table 3).
From the equation (6)

$$p = 1/(1 + e^{-(b0+b1x1+b2x2)})$$

we can employ stochastic gradient descent to the problem of finding coefficient for the logistic regression model as follows.

We start with initializing coefficient as:

Table 3.

x_1	x_2	y
2.78	2.55	0
1.46	2.36	0
3.39	4.40	0
1.38	1.85	0
3.06	3.00	0
7.62	2.75	1
5.33	2.08	1
6.92	1.77	1
8.67	-0.24	1
7.67	3.51	1

$b_0=0; b_1=0; b_2=0$

with the first labeled input data we calculate the prediction as:

x1=2.78 x2=2.55 p=1/2=0.5

we now update the coefficients using the equation

b=b+alpha*(y-p)*p(1-p)*x

Here alpha is the acceleration factor and it is taken to be 0.3 for this problem
For calculating b_0 x=1is taken,
Similarly for calculating b_1 and b_2, x values of 2.78 and 2.55 respectively are substituted in the update equation

$b_0=-0.037; b_1=-0.104, b_2=-0.09564$

The entire process is repeated with next training data and coefficients are updated
After 10 iterations the values are $b_0=-0.41; b_1=0.85, b_2=-1.10$

DISCRIMINANT ANALYSIS

Discriminant analysis is a classification technique based on the estimation of statistical distance of the raw input data and class centers under consideration. Statistical distance accounts for location size and shape of the class clouds. It is also called as Mahalanobis distance. On the assumptions that whenever the data come Gaussian distribution, the statistical distance employ a covariance matrix to evaluate the distance between new data and centroid of the class.

Consider two classes C_1 and C_2. Each data in these classes have three features and $\overline{F_{11}}$, $\overline{F_{12}}$, $\overline{F_{13}}$ represent average value of features for class C_1. The new input data has feature values as F_{1n}, F_{2n}, F_{3n}. The statistical distance between new data and class one can be evaluated as

$$F_1 = [\ \overline{F_{11}}\ \overline{F_{12}}\ \overline{F_{13}}\ ]^T \tag{7}$$

$$F_n = [\ F_{1n}\ F_{2n}\ F_{3n}]^T \tag{8}$$

$$D(F_n, F_1) = \sqrt{((F_n-F_1)^T S^{-1} (F_n-F_1))} \tag{9}$$

Here S represents covariance matrix between different predictors. Similarly the statistical distance between F_n and F_2 can be calculated. The lesser of the two values would identify the class for the new input. Similar procedure can be done for multiple class problems.

Example

As part of customer acquisition efforts, Bank A plans to run a campaign for current customers to purchase a loan. To improve target marketing, they want to identify the customers most likely to accept the loan offer. They use data from previous campaign on 5000 customers where 450 customers accepted.

So there are two classes: Acceptors and Non acceptors

For each of these class three attributes or features are employed (credit card average, age, income) and average of these features for both the classes are evaluated (using the database of customers).

So, if a new customer with feature as (CCavg=2.70, age=44, income=100) comes, the objective is to find which class he will fall into:

Now if the covariance matrix 'S' for acceptors is formulated (using the database) as:

Then, statistical distance of the input class with acceptor class can be calculated as:

$$D(x_0, x'_{acc}) = \sqrt{((x_0 - x'_{acc})^T S^{-1}(x_0 - x'_{acc}))}$$

x' denote the average values of the features.

x-x'=[2.7 44 100]-[3.91 45.07 144.75]

inverse(S)=

Substituting the values in equation ()

$D = \sqrt{15.22} = 3.9$

Table 4.

	Non Acceptors	**Acceptors**
Average CCavg	1.73	3.91
Average Age	45.37	45.07
Average Income	66.24	144.75

Table 5.

	CCavg	**Age**	**Income**
CCavg	995.5	14.21	7.77
Age	14.21	4.39	-0.06
Income	7.77	-0.06	134.07

Table 6.

0.0011	-0.0034	-0.0001
-0.0034	0.2388	0.0003
-0.0001	0.0003	0.0075

Figure 1.

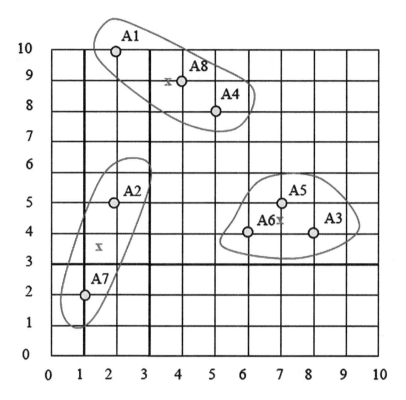

LINEAR SUPPORT VECTOR MACHINES

Support Vector Machines (SVMs) are a good example of the way in which current machine learning research combines ideas from different research areas. SVMs were introduced in the early nineties by Boser and his co-authors (1992), bringing together ideas that had been around since the 1960s—and the topic has developed into a very active research area.

Suppose classification is to be made in two classes: class red and class blue and there are two features, then the objective is to find the hyper-plane that would classify the labeled data into two classes. Now, there may be many such planes that would classify the data correctly. So now the point is which hyper-plane would be suitable. The decision is made on the basis of support vectors. For each qualifying hyper-plane there are support vectors on either side. These vector are passing through the closest elements from the hyperplane on either side of the plane. We select the hyperplane which has the maximum margin with respect to its support vectors. Suppose the equation of the hyperplane is given as:

$G(x) = w^t x + b$ (10)

Here w is weight vector and x is vector of feature and b is constant. Refer Figure 1 Vector $w = [w1, w2...]$ is perpendicular to the hyper-plane (shown in blue). We choose x such that $g(x^-) = -1$ and $g(x^+) = 1$

Also, $x^+ = x^- + r*w$ (11)

Now,

$wx^- + b = -1 \text{ and}$ (12)

$wx^+ + b = 1$ (13)

Substitution eq(11) in eq(13) we get

$w(x^- + r*w) + b = 1$ (14)

$r w^2 + w.x^- + b = 1$ (15)

$r w^2 - 1 = 1$ (16)

$r = 2 / w^2$ (17)

$M = x^+ - x^-$ (18)

$= r*w$

$r = 2 / w$ (19)

Objective problem becomes

$$Max(\frac{2}{\sqrt{w^T w}})$$ (20)

Such that all data lie on the correct side of the margin

We define $y^{(i)} = 1 \rightarrow wx^i + b \geq 1$

$$y^{(i)} = -1 \rightarrow wx^i + b \leq 1 \tag{21}$$

So the constraints can be written as

$$y^{(i)} \left(wx^i + b \right) \geq 1 \tag{22}$$

Now the optimization problem can be solved using done using Lagrangian function method and weights value (w) can be calculated. With these weights hyper-plane can be estimated. The variables of new input data are substituted in hyperplane equation to get a value and the sign of this value decides on which side of the hyper-plane the new data belongs to.

Now if the data is inseparable then SVM uses a mapping function to change the input data into another feature space in such a manner that the data becomes linearly separable. Such functions are called "Kernel' Functions.

K NEAREST NEIGHBOR ALGORITHM

K nearest Neighbor Algorithm (KNN) is a classification algorithm. Here the Euclidean distance between the raw input data and other labeled data is evaluated. K closest values are identified and ranked. The class which has majority of the closest values becomes the predicted class for the input data. The biggest advantage of the KNN is that it is robust to noisy training data. So, it can be said that KNN is an intuitive algorithm that identifies the class of unlabeled data based on its similarity with data in the training samples. So for classification purpose, KNN only requires: integer K, set of labeled example, and a metric to measure closeness (Euclidean Distance)

Example

We have data from the questionnaires survey and two attributes (acid durability and strength) to classify whether a special paper tissue is 'good' or 'bad'. Four training samples are given as:

Now a factory produces a new paper tissue with X1=3 and X2=7. The objective is to identify which class it belongs to but with exhaustive survey.

So, we start by taking k=3, then the distance between the query instance (new input) and all the training samples are evaluated

Table 7.

X1	X2	y
7	7	BAD
7	4	BAD
3	4	GOOD
1	4	GOOD

Distances evaluated are then ranked and 3 nearest neighbor are determined. We collect the classes of these nearest neighbors. So, since we have 2 'good' and '1 bad', we conclude that new tissue paper falls in 'good' class.

UNSUPERVISED MACHINE LEARNING

Unsupervised machine learning is the machine learning task of inferring a function that describes the structure of "unlabeled" data (i.e. data that has not been classified or categorized). Since the examples given to the learning algorithm are unlabeled, there is no straightforward way to evaluate the accuracy of the structure that is produced by the algorithm-one feature that distinguishes unsupervised learning from supervised learning and reinforcement learning. Unsupervised learning is where you only have input data (X) and no corresponding output variables.

The goal for unsupervised learning is to model the underlying structure or distribution in the data in order to learn more about the data.

These are called unsupervised learning because unlike supervised learning above there is no correct answer and there is no teacher. Algorithms are left to their own devises to discover and present the interesting structure in the data.

Unsupervised learning is the training of an artificial intelligence (AI) algorithm using information that is neither classified nor labeled and allowing the algorithm to act on that information without guidance.

Table 8.

X1	X2	Distance
7	7	$(7-3)^2+(7-7)^2=16$
7	4	$(7-3)^2+(4-7)^2=25$
3	4	$(3-3)^2+(4-7)^2=9$
1	4	$(1-3)^2+(4-7)^2=13$

In unsupervised learning, an AI system may group unsorted information according to similarities and differences even though there are no categories provided. AI systems capable of unsupervised learning are often associated with generative learning models, although they may also use a retrieval-based approach (which is most often associated with supervised learning). Chatbots, self-driving cars, facial recognition programs, expert systems and robots are among the systems that may use either supervised or unsupervised learning approaches.

In unsupervised learning, an AI system is presented with unlabeled, uncategorised data and the system's algorithms act on the data without prior training. The output is dependent upon the coded algorithms. Subjecting a system to unsupervised learning is one way of testing AI.

Unsupervised learning algorithms can perform more complex processing tasks than supervised learning systems. However, unsupervised learning can be more unpredictable than the alternate model. While an unsupervised learning AI system might, for example, figure out on its own how to sort cats from dogs, it might also add unforeseen and undesired categories to deal with unusual breeds, creating clutter instead of order.

Unsupervised learning methods are used in bioinformatics for sequence analysis and genetic clustering; in data mining for sequence and pattern mining; in medical imaging for image segmentation; and in computer vision for object recognition.

Unsupervised learning problems can be further grouped into clustering and association problems.

- **Clustering:** A clustering problem is where you want to discover the inherent groupings in the data, such as grouping customers by purchasing behavior.
- **Association:** An association rule learning problem is where you want to discover rules that describe large portions of your data, such as people that buy X also tend to buy Y.

Some popular examples of unsupervised learning algorithms are:

- k-means for clustering problems.
- Apriori algorithm for association rule learning problems.

CLUSTERING ALGORITHMS

The most common unsupervised learning method is cluster analysis, which is used for exploratory data analysis to find hidden patterns or grouping in data. The clusters are modeled using a measure of similarity which is defined upon metrics such as Euclidean or probabilistic distance. The most common clustering algorithms are:

- K-Means Clustering
- Hierarchical Clustering

K-Means Clustering

The k-means algorithm takes as input a parameter k and partitions a set of n objects into k clusters so that elements belonging to the same cluster possess similar properties. Or in other words we can say that the resulting intracluster similarity is high but the intercluster is low. We can measure the cluster similarity in terms of the mean value of the objects in the cluster. This mean can be viewed as the clusters center of gravity.

Method:

1. Randomly select k objects each of which initially represents a cluster mean or center.
2. For every other remaining object, find a cluster to which it is the most similar, based on the distance between the object and the cluster mean.
3. Compute the new mean of each cluster.
4. Continue Steps 1 to 3 until the criterion function converges. Typically the squared error criterion is used and it is defined as:

$$E= \sum i=1 \text{ to } k \sum p \in Ci \mid p\text{-}mi \mid 2$$

where E is the sum of square error for all objects in the database, p is the point in space representing a given object, and mi is the mean of cluster Ci (both p and mi are multidimensional).

The above mentioned criterion function E tries to make the resulting k clusters as compact and as separate as possible.

The method is relatively scalable and efficient in processing large data set because the computational complexity of the algorithm is O(nkt) where n is the total number of objects, k is the number of clusters and t is the number of iterations. Normally, k <<n and t<<n. The method terminates at local optimum.

This algorithm can be applied only when it is possible to define the mean of the objects. It is not always possible because in some applications categorical attributes are involved whose mean value cannot be determined. Another necessary condition is that the users must predefine the number of clusters k. The algorithm is sensitive to noise and outlier data points since the addition or deletion of small amount of data can substantially affect the mean value and hence the clusters obtained.

Example

Use the k-means algorithm and Euclidean distance to cluster the following 8 points into 3 clusters:

A1=(2,10), A2=(2,5), A3=(8,4), A4=(5,8), A5=(7,5), A6=(6,4), A7=(1,2), A8=(4,9).

Suppose that the initial seeds (centers of each cluster) are A1, A4 and A7. Run the k-means algorithm for 1 iteration only. At the end of this iteration show:

A. The new clusters (i.e. the examples belonging to each cluster)
B. The centers of the new clusters
C. Draw a 10 by 10 space with all the 8 points and show the clusters after the first iteration and the new centroids.
D. How many more iterations are needed to converge? Draw the result for each iteartion.

Solution: Part A

d(a,b) denotes the Eucledian distance between the points a=(x1,y1) and b=(x2,y2). It is obtained directly using the equation:

d(a,b)=$\sqrt{}$ (x2-x1)2+(y2-y1)2

The distance matrix based on the Euclidean distance is given in Table 9.

Let seed1=A1=(2,10), seed2=A4=(5,8), seed3=A7=(1,2)

Iteration-1

See Table 10.
This ends iteration1.
New Clusters after iteration 1:

Table 9.

	A1	A2	A3	A4	A5	A6	A7	A8
A1	0	$\sqrt{25}$	$\sqrt{36}$	$\sqrt{13}$	$\sqrt{50}$	$\sqrt{52}$	$\sqrt{65}$	$\sqrt{5}$
A2		0	$\sqrt{37}$	$\sqrt{18}$	$\sqrt{25}$	$\sqrt{17}$	$\sqrt{10}$	$\sqrt{20}$
A3			0	$\sqrt{25}$	$\sqrt{2}$	$\sqrt{2}$	$\sqrt{53}$	$\sqrt{41}$
A4				0	$\sqrt{13}$	$\sqrt{17}$	$\sqrt{52}$	$\sqrt{2}$
A5					0	$\sqrt{2}$	$\sqrt{45}$	$\sqrt{25}$
A6						0	$\sqrt{29}$	$\sqrt{29}$
A7							0	$\sqrt{58}$
A8								0

Table 10.

A1: $d(A1, seed1)=0$ as A1 is seed1 $d(A1, seed2)= \sqrt{13} >0$ $d(A1, seed3)= \sqrt{65} >0$ Hence, A1 $\in$ cluster1	A2: $d(A2,seed1)= \sqrt{25} = 5$ $d(A2, seed2)= \sqrt{18} = 4.24$ $d(A2, seed3)= \sqrt{10} = 3.16$ (smallest) Hence, A2 $\in$ cluster3
A3: $d(A3, seed1)= \sqrt{36} = 6$ $d(A3, seed2)= \sqrt{25} = 5$ (smallest) $d(A3, seed3)= \sqrt{53} = 7.28$ Hence, A3 $\in$ cluster2	A4: $d(A4, seed1)= \sqrt{13}$ $d(A4, seed2)=0$ as A4 is seed2 $d(A4, seed3)= \sqrt{52} >0$ Hence, A4 $\in$ cluster2
A5: $d(A5, seed1)= \sqrt{50} = 7.07$ $d(A5, seed2)= \sqrt{13} = 3.60$ (smallest) $d(A5, seed3)= \sqrt{45} = 6.70$ Hence, A5 $\in$ cluster2	A6: $d(A6, seed1)= \sqrt{52} = 7.21$ $d(A6, seed2)= \sqrt{17} = 4.12$ (smallest) $d(A6, seed3)= \sqrt{29} = 5.38$ Hence, A6 $\in$ cluster2
A7: $d(A7, seed1)= \sqrt{65} >0$ $d(A7, seed2)= \sqrt{52} >0$ $d(A7, seed3)=0$ as A7 is seed3 Hence, A7 $\in$ cluster3	A8: $d(A8, seed1)= \sqrt{5}$ $d(A8, seed2)= \sqrt{2}$ (smallest) $d(A8, seed3)= \sqrt{58}$ Hence, A8 $\in$ cluster2

1: {A1}, 2: {A3, A4, A5, A6, A8}, 3: {A2, A7}

Part B

The centers of the new clusters can be determined as:

C1=(2,10)

C2=((8+5+7+6+4)/5, (4+8+5+4+9)/5)= (6,6)

C3=((2+1)/2, (5+2)/2)= (1.5, 3.5)

Part C

See Figure 2-5.

Part D

We need two more iterations.

After the second iteration the result would be:

1: {A1, A8}, 2: {A3, A4, A5, A6}, 3: {A2, A7} with centers C1=(3, 9.5), C2=(6.5, 5.25) and C3=(1.5, 3.5).

Figure 2.

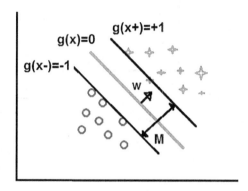

Figure 3.

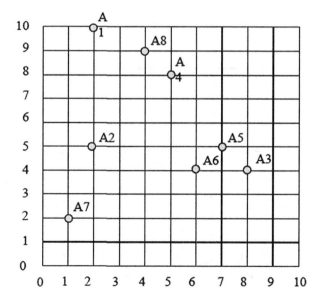

Figure 4.

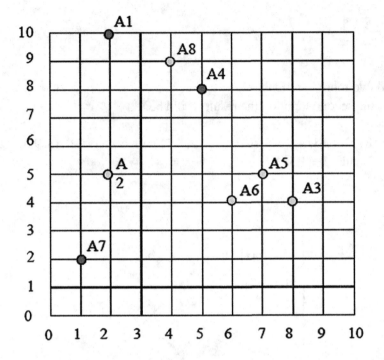

Figure 5.

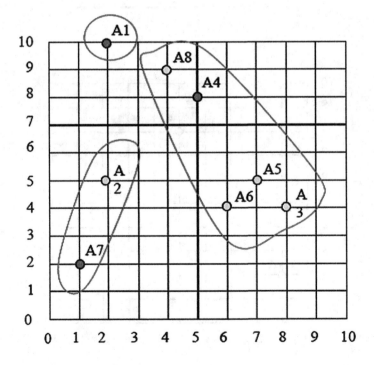

After the 3rd epoch, the results would be:

1: {A1, A4, A8}, 2: {A3, A5, A6}, 3: {A2, A7} with centers C1=(3.66, 9), C2=(7, 4.33) and C3=(1.5, 3.5).

Hierarchical Clustering

The second commonly used clustering method is the hierarchical clustering method. In this method of clustering the data objects are grouped into a tree of clusters. Depending on whether the hierarchical decomposition is formed in a top down or bottom up manner, hierarchical clustering can be further divided into two types:

- **Agglomerative Clustering:** This is a bottom up strategy of building a cluster. It starts by placing each object in its own cluster and then merges these atomic clusters into larger clusters until all the objects are there in a single cluster or until certain termination conditions are satisfied. Most of the hierarchical clustering algorithms belong to this category.

Figure 6.

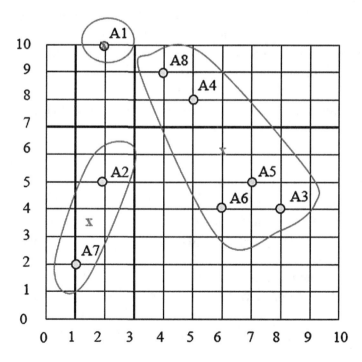

Figure 7.

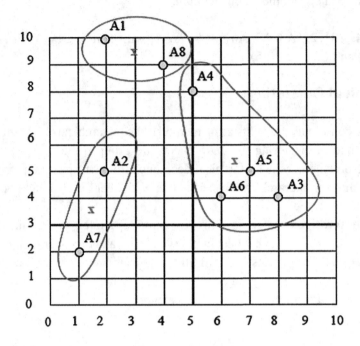

- **Divisive Clustering:** This method is the reverse of Agglomerative Clustering. It follows the top down method for clustering a set of data objects. Initially all the objects belong to a single cluster. It then subdivides the cluster into smaller fragments until each object forms a cluster on its own or until it satisfies certain termination conditions such as a desired number of clusters is obtained or the distance between the two closest clusters is above a certain threshold distance.

ASSOCIATION ALGORITHMS

Association algorithms are another way of implementing unsupervised learning. Due to the rapid growth of data generation and its storage every day, there is an increasing interest among the companies to find the association rules in their databases. The discovery of association rules or the relationships among the various data items in the databases can help in many decision making processes as it will represent the dependencies among the data items. Association rules are represented by using if/then statements that will help to reveal the relationships between seemingly unrelated data in a relational database or other information repository. An example of an association rule would be "If a customer buys a computer system he is likely to purchase the antivirus software." In data mining, association rules are useful for analyzing and predicting the behavior of the customer. They play an important part in market basket data analysis, product clustering, catalog design and store layout.

An association rule is composed of two parts: an antecedent (if) and a consequent (then). An item that is found in the data is referred to as an antecedent whereas a consequent is an item that is found in combination with the antecedent or that has a high probability of occurrence with the antecedent.

Association rules are created by analyzing data for frequent if/then patterns and using the criteria support and confidence to identify the most important relationships. Support is an indication of how frequently the items appear in the database and Confidence indicates the number of times the if/then statements have been found to be true. Association rules are considered to be interesting if they satisfy a minimum support threshold and a minimum confidence threshold. These thresholds can be either defined by the user or the domain experts.

Apriori Algorithm

The Apriori principle can reduce the number of itemsets we need to examine. Put simply, the apriori principle states that if an itemset is infrequent, then all its subsets must also be infrequent. This means that if {beer} was found to be infrequent, we can expect {beer, pizza} to be equally or even more infrequent. So in consolidating the list of popular itemsets, we need not consider {beer, pizza}, nor any other itemset configuration that contains beer.

Step 1: Finding Itemsets With High Support

Using the Apriori principle, the number of itemsets that have to be examined can be pruned, and the list of popular itemsets can be obtained in these steps:

1. Start with itemsets containing just a single item, such as {apple} and {pear}.
2. Determine the support for itemsets. Keep the itemsets that meet your minimum support threshold, and remove itemsets that do not.
3. Using the itemsets you have kept from Step 1, generate all the possible itemset configurations.
4. Repeat Steps 1 & 2 until there are no more new itemsets.

Step 2: Finding Item Rules With High Confidence or Lift

We have seen how the Apriori algorithm can be used to identify itemsets with high support. The same principle can also be used to identify item associations with high confidence or lift. Finding rules with high confidence or lift is less computationally taxing once high-support itemsets have been identified, because confidence and lift values are calculated using support values.

Take for example the task of finding high-confidence rules. If the rule has low confidence, all other rules with the same constituent items and with apple on the right hand side would have low confidence too.

```
{beer, chips -> apple}
```

Specifically, the rules would have low confidence as well.

```
{beer -> apple, chips}
{chips -> apple, beer}
```

As before, lower level candidate item rules can be pruned using the Apriori algorithm, so that fewer candidate rules need to be examined.

Limitations

- **Computationally Expensive**: Even though the Apriori algorithm reduces the number of candidate itemsets to consider, this number could still be huge when store inventories are large or when the support threshold is low. However, an alternative solution would be to reduce the number of comparisons by using advanced data structures, such as hash tables, to sort candidate itemsets more efficiently.
- **Spurious Associations**: Analysis of large inventories would involve more itemset configurations, and the support threshold might have to be lowered to detect certain associations. However, lowering the support threshold might also increase the number of spurious associations detected. To ensure that identified associations are generalizable, they could first be distilled from a training dataset, before having their support and confidence assessed in a separate test dataset.

CONCLUSION

Machine Learning is an evolving field of computer engineering where existing systems are given intelligence to assist humans in performing several tasks with increased efficiency and less computational time. Intelligence can be created through learning. Learning process can be classified as supervised and unsupervised. Thus this chapter aims to give readers an overview of the commonly used learning algorithms. These learning methods can be used to develop real time intelligent applications.

REFERENCES

Boser, B. E., Guyon, I. M., & Vapnik, V. N. (1992). A training algorithm for optimal margin classifiers. In *Proc. 5th Annual ACM Workshop on Computational Learning Theory*. Pittsburgh, PA: ACM Press. 10.1145/130385.130401

Clark, P., & Niblett, R. (1989). The CN2 induction algorithm. *Machine Learning*, 3.

Cohen, W. W. (1995). Fast effective rule induction. *Proceedings of the Twelfth International Conference on Machine Learning*.

Dietterich, T. G. (1997). Machine-learning research: Four current directions. *AI Magazine*, 18.

Han, J., Pei, J., & Kamber, M. (2011). *Data mining: concepts and techniques*. Elsevier.

Langley, P. (1996). *Elements of Machine Learning*. San Mateo, CA: Morgan Kaufmann.

Michalski, R. S., Bratko, I., & Kubat, M. (1988). *Machine learning and data mining: methods and applications*. John Wiley and Sons.

Mitchell, T. M. (1997). *Machine Learning*. New York: McGraw-Hill. Retrieved from http://www.cs.cmu.edu/~tom/mlbook.html

Mitchell, T. M. (1997). Does machine learning really work. *AI Magazine*, *18*(3).

Turing, A. M. (2009). Computing machinery and intelligence. In *Parsing the Turing Test* (pp. 23–65). Dordrecht: Springer. doi:10.1007/978-1-4020-6710-5_3

Witten, I. H., & Frank, E. (2000). *Data Mining: Practical Machine Learning Tools and Techniques with Java Implementations*. San Mateo, CA: Morgan Kaufmann. Retrieved from http://www.cs.waikato.ac.nz/ml/weka/

Chapter 10
Rainfall Prediction Model Using Exponential Smoothing Seasonal Planting Index (ESSPI) For Determination of Crop Planting Pattern

Kristoko Dwi Hartomo
*Satya Wacana Christian University,
Indonesia*

Muchamad Taufiq Anwar
*Satya Wacana Christian University,
Indonesia*

Sri Yulianto Joko Prasetyo
*Satya Wacana Christian University,
Indonesia*

Hindriyanto Dwi Purnomo
*Satya Wacana Christian University,
Indonesia*

ABSTRACT

The traditional crop farmers rely heavily on rain pattern to decide the time for planting crops. The emerging climate change has caused a shift in the rain pattern and consequently affected the crop yield. Therefore, providing a good rainfall prediction models would enable us to recommend best planting pattern (when to plant) in order to give maximum yield. The recent and widely used rainfall prediction model for determining the cropping patterns using exponential smoothing method recommended by the Food and Agriculture Organization (FAO) suffered from short-term forecasting inconsistencies and inaccuracies for long-term forecasting. In this study, the authors developed a new rainfall prediction model which applied exponential smoothing onto seasonal planting index as the basis for determining planting pattern. The results show that the model gives better accuracy than the original exponential smoothing model.

DOI: 10.4018/978-1-5225-7955-7.ch010

INTRODUCTION

An accurate rainfall prediction model is needed to overcome the problem of shifting rainfall patterns. Rainfall prediction models for determining cropping patterns recommended by the Food and Agriculture Organization (FAO) is the exponential smoothing to replace the linear models such as regressions which are still widely used. The weakness of this model is the innacuracy in short-term forecasting and inconsistencies for long-term forecasting. This study aims to develop a new model of rainfall prediction using the Exponential Smoothing Seasonal Planting Index (ESSPI) method which has a high degree of accuracy. The next goal is to formulate a new theoretical framework for grouping rainfall data based on the seasonal planting index, a new method of determining smoothing value (α) using the method seasonal planting index, and a new model for predicting rainfall using a seasonal planting index for determining rice cropping patterns.

RELATED WORKS

According to Naylor et al. (2007), some experts find and predict the direction of rainfall pattern changes in the western part of Indonesia, especially in the northern part of Sumatra and Kalimantan, where rainfall intensity tends to be lower, but with a longer period. In contrast, in the southern regions of Java and Bali rainfall intensity tends to increase but with a shorter period. Hartomo et al. (2015) also stated that in certain region such as in Boyolali, Central Java, there had been recorded some shifts in the peak rain pattern during 1969-1979, 1979-1989 and 2000-2010.

Shifting rainfall patterns affect agricultural resources and infrastructure which causes shifts in planting time, seasons, cropping patterns and land degradation. The tendency to shorten the rainy season and increase rainfall in the southern part of Java and Bali resulted in an initial change and duration of the planting season, thus affecting the planting index (PI), planting area, initial planting time and cropping patterns. The retreat of the beginning of the rainy season for 30 days can reduce rice production in West Java and Central Java by 6.5% and in Bali reach 11% of normal conditions. Rice productivity in Brebes Regency is the highest among rice productivity in other districts/cities, which is 65.19 quintals per hectare. The lowest productivity was recorded in Klaten Regency which was 43.19 quintals per hectare.

Rainfall prediction model recommended by the Food and Agriculture Organization (FAO) is the exponential smoothing to replace linear models such as regression which is still widely used for weather prediction in relation to agricultural cultivation. This model is recommended with high accuracy in short-term predictions. According to Ngopya (2009), the first weakness of this model is short-term forecasting inconsistencies, for example, the fact that there is a decrease in agricultural cultivation production in an area caused by drought but the model still illustrates the existence of rain. The second weakness, this model is not accurate for long-term forecasting (12 periods). Rainfall prediction model was then developed by Mara (2013), combining methods of hybridizing exponential smoothing and neural network for forecasting rainfall data. From the studies that have been done, it can be concluded that the weight parameter estimation with the least squares method in the model hybridizing exponential smoothing with the neural network does not provide optimal results. This is because square errors in the merging model will shift the fit of the curve to another point so as to reduce the accuracy of the predicted results.

Rainfall prediction models using ARIMA tested using RMSE produce low standard error values, indicating the predictive model is quite reliable (Mahsin, 2012). By comparing the predicted value and the actual value of the rainfall data using the ARIMA model it can be concluded that the results of rainfall forecasts are quite accurate. With the ARIMA model of two-year monthly rainfall can be predicted with a 90% confidence interval. According to Makridakis and Hibon (2000), for the long-term prediction of the shortcomings of the ARIMA method is a decrease in the level of accuracy and high complexity to be implemented into a prediction model rainfall so that it does not fulfill the aspect of parsimony/ simplicity.

Judging from the literature (Naylor et al., 2007; Murdohardono, 2007; Ngopya, 2009; Surmaini et al., 2010; Sari et al., 2010; Mahsin, 2012; Mara, 2013) rainfall prediction models used for determining cropping patterns cannot provide accurate long-term rainfall prediction results and still use methods with high complexity. The literature also shows that there is no rainfall prediction model that is integrated with the model of determining the planting period based on spatial connectivity between planting locations in one region and neighboring regions. Especially for rainfall prediction method with exponential smoothing there is a problem in determining the smoothing value (α, β, and γ) to minimize errors, the general approach used determines the smoothing value by trial and error (Hyndman et al., 2008) To overcome these weaknesses, this research proposed a rainfall prediction model usimg Exponential Smoothing Seasonal Planting Index (ESSPI) for determining cropping patterns.

Research on Rainfall Prediction

Makridakis and Hibon (2000) conducted a study using the exponential smoothing method for prediction, there are three types of exponential methods used, namely the simple exponential method (for data with stationary patterns), double exponentials which use two parameters known as the Holt method for smoothing data trend, and a three-parameter exponential forecasting method for smoothing seasonal data. Determining the value of smoothing parameters is still a weakness of the research of Makridakis and Hibon (2000), the approach used is trial and error. State space framework for automatic computational prediction using exponential smoothing method was developed by Hyndman et al. (2002), state space framework provides convenience for every possibility in computational prediction, computation of prediction intervals for each method, and is able to handle computational predictions with random simulations. This study has the disadvantage of high accuracy only for short-term predictions (prediction of a maximum of six periods), while for long-term predictions, it has large error values (predictive results are not accurate). Taylor's (2003) study was continued by Ai (2004) which uses exponential smoothing as a time series prediction method using past data weighting and uses exponential refining values as predictions of events in the future. The results show that some exponential smoothing methods meet the element parsimony (simplicity) and are suitable for short-term predictions but have shortcomings for predicting seasonal data because of the high error values in their predictions.

Khandakar et al. (2008) focused on conducting research on the computation and automatic prediction of a large number of univariate time series data. This research describing two automatic forecasting algorithms implemented in the R package. The first discussion uses an innovative model called the state space that underlies the exponential smoothing method, the second is the prediction algorithm using the ARIMA model. The algorithm applies to both seasonal and non-seasonal data, compared and visualized using four real time series. Subsequent research conducted by Ngopya (2009) discusses the short-term forecasting method using exponential smoothing method recommended by the FAO replacing linear models such as the regression that is still widely used for rainfall prediction in relation to the determination of planting time. The weakness of the model exponential smoothing is short-term forecasting inconsistencies (Burkom et al., 2009) as an example of the fact that there is a decrease in agricultural cultivation production in an area caused by drought but the model still illustrates an increase in production. According to Ngopya (2009), the method is exponential smoothing recommended with high accuracy in short term prediction (predictions in the period 1 - 2 periods in the future). Another problem in this study is in determining the smoothing value (α, β, and γ) to minimize errors, the general approach used determines the smoothing value by trial and error.

Research on forecasting the future rainfall was done by Sutrisno (2009) to determine the length of the rainy season by measuring the average monthly rainfall of an area. If monthly rainfall is greater than 150 mm, the length of the rainy season is 6 months and the length of the dry season is 6 months. If the results of rainfall measurements on a 10-days basis (*dasarian*) are greater or equal to 50 mm, and in the next 2 *dasarian* have the same rainfall, that '*dasarian*' is the beginning of the rainy season (Swarinoto, 2009). Research conducted by Swarinoto (2009) was improved by Tresnawati et al. (2010) by predicting monthly rainfall in Purbalingga area using the *Kalman filter* method with an SST 3.4 predictor. Validation of predictions to three years backwards (hindcast) 2006, 2007, 2008 showed a correlation coefficient of 75%. To obtain the SST Nino 3.4 predictor value, it was predicted using the ARIMA method. Validation of Nino 3.4 SST prediction during the three-year testing period shows that in 2006 r = 0.91, 2007 r = 0.64 and 2008 r = 0.82. Related to the research of Tresnawati et al. (2010) is the research by Mahsin (2012) with the main objective of improving predictive accuracy with the ARIMA model to forecast monthly rainfall in Dhaka, Bangladesh. Mahsin (2012) predicted the monthly rainfall in Dhaka, Bangladesh for the period of July 2010 to June 2012 using the ARIMA method. The results of this research testing using RMSE produce a standard error of low value. A common weakness in the application of the ARIMA method for forecasting rainfall is the high complexity in the implementation of ARIMA to become a rainfall prediction model (Dong et al., 2013).

Time series analysis and prediction have become the main tools in various applications in meteorological phenomena, such as rainfall, humidity, and temperature (Sofla et al., 2013). Subsequent research carried out by Edward (2013) is based on the interaction between the atmosphere and the sea which is very important to be studied related to its large influence on rainfall variability in Indonesia. This study aims to study the interaction of Monsun and Niño 3.4 in influencing rainfall fluctuations in Indonesia. The study area included Lampung, Sumbawa Besar, Indramayu, Banjarbaru, and Pandeglang for the period from January 1976 to December 2000. Power Spectral Density (PSD) analysis and wavelet analysis on rainfall anomalies and monsoon index data were strong at 12 months. The next theoretical and research studies on time series forecasting are carried out by Mara et al. (2013), a study conducted to study hybridizing exponential smoothing and neural networks for time series data forecasting. From the research and theoretical studies that have been carried out, it can be concluded that the parameter weight estimation with the least squares method in the hybridizing exponential smoothing model with the neural network does not provide optimal results. This is because square errors in the merging model will shift the fit of the curve to another point so it reduce the accuracy of the predicted results.

From the literature review related to research on rainfall prediction, it can be concluded that the application of methods exponential smoothing for short-term rainfall prediction (one or two periods in the future) has good accuracy with low errors and meets the principles of parsimony (simplicity) for application. The weakness of the exponential smoothing method is its low accuracy for long-term predictions (Hyndman et al., 2002; Ngopya, 2009; Mara et al., 2013; Prasetyo et al., 2013). According to Makridakis and Hibon (2000), the next weakness is determining the smoothing value (α, β, and γ) to minimize errors, the general approach used to determine the smoothing value was by trial and error. A common weakness in the application of the ARIMA method for forecasting rainfall is the high complexity in the implementation of ARIMA to become a rainfall prediction model. Table 1 shows the recap of journals from previous studies with topics related to rainfall prediction models.

Analysis of literature studies on the complexity of rainfall prediction with the ARIMA method, Box-Jenkins as the inventor admitted that the theoretical basis is very complex. The ARIMA method is complex because it combines time series models which include the models Auto-Regressive (AR) and Moving Average (MA). Among other things, because the process of differentiation includes non-

Table 1. Research on rainfall prediction

No	Reference	Topic	Method			Output		
			ARIMA	Exponential Smoothing	Holt-Winters	Spatial Patern	Cluster/Hotspot	Graph
1	Makridakis dan Hibon (2000)	Time series prediction		√				√
2	Hyndman et al. (2002)	Computation and prediction model		√				√
3	Ai (2004)	Time series prediction		√				√
4	Burkom et al. (2006)	Rainfall prediction model			√	√		√
5	Khandakar et al. (2008)	Computation and prediction model	√	√				√
6	Ngopya (2009)	Rainfall prediction model		√				√
7	Swarinoto (2009)	Rainfall prediction model	√					√
8	Tresnawati et al. (2010)	Rainfall prediction model	√				√	√
9	Fildes dan Kourentzes (2011)	Climate change model	√	√				√
10	Mahsin et al. (2012)	Computation and prediction model	√				√	√
11	Sofla et al. (2013)	Rainfall prediction model		√				√
12	Dong et al. (2013)	Computation and prediction model	√			√	√	√
13	Edward (2013)	Rainfall prediction model		√		√	√	√
14	Mara et al. (2013)	Rainfall prediction model		√				√

seasonal and seasonal factors coupled with the processes of Auto Regressive and Moving Average. The Holt-Winters method also has high complexity because it requires three smoothing parameters for rainfall prediction, each parameter can be any value between 0 and 1, and many combinations must be tried before the optimal smoothing value can be determined. Theoretically, rainfall prediction using the method exponential smoothing by Brown has a low complexity because it only has one smoothing parameter. ARIMA and Holt-Winters method can be used for seasonal pattern in time series and nonseasonal data simultaneously, while the exponential smoothing method by Brown only corresponds to the pattern of data trend and short-term predictions.

Exponential Smoothing Methods

Exponential Smoothing methods consist of three categories: (1) Single exponential smoothing, (2) Holt Exponential Smoothing, or so-called Double Exponential Smoothing (Holt) and (3) Holt-Winters Exponential Smoothing, or so-called Triple Exponential Smoothing (HW) (Kalekar, 2004). The Single Exponential Smoothing method is used to analyze time series data that is not seasonal and has no particular tendency. The Holt method is used to analyze data with certain tendency (trends) but not seasonal. The HW method is used to analyze data that is seasonal and has a certain tendency / trend (Rijpkema, 2012).

Single Exponential Smoothing is generally used for short-term predictions (1 month). The basic assumptions used as reference are the level of fluctuations in data that are still around the mean value without the formation of a trend. Single Exponential Smoothing (Makridakis and Hibon, 2000) can be seen in Equation (1):

$$F_{t+1} = \left(\frac{1}{n}\right)x_t + \left(1 - \left(\frac{1}{n}\right)\right)F_t \tag{1}$$

where:

F_{t+1} = Prediction for time t + 1

$\left(\frac{1}{n}\right)$ = Smoothing constant, denoted as α with a value between 0 and 1

$\left\{1 - \left(\frac{1}{n}\right)\right\}$ = Actual value of a time series

Double Exponential Smoothing is generally applied to the data which form the pattern of a tendency / trend. Trend is defined as the result of estimating the average growth smoothing in each data period. Double Exponential Smoothing, according to Holt, smoothes the trend value using different parameters from the parameters used in the original series. The prediction of Holt linear exponentials smoothing is obtained by using two smoothing constants (with values between 0 and 1) and three equations (Makridakis and Hibon, 2000):

$$S_t = \propto X_t + \left(1 - \propto\right)\left(S_{t-1} + b_{t-1}\right) \tag{2}$$

$$b_t = \gamma\left(S_t - S_{t-1}\right) + \left(1 - \,^3\right)b_{t-1} \tag{3}$$

$$F_{t+m} = a_t + b_t m \tag{4}$$

where:

b_{t-1} = Trend of previous period
S_{t-1} = Last smoothing value
$S_t - S_{t-1}$ = Trend in the last period
F_t = Result of prediction at time t
m = Period of data to be predicted
b_t = Trend
S_t = Base value

Triple Exponential Smoothing, according to Winters (Makridakis and Hibon, 2000), is used for seasonal data analysis. Often times, time series data shows seasonal trends. Seasonal refers to the tendency of time series data to show recurrent pattern at any given time period or in each period of T. For example, rainfall will increase in intensity in November, or air temperature will increase in April. This pattern will continue to repeat every year. However, the value of the increase will change relatively from year to year, although it remains with the same pattern. The Holt-Winters model is based on three smoothing equations, namely one stationary element, one for trend, and one for seasonal with equality (Makridakis and Hibon, 2000). The equations are as follows: smoothing for the entire *winters* in Equation (5), smoothing the trend in Equation (6), seasonal smoothing in Equation (7), and forecasting in Equation (8):

$$S_t = \propto \frac{X_t}{I_{t-L}} + (1 - \propto)(S_{t-1} + b_{t-1}) \tag{5}$$

$$b_t = \gamma(S_t - S_{t-1}) + (1 - {}^3)b_{t-1} \tag{6}$$

$$I_t = \beta \frac{X_t}{S_t} + (1 - \beta)I_{t-L} \tag{7}$$

$$F_{t+m} = (S_t + b_t m)I_{t-L+m} \tag{8}$$

where:

S_t = Smoothing data overall in period t

b_t = Smoothing trend data for period t

I_t = Seasonal smoothing data for period t

$\propto$ = Smoothing constant (value 0 to 1)

β = Trend constant (value 0 to 1)

γ = Seasonal constant (value 0 to 1)

X_t = Actual rainfall data in period t

m = Desired forecasting period

$F_t + m$ = Forecasting data in period t + m

According to Shmueli and Fienberg (2005), exponential smoothing method can be applied in the field surveilan with consideration that this method is simple, easy to interpret, adaptive and easy to develop in automation. Equivalence between exponential smoothing methods and other methods is done by Shmueli and Fienberg (2005) with results as shown in Table 2.

Empirically the prediction accuracy is influenced by data observed and form the prediction model chosen to process the data. One method that can be used for smoothing a group of observational data is to use a moving average model on period n which is formulated as in equation 9.

$$M_t = \left(\frac{x_t + x_{t-1} + x_{t-2} + \ldots + x_{t-n}}{n}\right) \tag{9}$$

Table 2. Equivalence between exponential smoothing methods and ARIMA / SARIMA

Exponential Smoothing	Equivalent ARIMA/SARIMA
Simple exponential smoothing	ARIMA (0, 1, 1)
Holt's (double) linear trend	ARIMA (0, 2, 2)
Damped – trend linear	SARIMA (1,1,2)
Additive Holt – Winters (triple)	SARIMA $(0,1, p+1)(0,1,0)_p$
Multiplicative Holt – Winters (triple)	

(Shmueli and Fienberg, 2005)

where x_t is the observation data and M_t is the smoothing of a group of data. This process uses past observation values (historical values) and current values. The exponential smoothing method works through the exponential use of the moving average model in a certain period (n) as in Equation (3.9). The exponential coefficient value of the moving average model is calculated in such a way that the sum of the residual squares between the actual data value and the predictive data value is minimal. Each value of data processed in period t is given the weight $\beta =$ (1- α) where β <1.0, the value of α is referred to as the smoothing factor. Every historical data (the closest data to the beginning of the process) will have a smaller weight compared to the latest data (Accardi, 1996).

Planting Patterns Determination Model Using Rainfall Prediction Data

The existence of a close relationship between rainfall and SST Nino 3.4 is used as a basis for constructing rainfall prediction models with Kalman filters (Estiningtyas et al., 2008). Based on the results of Hendon (2003) research, it is known that SST Nino 3.4 variability affects 50% of rainfall variation across Indonesia while the SST variability in the Indian Sea is 10-15%. This opinion was reinforced by Boer et al. (1999) which states that sea surface temperature anomalies in Nino 3.4 region have a stronger relationship to monthly rainfall anomalies compared to sea surface temperature anomalies in other zones. Prabowo and Nicholls in Boer and Faqih (2004) also stated that the climate of Indonesia and Australia is closely related to the Nino 3.4 region (170 - 120 West Longitude, 5 North Lattitude - 5 South Lattitude). The Kalman filter is related to the development of the autoregressive statistical forecasting model using recursive techniques to integrate the latest observation data into the model to update previous predictions and continue predictions in the future (Tresnawati, 2010). The analysis process is carried out by setting the model parameters given in such a way that the output produced is similar or resembles measured output. In this case, SST Nino 3.4 is a model input, while rainfall is the model output. Before being used for prediction, the model was first validated with 4 choices of equations, namely: ARX, ARMAX, BJ, and OE. The best equation is determined based on the highest validation correlation coefficient.

Cropping scenarios are arranged based on soil, plant, and rainfall data prediction results predicted by the method Kalman filter. Calculation of plant water balance needs daily rainfall data. To obtain daily rainfall data based on monthly rainfall prediction data is done by taking the value of daily rainfall chance in the same month during the period for which there is data. The level of water demand by plants is known by the plant water balance analysis which is expressed as a relative evapotranspiration deficit, namely the ETR and ETM ratios. ETR / ETM analysis is based on two approaches, namely 1) the relationship between plants (relative loss of yield) and water (relative evapotranspiration) which is a linear function which is generally relevant to be used to estimate crop losses when plants experience stress due to water stress, 2) greater yield loss if plants experience water stress during the critical phase. Good plant conditions are indicated by an ETR / ETM value of more than 0.8, while below 0.8 indicates that the plant will experience water shortages during its growth. This water balance analysis is carried out with the "crop water balance" program, (CWB-ETO) from CIRAD France which has been modified by the Bogor Institute of Agro-climate and Hydrology Research. The commodity used is dryland rice that is 120 days old. The water content of field capacity is 0.360 m3 / m3 and permanent wilting water content is 0.270 m3 / m3. Outline of the stages of analysis, prediction, and determination of the overall cropping pattern is presented in Figure 1.

Weather and climate are the main factors that greatly affect agricultural production. In this study, the most influential and highly variable weather and climate variables are rainfall, with air temperature as supporting variables. Variable exploration of monthly rainfall and air temperature based on the height of the region both primary variables and secondary variables are obtained from relevant agencies, such as the Agency of Meteorology, Climatology and Geophysics (BMKG). The data to be processed consists of monthly per-district rainfall data for 12 years, the use of monthly data in predicting rainfall is to determine the right prediction method seen from the pattern of data in historical accordance with the study of literature (Sutrisno, 2009; Tresnawati, 2010; Mahsin, 2012; Edward, 2013) and monthly data are also used for determining the planting period adjusted to rice planting time in accordance with the literature review (Surmaini et al., 2010; Aqil, 2010). The next step is to explore and analyze rainfall variables to see the data patterns. Variables from spatial data elements consist of area height, location coordinates, area boundaries, slope, irrigation, and drainage. Spatial data will be used on the map of the planting period to be overlaid with weather data.

PROPOSED SOLUTIONS

Rainfall Prediction Using Exponential Smoothing

Rainfall data in Boyolali were interpolated using n-degree polynomials. Fitting and prediction of rainfall uses the smoothing value of $\alpha = 0.1$ and $\alpha = 0.2$.

Fittings of Prediction Points for Actual Points (Training Phase)

The results of fitting the method exponential smoothing for rainfall data from 2003 to 2014 with smoothing values of 0.2 show an increase in the suitability of actual data line patterns and prediction line patterns at all observation points compared to fitting using a smoothing value of 0.1. The graph shows that some rainfall prediction points have values that are too high or too low compared to the actual rainfall value.

Different trends (incompatibility) of fittings for rainfall data due to the smoothing value used is not appropriate. To improve the results match the actual data with prediction data required new methods to determine the value of smoothing and modification of algorithms that can perform fitting with better data In the method, the exponential smoothing approach in adjusting the predictive value can follow changes in trends, but this method cannot easily track the impact of the initialization process on future predictions. Conceptually the analysis method exponential smoothing represents the point of fitting with elements that must be updated every time forming a new point fitting from all past (historical) data.

Rainfall Prediction With Exponential Smoothing

The predictive analysis shows that the method exponential smoothing with 0.1 smoothing value is not suitable to be used to predict rainfall data for cropping planning because the prediction patterns are trendy. The analysis also shows the tendency of methods to exponential smoothing has low accuracy for long-term predictions.

Graph of 2015 rainfall prediction results for Ngemplak District (Figure 2. (A)), Juwangi (Figure 2. (B)), and Andong (Figure 2. (C)) using the method exponential smoothing with a smoothing value of 0.1 and 0.2 indicate a discrepancy with historical data patterns (seasonal patterns). The prediction of data trend patterns with the exponential smoothing method cannot be used to plan cropping patterns. The analysis also shows the tendency of exponential smoothing methods to have low accuracy for long-term predictions.

Figure 1. Stages of rainfall prediction and determination of planting period according to Estiningtyas et al. (2008)

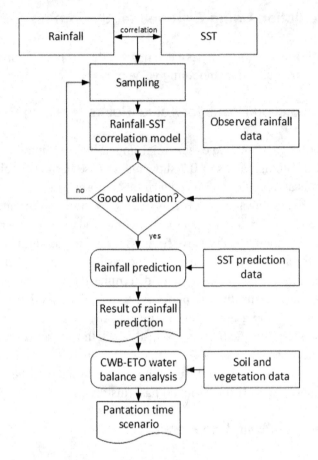

Rainfall Prediction With Exponential Smoothing Seasonal Planting Index

Data Grouping Based on Seasonal Planting Index (SPI)

Data grouping process based on SPI is done on the rainfall data of Ngemplak district at the period of 2003 until 2014. The process begins by grouping rainfall data into u, v, and vectors w vector. Each vector consists of four months, vector u consists of data for January, February, March, and April for the period 2003 to 2014. Vector v consists of data in May, June, July, and August for the period 2003 to 2014. The vector w consisted of data from September, October, November, and December for the period 2003 to 2014.

Determination of Smoothing Value Based on Seasonal Planting Index (SPI)

Based on the results of the analysis of annual rainfall patterns, natural weather phenomena in the research area, and the rice life cycle (time from planting to harvest) in a period of 12 months (1 year), it was decide the value of I_{SP} = ¾. A value of 3 is the number of planting periods in 1 year, the value of 4 is the number of months in a single life cycle of rice plants.

The determination the value of smoothing is based on SPI. According to Makridakis and Hibon, (2000) the value $\propto$ is $0 \leq \propto \leq 1$. For $\propto = 0$, the function exponential smoothing will not be defined . If $\propto = 1$ then S_t = α x_t/1_tL, clearly this is not appropriate because the data to be predicted S_(t is) only based on x_t data so that the data to be predicted is the previous data, therefore the smoothing value $0 < \alpha < 1$ is used. Literature shows that the smoothing value is $\propto$ obtained by trial error, this is considered to be very ineffective to improve the accuracy of predictions quickly and accurately. In this research, the value is $\propto$ formulated formally using an exponential function where $0 < \alpha < 1$.

The smoothing method using SPI provides a novelty on the value definition as one of the weight parameters smoothing because in general it still uses a trial and error method. By using an ISP, the parameters α symbolized as α_{ISP} is formulated as:

$$\alpha_{I_{SP}} = 1 - \exp(-I_{SP}) \tag{10}$$

The exp function is selected to determine the smoothing ($\propto$) value because the standard prediction method used is the method of exponential smoothing. The smoothing ($\propto$) value must be between $0 < \alpha < 1$ then the power - (negative) is selected. Based on the results of an analysis of annual rainfall patterns, natural weather phenomena in the research area, and the rice life cycle (time from planting to harvest) in a period of 12 months (1 year), the value of I_{SP} is determined as ¾ The value of 3 is the number of planting periods in 1 year, the value of 4 is the number of months in a single life cycle of rice plants.

The exponential smoothing method is characterized by setting parameters as weight parameters in the smoothing process. In this research, the smoothing parameter is determined by the approach of seasonal planting index, shown in equation 10, with the selection of I_{SP} = 3/4 it is obtained:

$$\alpha_{I_{SP}} = 1 - \exp(-3/4) = 0.527633 \tag{11}$$

Figure 2. Prediction of rainfall in 2015 for Ngemplak (a), Juwangi (b), dan Andong
(c) District using exponential smoothing with smoothing value of 0.1

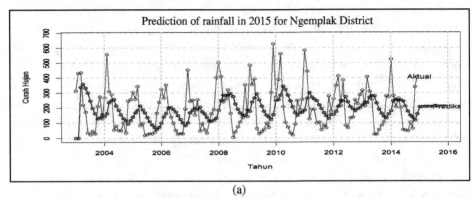

(a)

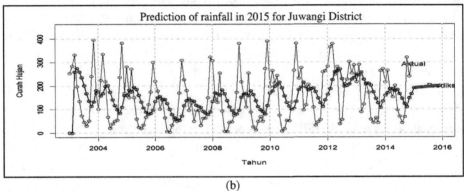

(b)

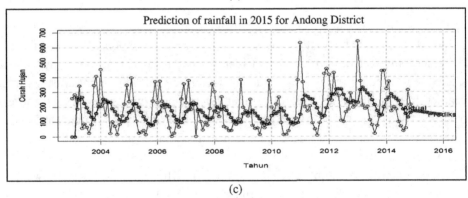

(c)

The smoothing parameter value (I_{SP}) may not equal to 3/4 if there are differences in annual rainfall pattern and difference in the number of corp life cycle (time from planting to harvest). For example, according to annual patterns, rainfall data are grouped into 2 types, namely: rainfall groups in January - June called the 1st type

Figure 3. Prediction of rainfall in 2015 for Ngemplak (a), Juwangi (b), dan Andong (c) District using exponential smoothing with smoothing value of 0.2

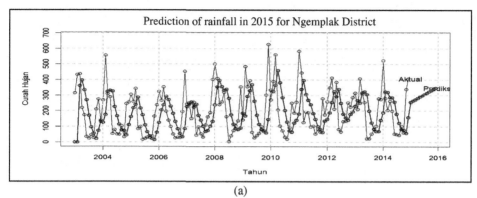

(a)

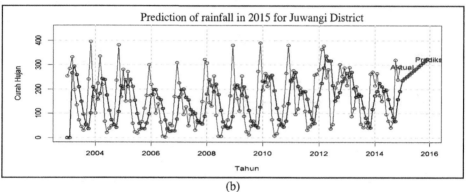

(b)

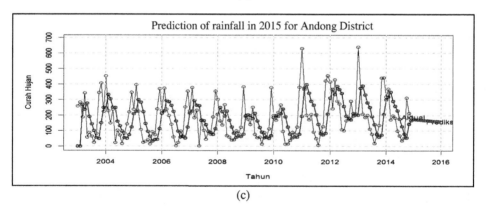

(c)

Table 3. Error testing for model fitting exponential smoothing

No	District	Error Measurement	Exponential Smoothing ($\alpha = 0.1$)	Exponential Smoothing ($\alpha = 0.2$)
1	Ngemplak	ME	0,59	0,65
		RMSE	154,72	157,38
		MAE	129,15	125,65
		MPE	149,64	126,88
		MAPE	186,37	167,16
		EE	40,99	42,41
2	Juwangi	ME	0,45	1,19
		RMSE	112,48	114,97
		MAE	92,07	90,56
		MPE	153,31	129,36
		MAPE	186,79	165,58
		EE	35,44	37,02
3	Andong	ME	1,71	0,41
		RMSE	139,63	142,85
		MAE	110,88	110,71
		MPE	195,17	176,61
		MAPE	226,64	214,16
		EE	38,38	40,17

and the rainfall group in July - December is called the second type. The number of groups measured is m = 2, while the length of the planting period (months) is L = 6 so it is determined = 2/6.

$$\alpha_{I_{SP}} = 1 - \exp(-2/6) = 0.283469 \tag{12}$$

Fitting and Prediction Data Rainfall Using Seasonal Planting Index

Graph showing the comparison data point predictions and the actual data for the District Ngemplak (Figure 4. (A)), Juwangi (Figure 4. (B)), and Andong (Figure 4. (c)), shows a match between the prediction line and the actual line on the graph of the looping pattern and the rain peak graph. The results of fitting rainfall data with the method seasonal planting index show the pattern of prediction lines with a tendency similar to the actual lines at almost all observation points. Most rainfall prediction points appear to have almost the same value compared to the actual rainfall value. Matching results of fitting rainfall data and actual data due to the smoothing value used is appropriate. The experimental results show that the algorithm seasonal planting index can do fitting rainfall data properly.

Figure 4. Prediction of rainfall in 2015 for Ngemplak (a), Juwangi (b), dan Andong District (c) using ESSPI

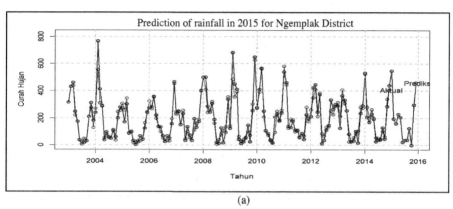

(a)

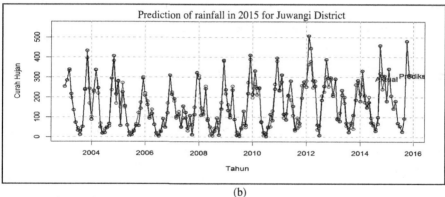

(b)

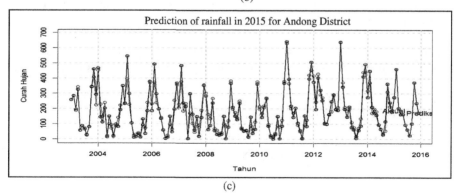

(c)

Table 3. Comparison of error between standar exponential smoothing and seasonal planting index model for Districts in Boyolali

No.	Error	Exponential Smoothing $\propto$ = 0,1	Exponential Smoothing $\propto$ = 0,2	E.S. Seasonal Planting Index (SPI)
1	ME	1,17	1,49	5,17
2	RMSE	163,74	166,10	51,37
3	MAE	132,09	129,26	35,19
4	MPE	291,42	243,95	32,05
5	MAPE	326,98	284,85	56,25
6	EE	43,45	44,75	4,27

CONCLUSION

The shift in the rain pattern had caused a decline to the crops yield of traditional farmers. A good rainfall prediction models is needed to provide recommendation for planting pattern (when to plant) so that the yield could me maximized. This research implemented exponential smoothing onto seasonal planting index as the basis for determining planting pattern. The results shows that our model give better accuracy than the original exponential smoothing model recommended by the FAO.

REFERENCES

Accardi, R. (1996). *A Comparison of Exponential Smoothing and Time Series Models for Forecasting Contract Estimate–At-Completion. US.ARMY Communication Electronic Command, Directorate of Resource Management.* Fort Monmouth: Cost Analysis Division.

Ai, T. J. (2004). Optimalisasi Prediksi Pemulusan Eksponensial Satu Variabel Dengan Menggunakan Algoritma Non Linear Programming. Jurnal Teknologi Industri, 3(3).

Aqil, M. (2010). *Pemetaan Spasial Varietas Jagung Berdasarkan Musim Tanam di Kabupaten Jeneponto, Sulawesi Selatan.* Prosiding Pekan Serealia Nasional.

Boer, R., Buono, A., Sumaryanto, E., Surmaini, A., Rakhman, W., Estiningtyas, K., & Kartikasari, F. (2009). Technical Report on Vulnerability and Adaptation Assessment to Climate Change for Indonesia's Second National Communication. Ministry of Environment and United Nations Development Programme.

Burkom, S.H., Muphy, S.P., & dan Shmuelli, G. (2006). *Automated Time Series Forecasting for Rainfall*. The Johns Hopkins University Applied Physics Laboratory, Department of Decision and Information Technologies, Robert H. Smith School, University of Maryland College Park.

dan Hermawan, E. (2013). Interkoneksi Monsun Dan El-Niño Terkait Dengan Curah Hujan Ekstrem. Prosiding Seminar Sains Atmosfer, LAPAN.

Dong, Z., Yang, D., Walsh, M. W., Reindl, T., & dan Aberle, A. (2013). Short-term Solar Irradiance Forecasting Using Exponential Smoothing State Space Model. Solar Energy Research Institute Of Singapore, National University of Singapore.

Estiningtyas, W., & dan Amien, L.I. (2006). *Pengembangan Model Prediksi Hujan dengan Metode Kalman Filter untuk Menyusun Skenario Masa Tanam*. Balai Besar Litbang Sumberdaya Lahan Pertanian.

FAO. (1976). *A Framework for Land Evaluation. Soil Resources Management and Conservation Service Land and Water Development Division. FAO Soil Bulletin No. 32*. Rome: FAO-UNO.

Fildes, R., & Kourentzes, N. (2011). Validation And Forecasting Accuracy In Models Of Climate Change. *International Journal of Forecasting, 27*, 968–995. doi:10.1016/j.ijforecast

Hartomo, K. D., & Winarko, E. (2015). Winters Exponential Smoothing And Z-Score, Algorithms For Prediction Of Rainfall. *Journal of Theoretical & Applied Information Technology, 73*(1).

Hendon, H. H. (2003). Indonesian Rainfall Variability: Impacts Of ENSO And Local Air –Sea Interaction. *Journal of Climate, 16*(11), 1775–1790. doi:10.1175/1520-0442(2003)016<1775:IRVIOE>2.0.CO;2

Hyndman, R. J. (2008). *Data Sets from Forecasting: Methods and Applications By Makridakis, Wheelwright and Hyndman*. R package version 1.11. Retrieved from http://CRAN. R-project.org/package=forecasting

Kalekar, P. S. (2004). *Time series Forecasting using Holt-Winters Exponential Smoothing*. Kanwal Rekhi School of Information Technology.

Khandakar, Y., & Hyndman, R. J. (2008). Automatic Time Series Forecasting: The forecast Package for R. *Journal of Statistical Software, 27*(3).

Mahsin, M. (2012). Modelling rainfall in Dhaka Division of Bangladesh Using Time Series Analysis. *Journal of Mathematical Modelling and Application, 1*(5), 67–73.

Makridakis, S., & Hibon, M. (2000). The M3-Competition: Results, Conclusions and Implications. *International Journal of Forecasting, 16*(4), 451–476. doi:10.1016/S0169-2070(00)00057-1

Mara, M. N., Satyahadewi, N., & dan Yundari. (2013). Kajian Teoritis Hybridizing Exponential Smoothing dan Neural Network Untuk Peramalan Data Runtun Waktu. Bimaster Ilmiah Mat. Stat. Dan Terapannya (Bimaster), 2(3), 205-210.

Murdohardono, D., Tobing Tigor, M.H.L., & dan Sayekti, A. (2007). Over Pumping of Groundwater as the Cause of sea Water Inundation in Semarang City. Prosiding dari Seminar Internasional Groundwater Management and Related Water Resources in East and Southeast Asia Region, Desember, Denpasar, Bali.

Naylor, R. L., Battisti, D. S., Vimont, D. J., Falcon, W. P., & dan Burke, M.B. (2007). Assessing risks of climate variability and climate change for Indonesian rice agriculture. *Proceeding of the National Academic of Science, 114*, 7752-7757. 10.1073/pnas.0701825104

Ngopya, F. (2009). *The Use Time Series in Crop Forecasting. Regional Early Warning System for Food Security, Food, Agriculture and Natural Resources*. Directorate, Botswana: FANR.

Prasetyo, S.Y.J.P., Subanar, Winarko, E., & Daryono, B.S. (2013). The Prediction of Population Dynamics Based on the Spatial Distribution Pattern of Brown Planthopper (Nilaparvata lugen Stal.) Using Exponential Smoothing – Local Spatial Statistics. *Journal of Agricultural Science, 5*(5).

Rijpkema, J. J. M. (2012). Time Series Analysis using R. Eindhoven University of Technology, Dept. Mathematics and Computer Science.

Sari, D. K., Ismullah, I. H., Sulasdi, W. N., & Harto, A. B. (2010). *Estimasi Produktivitas Padi Sawah Berbasis Kalender Tanam Heterogen Menggunakan Teknologi Pengindraan Jauh. Jurnal Rekayasa No. 3* (Vol. 14). Bandung: Institut Teknologi Nasional.

Shmueli, G., & dan Fienberg, S.E. (2005). *Current and Potential Statistical Methods for Monitoring Multiple Data Streams for Bio-Surveillance*. National Institute of Statistical Sciences, Carnegie Mellon University.

Sofla, M.J., & Silahi, B., & dan Masomi, M. T. (2013). Germi County Seasonal Precipitation Routing and Analysis, Using Holt-Winter Method for Times with Non-seasonal changes. *Technical Journal of Engineering and Applied Sciences, 3*(11), 950–953.

Surmaini, E., Runtunuwu, E., & dan Irsal, L. (2010). Upaya Sektor Pertanian Dalam Menghadapi Perubahan Iklim. Balai Besar Penelitian dan Pengembangan Sumberdaya Lahan Pertanian, Jalan Ir. H. Juanda No. 98, Bogor 16123.

Sutrisno, W. (2009). Pemodelan Curah Hujan Non Stasioner di Kota Surabaya Menggunakan Model ARIMA. *Conference on Information Technology and Electrical Engineering (CITEE)*.

Swarinoto, Y. S. (2009). *Validasi Spasial Data Estimasi Suhu Udara Turunan Dari Citra Satelit Landsat 7 - ETM+ Terhadap Data Observasi Stasiun Cuaca/IklimDarat (Kasus Provinsi Jawa Barat Bagian Selatan). In Jurnal Agroklimatologi*. Bogor: IPB.

Taylor, J. W. (2003). Exponential Smoothing with a Damped Multiplicative Trend. *International Journal of Forecasting, 19*(4), 715–725. doi:10.1016/S0169-2070(03)00003-7

Tresnawati, R., Nuraini, A.T., & Hanggoro, W. (2010). Prediksi Curah Hujan Bulanan Menggunakan Metode Kalman Filter Dengan Prediktor SST Nino 3.4 Diprediksi. *Jurnal Meteorologi Dan Geofisika, 11*(2), 106 - 115.

Chapter 11

Computer Forensic Investigation in Cloud of Things

A. Surendar

(iD) https://orcid.org/0000-0002-2421-9192

Vignan's Foundation for Science, Technology & Research (Deemed to be University), India

ABSTRACT

Digital data transformation is most challenging in developing countries. In recent days, all the applications are functioning with the support of internet of things (IoT). Wearable devices involve the most insightful information, which includes individual healthcare data. Health records of patients must be protected. IoT devices could be hacked, and criminals use this information. Smart cities with IoT use information technology to collect, analyze, and integrate information. Smart reduces the network traffic using the ground sensors, micro-radars, and drones monitor traffic to the traffic controller based on that signals are designed. The data collected includes the images and convey information to smart vehicles, which in turn, if data are hacked, may affect many people. Smart city includes important features such as smart buildings, smart technology, smart governance, smart citizen, and smart security. Cyber threat is a challenging problem, and usage of apps may increase malware that affects various customers.

DOI: 10.4018/978-1-5225-7955-7.ch011

INTRODUCTION TO IoT

The issue of security is becoming more crucial as IoT devices are becoming more relevant in people's lives. IoT devices may not be as secured as other traditional devices connected to the internet because of their sizes and restrictions on power, the increasing number of connected devices is bound to create challenges that are new and will thus require innovative security approaches (Elmaghraby, & Losavio, 2014). From a legal point of view, there are legal issues associated with the IoT which are not clear and require interpretation, notable amongst them being the impact that location has on privacy regulation and issues associated with ownership of data in the cloud as the data on IoT is stored in the cloud (Fremantle & Scott, 2015). Other challenges that could be associated with IoT devices include authentication, integrity, access control and confidentiality (Marinescu, 2017). Physical threats like theft and tampering, logical threats like denial of service and viruses are threats that can be directed at IoT based devices (Bos et al., 2009). As Data is kept on sites in the cloud, it is vulnerable to attacks such as SQL injection, side channel attacks and man in the middle attacks amongst others (Oriwoh et al., 2013). Today, discussions around IoT typically focus on applications, benefits and privacy, while there isn't much talk about incident response and forensic investigations. The need for an intelligent, adaptable forensic methodology to investigate IoT-related crimes, however, is becoming pertinent.

SMART CITY INFRA STRUCTURE DESIGN WITH SECURED INFORMATION TRANSFER

The security and privacy of information in a smart city has been interest of researchers. The reason behind it is that, in order to ensure the continuity of critical services like health care, governance and energy/utility issues in a smart city, the information security must be fool proof. The factors that are taken under consideration in order to identify the issues in information security in a smart city include governance factors, social/economic factors and most importantly economic factors. The researchers identify, explain and propose solutions to the information security issues by considering the mentioned factors. The IoT has been the key interest of the researchers as it is the core technology on which the smart cities are being developed and maintained (Mattern & Floerkemeier, 2010). For instance, in Marinescu (2017), the key hurdles and problems faced regarding security and privacy are discussed, keeping in the context of technological standards. This chapter particularly focuses on Machine to Machine (M2M) standard solutions that are helpful in better implementation of IoT in a smart city.

Though the mathematical and graphical model for the IoT, people and servers is given stating that it will help in locating the problems in security and privacy, but the methodology to do so is not discussed. Moreover, Mell and Grance (2011) propose a distributed framework for IoT applications, which promises security, trust and privacy in information delivery. As IoT applications play a key role on building the smarter city, so some information security issues in a smart city can be addressed through the distributive framework.

Data Security in Smart Cities: Challenges and Solutions

Trends as hyper connectivity, messy complexity, loss of boundary and industrialized hacking transform smart cities in complex environments in which the already-existing security analysis are not useful anymore. Specific data-security requirements and solutions are approached in a four-layer framework, with elements considered to be critical to the operation of a smart city: smart things, smart spaces, smart systems and smart citizens.

Data Vulnerabilities in a Smart City

Smart Things: In a smart city, objects are connected in order to provide seamless communication and contextual services. A large variety of things are used in a smart city. Data collected by smart things are at the heart of smart cities. The problem is that they are sensitive data, often gathered without our explicit consent. For example, messages, personal pictures, appointments, bank account information, contacts and others are stored in our smart phones in full awareness, with more or less security measures put in place.

- **Smart Spaces:** In a smart space, smart things are put in context, they form ecosystems that monitor and control our physical environment and our actions. There are different spaces: smart buildings, like home and offices, smart hospitals, hotels and malls, smart cars, and even smart streets.
- **Smart Infrastructure:** Smart cities are based on water and energy generation and transmission setups, transportation frameworks, waste disposal mechanisms, street and home lighting systems, connected healthcare, surveillance, and more. Huge amounts of data are produced by utility companies (use of electricity, gas, water, and lighting), transport providers (location/movement, traffic flow), mobile phone operators (location/movement, app use, and behaviour), travel and accommodation websites and smart hotels (reviews, location/movement, and consumption), Social Media sites (opinions, photos, personal info, location/movement), crowdsourcing

and citizen science (maps, local knowledge, urban incidents, weather), government bodies and public administration (services, performance, surveys) [3] and transmitted through a wireless, mobile and Internet of Things (IoT) infrastructure

- **Smart Citizens**: A smart city is about the relations between the everyday objects surrounding humans and humans themselves, and serving citizens is the main reason of a smart city. In consequence, a smart city will use e-government, will encourage individuals' participation in reporting issues and planning.

SMART GOVERNANCE

The attention for Smart governance, a key aspect of Smart cities, is growing, but our conceptual understanding of it is still limited. This article fills this gap in our understanding by exploring the concept of Smart governance both theoretically and empirically and developing a research model of Smart governance. On the basis of a systematic review of the literature defining elements, aspired outcomes and implementation strategies are identified as key dimensions of Smart governance. E-governance and involvement of the public in decision making process is the most important aspect of smart governance. The tools used to achieve them are following

- **Use of Information and Communication Technology:** This implies the use of computers, the internet, telecommunication, digital equipment's for collecting, processing, sharing and retrieving of data. Better penetration of telecommunication channels such as cable, radio, telephones and satellite systems for transmitting information. Use of Geographical Information System (GIS) for travel and transport, video conferencing, instant messaging in banking, healthcare, energy and security services.
- **E-Consultation:** People participation is the main feature of smart governance. There must be a proper channel of interaction between government and citizens. They must be empowered to voice their opinions, ideas about government programs, schemes etc. Their feedback should directly reach out to leaders, counsellors, city managers or local head.
- **E-Data:** Easy access to government funds, expenditure and investment data and public information must be available online. Except for critical information pertaining to security and safety of citizens, data must be provided freely and openly. This will make government more accountable and citizen participative in government's functioning.

Models of Smart Governance

- **Government to Citizen Model (G2C):** Under this approach government directly interacts with citizens through various communication channels like newspapers, web portals, forums, radios, Apps etc.
- **Government to Business Model:** Entrepreneurs play a crucial role in taking an economy ahead. The model is aimed towards the direct interaction between central and state government with the business sector and reduce 'red tapism' and bottlenecks faced by entrepreneurs, traders and startups.
- **Government to Government (G2G):** The model is targeted towards the direct interaction between government to government organizations, departments and agencies. The aim is to integrate all channels of governance for a simpler, holistic system.
- **Government to Employee (G2E):** The model aims to provide online software system and tools to create a channel of interaction between employees, government and companies. The idea is to maintain a personal account for each employee with his social security number, bank account number and personal information.

PROTOCOLS DESIGN IN WEARABLE DEVICES AND HEALTH CARE DATA

The Internet of Things (IoT) is a new concept, providing the possibility of healthcare monitoring using wearable devices. The IoT is defined as the network of physical objects which are supported by embedded technology for data communication and sensors to interact with both internal and external objects states and the environment

Wearable Devices in Health Monitoring

Motion Trackers

Wearable motion trackers are becoming increasingly popular for two main reasons. They can motivate the user during the daily workout to perform more exercise, while providing activity measurement information through a smartphone without manual calculation. In particular, to accurately observe motion of the human body, 3-axis accelerometers, magnetometers, and gyroscopes sensors obtain data, each for a specific purpose.

Vital Signs Measurement

A wearable health sensor monitoring system based on a multi-sensor fusion approach is outlined. The implemented device consists of a chest-worn device that embeds a controller board, an ECG sensor, a temperature sensor, an accelerometer, a vibration motor, a color-changing light-emitting diode (LED), and a push-button. To address privacy concerns, data is encrypted before transmission. Data collected for permanent storage are sent to cloud storage, while data to be visualized in real-time, are sent directly to a laptop or smart phone.

Challenges and Bottlenecks for Medical IoT

Leading wearable devices based on IoT platforms must provide simple, powerful application access to IoT devices. Many platforms and structures have been proposed by the scientific community, and commercial devices are already available for bio-metric/medical parameter measurement.

The following are four key capabilities that leading platforms must enable:

Simple and Secure Connectivity

A good IoT platform is expected to provide easy connection of devices and perform device management functions in three levels of data collection, data transmission to a hub, and permanent storage and observation in a medical station. These steps must be secured; therefore, data encryption is necessary.

Power Consumption

To provide the wearer with easy device management and long-term monitoring without interruption, power loss is becoming more important. This is strictly correlated to the number of parameters that are observed, efficient code programming, as well as good data packing, encryption, and compression.

Wearability

Wearable devices have been designed for various types of bio-medical monitoring to assisting users in living long, healthy lives. This point is more significant when these devices are intended to be worn by elderly users. Therefore, such devices must be easy to wear, easy to carry, and comfortable. These requirements are fulfilled with a light, small, and well-structured device. A wearable device is expected to be small and light weight, and should be able to be used for a long time.

Reduced Risk in Data Loss

When data is collected by a microcontroller and transmitted to a smartphone or cloud storage, there is a possibility of disconnection and consequently data loss. This must be reduced as much as possible to provide safe health monitoring. It may be possible through temporary data saving (buffering) in the microcontroller providing a large memory.

HEALTH SYSTEM MONITORING PROTOCOL

The *Connected Medical Device Architecture* approach allows distributed alarm notifications, device teaming (which means multiple devices can work with each other for alarm synchronization and escalation), connection to cloud services (for use in remote surveillance), cross-device application workflows, and many other important benefits. See Figure 2 for a summary of important capabilities on the enterprise IT side of the equation. All next-generation connected medical devices embrace and extend either XMPP, DDS, MQTT, or other IoT protocols as depicted in Figure 1.

The Internet Engineering Task Force (IETF) Extensible Messaging and Presence Protocol (XMPP, RFC 2779) is an open protocol optimized for IM, but it is extensible and robust enough for arbitrary messaging use in modern medical device platforms in figure 2. XMPP was defined to help with (a) presence management, (b) direct message exchange, and (c) querying for arbitrary data. XMPP is a reasonable choice for connected medical devices because it can eliminate polling for messages and

Figure 1. Enterprise IT benefits of the connected medical device architecture

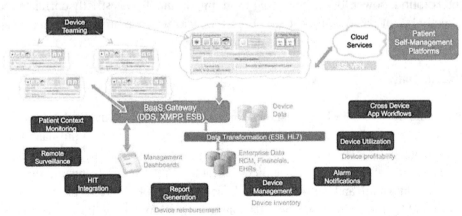

Figure 2. Device connectivity options

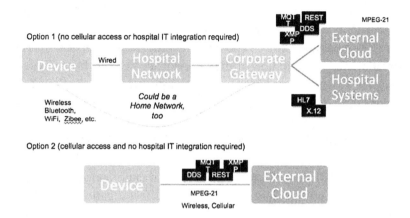

device states, can facilitate two-way data exchange without firewall and network path issues, can pass binary or text data, and knows when devices or servers are on- or offline.

While not as well-known as its more generalized SOAP (Simple Object Access Protocol) and REST (representational state transfer) protocol cousins, XMPP is a capable protocol with wide and deep open source and commercial software support. XMPP is scalable, has built-in access control capabilities, has HIPAA-compliant support for message encryption and authentication, can be implemented in a reliable manner, and has been demonstrated to be performant in production environments

XMPP's primary weakness is that it is more verbose and uses up a bit more bandwidth than competing methods, but in a modern network infrastructure, compression and faster network components can usually overcome that weakness. Keep in mind that while XMPP is a great choice, DDS and MQTT should also be considered based on device design requirements. XMPP is a client-to-server and server to server communications protocol. For our purposes, a client may be one or more medical devices, and a server is a device gateway.

DIGITAL FORENSICS

Digital forensics could be defined as a processing that use to identify the digital evidence in its most original form and then performing a structured investigation to collect, examine and analyze the digital evidence. There are several aspects of difference and similarity between traditional and IoT forensics. In terms of evidence sources, traditional evidence could be computers, mobile devices, servers or gateways. In IoT forensics, the evidence could be home appliances, cars, tags readers, sensor nodes, medical implants in humans or animals, or other IoT devices. Digital forensics is defined as the use of scientifically-derived and proven methods for the preservation, collection, validation, identification, analysis, interpretation, documentation and presentation of digital evidence derived from digital sources for the purpose of facilitating or furthering the reconstruction of events found to be criminal, or helping to anticipate unauthorized actions shown to be disruptive to planned operations (Bos et al., 2009).

A comprehensive forensic model can provide a common reference framework for investigation. These models can support the development of tools, techniques, training and the certification/accreditation of investigators and tools (Baryamureeba & Tushabe, 2004). The outcome of digital forensics investigation depends largely on the methodology adopted. Overlooking one step or interchanging any of the steps may lead to incomplete or inconclusive results, resulting in wrong interpretations and conclusions (Cassidy, 2014). IoT forensics shall include forensics in mobile devices, the cloud, computers, sensors and RFID technologies and many other areas (Oriwoh et al., 2013). The First Digital Forensics Research Conference (DFRW) made an initial effort at explaining the processes to follow in conducting digital forensics, they proposed a model known as the DFRW Investigative process (DIP) which in their estimation could be used in all digital forensic examinations (Palmer, 2001). The Forensics Automated Correlation Engine (FACE) presented by Case, Cristina, Marziale, Richard, and Roussev (2008) demonstrates completely automatic relationship of different sources of evidence. For the future they suggest there should be more work for an improved correlation, they suggest that rigorous logical methods should be employed. Researchers do not have a logical method for reverse engineering even though a lot of resources have been spent in researching into it, forensic tools are not well automated and data cannot be exchanged (Garfinkel, 2010). The model proposed by (Ademu, Imafidon, & Preston, 2011) results in forensic investigation taking a longer time to complete and so cannot produce effective and reliable results. Due to volatility this model cannot be applied in IoT forensics. Forensics in the IoT is classified by Zawoad and Hasan (2015) as a blend of forensics at the device level, network forensics and forensics in the cloud. They also argue that current forensic tools and its associated techniques are inadequate to deal with IoT infrastructure.

Digital Forensics in Cloud Environments

The following discussion is based principally on the DFRW Investigative Process (DIP) Model and the ACPO principles and guidelines. The DIP model provides a comprehensive review of the stages employed in the digital forensic process, and so is convenient for analysing the impact of cloud forensics on this process. Other models are also referenced where appropriate, in particular the ACPO principles and guidelines.

This section presents the challenges in every phase of cloud forensics.

- Identification
- Collection and Presentation
- Examination and Analysis
- Reporting and Presentation

The Identification phase mainly defines the purpose and process of Investigation. Identification of crime is the starting step in Digital Investigation Process model. Determining of a malicious activity that happen is simply identification step. Identification of crime in cloud is difficult compare to traditional forensics identification. Evidence collection collects the evidence from identified sources of evidence. Collected evidence need to be preserved. Preserving data is maintaining data integrity original data is not to be changed till investigation completes. In traditional system the investigation process starts by seizing the hard disk of the system and taking the bit wise copy of the same maintaining integrity of the system. In the Digital Imaging Process (DIP) model once the data is collected and preserved various examination techniques and several software tools are available to aid the investigators. FTK (Forensic Tool Kit) and Encase are widely used commercial forensic tool suites; another Open source tool is Sleuth tool kit. These all tools are used to perform filtering and pattern matching for searching the content or files or file types. The gathered evidence in the digital investigation process is needed to be submitted in the court of law to prove the crime. For that the investigator submits a report withsummarized investigation process and explained conclusion. At the end of investigation the investigator need to present a report and it must be useful for cross- examination. The result report should be used by an organization to improve their security policy and must be documented for future investigation.

IoT Forensics Challenges

Currently, the tools and technologies of digital forensics are mean for the conventional computing and not capable to accommodate the IoT infrastructure. (Zawoad and Hasan 2015). This paradigm change implies that advanced examinations progressively needed to encounter evidence that may be come from many source in the real environment. (Taylor et al. 2010). In this section, the challenges are identified, while dealing with the IoT environment. In forensic perspective, no significant work has been done except for a framework. (Oriwoh et al. 2013). IoT forensics has more areas of interest than traditional forensics. In addition to the traditional type of networks — wired, Wi-Fi, wireless and mobile — IoT also has the RFID sensor network. Different IoTware such as appliances, tags and medical devices should be considered as sources of evidence during investigation as well.

The main challenge in investigating an IoT crime is introduced by the dynamic nature of IoT solutions. IoT is a combination of many major technology areas, which includes cloud computing, mobile devices, computers and tablets, sensors and RFID technologies. As a result, forensics for IoT will encompass all of these aforementioned areas.

Sources of evidence on IoT can be categorized into three groups:

1. All evidence collected from smart devices and sensors;
2. All evidence collected from hardware and software that provide a communication between smart devices and the external world (e.g., computers, mobile, IPS, IDS and firewalls), which are included in traditional computer forensics; and
3. All evidence collected from hardware and software that are outside the network under investigation. This group includes cloud, social networks, ISPs and mobile network providers, virtual online identities and the internet.

Data Location: Many of IoT data are spread in different locations which are out of the user control. This data could be in the Cloud in third party's location, in mobile phone or other devices. Therefore, in IoT forensics, to identify the location of evidence is considered as one of the biggest challenges can investigator faced in order to collect the evidence. In addition, IoT data might be located in different countries and be mixed with other users information, which means different countries regulations are involved (Oriwoh et al., 2013).

Lifespan limitation of digital media: Because the limitation of stor- age in IoT devices,the lifespan of data in IoT devices is short and data can be easily overwritten. Resulting in the possibility of evidence being lost (Cassidy, 2014). Therefore, one of the challenges is the period of survival of the evidence in IoT devices before it is overwritten.

Cloud service requirement: Most of the accounts are anonymous users because Cloud service does not require the accurate information from user to sign up for their service. It could lead to impossible to identify a criminal (Palmer, 2001).

Security lack: Evidence in IoT devices could be changed or deleted because of lack of security, which could make these evidence not solid enough to be accepted in law court (Case et al., 2008; Garfinkel, 2010).

Device type: In identification phase of forensics, the digital investigator needs to identify and acquire the evidence from a digital crime scene. Usually, evidence source is types of a computer system such as computer and mobile phone. However, in IoT, the source of evidence could be objects like a smart refrigerator or smart coffee maker (Marinescu, 2017).

Data Format: The format of the data that generated by IoT devices is not matching to what is saved in the Cloud. In addition, user have no direct access to his/her data and the data presents in deferent format than that in which it is stored.

Limitations in the Currently Available Forensic Tools

The existing tools in digital forensics field cannot fit with the heterogeneous infrastructure of IoT environment. The massive amount of possible evidence that are generated by a large number of IoT devices, it will consequently bring new challenges in the aspect of collecting evidence from distributed IoT infrastructures. In addition, since a hacker can monopolize the evidence in IoT devices because the weakness of these devices in term of security, the extracting evidence from them maybe not acceptable in law court. Moreover, because most of IoT data are stored in the Cloud, the Cloud becomes one of the main sources of evidence in IoT. Hence, investigators will face some of the problems of collecting evidence from the Cloud, because the procedures of digital forensic and tools assume to have physical access to the evidence source.

CONCLUSION

Data acquisition in the cloud remains the biggest issue with many and varied problems. Much research is needed to develop procedures and tools that can be used by service providers to extract the data needed by investigators in a forensically sound way. Unlike traditional forensic computing investigations, cloud environments are shared between multiple users and the systems are usually located in multiple physical locations. This chapter provides a comprehensive overview on the threats, vulnerabilities and available solutions in order to facilitate much needed research in addressing the problem areas in smart city security. The technological factors are pivotal in deployment and maintenance of a smart city. In fact, technology is the driving force that establishes and maintains a smart city to deliver the promised services. Good governance with information technology support can create a smart city. Even this two concept is different but, they are in the same goal to provide excellent service and to enhance the quality of life of the human. Furthermore, we have come to the conclusion that forensic investigations biggest challenge is not technical but legal. Law enforcement agencies' power restrictions and the need for advice and legal training seem to be overlooked. From the above discussion, it is evident that IoT forensics is different from other forensics. Evidence must be produced timely and must be able to withstand rigorous cross examination in court. A significant number of literatures were reviewed for the purpose of finding gaps in current IoT Forensics.

REFERENCES

Ademu, I. O., Imafidon, C. O., & Preston, D. S. (2011). A new approach of digital forensic model for digital forensic investigation. *Int. J. Adv. Comput. Sci. Appl*, 2(12), 175–178.

Baryamureeba, V., & Tushabe, F. (2004, August). The enhanced digital investigation process model. In *Proceedings of the Fourth Digital Forensic Research Workshop* (pp. 1-9). Academic Press.

Bos, H., Ioannidis, S., Jonsson, E., Kirda, E., & Kruegel, C. (2009). Future threats to future trust. In Future of Trust in Computing (pp. 49-54). Vieweg+ Teubner. doi:10.1007/978-3-8348-9324-6_5

Case, A., Cristina, A., Marziale, L., Richard, G. G., & Roussev, V. (2008). FACE: Automated digital evidence discovery and correlation. *Digital Investigation, 5*, S65-S75.

Cassidy, A. (2014). *The "Internet of Things" Revolution and Digital Forensics*. NUIX.

Elmaghraby, A. S., & Losavio, M. M. (2014). Cyber security challenges in Smart Cities: Safety, security and privacy. *Journal of Advanced Research, 5*(4), 491–497. doi:10.1016/j.jare.2014.02.006 PMID:25685517

Fremantle, P., & Scott, P. (2015). *A security survey of middleware for the Internet of Things (No. e1521)*. PeerJ PrePrints.

Garfinkel, S. L. (2010). Digital forensics research: The next 10 years. *Digital Investigation, 7*, S64-S73.

Grispos, G., Glisson, W. B., & Storer, T. (2013, January). Using smartphones as a proxy for forensic evidence contained in cloud storage services. In *System Sciences (HICSS), 2013 46th Hawaii International Conference on* (pp. 4910-4919). IEEE. 10.1109/HICSS.2013.592

Guo, H., Jin, B., & Shang, T. (2012, August). Forensic investigations in cloud environments. In *Computer Science and Information Processing (CSIP), 2012 International Conference on* (pp. 248-251). IEEE.

Kunzmann, K. R. (2014). Smart cities: A new paradigm of urban development. *Crios*, *4*(1), 9–20.

Marinescu, D. C. (2017). *Cloud computing: theory and practice*. Morgan Kaufmann.

Marty, R. (2011, March). Cloud application logging for forensics. In *Proceedings of the 2011 ACM Symposium on Applied Computing* (pp. 178-184). ACM. 10.1145/1982185.1982226

Mattern, F., & Floerkemeier, C. (2010). From the Internet of Computers to the Internet of Things. In *From active data management to event-based systems and more* (pp. 242–259). Berlin: Springer. doi:10.1007/978-3-642-17226-7_15

Mell, P., & Grance, T. (2011). *The NIST definition of cloud computing*. NIST.

Oriwoh, E., Jazani, D., Epiphaniou, G., & Sant, P. (2013, October). Internet of things forensics: Challenges and approaches. In *Collaborative Computing: Networking, Applications and Worksharing (Collaboratecom), 2013 9th International Conference on* (pp. 608-615). IEEE.

Palmer, G. (2001). *A Road Map for Digital Forensic Research: Report from the First Digital Forensic Workshop, 7–8 August 2001*. DFRWS Technical Report DTR-T001-01.

Rimal, B. P., Choi, E., & Lumb, I. (2009, August). A taxonomy and survey of cloud computing systems. In *INC, IMS and IDC, 2009. NCM'09. Fifth International Joint Conference on* (pp. 44-51). IEEE. 10.1109/NCM.2009.218

Sang, T. (2013, January). A log based approach to make digital forensics easier on cloud computing. In *Intelligent System Design and Engineering Applications (ISDEA), 2013 Third International Conference on* (pp. 91-94). IEEE. 10.1109/ISDEA.2012.29

Surendar, A., Samavatian, V., Maseleno, A., Ibatova, A. Z., & Samavatian, M. (2018). Effect of solder layer thickness on thermo-mechanical reliability of a power electronic system. *Journal of Materials Science Materials in Electronics*, 1–10.

Zawoad, S., & Hasan, R. (2013). *Cloud forensics: a meta-study of challenges, approaches, and open problems.* arXiv preprint arXiv:1302.6312

Zawoad, S., & Hasan, R. (2015, June). Faiot: Towards building a forensics aware eco system for the internet of things. In *2015 IEEE International Conference on Services Computing (SCC)* (pp. 279-284). IEEE. 10.1109/SCC.2015.46

Chapter 12
Neural Network for Big Data Sets

Vo Ngoc Phu
Duy Tan University, Vietnam

Vo Thi Ngoc Tran
Ho Chi Minh City University of Technology, Vietnam

ABSTRACT

Machine learning (ML), neural network (NN), evolutionary algorithm (EA), fuzzy systems (FSs), as well as computer science have been very famous and very significant for many years. They have been applied to many different areas. They have contributed much to developments of many large-scale corporations, massive organizations, etc. Lots of information and massive data sets (MDSs) have been generated from these big corporations, organizations, etc. These big data sets (BDSs) have been the challenges of many commercial applications, researches, etc. Therefore, there have been many algorithms of the ML, the NN, the EA, the FSs, as well as computer science which have been developed to handle these massive data sets successfully. To support for this process, the authors have displayed all the possible algorithms of the NN for the large-scale data sets (LSDSs) successfully in this chapter. Finally, they have presented a novel model of the NN for the BDS in a sequential environment (SE) and a distributed network environment (DNE).

INTRODUCTION

We have already considered where many big data sets (BDSs) have been generated from. We have already found that: Many large-scale corporations, big organizations, and etc. have been created, built and developed more and more for many years in the

DOI: 10.4018/978-1-5225-7955-7.ch012

world from that lots of economies of countries in the world have been developed in the strongest way for the recent years. Each massive corporation (each large-scale organization, and etc.) has had thousands of branches in the countries in the world. Each branch has had thousands of employee certainly. Therefore, the big corporation could have had millions of the employees in the countries in the world. From its business process, many massive data sets (MDSs) have already been generated from the millions of the employees, and etc. certainly. Many hard problems and challenges have been generated and grown from which a lot. For example, these negative problems have been as follows: What are the problems? How to store the MDSs? How to handle the large-scale data sets (LSDSs)? How to extract many helpful values from the BDSs? Whether to necessarily save them or not? Where to store them? Whether to save them for a long time or not? Whether to necessarily store them for a long time or not? Whether to necessarily process them or not? Whether to successfully handle them or not? How long time to process them? How long time to handle them successfully? Whether to extract their significant values? Whether to get successfully their helpful values? And etc.

Besides, many different fields of the computer science have already been developed in the strongest way in the world. These fields such as machine learning (ML), neural network (NN), evolutionary algorithm (EA), fuzzy systems (FSs), and etc. have been very useful for many fields of everyone's life. Their algorithms, methods, models, and etc. have successfully been built, and in addition, they have also been applied to the BDSs. Thus, we have presented many simple concepts of the ML, the NN, the EA, the FSs, and etc. in this book chapter. In addition, we have also displayed a novel model of the NN for handling the LSDSs successfully.

According to our opinion, ML is a sub-area of the AI of the computer science which uses many statistical techniques to allow computers to be the ability to learn with data sets. The ML is also a method of data analysis which automates analytical model building. It is based on the idea which computer systems can learn from many data sets, identify many patterns, and make many decisions with minimal human intervention

NN based on our opinion is a computing system which is similar to the biological neural networks which constitute human brains. It comprises a set of connected units or nodes (called neural network) which look like the neurons in a biological brain. One connection looks like the synapses in a biological brain which can transmit a signal from one neuron to another. Then, one neuron can receive a signal which can process it and in addition, signal additional neurons connected to it.

According to our opinion, EA is a subset of evolutionary computation which is a type of meta-heuristic optimization algorithm. Many mechanisms inspired by biological evolution can be used by the EA as follows: reproduction, mutation, recombination, and selection. Many approximating solutions to all types of problems are often implemented well by the EAs

FS based on our opinion is a control system according to a fuzzy logic (a math system) which can analyze analog input values in terms of logical variables which take many values between 0 and 1.

We have found why these problems and challenges are important.

1. According to our opinion and the reviews which we have already referenced, these large-scale data sets have been needed to store certainly and successfully. Moreover, they must be saved in a time-saving way. Many reasons for these are as follows:

    a. The big data sets of the massive corporations, large-scale organizations, and etc. have been protected surely. If the massive data do not store surely, they are stolen. Thus, the secrets of the corporations, organizations, and etc. can be exploited for many bad purposes. In addition, the corporations, organizations, and etc. can be crashed.

    b. They must be stored regularly and fully: When there have any incidents, they can be rehabilitated surely.

    c. They must be backed up regularly and fully: When there have any incidents, they can be rehabilitated surely.

    d. They can be saved in the most economical way: They are very large and are increased every day. Thus, costs of computer hardware of the storing are very expensive.

    e. Human resources of the storing also need to be saved costs.

    f. We have also asserted that this stage has been performed with so much cost and time surely.

    g. ...

2. We have also confirmed that those massive data sets have needed to be handled carefully, effectively, fully, successfully, and etc. because of the below reasons as follows:

    a. The above items of (A) must be performed firstly.

    b. Processing them to store them as following above reasons in (A).

    c. Handling them as quick as possible, effectively, and etc. for aims of extracting them in a valuable way to get, save, and use many helpful values.

    d. Processing them to demonstrate professional levels of the corporations, organizations, and etc.

    e. Based on our opinion, we have also found that it has taken lots of cost and time to this stage clearly.

    f.   At the present time, there have been many problems and challenges to perform this stage certainly and successfully because of the below reasons as follows:

        i.   There have not been a lot of awareness fully and clearly yet about the massive data sets.

        ii.   There have not been many tools, software, hardware, algorithms, methods, models, and etc. of the large-scale data to implement this stage yet.

        iii.   Because of so much cost and time, the corporations, the organizations, and etc. still do not want to make this stage fully, and etc.

        iv.   …

    g.   …

3.   We have also asserted that those large-scale data have been very necessary for being extracted automatically the significant values from them:

    a.   The above items of (A) and the above items of (B) must be implemented firstly.

    b.   If this stage is not performed, the stage of (A) and the stage of (B) should not be implemented: The reason is as follows: In addition to the values of (A) and (B) presented in more details, this stage is performed for complementing to the previous two phases (A and B). If the stages of (A) and (B) are only implemented and this stage is not performed, lots of cost and time are spent in a wasteful way.

    c.   This stage brings core values to the massive corporations, the large-scale organizations, and etc.

    d.   We have also confirmed that we have already extracted automatically the crucial positive values from the large-scale data sets with a lot of cost and time certainly.

    e.   Based on our opinion, this stage is also a most expensive duration for the corporations, the organizations, and etc., and this stage also takes a lot of time for them.

    f.   …

According to our opinion, a big data set is a set of many records (many samples) which has a large of quantity comprising over 500,000 data samples – 1,000,000 data samples or this data set has a large of size about over millions of GB. Sometimes, a big data set has a large of quantity including over 500,000 data samples – 1,000,000 data samples and this data set also has a large of size about over millions of GB

The problem has been done so far by others as follows:

1. Some algorithms, methods, models, and etc. have been studied, developed, and deployed for the BDS but there is not a lot.
2. There have been not enough many algorithms, methods, models, and etc. for the LSDSs yet to be applied to many different areas for the economies, countries, societies, corporations, organizations, and etc.
3. There have been not a lot of those algorithms, methods, models, and etc. of the MDSs which have been implemented in sequential environments (SEs) – sequential systems (SSs)
4. Those algorithms, methods, models, and etc. of the LSDS in the SSs have already been developed with small samples.
5. There have also been not lots of those algorithms, methods, models, and etc. of the big data sets which have been performed in distributed network systems (DNSs) – parallel network environments (PNEs)
6. Those algorithms, methods, models, and etc. of the LSDS in the DNS have also already been performed with small samples.
7. …

The main contributions of this chapter to the problem from many studies related to lots of new computational models (related to the NN) for the massive data sets are as follows:

1. This chapter helps the readers have information and knowledge about the MDSs.
2. The chapter also helps the reader understand most of all novel computational models (related to the NN) of the LSDS certainly.
3. Most of those computational models (related to the NN) of the BDSs in many different fields are shown in both the SEs and the DNSs in more details in the below sections.
4. From lots of the information and knowledge above of (1), (2), (3), and (4), the readers (comprising scientists, researchers, CEO, managers, and etc.) can build, develop and deploy many commercial applications, studies, and etc. so much.
5. Many different technologies of those models have already been displayed carefully.
6. We also show that a novel computational model (related to the NN) of us for the LSDSs have successfully been built with over 500,000 data samples - 1,000,000 data samples in the SS and the PNE
7. …

The contribution original of this chapter is as follows:

1. This chapter helps the readers understand many simple concepts of the big data sets clearly.
2. This chapter also helps the readers know many novel models of the MDSs fully in the SEs and the DNSs
3. A novel model, which we have built and developed in the SE and the DNS successfully, is presented in this chapter.
4. Many techniques, algorithms, methods, models, and etc. to handle the large-scale data in the SE and the DNS are fully shown in this chapter.
5. Based on all the things displayed in this chapter, many commercial applications, researches, and etc. can be developed and deployed successfully.
6. …

The contribution non-trivial is as follows: In this book chapter, we have proposed a new model for the MDS sentiment classification (SECL) in the parallel network environment – a Cloudera system (CPNS) with Hadoop Map (M) and Hadoop Reduce (R). Our new model has used an Artificial Neural Network Algorithm (ANN) with multi-dimensional vector (MDV) and 2,000,000 documents of our training data set (TRADS) for document-level sentiment classification in English. We have tested the novel model in both a SE and a PNS. Our novel model can classify sentiments (positive, negative, or neutral) of millions of documents based on many documents in the parallel network environment in English. However, we tested our new model on our testing data set (TESDS) including 1,000,000 reviews (500,000 positive and 500,000 negative) and achieved 84.25% accuracy.

BACKGROUND

In this section, we describe summaries of many studies related to an Artificial Neural Network Algorithm (ANN), vector space model (VSM), Hadoop, Cloudera, etc.

There are many works related to vector space modeling in [(Vaibhav Kant Singh, & Vinay Kumar Singh, 2015), (Víctor Carrera-Trejo, & et al, 2015), and (Pascal Soucy, & Guy W. Mineau, 2015)]. First, we have transferred all English sentences into many vectors, which have been used in the VSM algorithm. In this research (Vaibhav Kant Singh, & Vinay Kumar Singh, 2015), the authors examined the vector space model, an information retrieval technique, and its variation. The rapid growth of the Internet and the abundance of documents and different forms of information available underscored the need for good information retrieval technique. The vector space model was an algebraic model used for information retrieval. It represented natural language documents in a formal manner using of vectors in a multi-dimensional space and allowed decisions to be made as to which documents are similar to each other and to the queries fired. This research attempted to examine the vector space model, an information retrieval technique that was widely used today. It also explained the existing variations of VSM and proposes the new variation that should be considered. In text classification tasks, one of the main problems (Víctor Carrera-Trejo, & et al, 2015) was to choose which features give the best results. Various features could be used like words, n-grams, syntactic n-grams of various types (POS tags, dependency relations, mixed, etc.); or a combination of these features could be considered. Also, algorithms for dimensionality reduction of these sets of features could be applied, such as latent Dirichlet allocation (LDA). In this research, the authors considered multi-label text classification tasks and apply various feature sets. The authors considered a subset of multi-labeled files of the Reuters-21578 corpus. The authors used traditional TF-IDF values of the features and tried both considering and ignoring stop words. The authors also tried several combinations of features, like bi-grams and uni-grams. The authors also experimented with adding LDA results into vector space models as new features. These last experiments obtained the best results. KNN and SVM (Pascal Soucy, & Guy W. Mineau, 2015) were two machine learning approaches to text categorization (TC) based on the vector space model. In this model, borrowed from information retrieval, documents were represented as a vector where each component was associated with a particular word from the vocabulary. Traditionally, each component value was assigned using the information retrieval TFIDF measure. While this weighting method seemed very appropriate for IR, it was not clear that it was the best choice for TC problems. Actually, this weighting method did not leverage the information implicitly contained in the categorization task to represent documents. In this research, the authors introduced a new weighting method based on statistical estimation of the importance of a word for a specific categorization problem. This method also had the benefit to make feature selection implicit, since useless features of the categorization problem considered get a very small weight. Extensive experiments reported in the research showed that this new weighting method improved significantly the classification accuracy as measured on many categorization tasks.

Many research projects related to implementing algorithms, applications, studies in parallel network environment in [(Hadoop, 2017), (Apache, 2017), and (Cloudera, 2017)]. In (Hadoop, 2017) and (Apache, 2017), Hadoop is an Apache-based framework used to handle large data sets on clusters consisting of multiple computers, using the Map and Reduce programming model. The two main projects of the Hadoop are Hadoop Distributed File System (HDFS) and Hadoop M/R (Hadoop Map / Reduce). Hadoop M/R allows engineers to program for writing applications for parallel processing of large data sets on clusters consisting of multiple computers.

A M/R task has two main components: (1) Map and (2) Reduce. This framework splits inputting data into chunks which multiple Map tasks can handle with a separate data partition in parallel. The outputs of the map tasks are gathered and processed by the Reduce task ordered. The input and output of each M/R task are stored in HDFS because the Map tasks and the Reduce tasks perform on the pair (key, value), and formatted input and output formats will be the pair (key, value). Cloudera (Cloudera, 2017), the global provider of the fastest, easiest, and most secure data management and analytics platform built on Apache™ Hadoop® and the latest open source technologies, announced today that it will submit proposals for Impala and Kudu to join the Apache Software Foundation (ASF). By donating its leading analytic database and columnar storage projects to the ASF, Cloudera aims to accelerate the growth and diversity of their respective developer communities. Cloudera delivers the modern data management and analytics platform built on Apache Hadoop and the latest open source technologies. The world's leading organizations trust Cloudera to help solve their most challenging business problems with Cloudera Enterprise, the fastest, easiest and most secure data platform available to the modern world. Cloudera's customers efficiently capture, store, process, and analyze vast amounts of data, empowering them to use advanced analytics to drive business decisions quickly, flexibly, and at lower cost than has been possible before. To ensure Cloudera's customers are successful, it offers comprehensive support, training and professional services.

There are the works related to the Artificial Neural Network Algorithm (ANN) in [(R.J. Kuo, & et al, 2001), (K. P. Sudheer, & et al, 2002), (Carsten Peterson, & et al, 1994), (D.C. Park, & et al, 1991), (Kuo-lin Hsu, & et al, 1995), (Xin Yao, 1999), (B. Samanta, & K.R. Al-Balushi, 2003), (V Brusic, & et al, 1998), (Muriel Gevrey, & et al, 2003), (C. Charalambous, 1992), (K. P. Sudheer, & et al, 2002), (Zhi-Hua Zhou, & et al, 2002), (Laurent Magnier, & Fariborz Haghighat, 2010), (Sovan Lek, & J.F. Guégan, 1999), and (Kyoung-jae Kim, & Ingoo Han, 2000)]. The authors in (R.J. Kuo, & et al, 2001) developed a genetic algorithm based fuzzy neural network (GFNN) to formulate the knowledge base of fuzzy inference rules which could measure the qualitative effect on the stock market. The research in (K. P. Sudheer, & et al, 2002) investigated the prediction of Class A pan evaporation using the artificial neural network (ANN) technique, etc.

The latest researches of the sentiment classification are [(Basant Agarwal, & Namita Mittal, 2016a), (Basant Agarwal, & Namita Mittal, 2016b), (Sérgio Canuto, & et al, 2016), (Shoiab Ahmed, & Ajit Danti, 2016), (Vo Ngoc Phu, & Phan Thi Tuoi, 2014), (Vo Thi Ngoc Tran, & et al, 2014), (Vo Ngoc Phu, & et al, 2017a), (Nguyen Duy Dat, & et al, 2017), (Vo Ngoc Phu, & et al, 2016), (Vo Ngoc Phu, & et al, 2017b), (Vo Ngoc Phu, & et al, 2017c), (Vo Ngoc Phu, & et al, 2017d),

(Vo Ngoc Phu, & et al, 2017e), (Vo Ngoc Phu, & et al, 2017f), (Vo Ngoc Phu, & et al, 2017g), (Vo Ngoc Phu, & et al, 2017h), (Vo Ngoc Phu, & Vo Thi Ngoc Tran, 2017a), and (Vo Ngoc Phu, & Vo Thi Ngoc Tran, 2017b)]. In the research (Basant Agarwal, & Namita Mittal, 2016a), the authors presented their machine learning experiments with regard to sentiment analysis in blog, review and forum texts found on the World Wide Web and written in English, Dutch and French. The survey in (Basant Agarwal, & Namita Mittal, 2016b) discussed an approach where an exposed stream of tweets from the Twitter micro blogging site were preprocessed and classified based on their sentiments. In sentiment classification system the concept of opinion subjectivity has been accounted. In the study, the authors presented opinion detection and organization subsystem, which have already been integrated into our larger question-answering system, etc.

In Figure 1, our training data set includes 2,000,000 documents in the movie field, which contains 1,000,000 positive documents and 1,000,000 negative documents in English. All the documents in our English training data set are automatically extracted from English Facebook, English websites and social networks; then we labeled positive and negative for them.

In Figure 2, our testing data set comprises 1,000,000 documents in the movie field, which have 500,000 positive documents and 500,000 negative documents in English. All the documents in our testing data set are automatically extracted from English Facebook, English websites and social networks; then we labeled positive and negative for them.

The accuracy of this novel model is dependent on many different factors. One of the factors is our data sets including a the TESDS and the TRADS

To improve the accuracy of our model, we can reform many aspects of the TESDS and the TRADS as follows:

Figure 1. Our English training data set

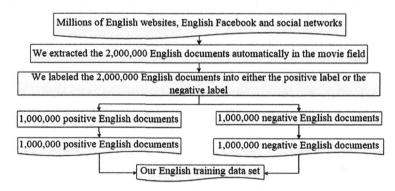

Figure 2. Our English testing data set

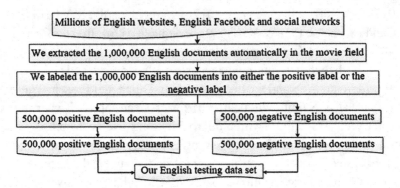

1. The TESDS must be similar to the TRADS
2. The documents of the TESDS must be standardized carefully.
3. The documents (or the sentences) of the TRADS must be standardized carefully.
4. The documents of the TESDS must be similar to the documents of the TRADS.
5. The sentences of the TRADS must be similar to the sentences of the TESDS

MAIN FOCUS OF THE CHAPTER

Issues, Controversies, Problems

In this part, we have presented many algorithms, methods, models, and etc. of the NN for the LSDSs in the SE and the DNS.

According to our opinion, we have not found any algorithms, methods, models, and etc. of the NN in the SS for the BDSs in the world.

This section, we have confirmed that all algorithms, methods, models, and etc. of the NN, which have been performed in the DNSs, can process for the BDSs certainly although their data sets can be many small data sets

The authors in (P. Chanthini, & K. Shyamala, 2016) used a NN which the distributed execution of the NN was achieved up to the level of the training process. This work could work well on hardware implementations, a software package, special purpose hardware and multicore CPUs through MPI. The authors used each neuron and full neural network to duplicate to multiple threads for achieving parallelism and speeding up the training process.

The authors displayed a technique to parallelize the training of NNs in (George Dahl, & et al, 2008). They designed this technique for parallelization on a cluster of workstations. Pattern Parallel Training was their solution to duplicate the full neural network et each cluster node. Each cooperating process in the cluster trained the neural network on a subset of the training set each epoch. The authors implemented and tested an MPI version of Pattern Parallel Training for the eight bit parity problem. The communication costs of our technique was analyzed and the authors discussed which types of common neural network problems would benefit most from their approach.

In (Dr. K. Usha Rani, 2010), the authors have proposed a parallel approach by using neural network technique to help in the diagnosis of breast cancer. The neural network was trained with breast cancer data base by using feed forward neural network model and back-propagation learning algorithm with momentum and variable learning rate. The performance of the network was evaluated.

A theoretical basis for a Hadoop - based neural network for parallel and distributed feature selection in BDSs was introduced in (Victoria J.Hodge, & et al, 2016). The implementation details of five feature selection algorithms was constructed using the authors' artificial neural network framework embedded in Hadoop YARN.

The authors of (Cristian Mihai BARCA, & Claudiu Dan BARCA, 2017) used the two main methods to distribute the patterns which were used for training – training set level parallelism or to distribute the computation performed by the neural network – neural network level parallelism. The first method was focused a lot in this research.

There have been many surveys of the NN for the BDSs which have not been displayed yet in this book chapter. However, there have not been enough researches of the NN for the LSDSs yet for many years.

In the below sub-section "Solutions and Recommendations", we have shown a novel model using a ANN algorithm and many MDVs of SECL for a MDS in a SE and a DNE in English.

Solutions and Recommendations

Many different algorithms of data mining, machine learning, and etc. have already been applied to sentiment analysis certainly. We have developed our models including the algorithms for the semantic classification.

To implement our new model, we have proposed the following basic principles:

1. Assuming that each English sentence has m English words (or English phrases).
2. Assuming that the maximum number of one English sentence is m_max; it means that m is less than m_max or m is equal to m_max.
3. Assuming that each English document has n English sentences.
4. Assuming that the maximum number of one English document is n_max; it means that n is less than n_max or n is equal to n_max.

5. Each English sentence is transferred into one one-dimensional vector (ODV). Thus, the length of the vector is m. If m is less than m_max then each element of the vector from m to m_max-1 is 0 (zero).
6. Each English document is transferred into one multi-dimensional vector (MDV). Therefore, the MDV has n rows and m columns. If n is less than n_max then each element of the MDV from n to n_max-1 is 0 (zero vector).
7. All the documents of the TRADS are transferred into the MDVs in English. The positive documents of the TRADS are transferred into the positive MDVs, called a positive vector group (PVP). The negative documents of the TRADS are transferred into the negative MDVs, called a negative vector group (NVP).
8. All the documents of the TESDS are transferred into the MDVs in English
9. One MDV (corresponding to one document in the TESDS in English) is the positive polarity if the vector is clustered into the PVP. One MDV (corresponding to one document in the TESDS) is the negative polarity if the vector is clustered into the NVP. One MDV (corresponding to one English document in the TESDS) is the neutral polarity if the vector is not clustered into either the PVP or the NVP

In this study, we have developed a new model by using the ANN to classify emotions (positive, negative, neutral) of the documents in the DNE. A study of semantic classification – SECL (emotional analysis - EMA) using the ANN does not currently exist in the world.

Our model has had many significant applications to many areas of research as well as commercial applications:

1. The ANN is applicable to the SECL of natural language processing.
2. This study also proves that different fields of scientific research can be related in many ways.
3. Millions of English documents are successfully processed for emotional analysis.
4. Many studies and commercial applications can use the results of this survey.
5. The semantic classification is implemented in the parallel network environment.
6. The principles are proposed in the research.
7. The opinion classification of English documents is performed on English documents.
8. The proposed model can be applied to other languages easily.
9. The Cloudera distributed environment is used in this study.
10. The proposed work can be applied to other distributed systems.

11. This survey uses Hadoop Map (M) and Hadoop Reduce (R).
12. Our proposed model can be applied to many different parallel network environments such as a Cloudera system
13. This study can be applied to many different distributed functions such as Hadoop Map (M) and Hadoop Reduce (R).
14. The ANN - related algorithms are proposed in this work.

This section has two parts: semantic classification for the documents of the testing in the SS is presented in the first part. In the second part, sentiment classification for the reviews of the testing in the DNE is displayed.

With the TRADS, there were two groups. The first group included the positive documents of the TRADS and the second group was the negative documents of the TRADS. The first group was called a positive cluster (POSC). The second group was called a negative cluster (NEGC). All the documents in both the first group and the second group went through the segmentation of words and stop-words removal; then, they were transferred into the MDVs (vector representation). The positive documents of the POSC were transferred into the positive MDVs which were called the PVP (or positive vector cluster). The negative documents of the NEGC were transferred into the negative MDVs which were called the NVP (or negative vector cluster). Therefore, the TRADS included the PVP (or positive vector cluster) and the NVP (or negative vector cluster).

In [(Vaibhav Kant Singh, & Vinay Kumar Singh, 2015), (Víctor Carrera-Trejo, & et al, 2015), and (Pascal Soucy, & Guy W. Mineau, 2015)], the VSM has been an algebraic model used for information retrieval. It has represented a natural language document in a formal manner by the use of vectors in a multidimensional space. The VSM has been a way of representing documents through the words they contain. The concepts behind vector space modeling has been that by placing terms, documents, and queries in a term-document space, it has been possible to compute the similarities between queries and the terms or documents and allow the results of the computation to be ranked according to the similarity measure between them. The VSM has allowed decisions to be made about which documents are similar to each other and to queries.

We have transferred all English sentences into one-dimensional vectors similar to VSM [(Vaibhav Kant Singh, & Vinay Kumar Singh, 2015), (Víctor Carrera-Trejo, & et al, 2015), and (Pascal Soucy, & Guy W. Mineau, 2015)].

Figure 3. Overview of transferring all English documents into the multi-dimensional vectors

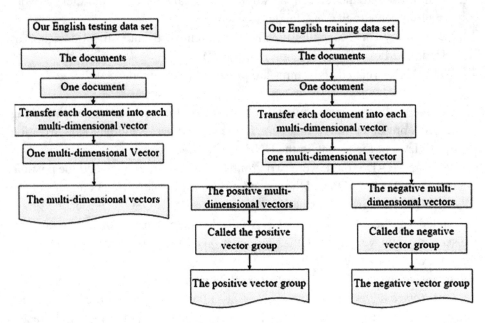

1. An Artificial Neural Network Algorithm (ANN) in a Sequential Environment

In Figure 3, in the SE, the documents of the TESDS were transferred to the MDVs: each document of the TESDS was transferred to each MDV (each sentence of one document in the TESDS was transferred to the ODV similar to VSM [(Vaibhav Kant Singh, & Vinay Kumar Singh, 2015), (Víctor Carrera-Trejo, & et al, 2015), and (Pascal Soucy, & Guy W. Mineau, 2015)]). The positive documents in the TRADS were transferred to the positive MDVs, called the PVP in the SS: each document of the positive documents was transferred to each MDV (each sentence of one document in the positive documents was transferred to the ODV similar to VSM [(Vaibhav Kant Singh, & Vinay Kumar Singh, 2015), (Víctor Carrera-Trejo, & et al, 2015), and (Pascal Soucy, & Guy W. Mineau, 2015)] in the SE). The negative documents in the TRADS were transferred to the negative MDVs, called the NVP in the SE: each document of the negative documents was transferred to each MDV (each sentence of one document in the negative documents was transferred to the ODV similar to VSM [(Vaibhav Kant Singh, & Vinay Kumar Singh, 2015), (Víctor Carrera-Trejo, & et al, 2015), and (Pascal Soucy, & Guy W. Mineau, 2015)] in the SE).

We have performed this part in Figure 4. In the SS, the ANN was implemented to cluster one MDV (called A) of the English TESDS to the PVP or the NVP. The document (corresponding to A) was the positive polarity if A was clustered to the PVP. The document (corresponding to A) was the negative polarity if A was clustered to the NVP. The document (corresponding to A) was the neutral polarity if A was not clustered to both the PVP and the NVP.

We built many algorithms to perform the ANN in the SE. We built the algorithm 1 to transfer one English document into one MDV. Each document was split into many sentences. Each sentence in each document was transferred to one one-dimensional vector based on VSM [(Vaibhav Kant Singh, & Vinay Kumar Singh, 2015), (Víctor Carrera-Trejo, & et al, 2015), and (Pascal Soucy, & Guy W. Mineau, 2015)] in the sequential environment. We inserted all the ODVs of the sentences into one MDV of one document

```
Input: one English document
Output: one MDV
Step 1: Split the English document into many separate sentences
based on "." Or "!" or "?";
Step 2: Each sentence in the n sentences of this document, do
repeat:
Step 3: Transfer this sentence into one one-dimensional vector
based on VSM [(Vaibhav Kant Singh, & Vinay Kumar Singh, 2015),
(Víctor Carrera-Trejo, & et al, 2015), and (Pascal Soucy, & Guy
```

Figure 4. An artificial neural network algorithm (ANN) in the Sequential Environment

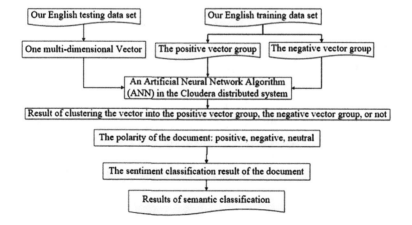

```
W. Mineau, 2015)];
Step 4: Add the transferred vector into one MDV
Step 5: End Repeat - End Step 2
Step 6: Return one MDV;
```

We proposed the algorithm 2 to create the PVP. Each document in the positive documents in the English TRADS was split into many sentences. Each sentence of the document was transferred to one ODV based on VSM [(Vaibhav Kant Singh, & Vinay Kumar Singh, 2015), (Víctor Carrera-Trejo, & et al, 2015), and (Pascal Soucy, & Guy W. Mineau, 2015)] in the SE. We inserted all the ODVs of the sentences of the document into one MDV of the document. Then, the positive documents in the TRADS were transferred to the positive MDVs.

```
Input: the positive English documents of the TRADS.
Output: the positive vector group - PositiveVectorGroup
Step 1: Each document in the positive documents of the TRADS,
do repeat:
Step 2: OneMultiDimensionalVector:= Call Algorithm 1 with the
positive English document  in the TRADS;
Step 3: Add OneMultiDimensionalVector into PositiveVectorGroup;
Step 4: End Repeat - End Step 1
Step 5: Return PositiveVectorGroup;
```

We developed the algorithm 3 to create the NVP. Each document in the negative documents in the English TRADS was split into many sentences. Each sentence of the document was transferred to one ODV based on VSM [(Vaibhav Kant Singh, & Vinay Kumar Singh, 2015), (Víctor Carrera-Trejo, & et al, 2015), and (Pascal Soucy, & Guy W. Mineau, 2015)] in the SE. We inserted all the ODVs of the sentences of the document into one MDV of the document. Then, the negative documents in the TRADS were transferred to the negative MDVs.

```
Input: the negative English documents of the TRADS.
Output: the negative vector group - PositiveVectorGroup
Step 1: Each document in the negative documents of the TRADS,
do repeat:
Step 2: OneMultiDimensionalVector:= Call Algorithm 1 with the
negative English document  in the TRADS;
Step 3: Add OneMultiDimensionalVector into NegativeVectorGroup;
Step 4: End Repeat - End Step 1
Step 5: Return Negative VectorGroup;
```

We built the algorithm 4 to cluster one MDV (corresponding to one document of the TESDS) into the positive vector group - PositiveVectorGroup, the negative vector group - NegativeVectorGroup, or not.

```
Input: one MDV A (corresponding to one English document of the
TESDS), the positive vector group - PositiveVectorGroup, the
negative vector group - NegativeVectorGroup;
Output: positive, negative, neutral;
Step 1: Implement the ANN based on the ANN in [(R.J. Kuo,
& et al, 2001), (K. P. Sudheer, & et al, 2002), (Carsten
Peterson, & et al, 1994), (D.C. Park, & et al, 1991), (Kuo-
lin Hsu, & et al, 1995), (Xin Yao, 1999), (B. Samanta, & K.R.
Al-Balushi, 2003), (V Brusic, & et al, 1998), (Muriel Gevrey,
& et al, 2003), (C. Charalambous, 1992), (K. P. Sudheer, & et
al, 2002), (Zhi-Hua Zhou, & et al, 2002), (Laurent Magnier, &
Fariborz Haghighat, 2010), (Sovan Lek, & J.F. Guégan, 1999),
and (Kyoung-jae Kim, & Ingoo Han, 2000)] with input is one
MDV (corresponding to one English document of the TESDS), the
positive vector group - PositiveVectorGroup, the negative
vector group - NegativeVectorGroup;
Step 2: With the results of Step 1, If the vector is clustered
into the PVP Then Return positive;
Step 3: Else If the vector is clustered into the negative
vector group Then Return negative; End If – End Step 2
Step 4: Return neutral;
```

The ANN uses Euclidean distance to calculate the distance between two vectors

2. An Artificial Neural Network Algorithm (ANN) in a Parallel Network Environment

In Figure 5, all documents of both the TESDS and the TRADS were transferred into all the MDVs in the CPNS. With the documents of the TRADS, we transferred them into the MDVs by using the M/R in the CPNS with the purpose of shortening the execution time of this task. The positive documents of the TRADS were transferred into the positive vectors in the CPNS and were called the PVP. The negative documents of the TRADS were transferred into the negative vectors in the CPNS and were called the NVP. Besides, the documents of the TESDS were transferred to the MDVs by using the M/R in the CPNS with the purpose of shortening the execution time of this task.

We have implemented this part in Figure 6. In the CPNS, by using the ANN, one MDV (called A) of one document in the TESDS was clustered into the PVP or the NVP. The document (corresponding to A) was the positive polarity if A was clustered into the PVP. The document (corresponding to A) was the negative polarity if A was clustered into the NVP. The document (corresponding to A) was the neutral polarity if A was not clustered into both the PVP and the NVP.

An overview of transferring each sentence into one vector in the CPNS has been presented in Figure 7.

In Figure 7, transferring each English document into one vector in the CPNS included two phases: the M phase and the R phase. The input of the M was one document and the output of the M was many components of a vector which corresponded to the document. One document which was input into the M, was split into many sentences. Each sentence in the document was transferred into one ODV based on VSM [(Vaibhav Kant Singh, & Vinay Kumar Singh, 2015), (Víctor Carrera-Trejo, & et al, 2015), and (Pascal Soucy, & Guy W. Mineau, 2015)]. This was repeated for all the sentences of the document until all the sentences were transferred into all the ODVs of the document. After finishing to transfer each sentence of the document into one ODV, the M of the CPNS automatically transferred the ODV into the R.

Figure 5. Overview of transferring all English documents into the multi-dimensional vectors in the Cloudera distributed system

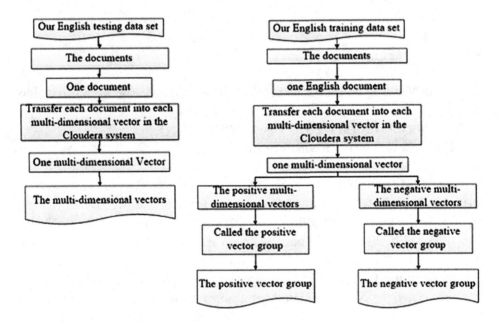

Figure 6. An artificial neural network algorithm (ANN) in the parallel network environment

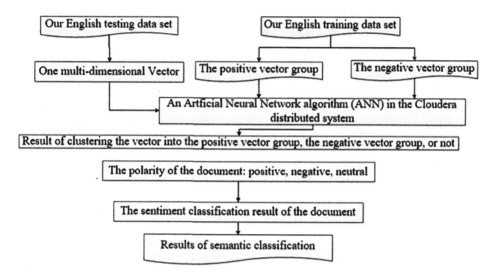

In Figure 7, the input of the R was the output of the Map phase, and this input comprised many components (many ODVs) of a MDV. The output of the R was a MDV which corresponded to the document. In the R of the CPNS, those components of the vector were built into one MDV. The documents of the TESDS were transferred into the MDVs based on Figure 7.

Figure 7. Overview of transforming each English sentence into one vector in Cloudera

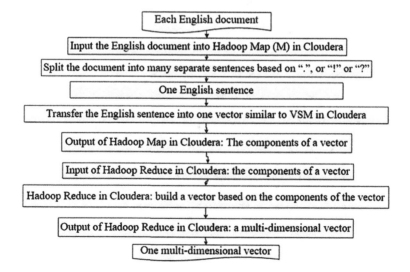

The ANN in the CPNS had two main phases: the first main phase was the M phase in the CPNS and the second main phase was the R phase in the CPNS. In the M of the CPNS, the input of the phase was the MDV of one English document (which was classified), the PVP, the NVP; and the output of the phase was the clustering results of the MDV of the document to the PVP or the NVP, or not. With the R of the CPNS, the input of the phase was the output of the M of the CPNS and this input was the clustering results of the MDV of the document to the PVP or the NVP or not; and the output of the phase was the sentiment classification result of the document into the positive polarity, the negative polarity, or the neutral polarity. In the R, the document was classified as the positive emotion if the MDV was clustered into the PVP; the document was classified as the negative semantic if the MDV into the NVP; and the document was classified as the neutral sentiment if the MDV was not clustered into the PVP, or the NVP, or not.

2.1 Hadoop Map (M) Stage

We have performed this stage in Figure 8. The ANN in the CPNS was based on the ANN in [(R.J. Kuo, & et al, 2001), (K. P. Sudheer, & et al, 2002), (Carsten Peterson, & et al, 1994), (D.C. Park, & et al, 1991), (Kuo-lin Hsu, & et al, 1995), (Xin Yao, 1999), (B. Samanta, & K.R. Al-Balushi, 2003), (V Brusic, & et al, 1998), (Muriel Gevrey, & et al, 2003), (C. Charalambous, 1992), (K. P. Sudheer, & et al, 2002), and (Zhi-Hua Zhou, & et al, 2002)]. The input was one MDV in the TESDS, the PVP and the NVP of the TRADS. The output of the ANN was the clustering results of the multi-dimensional vector into the positive vector group or the NVP, or not.

Figure 8. Overview of neural network

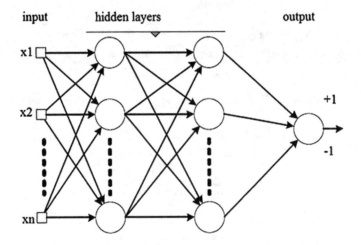

Algorithm 1. The basic algorithm of the supervised learning of our neural network

```
Supervised learning can be considered as mapping approximately:
X → Y, where X is the set of problems and Y is the
corresponding set of solutions to that problem. The samples (x,
y) with x = (x1, x2,..., Xn) ∈ X, y = (y1, y2,..., Ym) ∈ Y be
given.
Input: x = (x1, x2,..., Xn) ∈ X,
Output: y = (y1, y2,..., Ym) ∈ Y
begin
1. Build the appropriate structure for neural network,
for example with (n+1) neurons input (n neurons for input
variables and 1 neuron for threshold x0), m output neurons, and
initialize the weights of the network links.
2.  Input one vector x in the X TRADS input into network
3.  Calculate the output vector o of network.
4.  Compare the expected output vector y (is the given result
of TRADS) with the output vector o which network generated; if
can be then identify error
5.  Adjust the weights in some way so that in the next time,
when inputs vector x to the network, the output vector o will
resemble y more.
6.  Can repeat step 2 to step 5 if want, until converging. The
evaluation of error can perform in many different ways, using
the most used instant error: Err = (o - y), or Err = | o - y |;
mean squared error (MSE: mean-square error): Err = (o- y) 2/2;
end;
```

The NN in our model included the learning stage and the testing stage. An overview of our neural network was displayed in Figure 8.

In Figure 8, the input of the NN was a MDV X and the output of network was +1 or -1. If the output was +1 then this vector of the input was classified into the positive group. If the output was -1 then this vector of input was classified into the negative group.

Our learning stage: in this stage, we used the positive vectors of the PVP and the negative vectors of the NVP to identify the parameters of our neural network, such as weights, outputs, etc.

Our testing stage: with the parameters of our neural network, each vector of the TESDS was the input of our neural network.

There were two types of errors in the evaluation of a neural network. Firstly, called as clear error, assess approximately the training samples of a network have been trained. Second, called as test error, assess the ability of a total process of a network has been trained, the ability to react with the new input vector.

In this study, we used back-propagation algorithm of neural network for our new model.

The main ideal of the back-propagation algorithm: we wanted to train a multi-layer feed-forward network by gradient descent to approximate an unknown function, based on some training data consisting of pairs (x,t). The vector x represented a pattern of input to the network, and the vector t the corresponding target (desired output). As we have seen before, the overall gradient with respect to the entire training set was just the sum of the gradients for each pattern; in what follows we would therefore described how to compute the gradient for just a single training pattern. As before, we would number the units, and denoted the weight from unit j to unit i by w_{ij}.

1. **Definitions:**
   a. The error signal for unit j: $\delta_j = -\partial E / \partial net_j$
   b. The (negative) gradient for weight w_{ij}: $\Delta w_{ij} = -\partial E / \partial w_{ij}$
   c. The set of nodes anterior to unit i: $A_i = \{j : \exists w_{ij}\}$
   d. The set of nodes posterior to unit j: $P_j = \{i : \exists w_{ij}\}$

2. **The Gradient:** As we did for linear networks before, we expanded the gradient into two factors by use of the chain rule:

$$\Delta w_{ij} = -\frac{\partial E}{\partial net_i}\frac{\partial net_i}{\partial w_{ij}}$$

The first factor is the error of unit i. The second is

$$\frac{\partial net_i}{\partial w_{ij}} = \frac{\partial}{\partial w_{ij}}\sum_{k \in A_i} w_{ik} y_k = y_j$$

Putting the two together, we get

$$\Delta w_{ij} = \delta_i y_j$$

To compute this gradient, we thus needed to know the activity and the error for all relevant nodes in the network.

3. **Forward Activation:** The activity of the input units was determined by the network's external input x. For all other units, the activity was propagated forward:

$$y_i = f_i \left(\sum_{j \in A_i} w_{ij} y_j \right)$$

before the activity of unit i could be calculated, the activity of all its anterior nodes (forming the set Ai) must be known. Since feedforward networks did not contain cycles, there was an ordering of nodes from input to output that respects this condition.

4. **Calculating Output Error:** Assuming that we were using the sum-squared loss

$$E = \frac{1}{2} \sum_o (t_o - y_o)^2$$

the error for output unit o was simply

$$\delta_o = t_o - y_o$$

5. **Error Backpropagation:** For hidden units, we must propagate the error back from the output nodes (hence the name of the algorithm). Again using the chain rule, we could expand the error of a hidden unit in terms of its posterior nodes:

$$\delta_j = \sum_{i \in P_j} \frac{\partial E}{\partial net_i} \frac{\partial net_i}{\partial y_j} \frac{\partial y_j}{\partial net_j}$$

Of the three factors inside the sum, the first is just the error of node i. The second was

$$\frac{\partial net_i}{\partial y_j} = \frac{\partial}{\partial y_j} \sum_{k \in A_i} w_{ik} y_k = w_{ij}$$

while the third was the derivative of node j's activation function:

$$\frac{\partial y_j}{\partial net_j} = \frac{\partial f_j(net_j)}{\partial net_j} = f_j'(net_j)$$

For hidden units h that used the tanh activation function, we could make use of the special identity

$$f_h'(net_h) = 1 - y_h^2$$

Putting all the pieces together we got

$$\delta_j = f_j'(net_j) \sum_{i \in P_j} \delta_i w_{ij}$$

In order to calculate the error for unit j, we must first know the error of all its posterior nodes (forming the set Pj). Again, as long as there were no cycles in the network, there was an ordering of nodes from the output back to the input that respects this condition. For example, we could simply use the reverse of the order in which activity was propagated forward.

After finishing to cluster the MDV into the PVP, or the NVP, or not, the M transferred this results into the R in the CPNS.

2.2 Hadoop Reduce (R) Stage

We have performed this stage in Figure 9. After receiving the clustering result of the M, the R identified the semantics polarity for the MDV which was classified. Then, the output of the R would return the semantics polarity of one document (corresponding to the MDV) in the TESDS. One document was the positive polarity if the MDV was clustered into the PVP. One document was the negative polarity if the MDV was clustered into the NVP. One document was the neutral polarity if the multi-dimensional vector was not clustered into both the PVP and the NVP.

We have used an Accuracy (A) measure to calculate the accuracy of the results of emotion classification.

Figure 9. Overview of the Hadoop Reduce (R) in the Cloudera

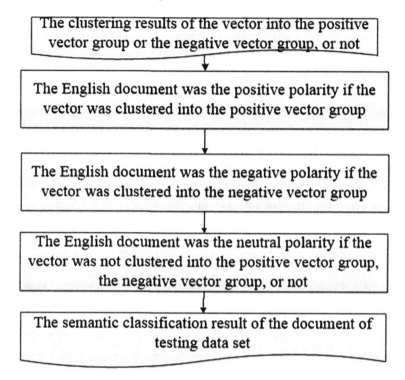

Java programming language (JAPL) have been used for programming to save data sets, implementing our proposed model to classify the documents of the TESDS. To implement the proposed model, we have already used the JAPL to save the TRADS, the TESDS, and to save the results of emotion classification.

The SE in this research included 1 node (1 server). The JAPL has been used in programming the ANN. The configuration of the server in the SE has been: Intel® Server Board S1200V3RPS, Intel® Pentium® Processor G3220 (3M Cache, 3.00 GHz), 2GB PC3-10600 ECC 1333 MHz LP Unbuffered DIMMs. The operating system of the server has been: Cloudera. We have performed the ANN in the Cloudera parallel network environment; this Cloudera system included 9 nodes (9 servers). The JAPL has been used in programming the application of the ANN in the Cloudera. The configuration of each server in the Cloudera system has been: Intel® Server Board S1200V3RPS, Intel® Pentium® Processor G3220 (3M Cache, 3.00 GHz), 2GB PC3-10600 ECC 1333 MHz LP Unbuffered DIMMs. The operating system of each server in the 6 servers has been: Cloudera. All six nodes had the same configuration information.

The results of the opinion mining of the documents of the TESDS are presented in Table 1.

The accuracy of the emotional classification of the documents of the TESDS is shown in Table 2.

In Table 3, the average times of the classification of our new model for the documents in TESDS are displayed

Although our new model has been tested on our English data set, it can be applied to many other languages. In this paper, our model has been tested on the 1,000,000 English documents of the TESDS in which the data sets are small. However, our model can be applied to larger data sets with millions of documents in the shortest time.

In this work, we have proposed a new model to classify the sentiments (position, negative, or neutral) of the documents using the ANN with the M and the R in the

Table 1. The results of the 1,000,000 English documents in the TESDS

	Testing Dataset	Correct Classification	Incorrect Classification
Negative	500,000	420,259	79,741
Positive	500,000	422,241	77,759
Summary	1,000,000	842,500	157,500

Table 2. The accuracy of our new model for the documents of the TESDS

Proposed Model	Class	Accuracy
Our new model	Negative	84.25%
	Positive	

Table 3. The average times of the classification of our new model for the documents of the TESDS

	Average time of the classification /1,000,000 English documents
The Artificial Neural Network Algorithm (ANN) in the sequential environment	5,461,091 seconds
The Artificial Neural Network Algorithm (ANN) in the Cloudera distributed system – 3 nodes	1,738,739 seconds
The Artificial Neural Network Algorithm (ANN) in the Cloudera distributed system – 6 nodes	874,378 seconds
The Artificial Neural Network Algorithm (ANN) in the Cloudera distributed system – 9 nodes	631,084 seconds

CPNS. With our proposed new model, we have achieved 84.25% accuracy of the TESDS in Table 2.

In Table 3, the average time of the EMA of the ANN algorithm in the SE is 5,461,091 seconds /1,000,000 English documents and it is greater than the average time of the SECL of the ANN in the CPNS – 3 nodes which is 1,738,739 seconds /1,000,000 English documents. The average time of the SECL of the ANN in the CPNS – 9 nodes, which is 631,084 seconds /1,000,000 English documents, is the shortest time. Besides, the average time of the SECL of the ANN in the CPNS – 6 nodes is 874,378 seconds /1,000,000 English documents

The execution time of the ANN in the CPNS is dependent on the performance of the CPNS and also dependent on the performance of each server on the CPNS.

The proposed model has many advantages and disadvantages. Its positives are as follows: It uses the ANN algorithm to classify the semantics of the documents based on the documents. The proposed model can process millions of documents in the shortest time. This study can be performed in distributed systems. It can be applied to other languages. Its negatives are as follows: It has a low rate of accuracy. It costs too much and takes too much time to implement this proposed model.

The accuracy of this novel model is dependent on many different factors as follows:

1. The algorithms
2. The data sets including the TESDS and the TRADS.

To improve the accuracy of our model, we can reform many aspects of the algorithms, the TESDS and the TRADS as follows:

1. We can improve the algorithms related to the ANN
2. We can combine the algorithms of the machine learning, the data mining, and etc.
3. The TESDS must be similar to the TRADS.
4. The documents of the TESDS must be standardized carefully.
5. The documents (or the sentences) of the TRADS must be standardized carefully.
6. The documents of the TESDS must be similar to the documents of the TRADS.
7. The sentences of the TRADS must be similar to the sentences of the TESDS.

The execution times of this model are dependent on several factors as follows:

1. The algorithms related to the ANN: we can improve them to get better execution times.
2. The performance of a parallel network system such as Cloudera, Hadoop and Hadoop Reduce

3. A number of nodes (servers) in the distributed environment: We can increase the number of nodes in the parallel system to get faster execution times

4. The performance of a server: We can increase the performance of a server to get better execution times

FUTURE RESEARCH DIRECTIONS

From those results of this novel model and according to the above proofs, we are going to study this model for applying to billions of English documents in both the SE and the PNE. In addition, we are also going to research this approach for being performed in the PNE with over 50 nodes. Furthermore, the accuracy of this new computational model can be studied to improve certainly.

From the results of this chapter, many algorithms, methods, models, and etc. are going to be developed more and more for handling the massive data sets fully in the near future.

CONCLUSION

In this chapter, we have displayed the simple concepts of the ML, the NN, the EA, the FSs, and etc. We have shown the possible novel computational models of the NN for the BDSs successfully in more details.

We have also shown a novel model using the ANN and the MDVs of the SECL for the LSDS in the SS and the PNE successfully.

These models can be performed in the SS or the DNS fully.

There can be many models of the NN for the LSDSs, which have not been presented in this chapter yet.

In the near future, many novel computational models are going to be developed more and more for the MDSs. This is very significant for many organizations, economies, governments, countries, commercial applications, researches, and etc. in the world.

REFERENCES

Agarwal, B., & Mittal, N. (2016a). Machine Learning Approach for Sentiment Analysis. In Prominent Feature Extraction for Sentiment Analysis (pp. 21–45). Academic Press. doi:10.1007/978-3-319-25343-5_3

Agarwal, B., & Mittal, N. (2016b). Semantic Orientation-Based Approach for Sentiment Analysis. In Prominent Feature Extraction for Sentiment Analysis (pp. 77–88). Academic Press. doi:10.1007/978-3-319-25343-5_6

Ahmed, S., & Danti, A. (2016). Effective Sentimental Analysis and Opinion Mining of Web Reviews Using Rule Based Classifiers. In Computational Intelligence in Data Mining (Vol. 1, pp. 171–179). Academic Press. doi:10.1007/978-81-322-2734-2_18

Apache. (2017). Retrieved from http://apache.org

Brusic, V., Rudy, G., Honeyman, G., Hammer, J., & Harrison, L. (1998). Prediction of MHC class II-binding peptides using an evolutionary algorithm and artificial neural network. *Bioinformatics (Oxford, England)*, *14*(2), 121–130. doi:10.1093/bioinformatics/14.2.121 PMID:9545443

Canuto, Gonçalves, & Benevenuto. (2016). Exploiting New Sentiment-Based Meta-level Features for Effective Sentiment Analysis. *Proceedings of the Ninth ACM International Conference on Web Search and Data Mining (WSDM '16)*, 53-62 10.1145/2835776.2835821

Carrera-Trejo, V., Sidorov, G., Miranda-Jiménez, S., Ibarra, M. M., & Martínez, R. C. (2015). Latent Dirichlet Allocation complement in the vector space model for Multi-Label Text Classification. *International Journal of Combinatorial Optimization Problems and Informatics*, *6*(1), 7–19.

Chanthini, P., & Shyamala, K. (2016). A Survey on Parallelization of Neural Network using MPI and Open MP. *Indian Journal of Science and Technology*, *9*(19). doi:10.17485/ijst/2016/v9i19/93835

Charalambous, C. (1992). Conjugate gradient algorithm for efficient training of artificial neural networks. *IEE Proceedings. Part G. Circuits, Devices and Systems*, *139*(3), 301–310. doi:10.1049/ip-g-2.1992.0050

Cloudera. (2017). Retrieved from http://www.cloudera.com

Cristian Mihai, B. A. R. C. A., & Claudiu Dan, B. A. R. C. A. (2017). Distributed algorithm to train neural networks using the Map Reduce paradigm. *Database Systems Journal*, *8*(1), 3–11.

Dahl, G., McAvinney, A., & Newhall, T. (2008). Parallelizing neural network training for cluster systems. *PDCN '08 Proceedings of the IASTED International Conference on Parallel and Distributed Computing and Networks*, 220-225.

Dat, N. D., Phu, V. N., Vo, T. N. T., & Vo, T. N. C. (2017). STING Algorithm used English Sentiment Classification in A Parallel Environment. *International Journal of Pattern Recognition and Artificial Intelligence*, *31*(07), 1750021. doi:10.1142/S0218001417500215

Gevrey, M., Dimopoulos, I., & Lek, S. (2003). Review and comparison of methods to study the contribution of variables in artificial neural network models. *Ecological Modelling*, *160*(3), 249–264. doi:10.1016/S0304-3800(02)00257-0

Hadoop. (2017). Retrieved from http://hadoop.apache.org

Hodge, V. J., O'Keefe, S., & Austin, J. (2016). Hadoop neural network for parallel and distributed feature selection. *Neural Networks*, *78*, 24–35. doi:10.1016/j.neunet.2015.08.011 PMID:26403824

Hsu, K., Gupta, H. V., & Sorooshian, S. (1995). Artificial Neural Network Modeling of the Rainfall-Runoff Process. *Water Resources Research*, *31*(10), 2517–2530. doi:10.1029/95WR01955

Kuo, R. J., Chen, C. H., & Hwang, Y. C. (2001). An intelligent stock trading decision support system through integration of genetic algorithm based fuzzy neural network and artificial neural network. *Fuzzy Sets and Systems*, *118*(1), 21–45. doi:10.1016/S0165-0114(98)00399-6

Kyoung-jae, K., & Han, I. (2000). Genetic algorithms approach to feature discretization in artificial neural networks for the prediction of stock price index. *Expert Systems with Applications*, *19*(2), 125–132. doi:10.1016/S0957-4174(00)00027-0

Lek, S., & Guégan, J. F. (1999). Artificial neural networks as a tool in ecological modelling, an introduction. *Ecological Modelling*, *120*(2–3), 65–73. doi:10.1016/S0304-3800(99)00092-7

Magnier, L., & Haghighat, F. (2010). Multiobjective optimization of building design using TRNSYS simulations, genetic algorithm, and Artificial Neural Network. *Building and Environment*, *45*(3), 739–746. doi:10.1016/j.buildenv.2009.08.016

Park, D. C., El-Sharkawi, M. A., Marks, R. J., Atlas, L. E., & Damborg, M. J. (1991). Electric load forecasting using an artificial neural network. *IEEE Transactions on Power Systems, Volume, 6*(2). doi:10.1109/59.76685

Peterson, C., Rögnvaldsson, T., & Lönnblad, L. (1994). JETNET 3.0—A versatile artificial neural network package. *Computer Physics Communications, 81*(1–2), 185–220. doi:10.1016/0010-4655(94)90120-1

Phu, Vo, Vo, Duy, & Duy. (2017g). Semantic lexicons of English nouns for classification. *Evolving Systems*. doi:. doi:10.100712530-017-9188-6

Phu, Ngoc, Ngoc, & Duy. (2017b). A C4.5 algorithm for english emotional classification. *Evolving Systems*, 1-27. doi:10.100712530-017-9180-1

Phu, V. N., Dat, N. D., Vo, T. N. T., & Vo, T. N. T. (2016). Fuzzy C-Means for English Sentiment Classification in a Distributed System. In International Journal of Applied Intelligence (pp. 1–22). APIN. doi:10.100710489-016-0858-z

Phu, V. N., & Tuoi, P. T. (2014). Sentiment classification using Enhanced Contextual Valence Shifters. *International Conference on Asian Language Processing (IALP)*, 224-229. 10.1109/IALP.2014.6973485

Phu, V. N., Vo, T. N. C., Dat, N. D., Vo, T. N. T., & Nguyen, T. A. (2017c). A Valences-Totaling Model for English Sentiment Classification. Knowledge and Information Systems. doi:10.100710115-017-1054-0

Phu, V. N., Vo, T. N. C., & Vo, T. N. T. (2017d). Shifting Semantic Values of English Phrases for Classification. International Journal of Speech Technology. doi:10.100710772-017-9420-6

Phu, V. N., Vo, T. N. C., & Vo, T. N. T. (2017e). SVM for English Semantic Classification in Parallel Environment. International Journal of Speech Technology. doi:10.100710772-017-9421-5

Phu, V. N., Vo, T. N. C., Vo, T. N. T., & Dat, N. D. (2017a). A Vietnamese adjective emotion dictionary based on exploitation of Vietnamese language characteristics. *Artificial Intelligence Review*, 1–69. doi:10.100710462-017-9538-6

Phu, V. N., Vo, T. N. C., Vo, T. N. T., Dat, N. D., & Khanh, L. D. D. (2017f). *A Valence-Totaling Model for Vietnamese Sentiment Classification. International Journal of Evolving Systems*. doi:10.100712530-017-9187-7

Phu, V. N., & Vo, T. N. T. (2017a). A STING Algorithm and Multi-dimensional Vectors Used for English Sentiment Classification in a Distributed System. American Journal of Engineering and Applied Sciences. doi:10.3844/ajeassp.2017

Phu, V. N., & Vo, T. N. T. (2017b). English Sentiment Classification using Only the Sentiment Lexicons with a JOHNSON Coefficient in a Parallel Network Environment. American Journal of Engineering and Applied Sciences. doi:10.3844/ajeassp.2017

Phu, V. N., & Vo, T. N. T. (2018a). English Sentiment Classification using A Gower-2 Coefficient and A Genetic Algorithm with A Fitness-proportionate Selection in a Parallel Network Environment. *Journal of Theoretical and Applied Information Technology, 96*(4), 1-50.

Phu, V. N., & Vo, T. N. T. (2018b). English sentiment classification using a Fager & MacGowan coefficient and a genetic algorithm with a rank selection in a parallel network environment. *International Journal of Computer Modelling and New Technologies, 22*(1), 57-112.

Phu, V. N., & Vo, T. N. T. (2018c). Latent Semantic Analysis using A Dennis Coefficient for English Sentiment Classification in A Parallel System. *International Journal of Computers, Communications and Control, 13*(3), 390-410.

Phu, V. N., & Vo, T. N. T. (2018e). English Sentiment Classification using A BIRCH Algorithm and The Sentiment Lexicons-Based One-dimensional Vectors in a Parallel Network Environment. *International Journal of Computer Modelling and New Technologies, 22*(1).

Phu, V. N., & Vo, T. N. T. (2018f). A Fuzzy C-Means Algorithm and Sentiment-Lexicons-based Multi-dimensional Vectors Of A SOKAL & SNEATH-IV Coefficient Used For English Sentiment Classification. *International Journal of Theoretical and Applied Information Technology, 96*(10).

Phu, V. N., & Vo, T. N. T. (2018g). A Self-Training - Based Model using A K-NN Algorithm and The Sentiment Lexicons - Based Multi-dimensional Vectors of A S6 coefficient for Sentiment Classification. *International Journal of Theoretical and Applied Information Technology, 96*(10).

Phu, V. N., & Vo, T. N. T. (2018h). The Multi-dimensional Vectors and An Yule-II Measure Used for A Self-Organizing Map Algorithm of English Sentiment Classification in A Distributed Environment. *Journal of Theoretical and Applied Information Technology, 96*(10).

Phu, V. N., & Vo, T. N. T. (2018i). Sentiment Classification using The Sentiment Scores Of Lexicons Based on A Kuhns-II Coefficient in English. International Journal of Tomography & Simulation, 31(3).

Phu, V. N., & Vo, T. N. T. (2018j). K-Medoids algorithm used for English sentiment classification in a distributed system. *Computer Modelling and New Technologies, 22*(1), 20-39.

Phu, V. N., & Vo, T. N. T. (2018k). A Reformed K-Nearest Neighbors Algorithm for Big Data Sets. *Journal of Computer Science*. Retrieved from http://thescipub.com/abstract/10.3844/ofsp.11819

Phu, V. N., Vo, T. N. T., & Max, J. (2018d). A CURE Algorithm for Vietnamese Sentiment Classification in a Parallel Environment. *International Journal of Computer Science*. Retrieved from http://thescipub.com/abstract/10.3844/ofsp.11906

Phu, V. N., Vo, T. N. T., Vo, T. N. C., Dat, N. D., & Khanh, L. D. D. (2017h). A Decision Tree using ID3 Algorithm for English Semantic Analysis. International Journal of Speech Technology. doi:10.100710772-017-9429-x

Rani. (2010). Parallel Approach for Diagnosis of Breast Cancer using Neural Network Technique. *International Journal of Computer Applications, 10*(3), 1-5.

Samanta, B., & Al-Balushi, K. R. (2003). Artificial Neural Network Based Fault Diagnostics Of Rolling Element Bearings Using Time-Domain Features. *Mechanical Systems and Signal Processing, 17*(2), 317–328. doi:10.1006/mssp.2001.1462

Singh & Singh. (2015). Vector Space Model: An Information Retrieval System. *Int. J. Adv. Engg. Res. Studies, 4*(2), 141-143.

Soucy, P., & Mineau, G. W. (2015). Beyond TFIDF Weighting for Text Categorization in the Vector Space Model. *Proceedings of the 19th International Joint Conference on Artificial Intelligence*, 1130-1135.

Sudheer, K. P., Gosain, A. K., Mohana Rangan, D., & Saheb, S. M. (2002). Modelling evaporation using an artificial neural network algorithm. *Hydrological Processes, 16*(16), 3189–3202. doi:10.1002/hyp.1096

Sudheer, K. P., Gosain, A. K., & Ramasastri, K. S. (2002). A data-driven algorithm for constructing artificial neural network rainfall-runoff models. *Hydrological Processes*. doi:10.1002/hyp.554

Vo, T. N. T., Phu, V. N., & Tuoi, P. T. (2014). Learning More Chi Square Feature Selection to Improve the Fastest and Most Accurate Sentiment Classification. *The Third Asian Conference on Information Systems (ACIS 2014)*.

Yao, X. (1999). Evolving artificial neural networks. *Proceedings of the IEEE, 87*(9). DOI: 10.1109/5.784219

Zhou, Z.-H., Wu, J., & Tang, W. (2002). Ensembling neural networks: Many could be better than all. *Artificial Intelligence, 137*(1–2), 239–263. doi:10.1016/S0004-3702(02)00190-X

Compilation of References

Abadeh, M. S., Habibi, J., & Lucas, C. (2007). Intrusion detection using a fuzzy genetics-based learning algorithm. *Journal of Network and Computer Applications*, *30*(1), 414–428. doi:10.1016/j.jnca.2005.05.002

Abadi, M., Barham, P., Chen, J., Chen, Z., Davis, A., Dean, J., . . . Kudlur, M. (2016, November). Tensorflow: a system for large-scale machine learning. In OSDI (Vol. 16, pp. 265-283). Academic Press.

Abraham, A. (2005). 129: Artificial Neural Networks. Handbook of Measuring System Design.

Accardi, R. (1996). *A Comparison of Exponential Smoothing and Time Series Models for Forecasting Contract Estimate–At-Completion. US.ARMY Communication Electronic Command, Directorate of Resource Management*. Fort Monmouth: Cost Analysis Division.

Aceituno-Cabezas, B., Mastalli, C., Dai, H., Focchi, M., Radulescu, A., Caldwell, D. G., ... Semini, C. (2018). Simultaneous Contact, Gait, and Motion Planning for Robust Multilegged Locomotion via Mixed-Integer Convex Optimization. *IEEE Robotics and Automation Letters*, *3*(3), 2531–2538.

Addo, P., Guegan, D., & Hassani, B. (2018). Credit Risk Analysis Using Machine and Deep Learning Models. *Risks*, *6*(2), 38. doi:10.3390/risks6020038

Ademu, I. O., Imafidon, C. O., & Preston, D. S. (2011). A new approach of digital forensic model for digital forensic investigation. *Int. J. Adv. Comput. Sci. Appl*, *2*(12), 175–178.

Adisasmito, W. (2007). Systematic Review Penelitian Akademik Bidang Kesehatan Masyarakat. Jurnal Makara Kesehatan, 11.

Agarwal, B., & Mittal, N. (2016a). Machine Learning Approach for Sentiment Analysis. In Prominent Feature Extraction for Sentiment Analysis (pp. 21–45). Academic Press. doi:10.1007/978-3-319-25343-5_3

Agarwal, B., & Mittal, N. (2016b). Semantic Orientation-Based Approach for Sentiment Analysis. In Prominent Feature Extraction for Sentiment Analysis (pp. 77–88). Academic Press. doi:10.1007/978-3-319-25343-5_6

Agi, I., & Gong, L. (1996). An Empirical Study of Secure MPEG Video Transmission. In *Proceeding of the Internet Society Symposium on Network and Distributed System Security (ISSoNDSS '96)*. IEEE. 10.1109/NDSS.1996.492420

Agrawal, R., & Srikant, R. (1994). Fast algorithms for mining association rules. *Proceedings of the 20th International Conference on Very Large Data Bases*, 487-499.

Agrawal, S., & Agrawal, J. (2015). Survey on Anomaly Detection using Data Mining Techniques. International Conference on Knowledge Based and Intelligent Information and Engineering Systems. *Procedia Computer Science*, *60*, 708–713. doi:10.1016/j.procs.2015.08.220

Ahmed, S., & Danti, A. (2016). Effective Sentimental Analysis and Opinion Mining of Web Reviews Using Rule Based Classifiers. In Computational Intelligence in Data Mining (Vol. 1, pp. 171–179). Academic Press. doi:10.1007/978-81-322-2734-2_18

Ahmed, A., & AL-Shaboti, M. (2018). Implementation of Internet of Things (IoT) Based on IPv6 over Wireless Sensor Networks. *International Journal of Sensors Wireless Communications And Control*, *7*(2). doi:10.2174/2210327907666170911145726

Ai, T. J. (2004). Optimalisasi Prediksi Pemulusan Eksponensial Satu Variabel Dengan Menggunakan Algoritma Non Linear Programming. Jurnal Teknologi Industri, 3(3).

Alcaide. (2016). Visual Anomaly Detection in Spatio-Temporal Data using Element-Specific References. *2016 IEEE VIS*.

AlEnezi, A., AlMeraj, Z., & Manuel, P. (2018). Challenges of IoT based Smart-government Development. *2018 IEEE Green Technologies Conference (GreenTech)*, 155-160. 10.1109/GreenTech.2018.00036

Alphonsa, A., & Ravi, G. (2016). Earthquake early warning system by IOT using Wireless sensor networks. *Proceedings of 2016 International Conference on Wireless Communications, Signal Processing and Networking (WiSPNET)*. 10.1109/WiSPNET.2016.7566327

Al-Sakran, H.O. (2015). Intelligent Traffic Information System Based on Integration of Internet of Things and Agent Technology. *International Journal of Advanced Computer Science and Applications, 6*(2).

Amjath Ali, J., Thangalakshmi, B., & Vincy Beaulah, A. (2017). IoT Based Disaster Detection and Early Warning Device. *International Journal of MC Square Scientific Research*, *9*(3), 20–25. doi:10.20894/IJMSR.117.009.003.003

Anand, M., & Susan, C. (2015). Artificial Intelligence Meets Internet of Things. *IJCSET, 5*(6), 149-151.

Anthi, E., Williams, L., & Burnap, P. (2018). Pulse: An adaptive intrusion detection for the Internet of Things. Living in the Internet of Things: Cybersecurity of the IoT - 2018, 1-4.

Apache. (2017). Retrieved from http://apache.org

Aqil, M. (2010). *Pemetaan Spasial Varietas Jagung Berdasarkan Musim Tanam di Kabupaten Jeneponto, Sulawesi Selatan.* Prosiding Pekan Serealia Nasional.

Arnold, T. (2017). kerasR: R Interface to the Keras Deep Learning Library. *The Journal Of Open Source Software, 2*(14), 296. doi:10.21105/joss.00296

Arora, M., Das, S. K., & Biswas, R. (2002). A Decentralized Scheduling and Load Balancing algorithm for Heterogeneous Grid Environments. *Proc. Of International Conference on Parallel Processing Workshops (ICPPW'02),* 499 - 505.

Atzori, L., Iera, A., & Morabito, G. (2010). *The Internet of Things: A survey.* Elsevier.

Azar, Y., Cohen, E., Fiat, A., Kaplan, H., & Racke, H. (2003). Optimal oblivious routing in polynomial time. *Proceedings of the 35th ACM Symposium on Theory of Computing,* 383–388.

Babu, A. S., Naidu, G. T., & Meenakshi, U. (2018). Earth Quake Detection And Alerting Using IoT. *International Journal of Engineering Science Invention, 07*(05), 14–18.

Barnaghi, P., Wang, W., Henson, C., & Taylor, K. (2012). Semantics for the Internet of Things. Early progress and back to the future. *International Journal on Semantic Web and Information Systems, 8*(1), 1–21. doi:10.4018/jswis.2012010101

Baryamureeba, V., & Tushabe, F. (2004, August). The enhanced digital investigation process model. In *Proceedings of the Fourth Digital Forensic Research Workshop* (pp. 1-9). Academic Press.

Beier, G., Niehoff, S., & Xue, B. (2018). More Sustainability in Industry through Industrial Internet of Things? *Appl. Sci., 8*(2), 219. doi:10.3390/app8020219

Blomquist, H., & Moller, J. (2015). *Anomaly detection with Machine learning.* Uppsala Universitet.

Boer, R., Buono, A., Sumaryanto, E., Surmaini, A., Rakhman, W., Estiningtyas, K., & Kartikasari, F. (2009). Technical Report on Vulnerability and Adaptation Assessment to Climate Change for Indonesia's Second National Communication. Ministry of Environment and United Nations Development Programme.

Bos, H., Ioannidis, S., Jonsson, E., Kirda, E., & Kruegel, C. (2009). Future threats to future trust. In Future of Trust in Computing (pp. 49-54). Vieweg+Teubner. doi:10.1007/978-3-8348-9324-6_5

Boser, B. E., Guyon, I. M., & Vapnik, V. N. (1992). A training algorithm for optimal margin classifiers. In *Proc. 5th Annual ACM Workshop on Computational Learning Theory.* Pittsburgh, PA: ACM Press. 10.1145/130385.130401

Braden, R., Clark, D., & Shenker, S. (1994). *Integrated services in t he Internet architecture: An overview.* RFC1633.

Breiman, L. (2001). Random Forests. *Machine Learning, 45*(1), 5–32. doi:10.1023/A:1010933404324

Briceno, M., Goldberg, I., & Wagner, D. (1999). *Voice Privacy, A Pedagogical Implementation of the GSM A5/1 AND A5/2.* Retrieved from the Internet http://cryptome.org/gsm-aS12.htm

Brous, P., & Janssen, M. (2015a). Advancing e-Government Using the Internet of Things: A Systematic Review of Benefits. In Lecture Notes in Computer Science: Vol. 9248. *Electronic Government. EGOV 2015*. Cham: Springer. doi:10.1007/978-3-319-22479-4_12

Brous, P., & Janssen, M. (2015b). A Systematic Review of Impediments Blocking Internet of Things Adoption by Governments. In Lecture Notes in Computer Science: Vol. 9373. *Open and Big Data Management and Innovation. I3E 2015*. Cham: Springer. doi:10.1007/978-3-319-25013-7_7

Brusic, V., Rudy, G., Honeyman, G., Hammer, J., & Harrison, L. (1998). Prediction of MHC class II-binding peptides using an evolutionary algorithm and artificial neural network. *Bioinformatics (Oxford, England)*, *14*(2), 121–130. doi:10.1093/bioinformatics/14.2.121 PMID:9545443

Budalakoti, S., Srivastava, A. N., & Otey, M. E. (2009). Anomaly Detection and Diagnosis Algorithms for Discrete Symbol Sequences with Applications to Airline Safety. *IEEE Transactions on Systems, Man, and Cybernetics Part C*, *39*(1), 101–113.

Burkhalter, M. (2018). How IoT infrastructure allows for more accurate weather forecasting. *Perle*. Available at https://www.perle.com/articles/how-iot-infrastructure-allows-for-more-accurate-weather-forecasting-40169629.shtml

Burkom, S.H., Muphy, S.P., & dan Shmuelli, G. (2006). *Automated Time Series Forecasting for Rainfall*. The Johns Hopkins University Applied Physics Laboratory, Department of Decision and Information Technologies, Robert H. Smith School, University of Maryland College Park.

Campbell, C., & Ying, Y. (2011). Learning with Support Vector Machines. *Synthesis Lectures On Artificial Intelligence And Machine Learning*, *5*(1), 1–95. doi:10.2200/S00324ED1V01Y201102AIM010

Canuto, Gonçalves, & Benevenuto. (2016). Exploiting New Sentiment-Based Meta-level Features for Effective Sentiment Analysis. *Proceedings of the Ninth ACM International Conference on Web Search and Data Mining (WSDM '16)*, 53-62 10.1145/2835776.2835821

Cao, Y. (2005). *Parallel and Distributed Computing techniques in Biomedical Engineering* (Ph.D thesis). National University of Singapore.

Carrera-Trejo, V., Sidorov, G., Miranda-Jiménez, S., Ibarra, M. M., & Martínez, R. C. (2015). Latent Dirichlet Allocation complement in the vector space model for Multi-Label Text Classification. *International Journal of Combinatorial Optimization Problems and Informatics*, *6*(1), 7–19.

Carta, J., Cabrera, P., Matías, J., & Castellano, F. (2015). Comparison of feature selection methods using ANNs in MCP-wind speed methods. A case study. *Applied Energy*, *158*, 490–507. doi:10.1016/j.apenergy.2015.08.102

Casas, P. (2016). *Machine-Learning Based Approaches for Anomaly Detection and Classification in Cellular Networks. 2016 The Traffic Monitoring and Analysis workshop*. TMA.

Casavant, T., & Kuhl, J. (1998). A Taxonomy of Scheduling in General Pupose Distributed Computing Systems. *IEEE Transactions on Software Engineering*, *14*(2), 141–154. doi:10.1109/32.4634

Case, A., Cristina, A., Marziale, L., Richard, G. G., & Roussev, V. (2008). FACE: Automated digital evidence discovery and correlation. *Digital Investigation, 5*, S65-S75.

Cassidy, A. (2014). *The "Internet of Things" Revolution and Digital Forensics*. NUIX.

Celik, M., Dadaser-Celik, W., & Dokuz, A. S. (2011). Anomaly detection in temperature data using DBSCAN algorithm. *11 International Symposium on Innovations in Intelligent Systems and Applications*. 10.1109/INISTA.2011.5946052

Cenci, K., Fillottrani, P., & Ardenghi, J. (2017). Government Data Interoperability: A Case Study from Academia. *Proc. o f the ICEGOV*. doi:10.1145/3047273.3047382

Chae, J., & Quick, B. (2014). An Examination of the Relationship Between Health Information Use and Health Orientation in Korean Mothers: Focusing on the Type of Health Information. *Journal of Health Communication, 20*(3), 275–284. doi:10.1080/10810730.2014.925016 PMID:25495418

Chandola, V., Banerjee, A., & Kumar, V. (2007). *Anomaly detection – a survey*. Technical Report 07-017. Computer Science Department, University of Minnesota.

Chandola, V., Banerjee, A., & Kumar, V. (2012). Anomaly detection for discrete sequences: A survey. *IEEE Transactions on Knowledge and Data Engineering, 24*(5), 823–839. doi:10.1109/TKDE.2010.235

Chanthini, P., & Shyamala, K. (2016). A Survey on Parallelization of Neural Network using MPI and Open MP. *Indian Journal of Science and Technology, 9*(19). doi:10.17485/ijst/2016/v9i19/93835

Charalambous, C. (1992). Conjugate gradient algorithm for efficient training of artificial neural networks. *IEE Proceedings. Part G. Circuits, Devices and Systems, 139*(3), 301–310. doi:10.1049/ip-g-2.1992.0050

Chase, J. (2013). *The Evolution of the Internet of Things*. Strategic Marketing, Texas Instruments.

Chatzigeorgiou, D. M., Youcef-Toumi, K., Khalifa, A. E., & Ben-Mansour, R. (2011, January). Analysis and design of an in-pipe system for water leak detection. In *ASME 2011 International Design Engineering Technical Conferences and Computers and Information in Engineering Conference* (pp. 1007-1016). American Society of Mechanical Engineers. 10.1115/DETC2011-48395

Chatzigeorgiou, D., Youcef-Toumi, K., & Ben-Mansour, R. (2015). Design of a novel in-pipe reliable leak detector. *IEEE/ASME Transactions on Mechatronics, 20*(2), 824–833. doi:10.1109/TMECH.2014.2308145

Chen, Y., Zhou, X. S., & Huang, T. S. (2001). One-class SVM for learning in image retrieval. In *Image Processing, 2001. Proceedings 2001 International Conference on* (Vol. 1, pp. 34-37). IEEE.

Chen, Y., Meng, F. W., & Guo, H. C. (2017). Design of detection system for mine oxygen concentration based on Internet of Things. *Electronic Design Engineering, 69*(12), 50–56.

Chen, Z., & Huang, X. (2017). End-to-end learning for lane keeping of self-driving cars. *IEEE Intelligent Vehicles Symposium (IV)*. 10.1109/IVS.2017.7995975

Chien, S.-Y., Chan, W.-K., Lee, C.-H., & Srinivasa Somayazulu, V. (2015). Distributed computing in IoT: System-on-a-chip for smart cameras as an example. In *The 20th Asia and South Pacific Design Automation Conference*. IEEE.

Chitrakar, R., & Chuanhe, H. (2012). Anomaly detection using Support Vector Machine classification with k-Medoids clustering. *Proceedings of IEEE Third Asian Himalayas International Conference on Internet (AH-ICI)*. 10.1109/AHICI.2012.6408446

Choi, H. R., & Roh, S. G. (2007). In-pipe robot with active steering capability for moving inside of pipelines. In *Bioinspiration and Robotics Walking and Climbing Robots*. InTech.

Chor, B., Israeli, A., & Li, M. (1987). On Processor Coordination using asynchronous hardware. *Proceedings of Sixth ACM symposium on Principles of Distributed Computing*, 86-97. 10.1145/41840.41848

Chou, B. C. C. H., Chou, B. C. C. H., Archive, F. D., Archive, F. D., Goethals, A., & Goethals, A. (2015). *An introduction to the European Interoperability Reference Architecture v0.9.0*. EIRA.

Chouhan, A., & Singh, S. (2015). Real Time Secure end to end Communication over GSM Network. In *Proceeding of the International Conference on Energy Systems and Applications (ICESA '15)*. Pune, India: IEEE. 10.1109/ICESA.2015.7503433

Chumchu, P., Phayak, A., & Dokpikul, P. (2012). A Simple and Cheap End-to-End Voice Encryption Framework over GSM-based Networks. In *Proceedings of the Computing, Communications and Applications Conference (ComComAp '12)*. Hong Kong, China: IEEE. 10.1109/ComComAp.2012.6154800

Clark, P., & Niblett, R. (1989). The CN2 induction algorithm. *Machine Learning*, 3.

Cloudera. (2017). Retrieved from http://www.cloudera.com

Cogswell, M., Ahmed, F., Girshick, R., Zitnick, L., & Batra, D. (2015). *Reducing Overfitting in Deep Networks by Decorrelating Representations*. arXiv:1511.06068

Cohen, W. W. (1995). Fast effective rule induction. *Proceedings of the Twelfth International Conference on Machine Learning*.

Collobert, R., & Bengio, S. (2004). Links between Perceptrons, MLPs and SVMs. *Proc. Int'l Conf. on Machine Learning (ICML)*.

Collobert, R., Bengio, S., & Mariéthoz, J. (2002). *Torch: a modular machine learning software library (No. EPFL-REPORT-82802)*. Idiap.

Columbus, L. (2018). *Where IoT Can Deliver The Most Value In 2018*. Retrieved from https://www.forbes.com/sites/louiscolumbus/2018/03/18/where-iot-can-deliver-the-most-value-in-2018/

Cooke, A. (2018). Realising the future and full potential of connected IoT devices with AI. *Silicon Republic*. Available at https://www.siliconrepublic.com/enterprise/ai-iot-automation-ibm

Corbett. (2013). Google's globally-distributed database. *ACM Transactions on Computer Systems*, *31*(8).

Cristian Mihai, B. A. R. C. A., & Claudiu Dan, B. A. R. C. A. (2017). Distributed algorithm to train neural networks using the Map Reduce paradigm. *Database Systems Journal*, *8*(1), 3–11.

Dahl, G., McAvinney, A., & Newhall, T. (2008). Parallelizing neural network training for cluster systems. *PDCN '08 Proceedings of the IASTED International Conference on Parallel and Distributed Computing and Networks*, 220-225.

dan Hermawan, E. (2013). Interkoneksi Monsun Dan El-Niño Terkait Dengan Curah Hujan Ekstrem. Prosiding Seminar Sains Atmosfer, LAPAN.

Das, M., & Parthasarathy, S. (2009). Anomaly detection and spatio-temporal analysis of global climate system. In *Proceedings of the Third International Workshop on Knowledge Discovery from Sensor Data*. ACM. 10.1145/1601966.1601989

Dat, N. D., Phu, V. N., Vo, T. N. T., & Vo, T. N. C. (2017). STING Algorithm used English Sentiment Classification in A Parallel Environment. *International Journal of Pattern Recognition and Artificial Intelligence*, *31*(07), 1750021. doi:10.1142/S0218001417500215

Datta, S., & Das, S. (2015). Near-Bayesian Support Vector Machines for imbalanced data classification with equal or unequal misclassification costs. *Neural Networks*, *70*, 39–52. doi:10.1016/j.neunet.2015.06.005 PMID:26210983

Daugherty, P., Negm, W., Banerjee, P., & Alter, A. (2016). *Driving Unconventional Growth through the Industrial Internet of Things*. Accenture.

Davis, J. (2009). *Attacks on Mobile and Embedded Systems: Current Trends*. Mocana whitepaper. Retrieved from www.mocana.com

Dean. (2006). *Experiences with MapReduce, an abstraction for large-scale computation*. Keynote I: PACT.

Dean, J., & Ghemawat, S. (2004). MapReduce: simplified data processing on large clusters. *Proc. of the 6th OSDI Symp.*

Deits, R., & Tedrake, R. (2014, November). Footstep planning on uneven terrain with mixed-integer convex optimization. In *Humanoid Robots (Humanoids), 2014 14th IEEE-RAS International Conference on* (pp. 279-286). IEEE. 10.21236/ADA609276

Deits, R., & Tedrake, R. (2015). Computing large convex regions of obstacle-free space through semidefinite programming. In *Algorithmic foundations of robotics XI* (pp. 109–124). Cham: Springer. doi:10.1007/978-3-319-16595-0_7

Deshpande, A., Pitale, P., & Sanap, S. (2016). Industrial Automation using Internet of Things (IOT). *International Journal of Advanced Research in Computer Engineering & Technology, 5*(2).

Despotovic, V., & Tanikic, D. (2017). Sentiment Analysis of Microblogs Using Multilayer Feed-Forward Artificial Neural Networks. *Computer Information, 36*(5), 1127–1142. doi:10.4149/cai_2017_5_1127

Di Pascale, Macaluso, Nag, Kelly, & Doyle. (2018). The Network As a Computer: A Framework for Distributed Computing Over IoT Mesh Networks. *IEEE Internet of Things Journal, 5*(3), 2107 – 2119.

Diaz-Sanchez, D., Almenarez, F., Marin, A., Proserpio, D., & Cabarcos, A. P. (2011). Media cloud: An open cloud computing middleware for content management. *IEEE Transactions on Consumer Electronics, 57*(2), 970–978. doi:10.1109/TCE.2011.5955247

Dietterich, T. G. (1997). Machine-learning research: Four current directions. *AI Magazine, 18*.

Din, S., Paul, A., Guizani, N., Ahmed, S. H., Khan, M., & Rathore, M. M. (2017). Features Selection Model for Internet of E-Health Things Using Big Data. *GLOBECOM 2017 IEEE Global Communications Conference*, 1-7.

Djurdjanovic, D., Liu, J., Marko, K. A., & Ni, J. (2007). Immune Systems Inspired Approach to Anomaly Detection and Fault Diagnosis for Engines. *2007 International Joint Conference on Neural Networks*. 10.1109/IJCNN.2007.4371159

Dong, Z., Yang, D., Walsh, M. W., Reindl, T., & dan Aberle, A. (2013). Short-term Solar Irradiance Forecasting Using Exponential Smoothing State Space Model. Solar Energy Research Institute Of Singapore, National University of Singapore.

Dwyer, B., & Hutchings, K. (1977, September). Flowchart Optimisation in Cope, a Multi-Choice Decision Table. *Australian Computer Journal, 9*(3), 92.

e-Estonia (2018). *Internet of Things paves the way for smart B2G solutions*. Available at https://e-estonia.com/internet-of-things-way-for-b2g-solutions/

El-Haddadeh, R., Weerakkody, V., Osmani, M., Thakker, D., & Kapoor, K. K. (2018). Examining citizens' perceived value of internet of things technologies in facilitating public sector services engagement. *Government Information Quarterly*. doi:10.1016/j.giq.2018.09.009

Elmaghraby, A. S., & Losavio, M. M. (2014). Cyber security challenges in Smart Cities: Safety, security and privacy. *Journal of Advanced Research, 5*(4), 491–497. doi:10.1016/j.jare.2014.02.006 PMID:25685517

El-Sayed, H., Mellouk, A., George, L., & Zeadally, S. (2008). Quality of service models for heterogeneous networks: Overview and challenges. *Annales des Télécommunications, 63*(11-12), 639–668. doi:10.100712243-008-0064-z

Ensafi, R., Dehghanzadeh, S., Mohammad, R., & Akbarzadeh, T. (2008). Optimizing Fuzzy K-means for network anomaly detection using PSO. *Computer Systems and Applications, IEEE/ACS International Conference.*

Ersue, M., Romascanu, D., Schoenwaelder, J., & Sehgal, A. (2014). *Management of Networks with Constrained Devices: Use Cases.* IETF Internet Draft.

Estiningtyas, W., & dan Amien, L.I. (2006). *Pengembangan Model Prediksi Hujan dengan Metode Kalman Filter untuk Menyusun Skenario Masa Tanam.* Balai Besar Litbang Sumberdaya Lahan Pertanian.

European Commission. (2017). *Digital Information Monitor: Industry 4.0 in Aeronautics: IoT applications.* Author.

Evans, P. C., & Annunziata, M. (2012). *Industrial Internet: Pushing the Boundaries of Minds and Machines.* General Electric.

FAO. (1976). *A Framework for Land Evaluation. Soil Resources Management and Conservation Service Land and Water Development Division. FAO Soil Bulletin No. 32.* Rome: FAO-UNO.

Farid, D. M., Harbi, N., & Rahman, M. Z. (2010). Combining naive bayes and decision tree for adaptive intrusion detection. *International Journal of Network Security & Its Applications, 2*(2).

Fattah, S., Sung, N., Ahn, I., Ryu, M., & Yun, J. (2017). Building IoT Services for Aging in Place Using Standard-Based IoT Platforms and Heterogeneous IoT Products. *Sensors (Basel), 17*(10), 2311. doi:10.339017102311 PMID:29019964

Feng, D. L. Y., & Liang, Y. D. (2010). A Survey of the Internet of Things. *The 2010 International Conference on E-Business Intelligence.*

Fildes, R., & Kourentzes, N. (2011). Validation And Forecasting Accuracy In Models Of Climate Change. *International Journal of Forecasting, 27*, 968–995. doi:10.1016/j.ijforecast

Fremantle, P., & Scott, P. (2015). *A security survey of middleware for the Internet of Things (No. e1521).* PeerJ PrePrints.

Freund, R. F., Gherrity, M., Ambrosius, S., Campbell, M., Halderman, M., Hensgen, D., ... Siegel, H. J. (1998). Scheduling resources in multi-user, heterogeneous, computing environments with SmartNet. *7th IEEE Heterogeneous Computing Workshop (HCW '98)*, 184-199. 10.1109/HCW.1998.666558

Fujimaki, R., Yairi, T., & Machida, K. (2005). An approach to spacecraft anomaly detection problem using kernel feature space. In *Proceedings of the eleventh ACM SIGKDD international conference on Knowledge discovery in data mining (KDD '05).* ACM. 10.1145/1081870.1081917

Fukuda, T., Hosokai, H., & Uemura, M. (1989, May). Rubber gas actuator driven by hydrogen storage alloy for in-pipe inspection mobile robot with flexible structure. In *1989 IEEE International Conference on Robotics and Automation* (pp. 1847-1852). IEEE. 10.1109/ROBOT.1989.100242

Fu, R., Li, B., Gao, Y., & Wang, P. (2018). Visualizing and analyzing convolution neural networks with gradient information. *Neurocomputing*, *293*, 12–17. doi:10.1016/j.neucom.2018.02.080

Fu, S., Liu, J., & Pannu, H. (2012). A Hybrid Anomaly Detection Framework in Cloud Computing Using One-Class and Two-Class Support Vector Machines. In *Advanced Data Mining and Applications*. Springer Berlin Heidelberg. doi:10.1007/978-3-642-35527-1_60

Gadea, C., Solomon, B., Ionescu, B., & Ionescu, D. (2011). A collaborative cloud-based multimedia sharing platform for social networking environments. In *Proceeding of the International Conference on Computer Communications and Networks (ICoCCN '11)*, Maui, HI: IEEE. 10.1109/ICCCN.2011.6006079

Gálvez, J. A., De Santos, P. G., & Pfeiffer, F. (2001). Intrinsic tactile sensing for the optimization of force distribution in a pipe crawling robot. *IEEE/ASME Transactions on Mechatronics*, *6*(1), 26–35. doi:10.1109/3516.914388

Garfinkel, S. L. (2010). Digital forensics research: The next 10 years. *Digital Investigation, 7*, S64-S73.

Gartner. (2017). *Gartner Says By 2020, More Than Half of Major New Business Processes and Systems Will Incorporate Some Element of the Internet of Things*. Available at http://www.gartner.com/newsroom/id/3185623

Gevrey, M., Dimopoulos, I., & Lek, S. (2003). Review and comparison of methods to study the contribution of variables in artificial neural network models. *Ecological Modelling*, *160*(3), 249–264. doi:10.1016/S0304-3800(02)00257-0

Global System for Mobile Communications (GSM). (2017). *From GSM to LTE-Advanced Pro and 5G*, 1–70. Doi:10.1002/9781119346913.ch1

Gomes, C., & Mayes, A. (2014). The kinds of information that support novel associative object priming and how these differ from those that support item priming. *Memory (Hove, England)*, *23*(6), 901–927. doi:10.1080/09658211.2014.937722 PMID:25051200

Goodfellow, I., Bengio, Y., Courville, A., & Bengio, Y. (2016). *Deep learning* (Vol. 1). Cambridge, MA: MIT Press.

Gornitz, N., Kloft, M., Rieck, K., & Brefeld, U. (2013). Toward supervised anomaly detection. Journal Artificial Intelligence. *Intestinal Research*, *46*, 235–262.

Goswami, S., Chakraborty, S., Laha, S., & Dhar, A. (2012). Enhancement of GSM Security Using Elliptic Curve Cryptography Algorithm. In *Proceedings of the Third International Conference on Intelligent Systems Modelling and Simulation (ISMS '12)*. Kota Kinabalu, Malaysia: IEEE. 10.1109/ISMS.2012.137

Grandinetti, L. (2013). *Pervasive Cloud Computing Technologies: Future Outlooks and Interdisciplinary Perspectives*. IGI Global.

Grispos, G., Glisson, W. B., & Storer, T. (2013, January). Using smartphones as a proxy for forensic evidence contained in cloud storage services. In *System Sciences (HICSS), 2013 46th Hawaii International Conference on* (pp. 4910-4919). IEEE. 10.1109/HICSS.2013.592

Grossman, R. (1977). *Data Mining: Challenges and Opportunities for Data Mining During the Next Decade.* Academic Press.

Gubbia, J., Buyya, R., Marusic, S., & Palaniswami, M. (2013). Internet of Things (IoT): A vision, architectural elements, and future directions. *Future Generation Computer Systems, 29*(7), 1645–1660. doi:10.1016/j.future.2013.01.010

Guo, H., Jin, B., & Shang, T. (2012, August). Forensic investigations in cloud environments. In *Computer Science and Information Processing (CSIP), 2012 International Conference on* (pp. 248-251). IEEE.

Guo, Y., Liu, Y., Georgiou, T., & Lew, M. (2017). A review of semantic segmentation using deep neural networks. *International Journal of Multimedia Information Retrieval, 7*(2), 87–93. doi:10.100713735-017-0141-z

Gupta, R. M. (2015). *Intelligent Data In The Context Of The Internet Of Things.* Academic Press.

Gupta, A., & Singh Chandel, P. (2014). Security Enhancement in GSM using A3 algorithm. *International Journal of Computers and Applications, 108*(1), 18–20. doi:10.5120/18875-0138

Hadoop. (2017). Retrieved from http://hadoop.apache.org

Hahsler, M., Grün, B., & Hornik, K. (2005). Introduction to a rules – A computational environment for mining association rules and frequent item sets. *Journal of Statistical Software, 14*(15). doi:10.18637/jss.v014.i15

Han, J., Pei, J., & Kamber, M. (2011). *Data mining: concepts and techniques.* Elsevier.

Han, J., Pei, J., & Yin, Y. (2000). Mining frequent patterns without candidate generation. *Proceedings of the 2000 ACM-SIGMID International Conference on Management of Data*, 1-12.

Harrelson, C., Hildrum, K., & Rao, S. (2003). A polynomial-time tree decomposition to minimize congestion. *Proceedings of the 15th Annual ACM Symposium on Parallel Algorithms and Architectures*, 34–43. 10.1145/777412.777419

Hartomo, K. D., & Winarko, E. (2015). Winters Exponential Smoothing And Z-Score, Algorithms For Prediction Of Rainfall. *Journal of Theoretical & Applied Information Technology, 73*(1).

Hendon, H. H. (2003). Indonesian Rainfall Variability: Impacts Of ENSO And Local Air –Sea Interaction. *Journal of Climate, 16*(11), 1775–1790. doi:10.1175/1520-0442(2003)016<1775:IR VIOE>2.0.CO;2

Herlihy, M. (1991). Wait-Free Synchronization. *ACM Transactions on Programming Languages and Systems, 11*(1), 124–149. doi:10.1145/114005.102808

Heylen, J., Iven, S., De Brabandere, B., Jose, O. M., Van Gool, L., & Tuytelars, T. (2018). From Pixels to Actions: Learning to Drive a Car with Deep Neural Networks. *IEEE Winter Conference on Applications of Computer Vision*. 10.1109/WACV.2018.00072

Hochreiter, S., & Schmidhuber, J. (1997). Long short-term memory. *Neural Computation*, *9*(8), 1735–1780. doi:10.1162/neco.1997.9.8.1735 PMID:9377276

Hodge, V. J., O'Keefe, S., & Austin, J. (2016). Hadoop neural network for parallel and distributed feature selection. *Neural Networks*, *78*, 24–35. doi:10.1016/j.neunet.2015.08.011 PMID:26403824

Hong, S., & Lee, Y. (2013). CPU Parallel Processing and GPU-accelerated Processing of UHD Video Sequence using HEVC. *Journal Of Broadcast Engineering*, *18*(6), 816–822. doi:10.5909/JBE.2013.18.6.816

Horng, S.-J., Su, M.-Y., Chen, Y.-H., Kao, T.-W., Chen, R.-J., Lai, J.-L., & Perkasa, C. D. (2011). A novel intrusion detection system based on hierarchical clustering and support vector machines. *Expert Systems with Applications*, *38*(1), 306–313. doi:10.1016/j.eswa.2010.06.066

Horodinca, M., Doroftei, I., Mignon, E., & Preumont, A. (2002, June). A simple architecture for in-pipe inspection robots. In Proc. Int. Colloq. Mobile, Autonomous, Systems (pp. 61-64). Academic Press.

Ho, T. K. (1995). Random Decision Forests. *Proceedings of the 3rd International Conference on Document Analysis and Recognition*, 278–282.

Hounsell, N. B., Shrestha, B. P., Piao, J., & McDonald, M. (2009). Review of urban traffic management and the impacts of new vehicle technologies. *IET Intelligent Transport Systems*, *3*, 419–428.

Hsu, K., Gupta, H. V., & Sorooshian, S. (1995). Artificial Neural Network Modeling of the Rainfall-Runoff Process. *Water Resources Research*, *31*(10), 2517–2530. doi:10.1029/95WR01955

Hu, Xu, Xiao, Chen, He, Qin, & Heng. (2018). SINet: A Scale-insensitive Convolutional Neural Network for Fast Vehicle Detection. *IEEE Transactions on Intelligent Transportation Systems*.

Huh, M., Agrawal, P., & Efros, A. A. (2016). *What makes ImageNet good for transfer learning?* arXiv preprint arXiv:1608.08614

Hyndman, R. J. (2008). *Data Sets from Forecasting: Methods and Applications By Makridakis, Wheelwright and Hyndman*. R package version 1.11. Retrieved from http://CRAN. R-project. org/package=forecasting

Ilg, W., Berns, K., Cordes, S., Eberl, M., & Dillmann, R. (1997, September). A wheeled multijoint robot for autonomous sewer inspection. In *Intelligent Robots and Systems, 1997. IROS'97., Proceedings of the 1997 IEEE/RSJ International Conference on* (Vol. 3, pp. 1687-1693). IEEE. 10.1109/IROS.1997.656584

Industries, I. B. M. (2017). *The incredible ways governments use the Internet of Things*. Available at https://medium.com/ibmindustrious/the-incredible-ways-governments-use-the-internet-of-things-1072d34b9821

Ioffe, S., & Szegedy, C. (2015). *Batch normalization: Accelerating deep network training by reducing internal covariate shift*. arXiv preprint arXiv:1502.03167

Jakimoski, G., & Kocarev, L. (2001). Chaos and Cryptography: Block Encryption Ciphers Based on Chaotic Maps. *IEEE Transactions on Circuits and Systems Fundamental Theory and Applications*, *48*(2), 163–169. doi:10.1109/81.904880

Jakimovski, B. (2011). Biologically Inspired Approaches for Anomaly Detection within a Robotic System. In Biologically Inspired Approaches for Locomotion. Anomaly Detection and Reconfiguration for Walking Robots (pp. 127-150). Springer. doi:10.1007/978-3-642-22505-5_7

Jang, Y. (2015). Big Data, Business Analytics, and IoT: The Opportunities and Challenges for Business. *Journal of Information Systems*, *24*(4), 139–152. doi:10.5859/KAIS.2015.24.4.139

Jatsun, S., Yatsun, A., & Savin, S. (2012). Pipe inspection parallel-link robot with flexible structure. In Adaptive Mobile Robotics (pp. 713-719). Academic Press. doi:10.1142/9789814415958_0091

Jatsun, S., Savin, S., & Yatsun, A. (2017, August). Walking pattern generation method for an exoskeleton moving on uneven terrain. *Proceedings of the 20th International Conference on Climbing and Walking Robots and Support Technologies for Mobile Machines (CLAWAR 2017)*. 10.1142/9789813231047_0005

Jatsun, S., Savin, S., & Yatsun, A. (2017, September). Footstep Planner Algorithm for a Lower Limb Exoskeleton Climbing Stairs. In *International Conference on Interactive Collaborative Robotics* (pp. 75-82). Springer. 10.1007/978-3-319-66471-2_9

Jha, D., & Kwon, G. (2017). Alzheimer's Disease Detection Using Sparse Autoencoder, Scale Conjugate Gradient and Softmax Output Layer with Fine Tuning. *International Journal Of Machine Learning And Computing*, *7*(1), 13–17. doi:10.18178/ijmlc.2017.7.1.612

Jia, Y., Shelhamer, E., Donahue, J., Karayev, S., Long, J., Girshick, R., ... Darrell, T. (2014, November). Caffe: Convolutional architecture for fast feature embedding. In *Proceedings of the 22nd ACM international conference on Multimedia* (pp. 675-678). ACM. 10.1145/2647868.2654889

Jun, C., Deng, Z., & Jiang, S. (2004, August). Study of locomotion control characteristics for six wheels driven in-pipe robot. In *Robotics and Biomimetics, 2004. ROBIO 2004. IEEE International Conference on* (pp. 119-124). IEEE.

Juneja, P., & Kashyap, R. (2016). Energy based methods for medical image segmentation. *International Journal of Computers and Applications*, *146*(6), 22–27. doi:10.5120/ijca2016910808

Juneja, P., & Kashyap, R. (2016). Optimal approach for CT image segmentation using improved energy based method. *International Journal of Control Theory and Applications*, *9*(41), 599–608.

Kajita, S., Kanehiro, F., Kaneko, K., Fujiwara, K., Harada, K., Yokoi, K., & Hirukawa, H. (2003, September). *Biped walking pattern generation by using preview control of zero-moment point* (Vol. 3). ICRA. doi:10.1109/ROBOT.2003.1241826

Kalekar, P. S. (2004). *Time series Forecasting using Holt-Winters Exponential Smoothing*. Kanwal Rekhi School of Information Technology.

Kao, A. R., Ganguly, S. C., & Steinhaeuser, K. (2009). Motivating Complex Dependence Structures in Data Mining: A Case Study with Anomaly Detection in Climate. *2009 IEEE International Conference on Data Mining Workshops*, 223-230. 10.1109/ICDMW.2009.37

Karami, A. (2016). *A Novel Fuzzy Anomaly Detection Algorithm Based on Hybrid PSO-Kmeans in Content-Centric Networking. In Handbook of Research on Advanced Hybrid Intelligent Techniques and Applications*. IGI Global.

Kartik, S., & Siva Ram Murthy, C. (1995). Improved Task- Allocation Algorithms to Maximize Reliability of Redundant Distributed Computing Systems, Wipro Infotech Limited, Bangalore Indian Institute of Technology, Madras. *IEEE Transactions on Reliability, 44*(4). doi:10.1109/24.475976

Kashyap, R., & Piersson, A. (2018). Big Data Challenges and Solutions in the Medical Industries. In Handbook of Research on Pattern Engineering System Development for Big Data Analytics. IGI Global. doi:10.4018/978-1-5225-3870-7.ch001

Kashyap, R., & Gautam, P. (2016). Fast level set method for segmentation of medical images. In *Proceedings of the International Conference on Informatics and Analytics (ICIA-16)*. ACM. 10.1145/2980258.2980302

Kashyap, R., & Tiwari, V. (2017). Energy-based active contour method for image segmentation. *International Journal of Electronic Healthcare, 9*(2–3), 210–225. doi:10.1504/IJEH.2017.083165

Kashyap, R., & Tiwari, V. (2018). Active contours using global models for medical image segmentation. *International Journal of Computational Systems Engineering, 4*(2/3), 195. doi:10.1504/IJCSYSE.2018.091404

Kavitha, B., Karthikeyan, D. S., & Maybell, P. S. (2012). An ensemble design of intrusion detection system for handling uncertainty using Neutrosophic Logic Classifier. *Knowledge-Based Systems, 28*(0), 88–96. doi:10.1016/j.knosys.2011.12.004

Kawale, J. (2011). *Anomaly Construction in Climate Data: Issues and Challenges. Technical Report*. Department of Computer Science, University of Minnesota.

Khan, S. R., & Bhat, M. S. (2014). *GUI Based Industrial Monitoring and Control System*. IEEE.

Khandakar, Y., & Hyndman, R. J. (2008). Automatic Time Series Forecasting: The forecast Package for R. *Journal of Statistical Software, 27*(3).

Kim, D., Jeong, Y., & Kim, S. (2017). Data-Filtering System to Avoid Total Data Distortion in IoT Networking. *Symmetry, 9*(1), 16. doi:10.3390ym9010016

Kitchenham, B., & Charters, S. (2007). *Guidelines for performing Systematic Literature Reviews in Software Engineering*. EBSE Technical Report Version 2.3.

Koakutsu, S. (2018). Deep Learning - Current Situation and Expectation of Deep Learning and IoT. *The Journal Of The Institute Of Electrical Engineers Of Japan, 138*(5), 270–271. doi:10.1541/ieejjournal.138.270

Kohavi, R. (1995). The Power of Decision Tables. *8th European Conference on Machine Learning*, 174-189.

Kohler, E., Morris, R., Chen, B., Jannotti, J., & Kaashoek, M. F. (2000). The click modular router. *ACM Transactions on Computer Systems, 18*(3), 263–297. doi:10.1145/354871.354874

Koopman, P. (2004). Embedded system security. *IEEE Computer, 37*(7), 95–97. doi:10.1109/MC.2004.52

Krizhevsky, A., Sutskever, I., & Hinton, G. E. (2012). Imagenet classification with deep convolutional neural networks. In Advances in neural information processing systems (pp. 1097-1105). Academic Press.

Kroumov & Yu. (2011). *Neural Networks Based Path Planning and Navigation of Mobile Robots*. Doi:10.5772/26889

Ksiezopolski, B. (2012). QoP-ML: Quality of protection modelling language for cryptographic protocols. *Computers & Security, 31*(4), 569–596. doi:10.1016/j.cose.2012.01.006

Kuindersma, S., Deits, R., Fallon, M., Valenzuela, A., Dai, H., Permenter, F., ... Tedrake, R. (2016). Optimization-based locomotion planning, estimation, and control design for the atlas humanoid robot. *Autonomous Robots, 40*(3), 429–455. doi:10.100710514-015-9479-3

Kumar, S. P. (2017). Internet of Things for sophisticated e-governance: A special focus on agricultural sector. *International Journal of Trend in Research and Development*.

Kundra, A., & Maheshwari, A. (2016). Design of Intelligent Traffic Management Systems using Computer Vision and Internet of Things. *International Journal of Information & Computation Technology, 6*(1), 11-18.

Kunzmann, K. R. (2014). Smart cities: A new paradigm of urban development. *Crios, 4*(1), 9–20.

Kuo, R. J., Chen, C. H., & Hwang, Y. C. (2001). An intelligent stock trading decision support system through integration of genetic algorithm based fuzzy neural network and artificial neural network. *Fuzzy Sets and Systems, 118*(1), 21–45. doi:10.1016/S0165-0114(98)00399-6

Kyoung-jae, K., & Han, I. (2000). Genetic algorithms approach to feature discretization in artificial neural networks for the prediction of stock price index. *Expert Systems with Applications, 19*(2), 125–132. doi:10.1016/S0957-4174(00)00027-0

Lachdhaf, S., Mazouzi, M., & Abid, M. (2018). Secured AODV Routing Protocol for the Detection and Prevention of Black Hole Attack in VANET. *Advanced Computing: An International Journal, 9*(1), 1-14. doi:10.5121/acij.2018.9101

Langley, P. (1996). *Elements of Machine Learning*. San Mateo, CA: Morgan Kaufmann.

Le Cun, Y., & Bengio, Y. (1994). Word-level Training of a Handwritten Word Recognizer Based on Convolutional Neural Networks. *Proc. of the International Conference on Pattern Recognition,* 88-92.

LeCun, Bengio, & Hinton. (2015). Deep learning. *Nature, 521*(7553), 436.

LeCun, Y., & Bengio, Y. (1994). Word-level training of a handwritten word recognizer based on convolutional neural networks. In *Proc. of the International Conference on Pattern Recognition* (pp. 88-92). IEEE.

Lee, H., Grosse, R., Ranganath, R., & Ng, A. Y. (2011). Unsupervised Learning of Hierarchical Representations with Convolutional Deep Belief Networks. Communication of the ACM, 10(10).

Lee, I., & Lee, K. (2015). The Internet of Things (IoT): Applications, investments, and challenges for enterprises. *Business Horizons, 58*(4), 431–440. doi:10.1016/j.bushor.2015.03.008

Lek, S., & Guégan, J. F. (1999). Artificial neural networks as a tool in ecological modelling, an introduction. *Ecological Modelling, 120*(2–3), 65–73. doi:10.1016/S0304-3800(99)00092-7

Lemke, K., Paar, C., & Wolf, M. (Eds.). (2006). Embedded Security in CarsSecuring Current and Future Automotive IT Applications. Springer-Verilag.

Levis, P., Madden, S., Gay, D., Polastre, J., & Szewczyk, R. (2004). The emergence of networking abstractions and techniques in TinyOS. *First USENIX/ACM Symposium on Networked Systems Design and Implementation (NSDI 2004).*

Liao, Y., & Vemuri, V. R. (2002). Use of k-nearest neighbor classifier for intrusion detection. *Computers & Security, 21*(5), 439–448. doi:10.1016/S0167-4048(02)00514-X

Li, H., Ota, K., & Dong, M. (2018). Learning IoT in Edge: Deep Learning for the Internet of Things with Edge Computing. *IEEE Network, 32*(1), 96–101. doi:10.1109/MNET.2018.1700202

Li, M., Fan, H., Xiang, Y., Li, Y., & Zhang, Y. (2018). Cryptanalysis and improvement of a chaotic image encryption by first-order time-delay system. *IEEE MultiMedia, 24*(1), 1–1.

Lin, J., Yu, W., Zhang, N., Yang, X., Zhang, H., & Zhao, W. (2017). A survey on Internet of Things: Architecture enabling technologies security and privacy and applications. *IEEE Internet Things J., 4*(5), 1125–1142. doi:10.1109/JIOT.2017.2683200

Liu, B., Hsu, W., & Ma, Y. (1998). Integrating Classification and Association Rule Mining. *Fourth International Conference on Knowledge Discovery and Data Mining,* 80-86.

Liu, C., Ghosal, S., Jiang, Z., & Sarkar, S. (2016). An unsupervised spatiotemporal graphical modeling approach to anomaly detection in distributed CPS. In *Proceedings of the 7th International Conference on Cyber-Physical Systems (ICCPS 2016)*. IEEE Press. 10.1109/ICCPS.2016.7479069

Lopez Research. (2013). *An Introduction to the Internet of Things (IOT)*. Author.

Lwowski, J., Kolar, P., Benavidez, P., Rad, P., Prevost, J. J., & Jamshidi, M. (2017). Pedestrian detection system for smart communities using deep Convolutional Neural Networks. *12th System of Systems Engineering Conference (SoSE)*, 1-6.

Lynggaard, P. (2013). *Artificial intelligence and Internet of Things in a "smart home" context: A Distributed System Architecture* (PhD dissertation). Aalborg University, Copenhagen, Denmark.

Magnier, L., & Haghighat, F. (2010). Multiobjective optimization of building design using TRNSYS simulations, genetic algorithm, and Artificial Neural Network. *Building and Environment*, *45*(3), 739–746. doi:10.1016/j.buildenv.2009.08.016

Mahsin, M. (2012). Modelling rainfall in Dhaka Division of Bangladesh Using Time Series Analysis. *Journal of Mathematical Modelling and Application*, *1*(5), 67–73.

Makonin, S., Popowich, F., Bartram, L., Gill, B., & Bajic, I. V. (2013). AMPds: A Public Dataset for Load Disaggregation and Eco-Feedback Research. In *Electrical Power and Energy Conference (EPEC)*. IEEE. 10.1109/EPEC.2013.6802949

Makridakis, S., & Hibon, M. (2000). The M3-Competition: Results, Conclusions and Implications. *International Journal of Forecasting*, *16*(4), 451–476. doi:10.1016/S0169-2070(00)00057-1

Malone, T. W., Fikes, R. E., & Howard, M. T. (1988). A market-like task scheduler for distributed computing environments. In B.A. Huberman (Ed.), The Ecology of Computation. North-Holland.

Mara, M. N., Satyahadewi, N., & dan Yundari. (2013). Kajian Teoritis Hybridizing Exponential Smoothing dan Neural Network Untuk Peramalan Data Runtun Waktu. Bimaster Ilmiah Mat. Stat. Dan Terapannya (Bimaster), 2(3), 205-210.

Maranda, A. P., & Kaczmarek, D. (2015). Selected methods of artificial intelligence for Internet of Things conception. *Proceedings of the Federated Conference on Computer Science and Information Systems, ACSIS, 5*, 1343–1348.

Marinescu, D. C. (2017). *Cloud computing: theory and practice*. Morgan Kaufmann.

Marty, R. (2011, March). Cloud application logging for forensics. In *Proceedings of the 2011 ACM Symposium on Applied Computing* (pp. 178-184). ACM. 10.1145/1982185.1982226

Mascaroa, S., Nicholson, A., & Korb, K. (2014). Anomaly detection in vessel tracks using Bayesian Networks. *International Journal of Approximate Reasoning*, 55.

Mason, S., Righetti, L., & Schaal, S. (2014, November). Full dynamics LQR control of a humanoid robot: An experimental study on balancing and squatting. In *Humanoid Robots (Humanoids), 2014 14th IEEE-RAS International Conference on* (pp. 374-379). IEEE.

Mattern, F., & Floerkemeier, C. (2010). From the Internet of Computers to the Internet of Things. In *From active data management to event-based systems and more* (pp. 242–259). Berlin: Springer. doi:10.1007/978-3-642-17226-7_15

Mazzei, D., Baldi, G., Montelisciani, G., & Fantoni, G. (2018). A full stack for quick prototyping of IoT solutions. *Annales des Télécommunications, 73*(7-8), 439–449. doi:10.100712243-018-0644-5

McKinsey. (2018). *The Internet of Things: How to capture the value of IoT*. McKinsey & Company. Available at https://www.mckinsey.com/featured-insights/internet-of-things/our-insights

Mell, P., & Grance, T. (2011). *The NIST definition of cloud computing*. NIST.

Meyer, J., & Gadegast, F. (1995). *Security Mechanisms for Multimedia Data with the Example MPEG_1 Video*. Berlin: Project Description of SECMPEG.

Michalski, R. S., Bratko, I., & Kubat, M. (1988). *Machine learning and data mining: methods and applications*. John Wiley and Sons.

Michell, T. (1997). *Machine Learning*. Mc Graw Hill.

Milutinovic. (1988). A Simulation Study of Two Distributed Task Allocation Procedures. *IEEE Transactions on Software Engineering, 14*.

Mitchell, T. M. (1997). Does machine learning really work. *AI Magazine, 18*(3).

Mochamad, V. G. A., Hindersah, H., & Prihatmanto, A. S. (2017). Implementation of Vehicle Detection Algorithm for Self-Driving Car on Toll Road Cipularang using Python Language. *4th International Conference on Electric Vehicular Technology (ICEVT)*.

Mohamed, N., Al-Jaroodi, J., Jawhar, I., Lazarova-Molnar, S., & Mahmoud, S. (2017). SmartCityWare: A service-oriented middleware for cloud and fog enabled smart city services. *IEEE Access: Practical Innovations, Open Solutions, 5*, 17576–17588. doi:10.1109/ACCESS.2017.2731382

Mohammadi, M., & Al-Fuqaha, A. (2018). Enabling Cognitive Smart Cities Using Big Data and Machine Learning: Approaches and Challenges. *IEEE Communications Magazine, 56*(2), 94–101. doi:10.1109/MCOM.2018.1700298

Mohammadi, M., Al-Fuqaha, A., Sorour, S., & Guizani, M. (2018). Deep Learning for IoT Big Data and Streaming Analytics: A Survey. *IEEE Communications Surveys and Tutorials, 20*(4), 2923–2960. doi:10.1109/COMST.2018.2844341

Mohammeda, Z. K. A., & Ahmedb, E. S. A. (2017). Internet of Things Applications, Challenges and Related Future Technologies. *World Scientific News, 67*(2), 126–148.

Moya, M., & Hush, D. (1996). Network constraints and multi- objective optimization for one-class classification. *Neural Networks, 9*(3), 463–474. doi:10.1016/0893-6080(95)00120-4

Murdohardono, D., Tobing Tigor, M.H.L., & dan Sayekti, A. (2007). Over Pumping of Groundwater as the Cause of sea Water Inundation in Semarang City. *Prosiding dari Seminar Internasional Groundwater Management and Related Water Resources in East and Southeast Asia Region*, Desember, Denpasar, Bali.

Naylor, R. L., Battisti, D. S., Vimont, D. J., Falcon, W. P., & dan Burke, M.B. (2007). Assessing risks of climate variability and climate change for Indonesian rice agriculture. *Proceeding of the National Academic of Science, 114*, 7752-7757. 10.1073/pnas.0701825104

Newman, P. (2017). The Internet of Things 2017 Report: How the IoT is Improving Lives to Transform the World. *Business Insider*. Available at http://www.businessinsider.com/the-internet-of-things-2017-report-2017-1

Ngopya, F. (2009). *The Use Time Series in Crop Forecasting. Regional Early Warning System for Food Security, Food, Agriculture and Natural Resources*. Directorate, Botswana: FANR.

Nishimura, T., Kakogawa, A., & Ma, S. (2012, August). Pathway selection mechanism of a screw drive in-pipe robot in T-branches. In *Automation Science and Engineering (CASE), 2012 IEEE International Conference on* (pp. 612-617). IEEE. 10.1109/CoASE.2012.6386388

Oishi, J. N., & Mahamud, A. (2016). Short Paper: Enhancing Wi-Fi Security Using a Hybrid Algorithm of Blowfish and RC6. In *Proceeding of the International Conference on Networking Systems and Security (NSysS '16)*. Dhaka, Bangladesh: IEEE. 10.1109/NSysS.2016.7400706

Omar, S. (2013). Machine Learning Techniques for Anomaly Detection: An Overview. *International Journal of Computer Applications, 79*(2).

Ong, J. K., Kerr, D., & Bouazza-Marouf, K. (2003). Design of a semi-autonomous modular robotic vehicle for gas pipeline inspection. *Proceedings of the Institution of Mechanical Engineers. Part I, Journal of Systems and Control Engineering, 217*(2), 109–122. doi:10.1177/095965180321700205

Oriwoh, E., Jazani, D., Epiphaniou, G., & Sant, P. (2013, October). Internet of things forensics: Challenges and approaches. In *Collaborative Computing: Networking, Applications and Worksharing (Collaboratecom), 2013 9th International Conference on* (pp. 608-615). IEEE.

Osuwa, A. A., Ekhoragbon, E. B., & Fat, L. T. (2017). Application of artificial intelligence in Internet of Things. *9th International Conference on Computational Intelligence and Communication Networks (CICN), Girne*, 169-173.

Palmer, G. (2001). *A Road Map for Digital Forensic Research: Report from the First Digital Forensic Workshop, 7–8 August 2001*. DFRWS Technical Report DTR-T001-01.

Park, D. C., El-Sharkawi, M. A., Marks, R. J., Atlas, L. E., & Damborg, M. J. (1991). Electric load forecasting using an artificial neural network. *IEEE Transactions on Power Systems, Volume, 6*(2). doi:10.1109/59.76685

Parker, R. (2014). *Internet of Things in Manufacturing: Driving Revenue and Improving Operations*. Academic Press.

Park, Y., Wang, H., Nobauer, T., Vaziri, A., & Priebe, C. E. (2015). Anomaly Detection on Whole-Brain Functional Imaging of Neuronal Activity using Graph Scan Statistics. *Computer Networks*, *51*, 3448–3470.

Patel, K. K., & Patel, S. M. (2016). IOT: Definition, Characteristics, Architecture, Enabling Technologies. Application & Future Challenges. IJESC, 6(5).

Peterson, C., Rögnvaldsson, T., & Lönnblad, L. (1994). JETNET 3.0—A versatile artificial neural network package. *Computer Physics Communications*, *81*(1–2), 185–220. doi:10.1016/0010-4655(94)90120-1

Pfeiffer, F. (1850). The TUM walking machines. *Philosophical Transactions of the Royal Society of London A: Mathematical Physical and Engineering Sciences*, *365*(1850), 109–131. doi:10.1098/rsta.2006.1922

Phu, Ngoc, Ngoc, & Duy. (2017b). A C4.5 algorithm for english emotional classification. *Evolving Systems*, 1-27. doi:10.100712530-017-9180-1

Phu, V. N., & Vo, T. N. T. (2017a). A STING Algorithm and Multi-dimensional Vectors Used for English Sentiment Classification in a Distributed System. American Journal of Engineering and Applied Sciences. doi:10.3844/ajeassp.2017

Phu, V. N., & Vo, T. N. T. (2018a). English Sentiment Classification using A Gower-2 Coefficient and A Genetic Algorithm with A Fitness-proportionate Selection in a Parallel Network Environment. *Journal of Theoretical and Applied Information Technology*, *96*(4), 1-50.

Phu, V. N., & Vo, T. N. T. (2018b). English sentiment classification using a Fager & MacGowan coefficient and a genetic algorithm with a rank selection in a parallel network environment. *International Journal of Computer Modelling and New Technologies*, *22*(1), 57-112.

Phu, V. N., & Vo, T. N. T. (2018c). Latent Semantic Analysis using A Dennis Coefficient for English Sentiment Classification in A Parallel System. *International Journal of Computers, Communications and Control*, *13*(3), 390-410.

Phu, V. N., & Vo, T. N. T. (2018e). English Sentiment Classification using A BIRCH Algorithm and The Sentiment Lexicons-Based One-dimensional Vectors in a Parallel Network Environment. *International Journal of Computer Modelling and New Technologies*, *22*(1).

Phu, V. N., & Vo, T. N. T. (2018f). A Fuzzy C-Means Algorithm and Sentiment-Lexicons-based Multi-dimensional Vectors Of A SOKAL & SNEATH-IV Coefficient Used For English Sentiment Classification. *International Journal of Theoretical and Applied Information Technology*, *96*(10).

Phu, V. N., & Vo, T. N. T. (2018g). A Self-Training - Based Model using A K-NN Algorithm and The Sentiment Lexicons - Based Multi-dimensional Vectors of A S6 coefficient for Sentiment Classification. *International Journal of Theoretical and Applied Information Technology*, *96*(10).

Phu, V. N., & Vo, T. N. T. (2018h). The Multi-dimensional Vectors and An Yule-II Measure Used for A Self-Organizing Map Algorithm of English Sentiment Classification in A Distributed Environment. *Journal of Theoretical and Applied Information Technology, 96*(10).

Phu, V. N., & Vo, T. N. T. (2018i). Sentiment Classification using The Sentiment Scores Of Lexicons Based on A Kuhns-II Coefficient in English. International Journal of Tomography & Simulation, 31(3).

Phu, V. N., & Vo, T. N. T. (2018j). K-Medoids algorithm used for English sentiment classification in a distributed system. *Computer Modelling and New Technologies, 22*(1), 20-39.

Phu, V. N., & Vo, T. N. T. (2018k). A Reformed K-Nearest Neighbors Algorithm for Big Data Sets. *Journal of Computer Science.* Retrieved from http://thescipub.com/abstract/10.3844/ofsp.11819

Phu, V. N., Dat, N. D., Vo, T. N. T., & Vo, T. N. T. (2016). Fuzzy C-Means for English Sentiment Classification in a Distributed System. In International Journal of Applied Intelligence (pp. 1–22). APIN. doi:10.100710489-016-0858-z

Phu, V. N., Vo, T. N. C., & Vo, T. N. T. (2017d). Shifting Semantic Values of English Phrases for Classification. International Journal of Speech Technology. doi:10.100710772-017-9420-6

Phu, V. N., Vo, T. N. C., & Vo, T. N. T. (2017e). SVM for English Semantic Classification in Parallel Environment. International Journal of Speech Technology. doi:10.100710772-017-9421-5

Phu, V. N., Vo, T. N. C., Dat, N. D., Vo, T. N. T., & Nguyen, T. A. (2017c). A Valences-Totaling Model for English Sentiment Classification. Knowledge and Information Systems. doi:10.100710115-017-1054-0

Phu, V. N., Vo, T. N. T., & Max, J. (2018d). A CURE Algorithm for Vietnamese Sentiment Classification in a Parallel Environment. *International Journal of Computer Science.* Retrieved from http://thescipub.com/abstract/10.3844/ofsp.11906

Phu, V. N., Vo, T. N. T., Vo, T. N. C., Dat, N. D., & Khanh, L. D. D. (2017h). A Decision Tree using ID3 Algorithm for English Semantic Analysis. International Journal of Speech Technology. doi:10.100710772-017-9429-x

Phu, Vo, Vo, Duy, & Duy. (2017g). Semantic lexicons of English nouns for classification. *Evolving Systems.* doi:. doi:10.100712530-017-9188-6

Phu, V. N., & Tuoi, P. T. (2014). Sentiment classification using Enhanced Contextual Valence Shifters. *International Conference on Asian Language Processing (IALP)*, 224-229. 10.1109/IALP.2014.6973485

Phu, V. N., Vo, T. N. C., Vo, T. N. T., & Dat, N. D. (2017a). A Vietnamese adjective emotion dictionary based on exploitation of Vietnamese language characteristics. *Artificial Intelligence Review*, 1–69. doi:10.100710462-017-9538-6

Phu, V. N., Vo, T. N. C., Vo, T. N. T., Dat, N. D., & Khanh, L. D. D. (2017f). *A Valence-Totaling Model for Vietnamese Sentiment Classification. International Journal of Evolving Systems.* doi:10.100712530-017-9187-7

Polyakov, E. V., Mazhanov, M. S., Rolich, A. Y., Voskov, L. S., Kachalova, M. V., & Polyakov, S. V. (2018). Investigation and development of the intelligent voice assistant for the Internet of Things using machine learning. *2018 Moscow Workshop on Electronic and Networking Technologies (MWENT)*, 1-5. 10.1109/MWENT.2018.8337236

Prasetyo, S.Y.J.P., Subanar, W. E., & Daryono, B.S. (n.d.). ESSA: Exponential Smoothing and Spatial Autocorrelation, Methods for Prediction of Outbreaks Pest In Indonesia. *International Review Computer and Software.*

Prasetyo, S.Y.J.P., Subanar, Winarko, E., & Daryono, B.S. (2013). The Prediction of Population Dynamics Based on the Spatial Distribution Pattern of Brown Planthopper (Nilaparvata lugen Stal.) Using Exponential Smoothing – Local Spatial Statistics. *Journal of Agricultural Science, 5*(5).

Priya, A., Sinha, K., Darshani, M. P., & Sahana, S. K. (2018). A Novel Multimedia Encryption and Decryption Technique Using Binary Tree Traversal. *Proceeding of the Second International Conference on Microelectronics, Computing & Communication Systems (MCCS 2017)*, 163–178. DOI: 10.1007/978-981-10-8234-4_15

Racke, H. (2002). Minimizing congestion in general networks. In *Proceedings of the 43rd Symposium on Foundations of Computer Science.* IEEE Computer Society.

Rani. (2010). Parallel Approach for Diagnosis of Breast Cancer using Neural Network Technique. *International Journal of Computer Applications, 10*(3), 1-5.

Rayner, M. (2011). The curriculum for children with severe and profound learning difficulties at Stephen Hawking School. *Support for Learning, 26*(1), 25–32. doi:10.1111/j.1467-9604.2010.01471.x

Redmon, J., Divvala, S., Girshick, R., & Farhadi, A. (2016). *You Only Look Once: Unified, Real-Time Object Detection.* arXiv:1506.02640

Redmon, J., Divvala, S., Girshick, R., & Farhadi, A. (2016). You Only Look Once: Unified, Real-Time Object Detection. *IEEE Conference on Computer Vision and Pattern Recognition (CVPR)*. 10.1109/CVPR.2016.91

Rembold. (2013). Using Low Resolution Satellite Imagery for Yield Prediction and Yield Anomaly Detection. *Yaogan Xuebao, 5*, 1704–1733.

Rijpkema, J. J. M. (2012). Time Series Analysis using R. Eindhoven University of Technology, Dept. Mathematics and Computer Science.

Rimal, B. P., Choi, E., & Lumb, I. (2009, August). A taxonomy and survey of cloud computing systems. In *INC, IMS and IDC, 2009. NCM'09. Fifth International Joint Conference on* (pp. 44-51). IEEE. 10.1109/NCM.2009.218

Rivest, L. R., Robshaw, B. J. M., Sidney, R., & Yin, L. Y. (1998). *The RC6 Block Cipher*. Version 1.1, Lab (M.I.T).

Roberts, C., & Nair, M. (2018). *Arbitrary Discrete Sequence Anomaly Detection with Zero Boundary LSTM*. arXiv preprint arXiv:1803.02395

Roh, S. G., & Choi, H. R. (2005). Differential-drive in-pipe robot for moving inside urban gas pipelines. *IEEE Transactions on Robotics*, *21*(1), 1–17. doi:10.1109/TRO.2004.838000

Roh, Y., Kim, J., Son, J., & Kim, M. (2011). Efficient construction of histograms for multidimensional data using quad-trees. *Decision Support Systems*, *52*(1), 82–94. doi:10.1016/j.dss.2011.05.006

Rosenschein, J. S. (1988). Synchronization of multiagent plans. In A. H. Bond & L. Gasser (Eds.), *Readings in Distributed Arti_cial Intelligence* (pp. 187–191). San Mateo, CA: Morgan Kaufmann. doi:10.1016/B978-0-934613-63-7.50020-6

Roslin, N. S., Anuar, A., Jalal, M. F. A., & Sahari, K. S. M. (2012). A review: Hybrid locomotion of in-pipe inspection robot. *Procedia Engineering*, *41*, 1456–1462. doi:10.1016/j.proeng.2012.07.335

Roßmann, T., & Pfeiffer, F. (1996). Control and design of a pipe crawling robot. *IFAC Proceedings Volumes*, *29*(1), 8162-8167.

Roßmann, T., & Pfeiffer, F. (1998). Control of an eight legged pipe crawling robot. In *Experimental Robotics V* (pp. 335–346). Berlin: Springer. doi:10.1007/BFb0112974

Ryew, S., Baik, S. H., Ryu, S. W., Jung, K. M., Roh, S. G., & Choi, H. R. (2000). In-pipe inspection robot system with active steering mechanism. In *Intelligent Robots and Systems, 2000.(IROS 2000). Proceedings. 2000 IEEE/RSJ International Conference on* (Vol. 3, pp. 1652-1657). IEEE. 10.1109/IROS.2000.895209

Samanta, B., & Al-Balushi, K. R. (2003). Artificial Neural Network Based Fault Diagnostics Of Rolling Element Bearings Using Time-Domain Features. *Mechanical Systems and Signal Processing*, *17*(2), 317–328. doi:10.1006/mssp.2001.1462

Sang, T. (2013, January). A log based approach to make digital forensics easier on cloud computing. In *Intelligent System Design and Engineering Applications (ISDEA), 2013 Third International Conference on* (pp. 91-94). IEEE. 10.1109/ISDEA.2012.29

Sari, D. K., Ismullah, I. H., Sulasdi, W. N., & Harto, A. B. (2010). *Estimasi Produktivitas Padi Sawah Berbasis Kalender Tanam Heterogen Menggunakan Teknologi Pengindraan Jauh. Jurnal Rekayasa No. 3* (Vol. 14). Bandung: Institut Teknologi Nasional.

Savin, S. (2017, June). An algorithm for generating convex obstacle-free regions based on stereographic projection. In *Control and Communications (SIBCON), 2017 International Siberian Conference on* (pp. 1-6). IEEE. 10.1109/SIBCON.2017.7998590

Savin, S. (2018). Enhanced Footsteps Generation Method for Walking Robots Based on Convolutional Neural Networks. In Handbook of Research on Deep Learning. Academic Press. (forthcoming)

Savin, S. (2018). RRT-based Motion Planning for In-pipe Walking Robots. In Dynamics of Systems, Mechanisms and Machines (Dynamics), 2018 (pp. 1-6). IEEE. doi:10.1109/Dynamics.2018.8601473

Savin, S., & Vorochaeva, L. (2017, June). Footstep planning for a six-legged in-pipe robot moving in spatially curved pipes. In *Control and Communications (SIBCON), 2017 International Siberian Conference on* (pp. 1-6). IEEE. 10.1109/SIBCON.2017.7998581

Savin, S., & Vorochaeva, L. (2017, May). Nested quadratic programming-based controller for pipeline robots. In *Industrial Engineering, Applications and Manufacturing (ICIEAM), 2017 International Conference on* (pp. 1-6). IEEE. 10.1109/ICIEAM.2017.8076142

Savin, S., & Vorochaeva, L. (2017, May). Pace pattern generation for a pipeline robot. In *Industrial Engineering, Applications and Manufacturing (ICIEAM), 2017 International Conference on* (pp. 1-6). IEEE. 10.1109/ICIEAM.2017.8076143

Savin, S., Ivakhnenko, A., & Medvedev, D. (2018). Pipeline branches detection using deep convolutional neural networks. Extreme Robotics 2018.

Savin, S., Jatsun, S., & Vorochaeva, L. (2017). Trajectory generation for a walking in-pipe robot moving through spatially curved pipes. In *MATEC Web of Conferences* (Vol. 113, p. 02016). EDP Sciences. 10.1051/matecconf/201711302016

Savin, S., Jatsun, S., & Vorochaeva, L. (2017, November). Modification of Constrained LQR for Control of Walking in-pipe Robots. In Dynamics of Systems, Mechanisms and Machines (Dynamics), 2017 (pp. 1-6). IEEE. doi:10.1109/Dynamics.2017.8239502

Savin, S., Jatsun, S., & Vorochaeva, L. (2018). State observer design for a walking in-pipe robot. In *MATEC Web of Conferences* (Vol. 161, p. 03012). EDP Sciences. 10.1051/matecconf/201816103012

Schölkopf, B., Williamson, R. C., Smola, A. J., Shawe-Taylor, J., & Platt, J. C. (2000). Support vector method for novelty detection. *Advances in Neural Information Processing Systems*, 582–588.

Schwertner, K., Zlateva, P., & Velev, D. (2018). Digital technologies of industry 4.0 in management of natural disasters. *Proceedings of the 2nd International Conference on E-commerce, E-Business and E-Government*.

Senov, A. (2015). Improving Distributed Stochastic Gradient Descent Estimate via Loss Function Approximation. *IFAC-Papersonline*, *48*(25), 292–297. doi:10.1016/j.ifacol.2015.11.103

Sezer, O., Dogdu, E., & Ozbayoglu, A. (2018). Context-Aware Computing, Learning, and Big Data in Internet of Things: A Survey. *IEEE Internet Of Things Journal*, *5*(1), 1–27. doi:10.1109/JIOT.2017.2773600

Shmueli, G., & dan Fienberg, S.E. (2005). *Current and Potential Statistical Methods for Monitoring Multiple Data Streams for Bio-Surveillance*. National Institute of Statistical Sciences, Carnegie Mellon University.

Short, A., & Bandyopadhyay, T. (2018). Legged Motion Planning in Complex Three-Dimensional Environments. *IEEE Robotics and Automation Letters*, *3*(1), 29–36. doi:10.1109/LRA.2017.2728200

Sideridis, A. B., Protopappas, L., Tsiafoulis, S., & Pimenidis, E. (2015). Smart Cross-Border e-Gov Systems and Applications. In S. Katsikas & A. Sideridis (Eds.), *E-Democracy – Citizen Rights in the World of the New Computing Paradigms. e-Democracy 2015. Communications in Computer and Information Science* (Vol. 570). Cham: Springer.

Sideridis, A., & Protopappas, L. (2015). Recent ICT Advances Applied to Smart e-Government Systems in Life Sciences. *Proceedings of the 7th International Conference on Information and Communication Technologies in Agriculture, Food and Environment (HAICTA 2015).*

Silva, M. F., & Tenreiro Machado, J. A. (2007). A historical perspective of legged robots. *Journal of Vibration and Control*, *13*(9-10), 1447–1486. doi:10.1177/1077546307078276

Singh & Chopra. (2017). The Internet of Things and Multiagent Systems: Decentralized Intelligence in Distributed Computing. *2017 IEEE 37th International Conference on Distributed Computing Systems (ICDCS).*

Singh & Singh. (2015). Vector Space Model: An Information Retrieval System. *Int. J. Adv. Engg. Res. Studies*, *4*(2), 141-143.

Singh, A., Sachdeva, E., Sarkar, A., & Krishna, K. M. (2017). *Design and optimal springs stiffness estimation of a Modular OmniCrawler in-pipe climbing Robot.* arXiv preprint arXiv:1706.06418

Sleman, A., & Moeller, R. (2008). Integration of Wireless Sensor Network Services into other Home and Industrial networks. *IEEE conference paper in 3rd International Conference on Information and Communication Technologies: From Theory to Applications.*

Smith & Davis. (1983). Negotiation as a metaphor for distributed problem solving. *Artificial Intell.*, *20*, 63-109.

Sofla, M.J., & Silahi, B., & dan Masomi, M. T. (2013). Germi County Seasonal Precipitation Routing and Analysis, Using Holt-Winter Method for Times with Non-seasonal changes. *Technical Journal of Engineering and Applied Sciences*, *3*(11), 950–953.

Soucy, P., & Mineau, G. W. (2015). Beyond TFIDF Weighting for Text Categorization in the Vector Space Model. *Proceedings of the 19th International Joint Conference on Artificial Intelligence*, 1130-1135.

Soyjaudah, S. M. K., Hosany, A. M., & Jamaloodeen, A. (2004). Design and Implementation of Rijindeal Algorithm for GSM Encryption. In *Proceedings of the Joint IST Workshop on Mobile Future & Symposium on Trends in Communications (SympoTIC '04)*, Bratislava, Slovakia: IEEE. 10.1109/TIC.2004.1409510

Spanos, A. G., & Maples, B. T. (1996). Security for Real-Time MPEG Compressed Video in Distributed Multimedia Applications. In *Proceeding of the International Phoenix Conference on Computers and Communications (IPcCC '96)*. Scottsdale, AZ: IEEE. 10.1109/PCCC.1996.493615

Srivastava, Hinton, & Krizhevsky, Sutskever, & Salakhutdinov. (2014). Dropout: A Simple Way to Prevent Neural Networks from Overfitting. *Journal of Machine Learning Research, 15*, 1929-1958.

Stack Exchange. (2017). *Difference between contextual anomaly and collective anomaly*. Retrieved from https://stats.stackexchange.com/questions/323553

Stojmenovic, I., Wen, S., Huang, X., & Luan, T. H. (2015). An Overview of Fog Computing and its Security Issues. *Concurrency and Computation*.

Subbulakshmi, T. (2017). A learning-based hybrid framework for detection and defence of DDoS attacks. *International Journal of Internet Protocol Technology, 10*(1), 51. doi:10.1504/IJIPT.2017.083036

Sudheer, K. P., Gosain, A. K., Mohana Rangan, D., & Saheb, S. M. (2002). Modelling evaporation using an artificial neural network algorithm. *Hydrological Processes, 16*(16), 3189–3202. doi:10.1002/hyp.1096

Sudheer, K. P., Gosain, A. K., & Ramasastri, K. S. (2002). A data-driven algorithm for constructing artificial neural network rainfall-runoff models. *Hydrological Processes*. doi:10.1002/hyp.554

Sun, B., Yu, F., Wu, K., Xiao, Y., & Leung, V. C. M. (2006). Enhancing Security Using Mobility-Based Anomaly Detection in Cellular Mobile Networks. *IEEE Transactions on Vehicular Technology, 55*(4), 1385–1396. doi:10.1109/TVT.2006.874579

Surendar, A., Samavatian, V., Maseleno, A., Ibatova, A. Z., & Samavatian, M. (2018). Effect of solder layer thickness on thermo-mechanical reliability of a power electronic system. *Journal of Materials Science Materials in Electronics*, 1–10.

Surmaini, E., Runtunuwu, E., & dan Irsal, L. (2010). Upaya Sektor Pertanian Dalam Menghadapi Perubahan Iklim. Balai Besar Penelitian dan Pengembangan Sumberdaya Lahan Pertanian, Jalan Ir. H. Juanda No. 98, Bogor 16123.

Sutrisno, W. (2009). Pemodelan Curah Hujan Non Stasioner di Kota Surabaya Menggunakan Model ARIMA. *Conference on Information Technology and Electrical Engineering (CITEE)*.

Swarinoto, Y. S. (2009). *Validasi Spasial Data Estimasi Suhu Udara Turunan Dari Citra Satelit Landsat 7 - ETM+ Terhadap Data Observasi Stasiun Cuaca/IklimDarat (Kasus Provinsi Jawa Barat Bagian Selatan). In Jurnal Agroklimatologi*. Bogor: IPB.

Tâche, F., Fischer, W., Moser, R., Mondada, F., & Siegwart, R. (2007). Adapted magnetic wheel unit for compact robots inspecting complex shaped pipe structures. In Advanced intelligent mechatronics, 2007 IEEE/ASME international conference on (No. LSRO-CONF-2007-013, pp. 1-6). IEEE Press. doi:10.1109/AIM.2007.4412506

Tamura, Tasaki, Sengoku, & Niigata. (2005). *Scheduling Problems for a Class of Parallel Distributed Systems*. Institute of Technology, Faculty of Engineering, Niigata University.

Tang, T., & Ho, A. T.-K. (2018). A path-dependence perspective on the adoption of Internet of Things: Evidence from early adopters of smart and connected sensors in the United States. *Government Information Quarterly*. doi:10.1016/j.giq.2018.09.010

Tariq, S., & Choi, H. (2016). Controlled Parking for Self-Driving Cars. *2016 IEEE International Conference on Systems, Man, and Cybernetics*.

Tătar, O., Mandru, D., & Ardelean, I. (2007). Development of mobile minirobots for in pipe inspection tasks. *Mechanika, 68*(6).

Tax, D. M., & Duin, R. P. (2004). Support vector data description. *Machine Learning, 54*(1), 45–66. doi:10.1023/B:MACH.0000008084.60811.49

Taylor, J. W. (2003). Exponential Smoothing with a Damped Multiplicative Trend. *International Journal of Forecasting, 19*(4), 715–725. doi:10.1016/S0169-2070(03)00003-7

Thibaud, M., Chi, H., Zhou, W., & Piramuthu, S. (2018). Internet of Things (IoT) in high-risk Environment, Health and Safety (EHS) industries: A comprehensive review. *Decision Support Systems, 108*, 79–95. doi:10.1016/j.dss.2018.02.005

Thielemann, J. T., Breivik, G. M., & Berge, A. (2008, June). Pipeline landmark detection for autonomous robot navigation using time-of-flight imagery. In *Computer Vision and Pattern Recognition Workshops, 2008. CVPRW'08. IEEE Computer Society Conference on* (pp. 1-7). IEEE. 10.1109/CVPRW.2008.4563167

Titanto, M., & Dirgahayu, T. (2014). Google Maps-Based Geospatial Application Framework with Custom Layers Management. *Applied Mechanics And Materials, 513-517*, 822-826. Retrieved from www.scientific.net/amm.513-517.822

Tresnawati, R., Nuraini, A.T., & Hanggoro, W. (2010). Prediksi Curah Hujan Bulanan Menggunakan Metode Kalman Filter Dengan Prediktor SST Nino 3.4 Diprediksi. *Jurnal Meteorologi Dan Geofisika, 11*(2), 106 - 115.

Tsai, C.-F., & Lin, C.-Y. (2010). A triangle area based nearest neighbors approach to intrusion detection. *Pattern Recognition, 43*(1), 222–229. doi:10.1016/j.patcog.2009.05.017

Tsubouchi, T., Takaki, S., Kawaguchi, Y., & Yuta, S. I. (2000). A straight pipe observation from the inside by laser spot array and a TV camera. In *Intelligent Robots and Systems, 2000. (IROS 2000). Proceedings. 2000 IEEE/RSJ International Conference on* (Vol. 1, pp. 82-87). IEEE. 10.1109/IROS.2000.894586

Turing, A. M. (2009). Computing machinery and intelligence. In *Parsing the Turing Test* (pp. 23–65). Dordrecht: Springer. doi:10.1007/978-1-4020-6710-5_3

Valiant, L. G., & Brebner, G. J. (1981). Universal schemes for parallel communication. *Proceedings of the 13th ACM symposium on Theory of Computing*, 263–277.

Vapnik, V. (1998). *Statistical learning theory*. Chichester, UK: Wiley.

Verma, K. H., & Singh, K. R. (2012). Performance Analysis of RC6, Twofish and Rijndael Block Cipher Algorithms. *International Journal of Computers and Applications*, *42*(16), 1–7. doi:10.5120/5773-6002

Vlajic, N., & Zhou, D. (2018). IoT as a Land of Opportunity for DDoS Hackers. *Computer*, *51*(7), 26–34. doi:10.1109/MC.2018.3011046

von Eicken, T., Culler, D. E., Goldstein, S. C., & Schauser, K. E. (1992). Active messages:A mechanism for integrated communication and computation. *SIGARCH Comput.Archit. News*, *20*(2), 256–266. doi:10.1145/146628.140382

Vo, T. N. T., Phu, V. N., & Tuoi, P. T. (2014). Learning More Chi Square Feature Selection to Improve the Fastest and Most Accurate Sentiment Classification. *The Third Asian Conference on Information Systems (ACIS 2014)*.

Vu, H., Gomez, F., Cherelle, P., Lefeber, D., Nowé, A., & Vanderborght, B. (2018). ED-FNN: A New Deep Learning Algorithm to Detect Percentage of the Gait Cycle for Powered Prostheses. *Sensors (Basel)*, *18*(7), 2389. doi:10.339018072389 PMID:30041421

Vukobratović, M., & Borovac, B. (2004). Zero-moment point—thirty five years of its life. *International Journal of Humanoid Robotics, 1*(1), 157-173.

Wahyono, T. (2017). Anomaly detection to evaluate in-class learning process using distance and density approach of machine learning. *International Conference on Innovative and Creative Information Technology (ICITech)*. 10.1109/INNOCIT.2017.8319138

Wang, Y. (2005). A multinomial logistic regression modeling approach for anomaly intrusion detection. *Computers & Security*, *24*(8), 662–674. doi:10.1016/j.cose.2005.05.003

Weber, R. (2010). Internet of Things – New security and privacy challenges. *Computer Law & Security Review*, *26*(1), 23–30. doi:10.1016/j.clsr.2009.11.008

Witten, I. H., & Frank, E. (2000). *Data Mining: Practical Machine Learning Tools and Techniques with Java Implementations*. San Mateo, CA: Morgan Kaufmann. Retrieved from http://www.cs.waikato.ac.nz/ml/weka/

World Bank Group. (2017). *Internet of Things: The New Government to Business Platform*. Available at: http://documents.worldbank.org/curated/en/610081509689089303/pdf/120876-REVISED-WP-PUBLIC-Internet-of-Things-Report.pdf

Wu, B., Wan, A., Iandola, F., Jin, P. H., & Keutzer, K. (2016). *SqueezeDet: Unified, Small, Low power Fully Convolutional Neural Networks for Real-Time Object Detection for Autonomous Driving*. arXiv:1612.01051

Xhafa, F., & Abraham, A. (2010). Computational models and heuristic methods for Grid scheduling problems. *Future Generation Computer Systems, 26*(4), 608–621. doi:10.1016/j.future.2009.11.005

Xie, M., Hu, J., & Guo, S. (2015). Segment-based anomaly detection with approximated sample covariance matrix in wireless sensor networks. Parallel and Distributed Systems. *IEEE Transactions on, 26*(2), 574–583.

Yairi, T., & Kawahara. (2006). Telemetry-mining: a machine learning approach to anomaly detection and fault diagnosis for space systems. *2nd IEEE International Conference on Space Mission Challenges for Information Technology (SMC-IT'06)*. 10.1109/SMC-IT.2006.79

Yang, S., Tiejun, L., Maunder, R., & Hanzo, L. (2013). From Nominal to True A Posteriori Probabilities: An Exact Bayesian Theorem Based Probabilistic Data Association Approach for Iterative MIMO Detection and Decoding. *IEEE Transactions on Communications, 61*(7), 2782–2793. doi:10.1109/TCOMM.2013.053013.120427

Yang, Y., Feng, S., Ye, W., & Ji, X. (2008). A Transmission Scheme for Encrypted Speech over GSM network. In *Proceeding of the International Symposium on Computer Science and Computational Technology (ISCSCT '08)*. Shanghai, China: IEEE. 10.1109/ISCSCT.2008.290

Yang, Y., & Liu, X. (1999). A re-examination of text categorization methods. In *Proceedings of the 22nd annual international ACM SIGIR conference on Research and development in information retrieval* (pp. 42-49). ACM.

Yang, Z., Meratnia, N., & Havinga, P. (2007). *Outlier Detection Techniques For Wireless Sensor Networks: A Survey*. Department of Computer Science, University of Twente.

Yao, S., Zhao, Y., Zhang, A., Hu, S., Shao, H., Zhang, C., ... Abdelzaher, T. (2018). Deep Learning for the Internet of Things. *Computer, 51*(5), 32–41. doi:10.1109/MC.2018.2381131

Yao, X. (1999). Evolving artificial neural networks. *Proceedings of the IEEE, 87*(9). DOI: 10.1109/5.784219

Yin, W., Kann, K., Yu, M., & Schütze, H. (n.d.). *Comparative Study of CNN and RNN for Natural Language Processing*. arXiv:1702.01923

Yi, Y., Wu, J., & Xu, W. (2011). Incremental SVM based on reserved set for network intrusion detection. *Expert Systems with Applications, 38*(6), 7698–7707. doi:10.1016/j.eswa.2010.12.141

Yu, Liang, He, Hatcher, Lu, Lin, & Yang. (2017). A Survey on the Edge Computing for the Internet of Things. *IEEE Access, 6*, 6900 – 6919.

Zagler, A., & Pfeiffer, F. (2003, September). "MORITZ" a pipe crawler for tube junctions. In *Robotics and Automation, 2003. Proceedings. ICRA'03. IEEE International Conference on* (Vol. 3, pp. 2954-2959). IEEE.

Zainuddin, Z., & Manullang, V. E. (2013). E-Learning Concept Design of Rijndael Encryption Process. In *Proceeding of the International Conference on Teaching, Assessment and Learning for Engineering (TALE '13)*. Bali, Indonesia: IEEE.

Zawoad, S., & Hasan, R. (2013). *Cloud forensics: a meta-study of challenges, approaches, and open problems.* arXiv preprint arXiv:1302.6312

Zawoad, S., & Hasan, R. (2015, June). Faiot: Towards building a forensics aware eco system for the internet of things. In *2015 IEEE International Conference on Services Computing (SCC)* (pp. 279-284). IEEE. 10.1109/SCC.2015.46

Zhang, Z. Y. (2010). Security, Trust, and Risk in the Digital Rights Management Ecosystem. In *Proceeding of the International Conference on High-Performance Computing and Simulation (HPCS '10)*. Caen, France: IEEE. 10.1109/HPCS.2010.5547093

Zhang, Z. Y. (2011). Digital Rights Management Ecosystem and its Usage Controls: A Survey. *International Journal of Digital Content Technology & Its Applications, 5*(3), 255–272. doi:10.4156/jdcta.vol5.issue3.26

Zhao, Y., Lee, E. A., & Liu, J. (2007). A programming model for time-synchronized distributed real-time systems. In *Real-Time and Embedded Technology and Applications Symposium (RTAS)* (pp. 259-268). IEEE. 10.1109/RTAS.2007.5

Zheng, Z., & Lyu, M. (2010). An adaptive QoS-aware fault tolerance strategy for web services. *Empirical Software Engineering, 15*(4), 323–345. doi:10.100710664-009-9126-8

Zhou, Z.-H., Wu, J., & Tang, W. (2002). Ensembling neural networks: Many could be better than all. *Artificial Intelligence, 137*(1–2), 239–263. doi:10.1016/S0004-3702(02)00190-X

Zhu, W., Luo, C., Wang, J., & Li, S. (2011). Multimedia cloud computing. *IEEE Signal Processing Magazine, 28*(3), 59–69. doi:10.1109/MSP.2011.940269

Zu, L. D. (2014, November). Internet of Things in Industries: A Survey. *IEEE Transactions on Industrial Informatics, 10*(4).

About the Contributors

Hindriyanto Dwi Purnomo is an Associate Professor in the Department of Information Technology, Universitas Kristen Satya Wacana (UKSW). He received B.SEng from Gadjah Mada University, Indonesia, Master of Information Technology from The University of Melbourne, and Doctor of Philosophy from Chung Yuan Christian University. His research interest are in the field of computational intelligence, applied soft computing and optimisation.

* * *

Amritanjali received B.E. degree in Computer Science, M.E. degree in Software Engineering and Ph.D. in Engineering from Birla Institute of Technology in the year 2000, 2005 and 2014 respectively. After completing B.E., she worked as Software Engineer at Computer Associates-TCG S/W Pvt. Ltd. for two years. She was responsible for software development and maintenance in the various industrial projects. In 2006, she joined the Birla Institute of Technology, Mesra, as Assistant Professor in the Department of Computer Science and Engineering. Her research interest is in the area of Bioinformatics, Parallel Computing and Wireless Networks.

Surendar Aravindhan is an Assistant Professor at Vignan's Foundation for Science, Technology and Research, India. He obtained his BE in Electronics and Communication Engineering from K.S.R. College of Engineering, (Anna University, Chennai), Tiruchengode, India, an ME from Anna University, Coimbatore, India, and pursuing PhD in Anna University, Chennai. His research interests include embedded system and bioinformatics. He has published research outcomes in several IEEE conferences and peer reviewed international journals like IEEE, Springer, Elsevier and has about 30 research publications to his credit. He is also a Reviewer for many reputed journals published by Springer, IGI Global and Inderscience Publishers; he is also Editor of International Journal of Communication & Computer Technology and guest editor for many special issues with Inderscience and IGI Global journals. He is also the Member of IEEE membership and ACM.

Arup Bhattacharjee did his Bachelors from University of Calcutta, Master of Computer Application from Kalyani University and MTech from West Bengal University of Technology. He is currently working as an Assistant Professor in RCC Institute of Information Technology, Kolkata, India. He has more than 14 years teaching experience. He has over 10 research publication in different national and international journal and conferences. He has contributed in over 20 internationally acclaimed books. He has edited 2 books. His research areas are software engineering, data mining and machine learning. He is member of various professional bodies like IETE, Indian Science Congress, Computer Society of India.

Debabrata Bhattacharya graduated in Electronics & Tele-Communications Engineering(1983) from Jadavpur University, Kolkata, India with first class honours and did M. Tech. degree in Electronics & Communication Engg. (specialization: Integrated Circuits and Systems Engg.) with first class distinction from IIT, Kharagpur, India in Dec. 1984. Worked in the Information Technology industry in various platforms(software and hardware) and applications with many MNCs for 17 years, both in India and abroad. Have been in academics for more than around 16 years since then. Involved in teaching and mentoring students in various Electronics, Computer, and Measurement (Instrumentation) related subjects, projects in undergraduate technical college curricula. Had been the founding HoD of the Applied Electronics and Instrumentation (AEIE) Engg. Dept. at RCCIIT, Kolkata, India.

Stuti Shukla Datta of ASET, Lucknow Campus has received her M.E. degree from Birla Institute of Technology, Mesra, Ranchi in the year 2007 and her Ph.D degree from the department of Electrical Engineering, Indian Institute of Technology Delhi in the year 2014. Her research interests include power quality assessment and improvement, deregulation of power system and its issues, energy market modeling and unit commitment. She has total 10 years of research experience including four years post Ph. D. During her days as a research scholar in Delhi she has worked on the software platforms like MATLAB, PSCAD and has working experience on the DSP processor dSpace. She is the recipient of POSOCO power system Award in the year 2014, She has publications in the peer reviewed journals including IEEE Transactions on Power Delivery, IEEE transactions on Industrial Informatics, IEEE transactions on Industrial Applications. She is also member of international societies including IEEE Power Electronics Society, IEEE Women in Engineering, IET UK. She is also an active reviewer for the journals IEEE Access, IEEE Industrial Informatics, IET Signal Processing. Some of her key publications are: S. Shukla, S. Mishra, B. Singh, "Implementation of Empirical Mode Decomposition Based Algorithm for Shunt Active Filter," IEEE Trans on Industrial Applications, 2016 S. Shukla, S. Mishra, B. Singh, "Empirical mode decomposition with hilbert transform for power quality assessment," IEEE Transaction on Power Delivery, vol. 24, no.4, Oct 2009, pp.2159-2165. S. Shukla, S. Mishra, B. Singh, "Power Quality Event Classification under Noisy Conditions using EMD based De-noising Techniques" IEEE Transactions on Industrial Informatics, vol. 10, no.2, Nov. 2013, pp.1044-1054.

Mudrika Dhanda completed their masters in data science and analytics and is currently working as a Data Analyst Intern at a renowned MNC in the United Kingdom.

Namrata Dhanda is working as a Professor in Department of Computer Science & Engineering, Amity School of Engineering & Technology, Amity University, Uttar Pradesh. Namrata Dhanda has about 18 years of teaching experience in various reputed Engineering Colleges and Universities located in India. They owe many subjects to their credit like Data Science, Machine Learning, Theory of Computation, Algorithm Design, Database Systems etc. Their qualifications include B.Tech (CSE), M.Tech (CSE) and Phd in Computer Science.

Charles Fayenuwo holds a Master with Honours in IS/IT from Griffith University. His Dissertation treated aspects of IoT in the Logistic sector in Nigeria. He is now in the process of enrolling in a PhD at Griffith University.

Stathes Hadjiefthymiades is a Professor in the Department of Informatics and Telecommunications (DIT) at the National and Kapodistrian University of Athens (NKUA). His research interests are in the area of distributed, mobile and pervasive computing and networked multimedia. He has participated in numerous EU projects in Programs like ACTS, ORA, TAP, INFO2000, IST, ICT, H2020 as well as National Research Initiatives. He leads the activities of the Pervasive Computing Research Group (p-comp) established in NKUA in 2003. He is currently the Director of the Network Technologies, Services and Applications (NETSA) Laboratory of NKUA and the Director of the MSc Programme on "Management and Economics of Telecommunication Networks and Information Systems". He also leads the H2020 RAWFIE project (http://www.rawfie.eu) establishing UxV testbeds for IoT experimentation.

Yaya Heryadi is a researcher and faculty member at Doctor of Computer Science Program, Binus Graduated Program, Bina Nusantara University in Jakarta, Indonesia. He received Bachelor degree in Statistics and Computation from Institut Pertanian Bogor, Bogor-Indonesia, Master of Science degree in Computer Science from Indiana University, Bloomington-USA, and Doctor of Computer Science from University of Indonesia, Depok-Indonesia. His teaching topics are mainly: Artificial

Intelligence, Machine Learning, Deep Learning, Softcomputing and Computational Mathematics. His research interests are in the field of Machine Learning, Deep Learning, Image Processing, Pattern Recognition, Signal Processing, Natural Language Processing, Video Understanding, and Computer Vision.

Ramgopal Kashyap's areas of interest are image processing, pattern recognition, and machine learning. He has published many research papers in international journals and conferences like Springer, Inderscience, Elsevier, ACM, and IGI-Global indexed by Science Citation Index (SCI) and Scopus (Elsevier) and many book chapters. He has Reviewed Research Papers in the Science Citation Index Expanded, Springer Journals and Editorial Board Member and conferences programme committee member of the IEEE, Springer international conferences and journals held in countries: Czech Republic, Switzerland, UAE, Australia, Hungary, Poland, Taiwan, Denmark, India, USA, UK, Austria, and Turkey. He has written many book chapters published by IGI Global, USA.

Kostas M. Kolomvatsos received his B.Sc. in Informatics from the Department of Informatics at the Athens University of Economics and Business in 1995, his M.Sc. in Computer Science - New Technologies in Informatics and Telecommunications and his Ph.D. from the Department of Informatics and Telecommunications at the National and Kapodistrian University of Athens (UoA) in 2005 and in the beginning of 2013 respectively. Currently, he serves as a Teaching Staff and Senior Researcher in the Department of Informatics and Telecommunications UoA. He also serves as an Adjunct Lecturer at the University of Thessaly, Department of Computer Science. He has participated in several European and National research projects. His research interests are in the definition of Intelligent Systems and techniques adopting Machine Learning, Computational Intelligence and Soft Computing for Pervasive Computing, Distributed Systems and the management of Large Scale Data. He is the author of over 70 publications in the aforementioned areas.

Soumen Mukherjee did his B.Sc (Physics Honours) from Calcutta University, M.C.A. from Kalyani University and ME in Information Technology from West Bengal University of Technology. He is the silver medalist in ME examination for the university. He has done his Post-Graduate Diploma in Business Management from Institute of Management Technology, Center of Distance Learning, Ghaziabad. He is now working as an Assistant Professor in RCC Institute of Information Technology, Kolkata. He has 15 years teaching experience in the field of Computer Science and Application. He has over 30 research paper published in different National and International Journal and Conferences. He has contributed in over 20 internationally acclaimed books in the field of Computer Science and Engineering. He has got best paper award in the international conference, ICCAIAIT 2018. He has edited 2 books. His research fields are Image Processing and Machine Learning. He is a life member of several institutions like IETE, CSI, ISTE, FOSET etc.

Panagiota Papadopoulou holds a BSc (hons.) in Informatics from the University of Athens, an MSc (distinction) in Distributed and Multimedia Information Systems from Heriot-Watt University and a PhD from the University of Athens. She teaches at undergraduate and postgraduate courses at several Universities, works in European and national research projects and provides evaluation and consulting services for public organisations. She has published in international journals such as the European Journal of Information Systems and has authored the book New Technologies and Management Information Systems. Her current research interests include information systems, trust, e-commerce, e-government and IoT.

Dharmendra Patel received Bachelor Degree in Industrial Chemistry- BSc. (Industrial Chemistry) from North Gujarat University, Gujarat, India and Master Degree in Computer Applications (MCA) from North Gujarat University, Gujarat, India. He completed his Ph.D., in the field of Web Usage Mining. He is HOD of MCA Department at Smt. Chandaben Mohanbhai Patel Institute of Computer Applications, under Charusat University of Science and Technology (CHARUSAT), Changa, Gujarat, India.

Partha Paul received the B.E(CS) and M.E(CS) degree from Moscow State University, Russia in 1998 & 1999 respectively. He did his Ph.D. degree from Birla Institute of Technology, Mesra, Ranchi, India in 2014. He is currently Assistant Professor in the Department of Computer Science& Engineering, Birla Institute of Technology, Mesra, Ranchi, India. He has authored or Co-authored more than 40 Papers published in Various International Journals and Conference Proceedings. His research interests include Cryptography and Network Security, Artificial Intelligence, Cloud Computing and Traffic Grooming in Optical WDM.

Jay Rodge is a Graduate student (2018~present) in Illinois Institute of Technology, Chicago pursuing Masters in Computer Science with a specialisation in Computational Intelligence. He has completed his Bachelors in Computer Engineering (2014-18) from Savitribai Phule Pune University. His interest areas mainly includes Machine Learning, Deep Learning and Autonomous Vehicles. He has done his final year project in Deep Learning and experience in Natural Language Processing. He is also a part of Self Driving Car Nanodegree class in Udacity.

Kuldeep Sandhu is an expert in Information Systems with research expertise in fields such as financial management information systems, human resource business intelligence, information systems, database modelling and management, e-government, e-business, e-commerce, and mobile technology. He has published 21 papers ranging from book chapters through to peer reviewed journal articles and is currently working on research projects relating to Valuation of Data, e-Health Systems, m-Commerce adoption and Security issue evaluation in Business Intelligence.

Louis Sanzogni is a member of Faculty at Griffith University in Brisbane Australia where he currently lectures in Management and Management Information System. His research interests are in the areas of Diffusion of Innovation and Technology Adoption. In his more recent publications Dr Sanzogni explored the effects of user perceptions on the adoption of innovations proposing a number of successful variations in pre-established as well as newly developed adoption models.

Sergei Savin obtained a bachelor degree in Automation and Control and an engineering degree in Mechatronics at Southwest State University. He finished a postgraduate program in Dynamics and Reliability of Machines and Equipment and obtained a candidate of science degree in 2014. He holds a senior researcher position at the laboratory of Robotics and Mechatronics. His areas of interest include walking robotics, in-pipe robots, optimal control, dynamics and machine learning. His current research is focused on exoskeletons, walking in-pipe robots and anthropomorphic bipedal robots. He also currently works as a docent at the department of Mechanics, Mechatronics and Robotics where he gives lectures on Mathematical Modelling in Mechatronics and Robotics, Information System in Mechatronics and Robotics and on Information System of Mobile Robots for bachelor and master student programs. He authored more than 70 papers and is a co-author of textbooks on applied simulation methods in Robotics.

Keshav Sinha was born in Dhanbad, India, in 1991. He received the B.E. Degree in Computer Science and Engineering from Sri Chandrasekharendra Saraswathi Viswa Mahavidyalaya, Kanchipuram, India, in 2013, and M.E. Degree in Software Engineering from the Birla Institute of Technology, Mesra, India, in 2016. Currently, as a research scholar, he is doing Ph.D. from BIT, Mesra in the field of Cryptography and Network security. As a research scholar, he published several papers in various conferences, journals, and ebook. His current research interest includes Soft Computing, IoT, and Cryptography & Network Security which provides the flexibility in the computer science society.

Teguh Wahyono is a lecturer at the Faculty of Information Technology, Satya Wacana Christian University. He received Bachelor degree in Informatics Engineering from Duta Wacana Christian University Yogyakarta, Master of Computer Science from Gadjah Mada University. He is doctoral student at Doctor of Computer Science Program, BINUS University since 2017. His teaching interest are information system analysis, software engineering and artificial intelligence. His research interest are in the field of spatial data mining, machine learning and deep learning.

Index

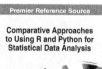

Ensure Quality Research is Introduced to the Academic Community

Become an IGI Global Reviewer for Authored Book Projects

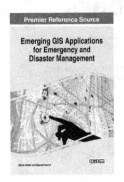

Premier Reference Source

Emerging GIS Applications for Emergency and Disaster Management

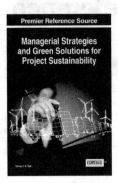

Premier Reference Source

Managerial Strategies and Green Solutions for Project Sustainability

Premier Reference Source

Comparative Approaches to Using R and Python for Statistical Data Analysis

Premier Reference Source

Solutions for High-Touch Communications in a High-Tech World

The overall success of an authored book project is dependent on quality and timely reviews.

In this competitive age of scholarly publishing, constructive and timely feedback significantly expedites the turnaround time of manuscripts from submission to acceptance, allowing the publication and discovery of forward-thinking research at a much more expeditious rate. Several IGI Global authored book projects are currently seeking highly qualified experts in the field to fill vacancies on their respective editorial review boards:

Applications may be sent to:
development@igi-global.com

Applicants must have a doctorate (or an equivalent degree) as well as publishing and reviewing experience. Reviewers are asked to write reviews in a timely, collegial, and constructive manner. All reviewers will begin their role on an ad-hoc basis for a period of one year, and upon successful completion of this term can be considered for full editorial review board status, with the potential for a subsequent promotion to Associate Editor.

If you have a colleague that may be interested in this opportunity, we encourage you to share this information with them.

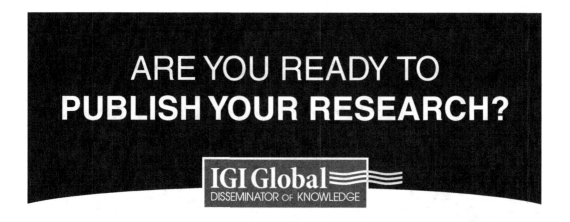

www.igi-global.com/infosci-ondemand

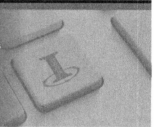

InfoSci®-OnDemand

Continuously updated with new material on a weekly basis, InfoSci®-OnDemand offers the ability to search through thousands of quality full-text research papers. Users can narrow each search by identifying key topic areas of interest, then display a complete listing of relevant papers, and purchase materials specific to their research needs.

Comprehensive Service

- Over 81,600+ journal articles, book chapters, and case studies.
- All content is downloadable in PDF format and can be stored locally for future use.

No Subscription Fees

- One time fee of $37.50 per PDF download.

Instant Access

- Receive a download link immediately after order completion!

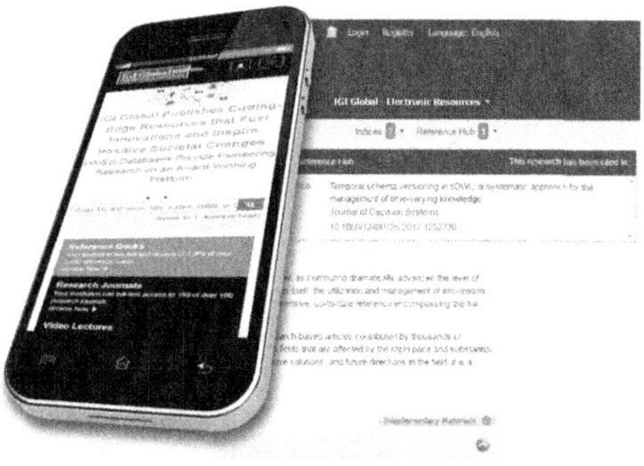

"It really provides an excellent entry into the research literature of the field. It presents a manageable number of highly relevant sources on topics of interest to a wide range of researchers. The sources are scholarly, but also accessible to 'practitioners'."

- Lisa Stimatz, MLS, University of North Carolina at Chapel Hill, USA

"It is an excellent and well designed database which will facilitate research, publication and teaching. It is a very very useful tool to have."

- George Ditsa, PhD, University of Wollongong, Australia

"I have accessed the database and find it to be a valuable tool to the IT/IS community. I found valuable articles meeting my search criteria 95% of the time."

- Lynda Louis, Xavier University of Louisiana, USA

Recommended for use by researchers who wish to immediately download PDFs of individual chapters or articles.

www.igi-global.com/e-resources/infosci-ondemand

IGI Global
DISSEMINATOR OF KNOWLEDGE
www.igi-global.com

Printed in the United States
By Bookmasters